What others are saying about *After Capitalism: Economic Democracy in Action*:

"In just a few pages I felt the brotherly embrace of a comrade-in-arms, a soul-mate, and a companion; further along his fierce intelligence and original insights challenged me to make new connections; by the end I was inspired to re-imagine next steps in my own efforts at movement-making. This is an essential book created by a gentle warrior."
 — *Left Eye on Books*, Bill Ayers, author of *Fugitive Days: Memoirs of an Anti-War Activist*.

"Well researched and written... The book shines... with a passionate and unique voice... A heartfelt and spiritual assertion of what must come next..."
 — *Win Magazine* of the War Resisters League

"Admirable...a thorough recounting of the Prout philosophy."
 — *ForeWord Reviews*

"*After Capitalism* is a crucial contribution towards figuring out where we want to go, not only after capitalism, but now, as we try to build the new world within the old. It is so important not only because of the thoroughly considered vision it presents, but also because it incorporates a spiritual dimension that is missing from most post-capitalist visioning."
 — Gregory Wilpert, author of *Changing Venezuela by Taking Power*

"The world is in urgent need of new ideas on how to house, feed and shelter us all, without destroying the planet we are on. *After Capitalism* is a rich and varied warehouse of new ideas and new thinking that will do much to contribute to a better humanity and a better world."
 — Kevin Cahill, author of *Who Owns the World*

"I enthusiastically recommend this book for a college classroom and for those who are organizing for economic and social justice."
 — Peter Bohmer, activist and faculty in Economics and Political Economy, The Evergreen State College

"The search is on for new ways to inhabit a strained earth. There are plenty of interesting leads in these pages that will get you thinking!"

— Bill McKibben, author *Earth: Making a Life on a Tough New Planet*

"The constitutional proposals of Prout are the ethical summary of everything that humanity needs to accomplish universal fraternity. The importance of Prout is that its vision of a new world is not just concerned with political, social and economic relationships, but also with education, gender relationships and spirituality."

— Frei Betto, activist and author of the bestseller *Fidel and Religion*

"From Caracas, where the author is putting his ideas into practice, comes this accessible guide to the spiritual socialism of P.R. Sarkar. Activists working on contemporary issues from local food production to economic inequality will find much of value in this innovative volume."

— Jeffery M. Paige, author of *Agrarian Revolution*

""The very concept of *After Capitalism* is liberating. This book is a must for those of us who are striving for a more equitable, ethical and just world–one which views society and the environment holistically and ethically."

— Frank Emspak, Professor Emeritus, University of Wisconsin; CEO and Executive Producer of Workers Independent News

"This is an amazing book, breathtaking in its range and ambition: an uncompromising critique of capitalism, an outline of new world economy centered on cooperatives and local, sustainable production, a theory of history, a compelling philosophical/spiritual vision, specific information about movements and experiments going on today all over the world... a treasure-trove."

— David Schweickart, Professor of Philosophy at Loyola University Chicago, author of another book entitled *After Capitalism*

AFTER CAPITALISM

Economic Democracy in Action

AFTER CAPITALISM

Economic Democracy in Action

Dada Maheshvarananda

InnerWorld Publications
San Germán, Puerto Rico
www.innerworldpublications.com

Library of Congress Control Number: 2012941494

Cover Design: Rodrigo Adolfo

Prout logo: José Albarrán

ISBN 978-1-881717-14-0

Publisher's Cataloging-in-Publication data

Maheshvarananda , Dada.
    After capitalism : economic democracy in action / Dada
    Maheshvarananda.
    p. cm.
    ISBN 978-1-881717-14-0
    Includes bibliographical references and index.
    1. Democracy --Economic aspects. 2. Economic development. 3.
Monetary policy. 4. Capitalism. 5. Sustainable development. 6.
Economics --Moral and ethical aspects. 7. Prout (Economic theory).
8. Sarkar, Prabhat Ranjan, 1921-1990. I. Title.

JC423 .M332 2012
321.8--dc23   2012941494

The author invites critical feedback and suggestions at email
maheshvarananda@prout.org.ve

The cover photo by Alex Fradkin shows an Occupy San Francisco
protest against economic injustice on October 15, 2011. Flying the
United States flag upside down is a distress signal, and was used here
to express that the country is in distress.

We would like to thank the following publishers for permission to reprint their material: Gurukula Press of Maleny, Australia,
for "Comparing Marx and Sarkar" by Ravi Batra, which appeared
in *Transcending Boundaries: Prabhat Ranjan Sarkar's Theories of
Individual and Social Transformation* (Inayatullah and Fitzgerald,
eds., 1999) and "The Future of the Prout Movement" by Sohail
Inayatullah, which appeared in his book *Situating Sarkar: Tantra,
Macrohistory and Alternative Futures* (1999); Publicações Ananda
Marga of São Paolo, Brazil, for "Prout and the Concept of Prama"
by Leonardo Boff, which appeared as the preface in *Democracia
Econômica* (by P.R. Sarkar, 1996).

Acknowledgements

It is very difficult to express in words my gratitude to the many people that have contributed to this project. Mirra Price, copyeditor, gave painstaking attention to detail that greatly enhanced this book. Those listed below, from six continents, are members of a growing, vibrant global network of Proutists and other fellow travelers working to realize our common dream of a better world. Their patient willingness to give their time, support, thoughts and encouragement leaves me very touched and humbled. My profound thanks to each one:

Abe Heisler, Alex Jackimovicz, Alanna Hartzok, Allan Rosen, Amal Jacobson, Andy Douglas, Ang KaSaMa, Arati Brim, Ary Moraes, Bradford Jones, Bo Lozoff (deceased), Bruce Dyer, Chuck Paprocki, Clark Webb, Dada Daneshananda, Dada Gunamuktananda, Dada Nabhaniilananda, David Hardwick, Delhi Prout magazine, Devashish Donald Acosta, Didi Ananda Rucira, Diego Esteche, Dieter Dambiec, Donald Moore, Doris Olivers, Edemilson Pereira dos Santos, Edvard Mogstad, Eugenio Mendoza, Fabio Barone, Frei Betto, Garda Ghista (deceased), Ghecimar Golindano, Howard Nemon, Jake Karlyle, Jehan De Soyza, Jeshua Pacifici, Jim Braun, Joan Russow, Johan Galtung, John Gross, José Albarrán, Kamala Alister, Katie Davison, Leonardo Boff, Liila Hass, Malcolm McDonell, Marcos Arruda, Mariah Branch, Mark A. Friedman, Mark L. Friedman, Matt Oppenheim, Michael Albert, Michael Towsey, Mike McSweeney, Mirra Price, Nada Khader, Noam Chomsky, Ole Brekke, Ossi Viljakainen, Paul Wildman, Peter Bohmer, Prabhakar, Prakash and Jody Laufer, Pranav Bihari, Raimundo Braga Filho, Ras Arthemio Selassie, Ravi Batra, Roar Bjonnes, Ron Baseman, Ron Logan, Satya Tanner, Silvia Valle (deceased), Sohail Inayatullah, Spencer Bailey, Steven Landau, Szakmáry Donát and Tom Barefoot.

For Prabhat Ranjan Sarkar, the founder of Prout, who devoted his life to "the good and happiness of all".

Contents

Chapter 10: "Our Culture is Our Strength!" Cultural Identity and Education 218

Chapter 11: Prout's Governance 239

Foreword

Dr. Marcos Arruda

The nine years that have passed since Dada Maheshvarananda first published this precious book have proven its validity and relevance. The first decade of the 21st century dramatically revealed the chaotic, dehumanizing and destructive nature of global capital. Capitalism's logic of maximum profit in the shortest time, with minimal government regulation and intervention has created a war economy of all against all – people against people, companies against workers and other companies, workers against workers, nations against nations, gender against gender, humans against God, nature and other species. And commercialized fiction still imagines wars between humans and aliens! Humanity seems to have forgotten its spiritual origin and been caught in the trap of fetishes: material wealth, money and power have become the goals not only of the economy, but of life itself.

Dada Maheshvarananda's book enriches the paradigm of P.R. Sarkar, who proposes that human development in its highest sense should be the goal of economic development. Dada emphasizes Sarkar's conception of an economy that is human-centered, that human beings are multi-dimensional, and that their wholeness encompasses the natural, the individual and the social, the physical, mental, psychic and spiritual. Such a being is in continuous evolution, self-directed in active and creative interaction with the great human family, life as a whole and with the natural environment, in a search for balance, harmony, wellbeing and happiness that is continually being recreated.

The radical nature of this proposal is the second feature of Sarkar's Prout, and lies in its viability – the act of making real the vision and dream of an economy that is just, equitable, and harmonious, and which produces wellbeing and happiness for all. Dada illustrates this feasibility with a great wealth of examples, narrated so that anyone reading the book feels confident that Prout – and every proposal for an economy that is centered on the whole human being, conscious and progressive – is historically viable.

In the holistic and systemic approach of Prout, which I greatly admire, no aspect of human existence is left out. There is critical reflection about the reality of the world, as well as the search for another way of constructing it.

The proposal to place human beings, individually and collectively, in the center of the social relations of production, demands that the economy be treated as valuable, but economics is not the only dimension of human existence on the planet, nor even the most important one. In the work of Sarkar, enriched by Dada, the economy exists alongside political, cultural, environmental and spiritual dimensions, creating a challenge that is just as complex and multidimensional as human beings are.

This is just one aspect of Prout's proposal that is close to what we have built under the name of "solidarity socioeconomy".[1] Other aspects of this convergence include a radical critique of capitalism and emphasis on human values such as altruism, a cooperative spirit, solidarity and mutual respect for human and cultural diversity. Our very survival as a species depends on our developing these qualities, applying them not only with other humans, but also with the Earth and the Cosmos.

Prout does not ignore the contradictory nature of our human reality, for that is what stimulates our evolving, dynamic character. It enhances our human consciousness, allowing us to adopt an attitude of active collaboration with the Creation. It achieves this by:

Working to overcome the pseudo-culture that subverts the spirit and will of many people, conditioning them to be self-centered, competitive and aggressive. In addition, deconstructing the illusion that individualism is the highest value, and the capitalist myth that, by maximizing self-interest, everyone benefits.

Promoting the culture of compassion,[2] altruism, cooperation and solidarity. Striving to realize the complementary dimensions of the human being: personal and collective, feminine and masculine, present and historical, active and contemplative, rational and sentimental, instinctive and volitional, material and spiritual, animal, human and superhuman.

Sarkar's critique of global capitalism is deeply radical, and the author applies it to the reality of Brazil, where he lived for 11 years, and to the world. It is revolutionary, because it examines capitalism not only as a system that organizes the social relations of production, but also for its ontological, ethical and epistemological assumptions. The author examines the fruits of capitalism, not in their abstract sense, but in their historical and social location.

Prout proposes that personal development has a role in changing the world. Great historical transformations begin with personal choice. Our everyday actions can contribute to significant social change. Each transforming act of improvement joins with others, like small lights merging to form a great effulgence.

This book presents some concepts that are completely redefined. For example, today's notion of wealth is purely material, centered on capital, money and goods. Prout greatly expands this concept, designing the economy to satisfy the material needs of human beings and supporting their mental and spiritual growth. Technological progress is also reinterpreted, as that which frees the time of workers from the tasks of mere survival, allowing people to dedicate more and more time to developing their higher capacities.

The author's analysis of global capitalism is deeply critical. Even as this capitalist system progresses technically and materially, producing an ever-growing abundance of products, it causes growing human suffering. Because of a compulsion to increase the concentration of wealth, capitalists construct increasing numbers of obstacles to the healthy distribution and circulation of money and resources. They commercialize and steal the dignity of not only everything in Nature, but also of the human being.

The book brings together prominent contributing authors from diverse cultures to construct a Proutist vision of socioeconomic and human transformation. The author shares with us Sarkar's opinion that Karl Marx was not opposed to spirituality or to superior human values.[3]

There are countless spiritual movements that propose that the solution for every human problem lies in the subjective sphere. However, this is not the case with Prout. Although it is deeply rooted in Indian culture and spirituality, this movement combines action with contemplation, and material human development with the spiritual. It contributes to an undeniable universalism. The book has another value: the author is one of the guides of this movement, combining all the wealth of these proposals with his practical experience and spiritual understanding.

The "utopian" aspect of this proposal may intimidate some readers. I would like to remind them that no system of social organization ever appeared in history based only on the abstract vision of an illuminated thinker. Prout's proposal is being lived, even as I write, in a diversity of forms and with different names, by millions of people and communities around the world. The "utopian" dimension of the proposal involves planning for an entire country, and hopefully, all of humanity. But it is practical in that it aspires to be a "realistic utopia." This vision is anchored in the human being's wholeness, and enacted in the enlightened lifestyle of a growing number of activists who search for concrete answers to the problems faced by contemporary humanity.

Global capitalism, with its single-minded desire to consume, fails to fulfill the deepest aspirations of humanity as a whole and of each individual. Prout's proposal has the power to construct itself in a post-capitalist project that embraces both existential values and the organization of human society.

This proposal is also being submitted to the hard test of the real world. Venezuela, where Dada currently lives, offers favorable conditions for its implementation. And it is exactly in the field of practice that I believe Prout will network and converge more and more with other grassroots groups that share similar principles, values and vision, such as the solidarity socioeconomy, the solidarity economy, the social economy and the agricultural revolution. Eventually this will become concrete in one or more experiences at the national level, leading towards a cooperative globalization based on solidarity. The ever-more likely potential of this movement is to transform the human species into ultra human beings.

Rio de Janeiro, March 17, 2012.

In 1970 the Brazilian dictatorship imprisoned and tortured Marcos Arruda. Amnesty International lobbied the government to release him. Once released, he was forced into exile for 11 years. He worked with Paulo Freire for four years at the Institute for Cultural Action based in Geneva. He also served as a consultant to the ministries of education in Guinea Bissau, Cape Verde and Nicaragua. He received his Master's degree in Development Economics from American University in Washington, DC, and a doctorate in Education from Universidade Federal Fluminense. He has contributed to several books and has written over one hundred articles and papers. With sociologist Herbert de Souza ("Betinho"), he founded the Brazilian Institute of Social and Economic Analysis (IBASE). Marcos Arruda is director of the Institute of Alternative Policies for the Southern

Cone (PACS), which helps educate and train groups of workers in Rio de Janeiro to manage their own enterprises.

Introduction

In 2003 I published *After Capitalism: Prout's Vision for a New World*. It was subsequently translated into nine other languages.[1] However, when I recently undertook to update it, I discovered that both the world and the development of Prout had changed so much that more than 80 percent of what I wanted to include was actually new material. Beyond this, economic democracy, a fundamental demand of Prout, is also starting to resonate with the *Indignados* Movement of Spain and Portugal and the global Occupy Movement. Hence a new title for this book is appropriate.

Whereas Noam Chomsky wrote the preface to the first book, the demands on his time precluded him from writing anything for this book. So I went with a team of professional filmmakers from Occupy Wall Street to interview him in his office at Massachusetts Institute of Technology. As always, he was very gracious and insightful. I have included the transcript, corrected by him, in Chapter 13, because the themes we discussed–economic democracy, cooperatives, limiting the accumulation of wealth, the Occupy Movement, consciousness raising and Latin America–are scattered throughout the book.

I have often said that the best part of the previous book was the acknowledgements, and it is even more true of this book. More than 70 friends, including economists, ecologists, activists, agriculturalists, and some very good writers have generously given their time to review, correct and improve the text. The book is much better because of them.

There are six new essays and two revised ones for this book. A number of resource tools and techniques for presenting Prout have been added, including the popular Sarkar Game. Appendix A is a list of discussion questions for each chapter so this book can be used as a study guide. Appendices B and C are tools to design your own Prout Study/Action Circle. Appendix D has the solutions to the block-level planning exercise at the end of Chapter 6. Appendix E is a list of Prout slogans.

People often ask me, who is my audience? My answer is always, "Anyone who'll read it!" In fact, this makes it a bit harder for the reader. Because I am writing for a diverse audience in different countries and on different continents, I explain things that seem obvious to many. For example, in Chapter 1 I list some of the inherent problems with global capitalism for readers in the economically wealthy countries, problems which are painfully obvious to most readers in the so-called Third World who are desperate for viable alternatives. I also use the internationally-accepted metric system for distances and weights, which is still foreign for many residents of a few former British colonies, like the United States. Finally, the vast majority of research data published in English is about the United States, and I apologize that I was not able to include more examples from other parts of the world. I would be grateful to hear from readers who have other examples to share in future editions.[2]

There are surprise entrances by the author, me, in chapters 9, 10 and 12. I apologize in advance for any shock my sudden appearances in the text may cause the reader!

Prabhat Ranjan Sarkar

Prabhat Ranjan Sarkar was born in 1922[3] in Jamalpur, Bihar, India into a respected family that had its roots in regional leadership and ancient spiritual traditions. To support the family after his father's death, Sarkar chose to discontinue his higher education in Calcutta, and in 1941 returned to Jamalpur to work as an accountant in the railways. About that time he began to teach the ancient science of Tantra meditation, insisting that every practitioner follow a strict code of moral conduct. In 1955, at the request of his followers, he founded the socio-spiritual organization Ananda Marga ("The Path of Bliss"). In 1959 he introduced the Progressive Utilization Theory (Prout), a blueprint for how to reorganize society and the economy for the welfare of everyone.

The Ananda Marga and Prout movements spread quickly in India during the 1960s. Many of Sarkar's followers – who held key positions in the Indian civil service – actively challenged the systemic corruption of the government as well as the Hindu caste system. Opposition therefore arose from nationalistic Hindu groups, eventually leading the government to declare Ananda Marga to be a politically subversive revolutionary organization, banning any civil servant from being a member. Perhaps surprisingly, the Communist Party of India-Marxist (CPI-M) – which for decades controlled the state government of West Bengal – also opposed Ananda Marga and Prout because Sarkar's unique blend of spiritual and social ideals was attracting members away from the Party.

The persecution and repression increased, and in 1971 Sarkar was arrested on fabricated charges of conspiracy to murder. He was imprisoned, and the government attempted to poison him. He began a long fast in protest, taking only two cups of yogurt mixed with water each day. On July 4, 1975, Prime Minister Indira Gandhi declared a "State of Emergency", in which she censored the press and declared all opposition groups illegal. Of the 26 organizations that she banned, the first 14 were affiliated with Ananda Marga and Prout.

All known activists and members of these groups were imprisoned without trial. During the suspension of democracy, Sarkar was convicted and sentenced to life imprisonment. The Emergency was repealed in 1977 when Indira Gandhi was suddenly voted out of office; in the following year Sarkar was acquitted of all charges on appeal. On his release he ended his fast, which had continued for more than five years.

My Experiences with Sarkar

In 1974, I learned meditation in the United States and began reading the books of Sarkar. The spiritual practices he designed transformed me, and I discovered a happiness and inner fulfillment greater than I had ever imagined. Sarkar's books offered an inexhaustible wealth of ideas on social change and the inner spiritual journey.

I met Sarkar for the first time in his prison cell in January 1978. Never before had I encountered such pure, unconditional love. He inspired me to dedicate my life in service to humanity as a monk. I have spent the succeeding years working in Southeast Asia, Europe and South America, organizing social service projects, teaching meditation to the public and in prisons, lecturing, and occasionally writing.

After our first meeting, I experienced the joy of meeting Sarkar many more times in the 12 years that followed until he passed away in 1990. During that period he remained intensely active in Kolkata (then called Calcutta), giving very detailed talks on spirituality, Prout, philosophy and science. He also provided leadership for his organizations, composed a new body of 5,018 songs called Prabhat Samgiit (Songs of the New Dawn), and presented discourses on the structure and grammar of dozens of different languages. During the same period he spent time teaching meditation to his growing number of disciples, including senior monks and nuns called *avadhútas* and *avadhútikás*, of which I am one.

My name, "Maheshvarananda", in Sanskrit means "one who experiences the bliss of the Supreme". I am usually called "Dada" which means, simply, "brother". I am an *ácárya*, "spiritual teacher", or, literally, "one who teaches others by example and personal conduct", a very high goal which I struggle to realize every day.

Prout's Holistic Macroeconomic Model

Sarkar's writings on Prout total nearly 1,500 pages, and include extensive details on how various states of India, especially the poorest ones, can become economically self-reliant. Prout is an integrated macroeconomic model designed to develop and benefit socio-economic regions and the people who live there, while at the same time preserving and enhancing the natural environment. It is a model of great depth and sophistication. This book can only offer an overview of Prout's basic concepts and structures.

It is important to understand that Prout is not a rigid mold to be imposed on any society. Rather, it comprises a holistic set of dynamic principles that can be applied appropriately to help any area prosper in an ecological way. When the citizens and leaders of a region or country choose to apply this model, they will still have to make many responsible decisions on how best to apply the principles to achieve success.

The most-asked question about Prout is: "Where has it been put into practice?" Although examples of Prout cooperatives and communities exist in various countries and on every continent, the world will be unable to see how this model can enrich the living standard and quality of life of all until an entire state or country chooses to materialize the whole integrated system.

I am one of many who believe that Sarkar was one of the greatest thinkers and spiritualists in the modern era, and that Prout's model for social change will revolutionize the world. One night in 1979, while I was walking with him in a park in Bangkok, Thailand, he explained why he had been opposed in and denied entry to different countries: "They say I am a dangerous man. No! I am not a dangerous man. I have love for each and every one. I have universal love. I am not a dangerous man – I am a strong man." Then his voice shifted. Speaking in a low, slow and measured voice, he said, "Only those who like the fishy smell of selfishness are afraid of me, because selfishness is a mental disease that Prout does not give scope to."

Chapter 1

The Failure of Global Capitalism and Economic Depressions

We must not forget, even for a single moment, that the entire animate world is a vast joint family. Nature has not assigned any portion of this property to any particular individual... When the entire wealth of the universe is the common patrimony of all living beings, how can there be any justification for the system in which some roll in luxury, while others, deprived of a morsel of food, shrivel up and starve to death bit by bit? [1]

—P. R. Sarkar

Capitalism supports a common belief, an unconscious assumption held by many people that rich countries, companies and people became rich because they were smarter and worked harder. This unspoken, unverified belief is not only widespread among the rich, but, sadly, many middle class, poor and uneducated people in the world also share it. Everyone who shares this belief will logically also believe that poor countries remain poor because their people are not as smart and do not work as hard.

The reality is quite different. For hundreds of years, the rich countries have stolen the wealth of and exploited people in the rest of the world. And though the global capitalist system has changed a lot in modern times, it is still unjust and based on profit, selfishness and greed. It excludes more people than it benefits. Today nearly half the world's population lives, suffers and dies in poverty. [2]

Global capitalism is terminally ill. It suffers from inherent contradictions that include growing inequity and concentration of wealth, addiction to speculation instead of production, and rising, unsustainable debt. Committed to growth at all costs, global capitalism has become a cancer, out of control and lethal to the world in which it lives. It is contributing to climate change and destroying our planet's life support systems. It cannot last.

To understand why, and what alternative should take its place, it is fundamental to explore first how capitalism has evolved and the nature of its critical flaws. This knowledge will help us realize how to prepare for the future–a future after capitalism.

From Colonialism to Political Independence

When Christopher Columbus first landed in the Bahamas in 1492, he encountered the Tainos. These people lived in village communes, grew corn, yams and cassava, and were remarkable for their hospitality and belief in sharing. Columbus and his men enslaved them by the hundreds, carrying them back to Spain. Many Tainos died en route when the weather turned cold and the rest died later in captivity.

On subsequent expeditions, his men brutally killed more native people in their desperate search for gold. They craved it both for themselves and to repay Queen Isabella of Spain who had financed the expeditions. It is estimated that upward of two million Taino Indians lived on Hispaniola when Columbus arrived. Enslaved, they were worked to death in the mines and on huge plantations. After two decades, their population had dwindled to fifty thousand. By 1550, only five hundred remained, and a report in 1650 confirmed that none of the original Tainos or their descendants lived on the island.[3]

Lust for gold, silver, land and other riches propelled the Spanish and Portuguese to invade almost every part of South and Central America, enslaving and massacring the native populations. The scale of wealth they stole was incredible: within 100 years of Columbus' first voyage, the total amount of gold and silver throughout Europe had increased eightfold![4] The English, French, Dutch and other European powers followed this example on other continents. These colonies provided entrepreneurs tremendous wealth in the form of raw materials.[5]

Another great source of wealth was the slave trade. Muslim countries began kidnapping slaves from Africa in the ninth century; European nations later carried between eleven and twenty million people across the Atlantic Ocean.[6] Robbed of their humanity, their children made slaves as well, their culture, language and religion destroyed, these Africans encountered a racism and contempt which still lingers today. Slave labor in the plantations and mines of the Americas enriched the European elites and helped finance the Industrial Revolution.

Adam Smith, the first theorist of capitalism, observed the enrichment of the colonizing nations in his book, *An Inquiry into the Nature and Causes of the Wealth of Nations*, published in 1776. He asserted that those individuals with the ability to create wealth would always do so, to the benefit of the whole population, if the government did not impede them. This approach later became known as 'laissez-faire', a theory which argues that capitalists should be free of all government regulation and should face no limits on accumulation of wealth. Yet the so-called "Father of Capitalism" also expressed concerns about the behavior of unchecked capitalism. He proposed an economy in which all capital was invested locally and productively, based upon strong humanitarian values and avoiding exploitation. During his time, no one could have envisioned the global speculative economy of today.

As the Industrial Revolution developed in the nineteenth century, colonies became a captive market. Clever entrepreneurs discovered they could force the colonies to buy the colonizer's industrial goods. For example, India was called "the jewel in the crown" of the British Empire because of the vast wealth it provided. Until the beginning of the nineteenth century, it had a flourishing weaving industry and exported its cotton products. The English destroyed these traditional trades and crafts by passing laws prohibiting textile export and forcing the Indian people to buy cloth from the mills of Manchester.[7] The British Empire even waged war with China twice to force them to allow the open sale of the opium they were producing in India to the Chinese population.

Resistance to this exploitation, however, also grew. Through long struggles for social justice, the consciousness of people evolved. Outright slavery was eventually outlawed in all the developed countries. When the fascist regimes of Germany, Japan and Italy invaded other nations in the twentieth century, triggering the Second World War, people could, for the first time, see and hear the carnage through newspaper photos, cinema and radio. Nearly seventy million people were killed in that war that vividly demonstrated the folly of "master races", making the words "empire" and "colonialism" shameful throughout the world.

After the war, liberation movements, long smoldering, began to burn in nearly every colony. Within two decades of their victory, the Allied powers of Britain, France, the United States, Belgium and the Netherlands were forced to grant political freedom to almost all their former colonies. Spain and Portugal had long since lost their colonies in the Americas.

Invading and plundering other countries by military force was now considered to be politically inexpedient. So capitalists in the rich countries searched for new and subtler ways to continue taking the wealth.

The Economics of the Cold War

Towards the end of the Second World War, in 1944, economic advisers of the allied powers met in the U.S. town of Bretton Woods, New Hampshire, to discuss how to organize business in a post-colonial world. Each government agreed to regulate their currencies based on the convertibility of the U.S. dollar for gold. This and many other rules essentially made the United States the world's banker. Playing such a key financial role was advantageous for the country in the 1950s and 1960s, facilitating enormous overseas investment by American corporations.[8]

The Cold War of the United States and its allies against the Soviet Union and its satellite states wielded political conflict, military tension, proxy wars, espionage, propaganda and arms races to contain communism. However the economic aspect of that struggle aimed to maintain dominance over poorer nations and thereby prevent socialists from taking over the sources of their raw materials. For example, in 1973 the democratically-elected president of Chile, Salvador Allende, nationalized the huge mines of the U.S.-owned Anaconda Copper Mining Corporation. Soon after, the Chilean military commanded by General Augusto Pinochet murdered Allende and thousands of others in a violent military coup, overthrowing his popular government. *The New York Times* later revealed that the coup was both encouraged and financed by the U.S. Central Intelligence Agency.[9]

Throughout Latin America, Africa and Asia, popular governments were overthrown and military dictators supported because of their ability to maintain order and favorable conditions for international business. Dissidents, activists, journalists, teachers and priests who protested against the abuses of these regimes were labeled communists. Those who demanded human rights and economic self-determination faced torture and murder.

In the 1970s, huge petrol profits from the Orgnization of Petroleum Exporting Countries (OPEC) countries were deposited in U.S. banks. The banks in turn became desperate for somewhere to invest all their money and earn respectable profits. So they began lending billions of dollars to developing countries, many of whom were controlled by dictators. Corrupt politicians, generals and business leaders in these countries siphoned off much of this money that had been allocated for public works. For example, the Brazilian military dictatorship borrowed billions to build highways and huge hydroelectric dams at grossly inflated costs. The Western press lauded the "Brazilian economic miracle", but this left the country burdened with huge debts. U.S. interest rates then rose in the 1980s, just as democratic elections were beginning to be held again in Brazil and other Latin American countries. The interest payments on the debt began to multiply.

Hundreds of billions of dollars began flowing from South to North. Part of this was to service the debt, which by the end of the 1980s far exceeded new aid. The rest was "capital flight", as the wealthy classes sent their profits overseas. The Latin American economies began to fail.

The International Monetary Fund (IMF) was created at the 1944 Bretton Woods Conference to supply member nations with money to help them overcome short-term balance-of-payment difficulties. It is often the *only* source of funding when a country has large external debts, as is the case with many of the poorer countries of the Southern Hemisphere. However, this money is only loaned if the recipients have agreed to extreme forms of "austerity" to attack inflation and stabilize the currency, a so-called structural adjustment program. These measures include:

Reducing the government budget by trimming payrolls and social spending, which can lead to massive layoffs; and introducing fees for education and medical care, which ultimately results in higher rates of illiteracy, suffering and death.

Raising interest rates to combat inflation, which hurts small farmers and businesses struggling to repay their loans. This makes the country more profitable for foreign investors, though they are free to pull their money out at any moment.

Eliminating customs tariffs charged on imported goods, which allows multinationals to undercut and bankrupt domestic manufacturers.

Eliminating laws that prohibit foreign ownership of land, resources and businesses. This permits multinational corporations to open factories in these poorer countries, where they are usually offered tax breaks and are free to pay low wages, often resulting in "sweatshop" conditions.

Cutting subsidies for basic necessities, freeing up more money for debt repayments while forcing the poor to pay more for basic foodstuffs.

Reorienting economies from subsistence to export by giving incentives to farmers to produce cash crops instead of food for domestic consumption, and encouraging the export of raw materials.[10]

These are the hallmarks of neoliberal free market economics. The wealthy elite of a 'structurally-adjusted' country greatly benefit from these policies. With fewer currency controls, they are able to invest their profits overseas or in foreign currencies. However, these programs have been disastrous for the common people. The people of Eastern Europe, Russia, Africa and Latin America have suffered terribly under these IMF structural policies. The World Bank recently estimated that the anti-protectionist measures imposed by the rich countries cost the undeveloped countries more than twice as much as the total aid flowing from the North to the South. [11]

Common Practices by Multinational Corporations

Small-scale free enterprise encourages invention, innovation and diversity, and contributes to local communities. The economics faculties of most Western universities highlight these benefits of a transparent market in which many small firms are fully competitive. Unfortunately, since 1600 when the British East India Company and the Dutch East India Company were formed, multinational corporations have played by different rules. These first two corporations were chartered as monopolies that issued stocks, and had quasi-governmental powers, including the ability to wage war, negotiate treaties, coin money, and establish colonies. Fabulously lucrative, they inspired future generations of capitalists to invent ingenious strategies to turn their corporations into the most wealthy and powerful entities on the planet.

Large-scale corporations do not reinvest their profits in local communities. Instead their earnings are paid to stockholders who live far from the production sites and often use the money for speculation. In addition, multinational corporations construct barriers to entry to protect their dominance. These obstacles make it difficult or impossible for other companies to compete. Some of the most significant barriers include:

Startup capital, economy of scale and predatory pricing: Huge multinationals have tremendous capital on hand to pour into new endeavors, a resource that can't be matched by smaller competitors. They can produce enormous quantities of goods at lower costs, and even sell at a loss to bankrupt the competition. In most Western countries predatory pricing and other actions intended to bankrupt a competitor are illegal, but these are difficult to prove and rarely prosecuted. Even when they are prosecuted, it's almost always too late to prevent the harm. By the time Microsoft Corporation was brought to trial for violating the Sherman Antitrust Act, it had already effectively destroyed Netscape, once the most widely used web browser.

Walmart Stores, Inc. is the world's third largest public corporation by revenue (US$446 billion) with 10,185 stores in 27 countries.[12] The corporation builds big box stores in the countryside where the price of land is cheap and the company doesn't have to pay city taxes for schools and other social services. Like McDonald's, they hire dozens of young people from the area at minimum wage. Because of their huge volume of business, they are able to stock their store with every type of product and price them cheaper than any other business. Their stores effectively bankrupt nearly every family-owned clothing store, drug store, hardware store, stationary store and other local business in nearby towns, enterprises which have served their customers and paid city taxes for decades. The local towns lose tax revenues, which hurts schools and infrastructure, and many experienced workers lose their jobs. In 2012 the widow and children of the founder, Sam Walton, together had a net worth of US$95.4 billion dollars, much more than the richest person in the world.[13]

Advertising: The ability to conduct large-scale promotional campaigns is a powerful advantage that large companies have over smaller competitors. They conduct scientific studies to learn how to effectively manipulate behavior and create artificial desires in the public. It is estimated that U.S. corporations would spend US$368 billion on advertising and marketing in 2010[14].

Coca-Cola, the largest producer of soft drinks in the world, has certainly been effective in its publicity. Since the company began in 1886, Coca-Cola has convinced the majority of people in the world that its product–a clearly unhealthy sugar-laden beverage containing caffeine and phosphoric acid–will quench a thirst better than water, and bring happiness at the same time. In addition to major sponsorship of sports teams, the Olympics and the World Cup, Coca-Cola has struck multi-million dollar deals with Colombia Pictures, Universal Studios and the popular Brazilian soap operas to have their actors drink Coke in their films.[15]

Buyouts and takeovers: Deregulation in the United States during the last three decades has allowed corporations to buy out or take over competing companies. Today the world is awash with speculation capital for mergers, partly because many retirement savings plans have been put into mutual funds and hedge funds, and partly because the money supply has grown at an alarming rate due to tremendous credit creation. In 2006 mergers and acquisitions in the world totaled US$2.2 trillion.[16]

In most corporate takeovers, large numbers of workers are laid off to make the companies more profitable. The intense competition for bottom-line profits each quarter renders corporate entities mostly unconcerned about worker rights or the environment.

Lawyers, lobbyists and government regulations: Because corporations often try to bankrupt or buy out competing firms, and to secretly or informally fix price deals, they have sometimes been targeted in anti-trust suits. Their response has been to delay any case until a more sympathetic government is elected. They also cultivate that sympathy by donating heavily to the political campaigns of both parties! An IBM lawyer said he learned at the beginning of his career that, "I could take the simplest anti-trust case... and protract it for the defense almost to infinity".[17] Even after the Microsoft Corporation *lost* its anti-trust case in 2000 and its appeal in 2001, it was still able to broker a favorable deal with the U.S. Justice Department.

Additionally, large firms often weight the probability of legal costs and fines upon getting "caught" against the profit from illicit behavior. As long as the payoff exceeds the expected cost of being caught, the illicit behavior is approved.

Domestically, through the use of lobbyist and campaign contributions, corporations reduce the effectiveness of government oversight and regulation. In the United States, it is not uncommon for lobbyists and industry representatives to write the language for laws that regulate their industry, thus assuring that the regulations are ineffective.

On the international front, corporations push their governments to create favorable regulations and trade agreements through agencies like the World Trade Organization. With the pretense of creating a "level playing field", these agreements attempt to bring down all national trade barriers that have served to protect the manufacturing and agriculture sectors of each country. Edward Goldsmith, founding editor of the respected English magazine *The Ecologist*, pointed out how absurd these economic globalization agreements are. "They kill domestic economies and result in a new colonization. If I had to confront world heavyweight boxing champion Mike Tyson, I wouldn't want to confront him on a 'level playing field'–I'd need a hell of a lot of bodyguards!"[18]

To push for these types of agreements, in 1994 the U.S. government sent more than 800 delegates to the last trade meeting of the Uruguay Round of the General Agreement on Tariffs and Trade (GATT, which later became the World Trade Organization).[19] Of course these lobbyists were not democratically chosen to reflect a diversity of opinions–all 800 of them were business executives and consultants pressing for agreements to make it illegal to diminish the profits of U.S. corporations, even at the expense of the environment.

Intellectual property control: Corporations pay for the best legal teams to file endless patents on their products and processes with the intent of preventing competition. Corporate lawyers also file harassing patent infringement suits that often bankrupt their competitors. The Monsanto Corporation's genetic engineering and its patents on agricultural genes are designed to monopolize their control of agriculture and to prohibit farmers from practicing, as they have for 10,000 years, the selection of their best seeds, maintaining biodiversity and ensuring food security. Pharmaceutical corporations routinely do "patent evergreening," making minor, irrelevant changes to existing molecules to extend their patent monopolies.

Vertical integration and control of resources: Corporations extend their coverage over all levels of production, while favoring their own operations at each level. They also seek to control essential resources to prevent rival companies from competing.

Another trick corporations use to raise the value of their stocks and reduce taxes is "creative accounting". Because corporate managers are usually rewarded with stock options, they are motivated to do anything to raise their stock prices artificially. For example, the accountants at Rupert Murdoch's Newscorp Investments were so skillful that the company paid no net British corporation tax from 1987 to 1997, despite announcing group profits of £1.4 billion during that period![20] Court-appointed investigators found that executives of Lehman Brothers Holdings Inc., the global financial services firm that filed the largest bankruptcy case

in history in 2008, had used cosmetic accounting gimmicks at the end
of each quarter to make its finances appear less gloomy than they really
were. They falsely showed that securities from the company's balance
sheet had been sold, and created "a materially misleading picture of the
firm's financial condition in late 2007 and 2008."[21]

A few corporations sincerely try to practice responsible investing,
environmental care and concern for local populations. However their
corporate structure with its separation of shareholder owners from
management and workers prevents any significant change of the exploitative system.

Such examples demonstrate how multinational corporations concentrate power and wealth in fewer and fewer hands. Their accounting
ledgers do not reflect the damage done to individuals, local economies
and the environment. Capitalism's claim that, left unhindered, market
forces will benefit everyone, is clearly a lie.

The Global Financial Crisis of the 2000s

Between 1997 and 2006, the price of the typical American house
increased by 124 percent.[22] As prices rose dramatically, an US$8 trillion
housing bubble was formed, encouraging many homeowners to refinance
their homes at lower interest rates, or to borrow money by taking out
second mortgages secured by the rising value of the house. As a result,
average U.S. household debt as a percentage of annual disposable personal
income rose from 77 percent in 1990 to 127 percent at the end of 2007.[23]
The subprime mortgages were resold to banks, and the total increased
from US$35 billion in 1994, to US$600 billion by 2006.[24]

Approximately 80 percent of U.S. subprime mortgages were adjustable-
rate.[25] After house prices peaked in mid-2006 and began a steep decline,
these adjustable-rate mortgages began to reset at higher rates. Many
homeowners were shocked to learn that they owed more on their mortgage than their house was now worth. Mortgage delinquencies soared
and foreclosures began. More than 2.3 million homes were repossessed
from December 2007 to August 2010.[26]

Securities backed with subprime mortgages, widely held by banks,
lost most of their value. Then on September 15, 2008, Lehman Brothers
Holdings Inc., a global financial services firm worth US$691 billion, filed
the largest bankruptcy case in history. This crashed the New York Stock
Exchange, causing the Dow its largest one-day point loss and creating a

"perfect storm" of economic distress. Citigroup, Bank of America and all the other major U.S. banks and many European banks were also on the brink of bankruptcy because of the subprime mortgage crisis and the toxic assets they held. On October 8, the British government announced a bank rescue package of £500 billion (approximately US$850 billion) to save their banks. Two weeks later a US$700 billion bailout package (Troubled Asset Relief Program) was approved by U.S. Congress to save these huge corporations. They were considered "too big to fail", meaning they were so central to the U.S. economy that their collapse would be disastrous and hence the taxpayers should save them.

In this bailout, the Federal Reserve Board loaned a total of US$3.3 trillion to the same U.S. banks and corporations and even to some European banks (Deutsche Bank and Credit Suisse) which caused the crisis, but with no conditions to restrict executive pay or to help homeowners with mortgages.[27] Questions arise: Why are the taxes of the public bailing out the big bankers? How much money can the United States or any government spend before it itself goes broke? Why are the firms "too big to fail" so badly mismanaged? And why were many smaller banks allowed to collapse without bailouts? Twenty-five US banks failed in 2008, 140 failed in 2009 and 157 failed in 2010.[28]

The human costs of the crisis are devastating. Unemployment has soared: 2 million factory jobs and 6.5 million other jobs disappeared from November 2007 to April 2010, the nation's worst slump since the Great Depression of the 1930s.[29] In addition, the retirement accounts of U.S. workers lost US$3.4 trillion in value between September 30, 2007 and March 6, 2009.[30]

In early 2010, the global financial crisis sparked a sovereign debt crisis in Europe, because taxpayers' money was used to bail out the private banks. At the time of this writing, the governments of Greece, Ireland and Iceland were in financial crisis due to the activities of their banking sector, and other countries and banks were refusing to finance their deficits. Portugal, Italy, Spain and Belgium were also rumored to be on the brink of debt collapse. Meanwhile, angry German voters believe that they are being asked to pay for the excesses of their neighbors. Conservatives argue that the sovereign debt crisis is due to government overspending, conveniently ignoring the ever-increasing burden of corporate welfare. However, much government expenditure is unavoidable and more to the point, the middle-class tax base is shrinking while big business and the rich pay a decreasing proportion of tax.

Economic Depressions

An economic recession is defined by the National Bureau of Economic Research as a period in which there is negative real economic growth for three quarters (nine months). There is no agreed-upon definition for a depression, though most economists consider it a longer, more severe downturn with abnormally large increases in unemployment and an element of panic.

Before the development of modern industrial economies, there were no economic depressions as such. Local economies were based on "production for subsistence," and were less market-oriented. Economic disasters did occur, but they were localized, caused by natural calamities, scarcity, famine or war.

In the last 150 years, however, capitalist economies have consistently moved through cycles of boom and bust. Years of industrial expansion have been followed by years of depression — the bull market by the bear market. These depressions have not been due to scarcity. Rather they have been characterized by surplus production, while the people lacked the money to buy goods.

At the root of economic depressions lie the inherent contradictions of capitalism. Firms seek to maximize profits and reduce costs, while maintaining or increasing their market share. Hence there is a constant pressure to increase efficiency and reduce labor costs. When business slows, companies lay off workers. When unemployment rises and real wages shrink, the purchasing capacity of the common people decreases and they buy less, resulting in reduced sales for all industries. In this way global capitalism constantly saws away at the branch upon which it sits.

Consider the issue of unemployment. The unemployed are defined as people who are without jobs and who have actively looked for work within the past four weeks. It does not count the chronically unemployed who have given up hope and stopped looking. In the United States, 9.8 percent of the workforce, 15.1 million people, were unemployed in November 2010, but "total unemployment" was nearly double that at 16.8 percent.[31] Unemployment among African Americans is higher than in the general public (in five states the official rates exceed 20 percent)[32] and among native Americans on the Pine Ridge Indian Reservation, unemployment nears 80 percent.[33] Every person in the world who wants to work but cannot find a job is experiencing economic depression. Many communities, regions and even countries are suffering depression as well.

Economics Professor Jaroslav Vanek of Cornell University is a prominent advocate of cooperatives and "economic democracy." He suggests that because the essential condition of capitalism is profit maximization, the system's defining equation can be written as:

Profit = income - labor and other expenses

As profit is the foremost goal of capitalist enterprises, capitalists are continually seeking to reduce the money paid to workers in order to maximize earnings. This naturally leads to exploitation of the labor force.[34]

P. R. Sarkar, the founder of Prout, blames depressions on capitalist exploitation:

> In the economic sphere depressions are inevitable in both capitalist and communist countries due to this very inherent, intensive and innate staticity. Economic depressions are actually the net result of suppression, repression and oppression–that is, exploitation. When exploitation reaches the culminating point, the mobility and the speed of the society become virtually nil. In such a stage, that is, in this culminating point, a natural explosion takes place.[35]

This perspective, that both capitalist and centralized state economies face the same danger, is uncommon. When the majority of people in any economy are not benefited by economic growth, when in fact their labor is exploited, society loses its dynamism and becomes static.

The way to avoid economic depressions is by creating a local cooperative-based economy. Designed to meet the needs and aspirations of the population, a cooperative economy may sometimes experience periods of little or no economic growth, because pause is a natural phenomenon. But when production exceeds demand, for example, instead of laying off workers, cooperatives would reduce the working hours for everyone.

The following section explains why increasingly severe economic depressions are inevitable in the corporate economy.

Global Capitalism's Four Fatal Flaws

There are four inter-related defects inherent in global capitalism.

The first fatal flaw is great concentration of wealth. Greed is the excessive and selfish pursuit of wealth or other material things, without concern about whether one's actions deprive others of necessities. Rather than controlling this instinct, unregulated capitalism encourages it. Some proponents of free market capitalism go so far as to argue that greed should be considered a positive trait because the race to maximize profits propels the global economy forward. As the character Gordon Gekko in the film *Wall Street* said, "*Greed... is good!*"

Though the wealth of the world is steadily increasing, the world's richest people are hoarding almost all of it. And because of this huge, increasing gap between the rich and the poor, common people can afford to buy very little.

For example, the chief executive officers (CEOs) of multinational corporations are paid salaries with stock options that *Fortune* magazine describes as "outrageous!"[36] In 2009 Aubrey McClendon of Chesapeake Energy received US$114 million, Lawrence Ellison of Oracle received US$130 million, and H. Lawrence Culp Jr. of Danaher received US$141 million.[37] On average the CEO of a Standard & Poor's 500 index company was paid US$9.25 million in compensation in 2009.[38] During the same year, millions of U.S. workers lost their jobs, their homes and their retirement savings in the worst financial crisis since the Great Depression.

The disparity between rich and poor continues to grow. The wealth of the world's 51 richest people more than doubled during the last eight years, to more than US$1 trillion.[39] This is more than the combined annual income of half the world's population–three billion human beings.

When wealth is concentrated in the hands of a few and not circulating productively, ordinary people have less and less purchasing power. As Australian artist Angela Brennan wrote in one of her paintings, "Every morning I wake up on the wrong side of capitalism."

Poverty and suffering on our planet is increasing. Currently, over half of the rural population in Latin America and the Caribbean is poor and almost a third lives in conditions of extreme poverty.[40] The World Bank estimates that in 2008, 1.4 billion people suffered what they call "absolute poverty," living on less than US$1.25 a day, and 2.7 billion lived on less than US$2 a day.[41]

Richard Wilkinson and Kate Pickett, in their book, *The Spirit Level: Why More Equal Societies Almost Always Do Better*, demonstrate the "pernicious effects that inequality has on societies: eroding trust, increasing anxiety and illness, and encouraging excessive consumption."[42] They claim that in more unequal rich countries, results are substantially worse for each of eleven different health and social problems: physical health, mental health, drug abuse, education, imprisonment, obesity, social mobility, trust and community life, violence, teenage pregnancies, and child well-being.

The greatly unequal distribution of wealth throughout the 1920s is now viewed as one of the main causes of the Great Depression. According to a study done by the Brookings Institute, in 1929 the top 0.1 percent of Americans had a combined income equal to the bottom 42 percent.[43] Yet mainstream economists did not predict that depression, nor did they foresee the global financial crisis that began in 2007, because they do not consider wealth concentration a chronic and fatal problem of capitalism.

The second fatal flaw of global capitalism is that the vast majority of investments are now made in speculation instead of production. The tremendous wealth held by the richest people is rarely invested in starting companies, paying salaries, or producing goods. We can understand why this happens by observing what motivates big investors. To start a new enterprise takes capital, careful planning and constant work. Many people have to be hired; managing them and confronting the daily problems that arise is a big responsibility. Most new enterprises fail; even the successful ones generally make no more than ten or twenty percent profit during the first few years of operation.

Wealthy individuals have the capital to invest in new enterprises, but few of them are interested in all that work for such a small profit. Instead, they prefer to gamble on ventures that offer the chance to earn big profits quickly, such as the stock market, the futures market, real estate, currency trading, derivatives, etc. This has been termed the financialization of the economy, in which financially-leveraged wealth surpasses that of the industrial economy. Consequently, the majority of people lose out as these speculative investments create only a few new jobs and tend to concentrate the wealth of the society in the hands of fewer and fewer individuals.

This results in the grossly inflated "bubbles" of speculative capital, when prices that investors are willing to pay soar far higher than the intrinsic value of the product. Economic bubbles burst from time to time and place to place, causing economic depressions with widespread unemployment and suffering.

About $3.98 trillion per day is shuffled around in this great casino of speculation as investors gamble in foreign exchange and related markets and try to get rich quick.[44] The prices of stocks, real estate and other markets have grown into speculative bubbles of incredible proportions, completely based on investor confidence–a misplaced confidence.

Sadly, more than half of U.S. households have invested their savings in the stock market, sometimes involuntarily through their employers' retirement programs. Families should not have to risk losing all their savings in the inevitable downturns of the ever-volatile stock markets.

What significance do the investments of the super-rich have for the rest of the world? A lot! Today the capitalist economies of most nations are ever more interconnected and interdependent. If the New York Stock Market falls, or the value of the dollar falls, within minutes the world's other stock markets and economies will also begin to fall.

The International Monetary Fund in 2009 estimated the total value of the world's economy to be US$70.21 trillion.[45] And yet the total world derivatives market in the second half of 2009 has been estimated at about US$615 trillion, more than eight times the size of the entire global economy![46] This explosion of financial assets destabilizes and endangers the world's economic health.

The third fatal flaw of global capitalism is debt, encouraging consumers and businesses to buy on credit. Corporations spend hundreds of millions of dollars on advertising campaigns to make debt sound desirable and risk-free. Their sophisticated global ad campaigns and direct mail programs are aimed at every age group, from young teenagers to the elderly. The largest credit card companies have launched campaigns such as "Life Takes Visa," MasterCard's "Priceless" and Citibank's "Live Richly." The insidious goal of each of these campaigns was to eliminate negative feelings about going into debt. The creative director of MasterCard's campaign, Jonathan B. Cranin, explained, "One of the tricks in the credit card business is that people have an inherent guilt with spending. What you want is to have people feel good about their purchases."[47]

American consumers have dug themselves into a terrible debt trap. In March 2010 the total consumer debt was US$2.45 trillion, which averages US$16,046 for each household.[48] The effects of debt are terrible on families. A 2010 survey in Great Britain found that debt problems have a negative impact on people's close relationships, their health and their ability to carry out their jobs. The majority of respondents hid the fact of the debt problems from their partners, their friends and their parents, expressing they felt "shame" and "embarrassment."[49]

It gets nastier, because financial companies prey on people who urgently need loans to pay for health care and other necessities. Lenders use unfair, deceptive, or fraudulent practices to induce people to take on more and more high-interest debt. To squeeze more profit from borrowers, U.S. credit card companies increased interest rates from 17.7 percent in 2005 to 19.1 percent in 2007, a difference that gave them billions of dollars in extra profits. Average late fees rose from less than US$13 in 1994 to US$35 in 2007, and fees charged when customers exceed their credit limits more than doubled from US$11 to US$26 a month.[50]

The lucrative lending practices of these merchants of debt have led millions of North Americans — young and old, rich and poor — to the brink of disaster. And yet in 2005 the U.S. bankruptcy laws were changed, making it much harder for consumers with modest incomes to escape their debt by filing for bankruptcy. The new laws encouraged more reckless lending on the part of lenders, because they could more easily force poor borrowers to repay. Still, more than one-and-a-half million Americans filed for bankruptcy in the 12-month period ending June 30, 2010.[51]

What is true for individuals is also true for countries. The largest debtor nation is the United States, with US$13.6 trillion national debt. The government constantly issues new bonds, bills and notes to finance this debt, borrowing an additional US$3.8 billion every day. In 2009, the budget deficit was US$1.4 trillion.[52] It is estimated that 48 percent of the federal budget is devoted to current and past military expenditure.[53] The goods trade deficit in 2009 was US$517 billion.[54] If for any reason the confidence of the world's investors in the US economy were to fail, the largest economy in history would come tumbling down like a house of cards.

The fourth fatal flaw of global capitalism is its tendency to exploit and ignore the natural environment. In addition to causing terrible human suffering, capitalist greed and mismanagement are destroying the environment. Unsustainable by its very nature, capitalism strives for ever-expanding markets, increasing consumption and production on a finite planet. The insatiable drive for profits results in corporations wielding their influence, money and power to get around or limit environmental laws and regulations. U.S. industries publicly admit to releasing 2.2 million tons of toxic chemicals a year,[55] and many companies open factories in other poorer countries with less strict laws about pollution.

Petroleum is one of the main problems. Our modern economy is very dependent on cheap fossil fuels, driving all transportation and much of industrial production, including all plastics. Corporations make great profits extracting oil from the earth, but they externalize the costs. For example, the companies externalize the cost of pollution caused by burning the petroleum. In 2007, due to the burning of fossil fuels and cement manufacture, China emitted 6.1 billion tons of carbon dioxide into the atmosphere, 21.5 percent of the world's total, closely followed by the United States, at 5.7 billion tons, 20.2 percent.[56] Air pollution kills people–2.4 million each year, according to the World Health Organization.[57] Yet the costs of those deaths and other problems caused by fossil fuels are paid for by individuals and society, not the petroleum corporations.

Carbon dioxide and other pollutants contribute to global warming. This puts at risk unique ecosystems and endangered species, causes sea levels to rise, and increases the frequency and intensity of extreme weather events, wildfires and famine. Millions of poor people living in the tropical regions are in the greatest danger. The planetary ecosystem is also at risk of reaching "tipping points", such as the melting of the permafrost releasing methane gas, or the slowing of the Gulf Stream Current in the Atlantic Ocean, beyond which change progresses much faster and is largely irreversible.

BP's Deepwater Horizon oil spill, from April 20 to July 15 2010, released 4.9 million barrels of crude oil into the Gulf of Mexico. The causes of the explosion and ensuing leakage, according to the White House oil spill commission's final report, were the efforts of the corporations to work more cheaply. The report states: "Whether purposeful or not, many of the decisions that BP, Halliburton, and Transocean made that increased the risk of the Macondo blowout clearly saved those companies significant time (and money)."[58]

The disaster was also related to peak oil. This refers to the point in time when the maximum rate of global petroleum extraction is reached, after which the rate of production enters a terminal decline. Whereas scientists have warned of this approaching crisis for decades, it is well understood that the only reliable way to identify the timing of peak oil is in retrospect, after the fact, due to the unreliability and inconsistency with which petroleum companies estimate the capacity of known reserves. The situation is further complicated due to the discovery of new reserves (which happens rarely now) and changes in consumption patterns. In other words, we cannot really know when it happens, until afterwards.

The BP corporation found that out of 54 oil-producing countries and regions in the world, 30 have definitely passed their production peak,

and ten more appear to have flat or declining production.[59] Because
of peak oil, and the global economy's addiction to oil, BP and other
companies drill in ever-deeper waters, squeeze oil from the tar sands
of Canada and do hydraulic fracturing of shale rock, at ever increasing
environmental costs.

The International Energy Agency finally announced on November
9, 2010 in their World Energy Outlook report that the milestone of
peak crude oil already passed in 2006.[60] And in 2012 the International
Monetary Fund predicted "...a near doubling, permanently, of real oil
prices over the coming decade... In that case the macroeconomic effects
of binding resource constraints could be much larger, more persistent,
and they would extend well beyond the oil sector."[61] As oil demand and
prices rise, the global economy, so heavily dependent upon petroleum-
based export agriculture and global shipping, will come under greater
and greater strain.

Crisis and Opportunity

We do not live in a world at peace. The systemic violence of the global
economy kills nearly 50,000 of the poor every day, through hunger,
preventable infectious diseases and AIDS.[62] This genocide goes on even
though the planet has enough food and basic necessities for everyone. Sadly, popular campaigns such as Great Britain's "Make Poverty
History" have failed to significantly impact the power structure of
global capitalism.

Today's multinational corporations are so big and powerful that they
are out of control. Their structure and practices increase the gap between
the rich and the poor, a gap that is dividing humanity. Because most
investments are speculative instead of productive, and because of rising
debt, the global economy is in serious trouble. Greed, the engine behind
global capitalism, is a mental disease.

Even though the majority of the scientific community is well aware of
the dangers of environmental destruction, climate change and peak oil,
they have no means to compel nations to sacrifice comforts and take the
radical and costly steps necessary to properly deal with these problems.
The world needs a powerful "wake-up call" to make everyone realize
that to survive, we have to change now.

Clearly, we require an economic system that is democratic, protective
of the environment, and that offers a higher quality of life to all. We

should not wait for the next economic disaster, depression or financial collapse, though any of these might strike tomorrow. Let us start building an alternative economy today to help our communities, our countries and the world overcome economic depression and minimize the suffering it causes.

How to Live Through Economic Turmoil

by Mark A. Friedman

I have worked for twenty years with low-income families as the Chief Executive Officer of the First 5 Alameda County, Every Child Counts, which serves children aged 0 to 5 and their families in California. I have seen first-hand the physical deprivation and emotional suffering that those who live below the poverty line undergo. Many people suffer from poor nutrition, inadequate public education, and lack of access to health care. American economic growth does not trickle down to those without education or economic opportunities. Often people of color and new immigrants are unable to share in the fruits of American society.

The ongoing economic turmoil necessitates preparing for possible worst-case scenarios, notably that the global economy could continue in a prolonged period of recession or slide into depression. The current economic crisis has featured significant corporate downsizing and although profits have rebounded quite well for most multi-national companies, rehiring or new hiring lags way behind. Real estate in many parts of the world continues to slump. Government tax coffers that depend on income, sales, and real estate taxes are under tremendous pressure leading to almost global cuts in public education, health and human services at a time when families need those services more than ever.

The lifestyle and economic changes that will help you live through the current economic downturn will generally benefit you, your family and your community regardless of economic ups and downs. Those changes include the following:

Simplify Your Life

• Purchase only what you and your family need.

- Excess material goods will burden you and take away money you may need.
- Get rid of unused, unwanted, and unnecessary goods.
- The market for used goods is not great in many places, but you may be able to get significant tax benefits for donating your goods for charitable purposes.

Emphasize non-material happiness and family togetherness.

No lasting happiness comes from external objects. Emphasizing the non-material joys of life now and in the future prepares you and your loved ones for enduring scarcity with minimal emotional damage.

Look Into Recession/Depression-Resistant Professions

In any economic downturn there are certain areas that have more job and economic security. Job categories that may provide more stability include:

Government employment: Although tax revenues have declined significantly leading to layoffs in many branches of government, there is be a great need for government workers in the area of health and human services to deal with the increased numbers of unemployed and impoverished people. A major advantage of government employment is that is often much more heavily unionized than the private sector and comes with greater benefits and job security.

Repair Shops: Fewer people will be able to afford new cars, computers, stereo equipment, furniture, clothes, and appliances. Shops that repair these things will flourish as a result.

Second Hand and Consignment Shops: Stores that sell used goods will do well, as fewer people can afford to buy new. Consignment shops that have people leave their goods for the store to sell require less money to start, because the store doesn't pay for inventory, but instead only pays the original owner once the goods are sold.

Education: Many people who get laid off will look into going back to school to gain more marketable skills. There will be a need for teachers and trainers who can help the returning students gain the skills they seek.

Cooperatives and Community Services: Both producer and consumer food cooperatives will flourish, as farmers seek reasonable prices for their produce and people in the cities seek ways to decrease the high cost of food. As large companies fail, there will be a need for cooperative consultants to show employees how to save them through worker management strategies. Community organizers, drug rehabilitation programs, crisis centers and other programs that can mend the social fabric of neighbor-hoods and create support networks will all be needed.

Diversify Your Potential Sources of Income

If your primary source of income suffers during an economic downturn, you will be much better able to weather that loss if you have developed other sources of income.

Among the potential additional sources of income you can begin to explore are the following:

Go back to school to develop marketable skills such as the ability to repair electronics or automobiles.

Look into acquiring a part-time job: If you lose your primary job in an economic downturn, your part-time job could become your primary source of income.

Look at renting out a room in your home: If you have children who now live on their own, you may have underused rooms that you can rent out for a significant income.

Think about ways to serve others and earn extra income: Many places have a critical need for foster parents or adoptive parents of children with special needs. Foster parents are compensated and often adopting a child with special needs has an ongoing subsidy attached. Tutoring and substitute teaching are other ways to help your community and bring in additional income.

Bartering: The time honored tradition of exchanging goods and services without a monetary exchange with your neighbors and community members is an excellent way to go about meeting the needs of your family. You might be surprised at how much you have to offer others and what they might have to offer you.

Be creative: Think of hobbies or interests that you may be able to convert into an income-producing activity. Increasing numbers of people who have found creative ways to use the Internet to generate incomes.

Develop and Strengthen Your Community and Put Your Priorities in Order

Economic difficulties can present a tremendous opportunity for your family and your community to unite to meet those challenges. Conversely, the failure to come together could allow the economic stress to create disharmony and conflict.

Both in your family and in your community, a depression tests all your inner strength and requires you to tap all of your inner resources. Love, compassion, emotional health, generosity, and friendship are resources that grow when they are used. Strengthening family ties is vital as when one or more members of a family lose their jobs the others can pick up the slack and help out. Many families have found joy and success by switching roles where previously one partner had been the primary breadwinner and the other the primary caregiver of children.

Some people react to economic hard times by becoming more fearful and greedy. Reacting that way will be a disservice to yourself, your family, and your community.

Finally, Prout is an alternative economic model that seeks to remedy the underlying causes of economic turmoil. By studying the principles of economic democracy and planning how to implement this model in your community, your state or your country, you can contribute to a solution that benefits all.

Chapter 2

A New Social Paradigm Based on Spiritual Values

Materialism can never be the base of human life in any country because it is detrimental to the all-round development of human beings.... The application of material science and technology may help increase the wealth of the country and thereby alleviate the financial distress of the people to some extent, but by solving economic problems one does not solve all problems. If that were the case, the affluent countries of the West would be utopian. Human beings are not merely destined to fill their bellies. There is much more to human life than that. Human beings are veritable children of God having a thirst for unlimited happiness. Limited physical wealth can never quench their infinite thirst.

— P.R. Sarkar[1]

Free market economists, staunch advocates of privatization, claim that any country can achieve economic efficiency and success through free market trade. Often called neoliberal economists or supporters of the "Washington Consensus", they portray economics as a value-free, objective science that describes timeless truths independent of ideology or cultural norms. Yet such free market analysts are woefully unable to predict accurately future currency rates, property values, inflation, and the like because the very implementation of their discipline has created a highly volatile and extremely aggressive global economy in which the quest for profits is the ultimate goal.

A clever trick of neoliberal economists has been to call the license of individuals and corporations to amass wealth beyond measure "economic freedom," as though it were equal to human rights. They claim the *right* to maximize one's wealth.

The idea of "economic freedom" conflicts with the reality that the world's resources are limited and that some actions limit the opportunities of others. In law, we grant individual rights only to the extent that they do not harm others. Prout includes this idea in economics.

Let us compare capitalism's concept of property rights with that of Prout. The seventeenth-century English philosopher John Locke asserted that a human being had the right to use his or her labor to alter the gifts of nature and to make them productive. Locke argued that by clearing an area of forest, cultivating the soil and collecting the harvest, a person made the land productive and hence had a right to own it and use it as he or she pleased. This theory is the basis of "property rights", that an owner of land or other physical property has the right to use it, not use it, rent or sell it, exclude others from using it, and even destroy it.

The founders of the United States combined this theory with a deep passion for personal freedom and the belief that it is everyone's *right* to strive to become as prosperous as possible. Any limits on property rights, assert neoliberal economists, would compromise efficiency, decrease output, and jeopardize the growth of the entire society. They also maintain that no government should be allowed to take away a significant portion of personal wealth through taxes.

This view of property rights dominates the world today, and is so fundamental to economically developed societies that it is taught and learned without question. Prout, however, has quite a different view.

An Ecological and Spiritual Perspective

Prout offers an ecological and spiritual perspective that most economic philosophies lack[2], but which is present in many traditional societies. Indigenous spirituality throughout the Americas, Africa, Asia and Australasia invariably revolves around nature. Indigenous people do not believe that the land belongs to them; rather they believe that they belong to the land. They express intense pain at seeing miners rip open the earth, loggers fell the trees, the poisoning of water and air, and the wanton slaughter of animals. Traditional cultures were and are more cooperative, living in harmony with nature and usually treating land as a common resource.

Black Elk, Oglala Lakota spiritual leader, said, "The first peace, which is the most important, is that which comes within the souls of people when they realize their relationship, their oneness, with the universe and all its powers, and when they realize that at the center of the universe dwells Wakan Tanka (the Great Spirit), and that this center is really everywhere, it is within each of us."[3]

"Aboriginal spirituality is the belief that all objects are living and share the same soul or spirit that Aboriginals share" said Eddie "Kookaburra" Kneebone.[4] Aboriginal author Mudrooroo wrote, "Our spirituality is a oneness and an interconnectedness with all that lives and breathes, even with all that does not live or breathe."[5]

In Nigeria, the Yoruba elders say: "Olorun [the Supreme Being] is hidden at the center of all things. All the worlds and their fullness are His. He cannot be contained because of His presence. Not a stone, a shell, not a tree is His person, but He is within all, He is invisible."[6]

Prout echoes this ecological perspective of traditional peoples that we all are part of the natural world, of Mother Earth. Proutist Roar Bjonnes writes:

> As long as the basic tenet of unlimited hoarding of wealth remains fundamental to our economy, economic disparity and environmental degradation will continue. We will continue to accept as fair and inevitable that economic growth creates concentration of wealth, on the one hand, and unemployment, displacement of people and poverty, on the other. Without a fundamental rethinking of the current economic dogma of private property rights as an absolute right above all other values, and that human progress is best measured as increased material consumption, we cannot create an environmentally sustainable and poverty-free society.[7]

Prout's Philosophical Base

Though Prout is a socio-economic theory that offers practical solutions to current problems, it is not a materialistic philosophy. To understand

Prout's holistic paradigm, it is helpful to look briefly at the founder's philosophy. Besides being a social philosopher and revolutionary thinker, Prabhat Ranjan Sarkar was, first and foremost, a great master of Tantra Yoga.

Tantra means "that which liberates one from the bondages of darkness." Both a spiritual outlook and a set of spiritual practices, Tantra is the oldest type of yoga, with roots going back 15,000 years. It is one of the most ancient spiritual paths in the world, and has had a profound influence on Hinduism, Taoism, Zen and Buddhism as a whole.

Tantra is a spiritual way of life, and one should not be confused with the misperception that it teaches sex practices. It is also not an organized religion; Sarkar vehemently opposed all kinds of dogmas, and went to considerable lengths to distance himself and his philosophy from Hindu dogma and the caste system in particular.

Tantra recognizes the fundamental oneness of which all mind and matter are composed. The all-pervasive awareness of this universal consciousness makes us self-aware. Our own feeling of existence is actually a reflection of the cosmic sense of existence.

Universal principles of ethics are also fundamental to Tantra. These are discussed at length in Chapter 9.

As Alan Watts wrote, "We do not 'come into' this world; we come out of it, as leaves from a tree. As the ocean 'waves,' the universe 'peoples.' Every individual is an expression of the whole realm of nature, a unique action of the total universe."[8]

Since the 1920s, when Albert Einstein and other physicists revolutionized the world of science, views about reality have been converging between physicists studying quantum mechanics, and mystics pursuing the ancient spiritual paths of Tantra Yoga, Buddhism and Taoism. Common to both are ideas of connectivity throughout the universe, a cosmic oneness and that the physical laws of the universe are guided by some intelligent process.[9]

Universal Spirituality

Dr. Peter L. Benson proposes the following definition of spirituality: "the intrinsic human capacity for self-transcendence, in which the self is embedded in something greater than the self, including the sacred" and which motivates "the search for connectedness, meaning, purpose, and contribution."[10]

Prout values this spiritual perspective focusing on the personal journey of self-development, and on service to humanity. This mystical search for truth[11] is quite different from fundamentalist religions that divide people into believers and non-believers, us versus them. Universal spirituality promotes love, while dogmas instill fear.

Ultimate truths are beyond the grasp of the intellect and can only be experienced through intuition. The divine essence resides deep within every human being; one way to experience this is to use the techniques of meditation that Sarkar called the "intuitional science." Just as the movements of the ocean currents govern the dance of the waves on the surface, so the invisible Consciousness underlying our reality guides the circumstances of our lives.

Daily meditation and other holistic lifestyle techniques of Tantra are very practical and can be done by anyone, anywhere. They are keys to personal transformation, powerful tools to overcome one's negative instincts and mental complexes, while cultivating compassion, unconditional love and altruism.

Cosmic Inheritance

Planet Earth, her wealth of resources, and even the entire universe, are the *common inheritance* of all living beings.

According to Sarkar, "This universe is the thought projection of Brahma [the Supreme Consciousness], so the ownership of the universe lies with the Supreme Entity and not with any of His imagined beings. [Note: Whereas Sarkar usually speaks of Brahma in neuter gender, here he uses "His" to emphasize the close, family relationship that exists between Supreme Consciousness and living beings.] All living beings can enjoy their rightful share of this property... As members of a joint family, human beings should safeguard this common property in a befitting manner and utilize it properly. They should also make proper arrangements so that everyone can enjoy it with equal rights, ensuring that all have the minimum requirements of life to enable them to live in a healthy body with a sound mind."[12]

Sarkar taught that every living being has both a utility value and a subtler, existential value. Nothing and no one can live independently; every complex human body depends on humble bacteria for its survival. Whether or not we can yet understand the utility and purpose of every animal and plant on this planet, we have a duty to try to preserve their habitats, and not to kill or exploit them needlessly.

Prout's notion of ownership is based on the concept that the Creator and the manifest universe are one, and that the Creator permeates and resonates in every particle of it. Even so-called inanimate objects are vital with latent consciousness. The Creator invites us to use these with respect, not to abuse them.

Because of this spiritual outlook, Prout does not give the same importance to the system of individual ownership of property that capitalism does. Collectively, like brothers and sisters in a human family, we have a duty and a responsibility to utilize and distribute fairly the world's resources for the welfare of all. Prout therefore encourages the protection of biodiversity and natural habitats through reforestation, aggressive control of air, water and soil pollution, and efforts to reduce carbon emissions and greenhouse gases.

All this represents a very different perspective from the current legal and economic systems of our world. Private property rights and the pursuit of unlimited wealth have become pre-eminent values. In the United States, for example, not more than three percent of the population owns 95 percent of the privately held land.[13] In Great Britain, the richest two percent own 74 percent of the land.[14]

According to Sarkar, "Uncultivated [farm]land is a liability for the human race." He further states, "In Prout's system of agriculture there is no place for intermediaries. Those who invest their capital by engaging others in productive labor to earn a profit are capitalists. Capitalists, like parasites, thrive on the blood of industrial and agricultural laborers."[15] Prout's solution, elaborated in the following chapters, includes starting agricultural cooperatives to better utilize land and provide jobs to the unemployed.

The spiritual concept of cosmic inheritance also suggests that the life and well-being of humans must be society's first priority, always taking precedence over other financial considerations. Hence a Proutist economy begins by providing the minimum necessities of life to all people in every region, and then gradually elevates their quality of life in a sustainable way. This is explained in the next chapter.

The Problems with Materialism

Materialist outlooks developed historically in ancient India (the Carvaka school), China (a branch of Confucianism), and Greece, later

during the European Enlightenment and finally among contemporary
scientists and Marxists. Western societies are generally concerned with
the pursuit of material wealth, possessions and luxury. Sarkar pointed
to a number of problems with what he called a "matter-centered" or a
"self-centered" approach.

First, the infinite longing for happiness, which all human beings share,
cannot be fulfilled through material objects, because they cannot be
enjoyed infinitely. When people are encouraged to seek sensory gratification, they spend their energy trying to accumulate physical possessions.
But no matter how rich they become, without a higher purpose in life,
they will inevitably experience frustration, alienation and sorrow. Even
intellectuals and scholars of materialism often run into ego conflicts,
as they argue from fragmented viewpoints; this inhibits them from
experiencing a more comprehensive, inclusive personal development
toward true wisdom.

Second, one's self-interest and greed for wealth will eventually conflict with the self-interest and greed of others. Because physical things
are limited, suspicion and distrust grow, and one competitively tries
to accumulate more by depriving others. This exploitation in turn
breeds dishonesty and corruption. The apparent morality and justice
of materialistic societies hide an immoral alliance between capitalists
and politicians to protect self-interests.

Third, materialism makes people more narrow-minded and shortsighted regarding the environment. Greed for profit is unsustainable,
because the resources of our planet are finite, and greed diminishes or
ignores the value of other species. Both capitalist and communist societies have been terribly destructive of the environment.

Human Sentiments and Neohumanism

A sentiment is an emotional tendency to identify with things we
like, with whatever gives us pleasure. It is common to feel allegiance
to one's family and close circle of friends. In addition, in many parts of
the world, membership in a clan, tribe or community is very important. Most people also consider themselves to be members or citizens
of a particular region or nation, often believing that their country is
somehow better and more important than any other. Sarkar calls this
patriotism or nationalism *geo-sentiment*. Believing that one's nation is
superior to others is expressed negatively in the slogan "My country,

right or wrong!" and in discrimination against foreigners. It was this sentiment that provided the emotional justification for colonialism and imperialism.

Identifying more with one's own race, religion, class or sex, to the exclusion of other groups, is known as *socio-sentiment*. Both geo-sentiment and socio-sentiment have led to countless tragic conflicts and wars that are, in the words of Sarkar, "the black spot of human character."[16] Politicians who exploit these sentiments to gain popularity may become quite powerful, but they can lead their entire community or nation to destruction.

"Neohumanism" is a term coined by Sarkar, and explained at length in his book, *The Liberation of Intellect: Neohumanism*. It expresses the process of expanding one's sentiment or allegiance outward from mere self-interest to one of empathy and identification with an ever-larger share of humanity and the universe.

Enlightened education that develops the rational, questioning mind can be an antidote to limiting sentiments and prejudices. If education expands our sense of identity to include all humanity, we will inevitably feel pain at the suffering of others, wherever they may be. This in turn inspires us to commit ourselves to social justice and service.

Why Neohumanism? The philosophy of humanism originated in Europe during the Renaissance in reaction to the illogical dogmas, predation and domination of the Catholic Church. In that era, powerful clergy demanded blind faith and total obedience. Later, during the Age of Enlightenment, many Western humanists rejected the idea of a transcendent God outside of human experience. Instead they relied on logic, scientific inquiry and reason, trusting only what could be observed and measured. This freed them from ecclesiastical rule, but it led to a new dogma of material physics and "scientific" materialism as the sole arbiter of truth and fact.

The rejection of God forced humanists to search deeply for the personal and political significance of such concepts as "liberty, equality and fraternity," a slogan of the French Revolution. Humanists struggled to find a more natural and rational morality. Soon, however, they ran into the problem of moral relativism. Liberty from what? Equality in relation to what? Good and evil seemed to depend on who was judging.

Within such a relative framework, the purpose of life is not always clear. This can leave the humanist in a spiritual vacuum, without transcendent values or direction–adrift on a sea of shifting, conflicting ideas.

Humanism has other limitations. When tied to internationalism, as in the case of the United Nations, its adherents may be plagued by political differences and jealousies.[17] If it is based on the belief that there is nothing greater than the human ego, that there is no higher consciousness within us, humanists can become cynical and materialistic.

The philosophy of humanism may also lead a person to neglect other species, to consider them inferior and exploit them for profit. This attitude has been called *speciesism* or *anthropocentrism*. Sarkar's Neohumanism urges us to overcome this limitation by including all of life in our definition of what is real, important and deserving of respect. Although human beings are the most evolved species on this planet, other animals have awareness and feelings, too. Our actions and conduct should demonstrate ever-increasing love and respect toward all beings and inanimate objects in the universe.

Thus, an outlook based on universalism and Neohumanism is one that recognizes the spiritual family of humanity, a family that transcends nations and is rooted in spiritual ecology. Neohumanism is an expansive concept promoting physical welfare and security, intellectual stimulation and encouragement, and spiritual growth and fulfillment. Neohumanism frees the intellect from narrow sentiments and established doctrines, as well as creating a shared sense of compassion. Viewing all human beings and the rest of this manifest universe as the children of one Supreme Consciousness, one feels that the world's sorrow is his or her own sorrow, and the world's happiness is his or her own happiness.

A New Definition of Social Progress

Every entity in this universe is moving–even inanimate objects vibrate on the atomic level. However, movement only has meaning or purpose when it is directed toward a goal. Prout defines social progress as movement directed towards the goal of well-being for all, from the first expression of ethical consciousness to the establishment of universal Neohumanism.

The concept is similar to the hierarchy of human needs developed by Abraham Maslow, who founded the field of humanistic psychology. These needs range, in ascending order, from basic physiological needs, to safety, a sense of belonging and love, esteem, and self-actualization. Lower needs must be met before meeting higher ones. Individuals whose physical and psychological needs are met can more easily develop altruism and their higher potentialities.

Maslow termed the state above self-actualization the transpersonal level. Activity here is purely spiritual, characterized by meditative introspection, contentment, unselfishness, feelings of harmony and oneness with the universe, and the experience of subtler states of consciousness. According to Maslow, this model enables one to distinguish "better" and "poorer" societies, the better ones gratifying all basic human needs of the population while fostering self-actualization.[18]

P. R. Sarkar often used the analogy of humanity as a family, or a group of people traveling on a pilgrimage, who stop whenever any member of their group is injured or falls sick. He quoted the American poet, Carl Sandburg:

> There is only one man, and his name is all men.
> There is only one woman, and her name is all women.
> There is only one child, and its name is all children.[19]

Human society should facilitate the collective movement and growth of all individuals. This requires a degree of collective consciousness and social cohesion or solidarity.

Progress is commonly associated with increases in material comfort, or advances in technology. Sarkar, however, asserted that no true progress is ever really possible in the physical realm. This is because all physical things eventually decay, and whatever physical strength one builds up will eventually be lost by accident, illness or old age. Physical inventions, while making our lives easier and more comfortable, also create problems, dangers and side effects. In the past, for example, when people walked or rode animal carts, few suffered critical injuries in accidents–now tens of thousands die in automobile accidents every year.

The well-known environmentalist Paul Hawken reports that according to the National Academy of Engineering, 94 percent of all original materials processed in the United States become waste before the final product is made. Of the products that are finished, 80 percent in turn become waste within six months after manufacture.[20] In other words, from an environmental perspective, the system is less than one percent efficient. If pollution and the treatment of waste were included, this may actually be a negative number.

It is also evident that increases in knowledge, communication and mental activity are not always truly progressive and conducive to one's deeper well-being. Whatever we learn can be forgotten. Stress, nervousness, depression and mental disease are much more common amongst educated urban populations in industrialized societies than among less educated rural people.

The speed with which human knowledge increases now is staggering. For example the number of different books published in the United States has doubled in the last 19 years. Scientific knowledge is increasing even faster, as represented by the number of journals published about oncology doubling in the last seven years, about programming (five years), stem cells (four years), global warming (three years) and nanotechnology (two years).[21] It is clearly impossible for any human being to assimilate even a tiny fraction of the world's knowledge in any subject. It is utter foolishness to be proud of how much one knows.

However, spiritual learning — wisdom — is very different. The deepest truths of life are an eternal fountain of inspiration. Spiritual, transpersonal development is a process of expanding one's consciousness to link with the Infinite, to reach a state of deep peace and happiness.

Prout asserts that spiritual longing in fact motivates every human being, though individuals experience it at different times and in different ways. Whereas absolute freedom from mundane duties and bondages is not possible in the physical and mental realms as long as we live, spiritual freedom or liberation is ours if we want it.

Prout recognizes that only those physical actions and intellectual expressions that promote progress toward the state of infinite well-being are truly progressive. For example, guaranteeing all the right to work and earn the minimum necessities of life ensures collective peace of mind. When people no longer have to worry about how they will pay the rent, or provide education and medical care for their families, they will be free to develop their higher mental and spiritual qualities.

The Dynamic Web of Life: "Pramá"

The environmental sciences demonstrate that an inter-connected web of living systems and organisms in dynamic balance exists throughout nature. Everything is changing and moving; nothing is static. The struggle to survive, the interdependence of animal and plant species, the rapid adaptation to changing conditions caused by the seasons, storms, fires, floods and other phenomena, account for the constant dynamism in nature.

To describe this relationship of shifting, vibrant forces, P. R. Sarkar introduced a Sanskrit word, *pramá*, which means dynamic equilibrium and dynamic equipoise–a fully balanced system. From the single-cell bacteria to the most complex animal, each creature inhabits its niche and expresses its unique role. The cycles of birth, life, death and decay continue in a fluctuating state of balance. In fact, one can view the environment as a factory that produces no waste at all–everything is recycled.

There are presently about 40,000 species of vertebrate animals, 250,000 species of plants, and several million species of insects and micro-organisms inhabiting our planet. Each depends on others, so on the survival of one may hang the continued existence or extinction of up to ten other species.

Today a third of the world's amphibians, a fifth of all mammals and 70 per cent of all plant species are threatened with extinction–as many as six million unique and irreplaceable forms of life.[22] Deforestation, agricultural expansion, overfishing, invasive alien species and climate change are the specific causes, all related to human activity. However, as ecologist Stephen Leahy writes, "The main engine of destruction is an economic system that is blind to the reality that there is no economy or human well-being without nature."[23]

Sadly, ecological destruction extends far beyond national boundaries, threatening the very potential of our planet to sustain life.

We have disturbed the pramá of Nature–its dynamic equipoise–because our human society has also lost its pramá. This lack of balance in society is apparent in all three spheres of existence–physical, mental and spiritual–and has occurred in both individual and collective life.

On December 6, 2001, at the Nobel Peace Prize Centennial Symposium in Oslo, Norway, 100 Nobel laureates issued a brief but dire warning of the profound dangers facing the world. Their statement, for the most part ignored by the mainstream press, predicts that our security depends on immediate environmental and social reform:

> The most profound danger to world peace in the coming years will stem... from the legitimate demands of the world's dispossessed. Of these poor and disenfranchised, the majority live a marginal existence in equatorial climates. Global warming, not of their making but originating with the wealthy few, will affect

their fragile ecologies most. Their situation will be desperate and manifestly unjust...

The only hope for the future lies in cooperative international action, legitimized by democracy... to counter both global warming and a weaponized world. These twin goals will constitute vital components of stability as we move toward the wider degree of social justice that alone gives hope of peace...

To survive in the world we have transformed, we must learn to think in a new way. As never before, the future of each depends on the good of all.[24]

Sarkar wrote that when pramá is lost, systems pass through three stages: first derangement, then disruption and finally degeneration. This means that first the biosystem or social system is disturbed, then its normal functioning must change drastically to cope, and finally its very existence is endangered. In the words of Sarkar, "Human society today has reached the stage of degeneration and, as a result, is lost in the wilderness of economic bankruptcy, social unrest, cultural degeneration and religious superstition."[25]

The North American Hopi Indians have a word describing this state, koyaanisqatsi, which means "life out of balance." Examples of this are not hard to find in society: intolerance, breakdown of the family, exploitation, religious fanaticism, widespread pornography and exploitation of women, drug and alcohol abuse, ever-rising crime rates, children killing other children, and environmental destruction.

This same type of breakdown can be observed taking place in the personal lives of many individuals as well. Nervousness, confusion, and doubt, which often result in eating disorders, and alcohol and drug abuse are common; then distrust, selfishness, lack of purpose, recklessness, uncontrollable anger and self-destructive behavior can follow; and finally hopelessness, depression and thoughts of suicide may develop.

Three-and-a-half million American teenagers between 14 and 17 years of age, 13.8 percent, considered suicide in the year 2008, and nearly one-half of those actually attempted it, reported the U.S. Department of Health. Incidents of depression and behavior risky to health are much more common, and each year the percentages climb.[26] More than one million teenagers under 18 years of age were arrested for violent crimes in 2009.[27] Statistically, youth in one of the wealthiest countries are the most troubled, depressed and violent in the world.

How Pramá Can be Restored

To restore pramá in individual life means adopting a wholesome lifestyle. Eating a nutritious and balanced diet, doing regular physical exercise, abstaining from tobacco and intoxicants, being part of a positive support group or community, volunteering service to the needy, practicing some form of daily inner reflection–all these are well-known to promote good health, a balanced mind and inner fulfillment.

To restore pramá in collective life, a systematic, step-by-step approach is also necessary. First, balance must be restored in the most fundamental physical level. This requires that we guarantee the minimum necessities of life to every human being.

Pramá, proper balance, will also have to be re-established in each field of work. For example, the agricultural system needs to be redesigned to sustainably provide a sufficient supply of the basic foodstuffs for the entire population. Only after this goal is achieved at local levels can the export and trading of excess food take place.

Industries need to be redesigned using appropriate technology to meet the needs of local populations. Converting global profit-motivated companies into locally-managed cooperatives will help accomplish this. Each industrial enterprise must also be environmentally safe. (This model is detailed further in subsequent chapters.)

To restore pramá on the mental level, the use and development of local languages, cultures and the historical wisdom of indigenous peoples should be encouraged. This will lead to a stronger sense of cultural identity and self-worth, and will eliminate feelings of inferiority caused by indoctrination by the current dominant culture. Governmental indoctrination and commercial influence over education must end. Universal ideas and values should be promoted instead of superstition and dogma; an ecological and spiritual outlook instead of a materialistic one needs to be taught at every level of education.

A spiritual perspective includes respect and gratitude for all beings, and gradually ever-expanding feelings of compassion, altruism and unconditional love for all. This involves self-transcendence, wisdom and connecting with the sacred, the infinite, to reach states of peace and transcendent happiness.

Society needs to encourage tolerance and acceptance of different beliefs and religious traditions. Recognition of and appreciation for common spiritual truths among these traditions should be taught and emphasized throughout society, and free instruction in universal spiritual practices available to all.

Finally, the balanced physical, mental and spiritual realms should be integrated to create a healthy, holistic society. These steps can transform the present materialistic society into a spiritually-oriented, global human family–a community of Earth.

By re-establishing pramá in human society, the destruction of our natural environment will cease. Instead of being despoilers of nature, we can strive to work in harmony with natural systems to reverse the damage that has been done.

Meditation

In the struggle for peace and justice in the world, we should not neglect our own internal peace. Human beings possess an inherent thirst for peace and happiness. External objects cannot satisfy this inner longing, because the pleasure they offer is only temporary; instead we have to journey within ourselves to find true peace and deepening happiness.

Meditation is a profound practice dating back thousands of years. The process is simple: by closing your eyes, sitting up straight and still, breathing deeply, concentrating the mind according to certain techniques, and practicing every day, one can gradually achieve deep peace and fulfillment.

One of the best techniques to concentrate the mind is to silently repeat a mantra. A mantra is a sound or collection of sounds which, when meditated upon, will lead to spiritual liberation. A very effective universal mantra, which anyone can meditate with, is *Baba Nam Kevalam*. In Sanskrit, this means "Only the essence of the Supreme Consciousness", or simply, "Love is all there is."

Meditation is a form of deep reflection on who we really are, a procedure for revealing hidden aspects of our identity. By penetrating beneath the social conditioning of everyday thoughts, meditation frees the mind from repressive dogmas. It can help us see through the veil of legitimacy that exploiters use to cover their destructive and selfish deeds.

Meditation offers many personal benefits, too: overcoming anger and aggression; cultivating willpower and self-control; improving self-esteem and mental health; increasing memory and concentration; surmounting insomnia, depression and loneliness; overcoming inferiority, superiority, fear, guilt and other complexes; calming the mind; expanding

understanding and tolerance; developing a balanced, integrated personality; and awakening wisdom, compassion and unconditional love.
Research supports many health-related benefits of meditation. For example, Paul Grossman and others did a comprehensive review and meta-analysis of 20 health-related studies that use mindfulness meditation. They found that meditators suffered 87 percent less heart disease, 55 percent fewer tumors, 50 percent fewer hospitalizations, 30 percent fewer mental disorders and 30 percent fewer infectious diseases.[28] Other studies show the benefits of meditation-based therapies for chronic pain,[29] anxiety and depression,[30] substance abuse,[31] and recurrent suicidal behavior.[32]

The field of transpersonal psychology recognizes seven elements common to authentic spiritual practice:[33]

1. *Ethics*: Practicing universal moral principles is an essential discipline for training the mind. Unethical behavior that inflicts harm arises from destructive instincts including greed, anger and jealousy. Conversely, ethical behavior, which aims at the well-being of others, purifies one's character and cultivates healthy tendencies such as kindness, compassion and peace. (See chapter 9.)

2. *Emotional transformation*: This process overcomes problematic emotions such as fear, anger and hatred by cultivating the positive emotions of happiness, love and compassion. A spiritualist's love and compassion is realized when they become unconditional and embrace all beings. The highest transformation allows one to develop equanimity, to stay positive whatever the obstacles, and to experience mental peace in both pain and pleasure.

3. *Redirecting Motivation*: Meditation gradually makes one less concerned with material wealth and status, and more concerned with subtle and internal goals of self-actualization, self-transcendence and selfless service. It is analogous to moving up Maslow's hierarchy of needs. By purifying our intention, we gain psychological maturity as we move away from selfishness towards a greater concern for others and magnanimity.

4. *Training Attention*: Training to concentrate the mind is essential for psychological well-being. The yogis state, "What you think, so you become." If one focuses on an angry person,

feelings of anger arise, whereas if one thinks of a loved one, love fills the heart. Therefore meditation teaches us how to calm, center, and direct our mind in order to master and transform it. As a recent Harvard University psychology study found, people were happier when they focused on whatever activity they were engaged in, instead of thinking about something else.[34]

5. *Refining Awareness*: Meditation makes us more perceptive, sensitive and appreciative of the freshness and wonder of every moment. To live in the present, to "be here now," helps us overcome boredom with routine, emotional instability and cravings that are out of control. Clarity is healing and transformative. It develops our inner orientation and intuition, allowing us to tune into the subconscious layers of the mind.

6. *Wisdom*: Cultivating wisdom means finding meaning and purpose in our lives, deeper insights about what it means to be human. It requires balancing social responsibilities with periods of quiet and solitude, especially in nature. By seeking the company of the wise and learning their teachings, and by ever deeper meditation, we realize universal truths and cultivate unconditional love for others.

7. *Altruism and Service*: Selfless service leads to psychological well-being. "It is better to give than to receive", because generosity facilitates personal happiness, lightens our heart and expands our mind. If we desire happiness for others, we tend to feel it ourselves, what the Buddhists call "sympathetic joy". As psychotherapist Sheldon Kopp said, "You only get to keep what you give away." Because meditation helps us perceive the divinity in all people, service to humanity becomes a natural expression of love for the Supreme.

These seven elements are integral to any authentic meditation practice. They illustrate well the link between personal spiritual development and social change.

The world needs not only new social and economic structures that are just and democratic; it also needs people who are better, stronger and less selfish. For this we need to make systematic, liberating changes in ourselves. Revolution begins from within.

The Importance of Prout and its Concept of Pramá [35]

By Dr. Leonardo Boff

Dr. Leonardo Boff is a theologian, professor and author of more than 100 books. He is one of the founders of Liberation Theology, a movement within the Catholic Church which blends a socialist perspective and struggle for justice with radical Christianity. He is a winner of the Right Livelihood Award, often considered the alternative Nobel, for his work promoting human rights.

The exceptional importance of the Prout system resides in two fundamental points: its completeness and its viability. The entire system comes from a correct understanding of the human being, personal and collective, and authentic human development...

In every person there are three dimensions: the physical, the mental and the spiritual. The three of them are to be developed together. If not, there is either no development or development that produces injustice and many victims. Prout was carefully thought out to create a development with equilibrium ("pramá") and with harmony. The result will be the welfare and happiness of all.

The physical occupies all of the physical dimensions such as the physical body, the world of measurable phenomena, nature, natural resources, the fertility of the earth, the physical chemical elements, and the cosmic energy which acts on our world. The Prout system teaches how to utilize to the maximum the physical resources in such a way that is sustainable enough for all who live in the world today and for all who will come after us. But not only the humans, also the other created beings: rocks, plants and animals.

The mental consists of the universe of the human mind, the intelligence, the will, the imagination, the psychic life formed by emotions and our inner and archetypal sensibility. The human being should develop his or her mental capacities for self-development and the development of others, through just behavior, the eradication of exploitative mechanisms, and continual creativity in the face of new problems.

The spiritual is that disposition of the human being to link the microcosms with the Macrocosm, to perceive the totality, to discover the other side of all things, the message that comes from the greatness of the universe. It is the capacity to contemplate, to venerate and to dialog with the Mystery that the religions call God or the Force that guides the universe. By the actuation of this dimension, the human being turns into a cosmic being. This is an infinite practice. We should strive to encompass all these dimensions in the process of sustainable development.

The second characteristic of the Prout system is its viability. The followers of P. R. Sarkar in the entire world, do not stop with the theoretical comprehension of the human being. They are preoccupied with the viability of a practical and effective way. It is here that the system becomes attractive...

The result of this pragmatic logic is a balanced economy... in which the necessities and amenities assist the three dimensions of the human: the physical, the mental and the spiritual. This system represents a humanistic approach to economics. It leaves behind the capitalist economy, with its unlimited accumulation of goods and material services, and instead rescues the classic sense of attending to all human demands, including the radiant communion with the Supreme...

I strongly recommend the reading and the application of this system in all fields. It will be especially useful in the ecclesiastical base communities of the Catholic Church and other grassroots groups of reflection and action that try to improve the purchasing power of people. It functions as a critique of the dominant capitalist economic system and neoliberal approach that excludes and causes massive injustice. It also critiques the system of real socialism because of its centralization and the rigid conformity that it demands. But principally Prout serves as an alternative for a truly human economy which, when it functions, will produce life and happiness for the people.

Leonardo Boff, Rio de Janeiro

Chapter 3

The Right to Live!

These days, a person who possesses wealth is respected and revered whereas a person without money is a person honored by none... Bereft of everything, people toil 'round the clock to earn a mere pittance... The railway stations and market places are full of half-clad beggars and lepers desperately stretching out their begging bowls... The poor live in shantytowns, barely protected from the elements... Village people die for want of medicine... The pavements have become the home for so many people.

— P.R. Sarkar[1]

Planet Earth has enough resources for everyone–if we share. As explained in the previous chapter, according to the principle of Cosmic Inheritance, it is unacceptable to hoard wealth or resources. The goal of Prout is to utilize and distribute our shared inheritance in a rational way for the benefit of everyone.

Material incentives for those who work harder, are more skilled, and who contribute more to society are integral to a Proutist economy, but the incentives must be reasonable. The goal is gradually to raise the standard of living and quality of life of everyone, while reducing damage to the natural world and other creatures.

The Minimum Necessities of Life

The first requirement of Prout is to guarantee the minimum necessities to everyone: "The minimum necessities of all should be guaranteed in any particular age."[2] Guaranteeing the right to live has to be the first priority of every country. The Brazilian spiritualist Frei Betto called attention to this need when he said, "The degree of justice in a society can be evaluated by the way food is distributed among all citizens."[3]

Prout recognizes five fundamental necessities of life: food (including pure drinking water), clothing, housing (including adequate sanitation and energy), medical care, and education. Supplemental requirements are local transportation and water for irrigation. According to the principle of Neohumanism, this birthright transcends citizenship -- meaning that every human being, whether native or visitor to a country, must be guaranteed these necessities.

Providing the basic necessities should be the primary function and duty of any economy. Human beings require these in order to realize their individual potentialities, to develop culturally, to achieve inner fulfillment. Without necessities, the "pursuit of happiness" remains beyond the reach of the world's poor.

Most governments provide a safety net to help guarantee that the poor and most vulnerable do not fall below a minimally accepted level of poverty and destitution. Unfortunately most government safety nets provide a very low bar that prevents only the worst suffering. Increasing numbers of citizens face great hardship without access to housing, health care, and food.

As many as 3.5 million people in the United States experience homelessness each year.[4] More than 60 million Americans have no health care insurance and many more have only limited coverage, causing millions to fall into poverty when their family is hit by a medical emergency. [5] And 46 million Americans are receiving food stamps.[6]

The right to meaningful employment with fair wages is also a fundamental human right. The minimum requirements should not be handed out by a government agency, as in the current welfare systems of liberal democratic countries. Rather, people should pay for them with the income they earn from honest work. It is the responsibility of all levels of government to pursue policies which achieve and maintain full employment, with jobs that utilize each worker's skills and capabilities. A just minimum wage, often called a "living wage," must be set high enough so that people can purchase the necessities. Increasing employment will reduce the numbers requiring the safety net.

Welfare systems create disincentives for their recipients to work. In the United States, for example, those who receive welfare must immediately report any dollar they earn, which is usually deducted from their next welfare check. They are not allowed to borrow money to start a small business without immediately sacrificing their monthly assistance. In this way, welfare recipients sometimes become emotionally dependent, prisoners of both poverty and the welfare system which seeks to alleviate it. Thus a whole class of people who should be employed remains jobless or becomes part of the underground informal economy. Prout, on the other hand, by guaranteeing a livable minimum wage, would limit welfare as a special contingency for those who are physically or mentally unable to work.

The determination of what are the minimum necessities should be done in a progressive way; there must be continual adjustment of these basic requirements depending upon the available resources and scientific standard of the locality. As with all the principles of Prout, the standard for minimum necessities will change with time and place.

For example, staple foods are different in different cultures, yet they must meet adequate nutritional standards. Clothing varies according to climate and culture. Minimum housing standards appropriate to the climate and culture must also be determined. The availability of better housing will also be an incentive–such incentives will be built into the system, unlike in the Soviet Union, for example, where "dacha" vacation homes for the Party elite were kept secret. Everyone, however, will be guaranteed a roof over their head, regardless of their social standing.

In a Proutist framework, the people's purchasing capacity will be taken as the measure of economic advancement. In order to facilitate a continually increasing purchasing capacity, a number of factors are required. These include the guaranteed availability of basic goods and services, stable prices, appropriate wage increases, and increasing collective wealth and productivity.

Imagine a world in which no one need worry about getting enough money to buy food, clothes, housing, education and medical care for his or her family!

Pharmaceutical Corporations vs. Generic Medicines

Poverty breeds ill-health and encourages the spread of infection. Infectious diseases are now the world's biggest killer of children and young adults. Six deadly infectious diseases - pneumonia, tuberculosis, diarrheal diseases, malaria, measles and HIV/AIDS - account for half of all premature deaths, killing mostly children and young adults.[7] More than 13 million people die each year from preventable diseases. AIDS killed 1.8 million people in 2009.[8] In addition, each day hundreds of millions of people undergo pain and suffering from these diseases. In poor countries, neither the people nor the governments can afford the medicines to treat these illnesses.

The economic and political story behind AIDS medicines is especially revealing. In 1996 an effective combination therapy that delays the onset of AIDS went on sale -- at a cost of US$10,000-15,000 per person per year! These drugs lowered the death rate for people with HIV/AIDS in rich countries by 84 percent over the next four years, but fewer than 8,000 of the millions of patients in sub-Saharan Africa could afford them.[9] Then in 2000, an Indian pharmaceutical company started to produce generic antiretrovirals that were exactly the same as those made by the multinationals, but cost only US$295 per patient per year.

The development of generics has allowed India to produce 95 percent of the bulk drugs it consumes and become a net exporter of medicines. Egypt, Thailand, Argentina, Brazil and Cuba are also becoming more self-reliant. Other developing countries benefit, too, because by purchasing these cheaper versions, they can afford to treat more patients. More than 50 developing countries as well as a few developed ones have exempted medicines from being patented to allow these cheaper versions that save lives.

Pharmaceuticals are the third most profitable industry in the United States.[10] Just a few multinational corporations dominate the field. They claim that tremendous profits are their right because of the money they spend in research developing new medicines; yet that budget is dwarfed by their billion-dollar advertising campaigns. Furthermore, only about 10 percent of their research and development budget is used to develop drugs that combat 90 percent of global disease–the rest is spent on afflictions of the rich countries such as obesity.[11]

Multinationals pressured the World Trade Organization (WTO) to create a set of tough laws called the Trade Related Intellectual Property Rights (TRIPS). These laws have received growing criticism from developing countries, academics, and NGOs, who claim that they embody all that is socially, politically and economically unjust about globalization. The big pharmaceuticals have also employed an army of lobbyists and lawyers to close the loopholes in the TRIPS agreement. Infringements are brought to a WTO disputes panel, and unlike in a criminal trial, the burden of proof is put on the defendant country.

When in 2001 South Africa passed a law facilitating the production and importation of generics, 39 pharmaceutical corporations filed a suit against the government. However, activist organizations and the European Parliament fought back alongside the South African government and forced the pharmaceutical industry to drop the case. Now Zambia, Ghana, Tanzania, Uganda and Zimbabwe have joined South Africa in manufacturing generic AIDS medicines. By 2008 the most widely used generic drug combination was available for only US$88 per year.[12]

Unfortunately about 15 percent of HIV/AIDS patients eventually develop toxicity or resistance and need what is called a second-line regime. This is problematic, because since 2005, developing countries that are members of the WTO, including India, Thailand and Brazil, have been required by TRIPS to comply with patent legislation. Though patents have expired on most first-line AIDS drugs, allowing generic producers to continue making them, patents still exist on most new and second-line medicines. After a long struggle, the large pharmaceutical corporations gave in to 'tiered' pricing, charging poorer countries less, so that in 2009 the median cost of the most commonly used second-line regime was US$853 in low-income countries, US$1,378 in lower-middle-income countries, and US$3,638 in upper-middle-income countries.[13]

Because the Brazilian government was committed to providing universal access to medicine for all, its Ministry of Health was spending 80 percent of its health budget importing these patented second-line regime medicines, even though they went to only a small proportion of HIV/AIDS patients. Despite potential sanctions, in 2007 the government ordered its laboratories to ignore the patent and produce a generic second-line medicine. President Luiz Inacio Lula da Silva said: "Between our trade and our health, we have chosen to look after our health."[14]

Malaria is another global killer–781,000 died in 2009, mainly children under age five, down slightly from nearly one million in 2000. The World Health Organization insists that present control measures are working and can end malaria deaths by 2015. All that is needed is US$6 billion to distribute insecticide-treated mosquito nets to everyone at risk.[15] Sadly, saving lives is not a priority to most financial investors.

Quality Health Care for All

Modern Western medicine, otherwise known as allopathy, uses powerful medicines to fight disease. However because the human body is so complex, it is sometimes difficult to make a correct diagnosis based on the symptoms. Studies of autopsies in the United States have shown that doctors seriously misdiagnose fatal illnesses about 20 percent of the time.[16] A conservative average of both the Institute of Medicine and HealthGrades reports indicates that there have been between 400,000 to 1,200,000 error-induced deaths between 1996 and 2006 in the United States.[17]

As shocking as this percentage of misdiagnosis is, the *Journal of the American Medical Association* reported that this rate has not changed since the 1930s.[18] Complicated technologies, powerful drugs, fatigue and sleep deprivation of interns, and poor communication among care providers, patients and family members all contribute to the problem. According to the WHO, 50 percent of medical equipment in developing countries is only partly usable due to lack of skilled operators or parts, forcing medical staff to rely on guesswork when diagnosing.[19]

Because powerful medicines and intrusive medical procedures have significant side effects, and if administered wrongly can harm or kill the patient, Prout recommends that health care systems and hospitals also offer alternative forms of medical treatment. Homeopathy, naturopathy, herbal medicine, acupuncture and yoga treatments, for example, are much less risky and less expensive, and often restore health in non-life threatening conditions. The goal of medicine should be the physical and mental welfare of the patient, utilizing whichever treatment works best.

P. R. Sarkar wrote, "The healing power of nature cures disease; medicine only helps nature. The mind of the patient helps to activate the healing power of nature."[20] He pointed out that when a patient has complete faith in the doctor, even an inert pill can cure, the so-called placebo effect. Hence psychological consideration should also be included in any effective healing strategy. In many cases, changing diet, lifestyle and social environment is crucial for both prevention and cure. Therefore health care systems should also emphasize health awareness education.

Comparing Prout to Marxism and Communism

Sarkar respected Karl Marx, saying he was "a good person, a thoughtful person, and a prophet for the poor."[21] Marx wrote a brilliant, methodical analysis of capitalism in the 1800s, *Das Kapital, Volumes 1-3,* approximately 3,000 pages in length, in which he demonstrated that capitalism is exploitive in nature and suffers from internal contradictions or weaknesses that contribute to its decay. Marx's compassion for the oppressed and his compelling call to end exploitation is extraordinary. (His class analysis is compared with Sarkar's in Chapter 7.)

While Marx was a champion of the poor and a genius in his critique of capitalist excesses, he was much less clear about what should replace it. He called for "an association of free men, working with the means of production held in common, and expending their many different forms of labor power in full self-awareness as one single social labor force."[22] That vague statement and a handful of others is the extent of Marx's economic alternative.

While it is important to acknowledge that many of the social and economic improvements in contemporary society were championed by Marxists and socialists, critics have pointed out that his economic analysis is internally inconsistent. For example, Marx's "labor theory of value" stated that the value of an object equals the cost of labor to produce or extract it. But in the 21st century, we are painfully aware that all resources are limited, and some are non-renewable. Scarcity increases value. Each resource has an intrinsic value and should be maximally utilized and rationally distributed.

The Marxist axiom, "from each according to his ability, to each according to his need" sounded good in theory, Sarkar wrote, but was an inadequate incentive to motivate most people. And, he argued, to distribute surplus wealth equally would not be reasonable. "Diversity, not identity, is the law of nature... Those who want to make everything equal are sure to fail because they are going against the innate characteristic of [nature]."[23] Leaders who tried to materialize Marx's ideas in different countries, Sarkar said, invariably encountered many practical difficulties because incentives are an important factor in economics.

Materialism holds that the only thing that exists is matter, and all phenomena, including consciousness, are the result of material interactions. Marx spoke of the "materialist conception of history", and later Friedrich Engels and others coined the term "dialectical materialism" to describe the Marxist perspective. The problem is that when the possibility of spiritual experience is denied, people's mental longings turn towards material objects of gratification. When one constantly focuses on material reality, the mind becomes materialistic and the baser instincts are aroused.

Soviet leader Vladimir Lenin repeated throughout his life that "the concrete analysis of the concrete situation" was the very soul of Marxism.[24] Sarkar, on the other hand, rejected this narrow, materialistic outlook, and propounded a much more expansive idea–"as you think, so you become."

At the same time, Sarkar promoted social equality and called Prout "progressive socialism."[25] This model certainly advocates public or common ownership and cooperative management of the means of production and allocation of resources, which is a common definition of socialism. Yet it differs markedly from Marxism in many ways.

Marx and Engels published *The Communist Manifesto* in 1848, analyzing the need for a revolutionary Communist Party to lead the working class in revolt against capitalist exploitation. It reviewed the history of class struggle and the problems of capitalism, but made few predictions or prescriptions about how Communist Parties should rule.

In fact, communist governments have frequently engendered mass alienation among their workers.[26] Fifty years after leading the communist revolution in Cuba, when asked if their economic system was still worth exporting to other countries, Fidel Castro replied: "The Cuban model doesn't even work for us anymore."[27] His brother, President Raul Castro, has indicated that the state has had too big a role in the economy, and that gradual but widespread reform is needed.

With the centralization of both political and economic power in the hands of the state, many communist leaders fell victim to a myopic belief in their own infallibility. This arrogance, combined with a materialist philosophy and belief that the ends justified the means, has resulted in Communist Party tyranny.

Communist regimes throughout the world have subjugated their own people under a yoke of oppression. Political repression, imprisonment, forced labor camps, executions, and famines caused by the forced collectivization of land and centralized economic policies were the worst crimes. The estimated combined death toll in Stalin's Soviet Union, Mao's China and Cambodia under the Khmer Rouge range from 21 million to 70 million.[28]

Party dictators have ordered their military to imprison or kill people if they tried to protest or escape. These autocratic governments censored artistic expression, banned private enterprise, stifled personal initiative, and prohibited religious and spiritual freedom. These same dictatorships have now been overthrown by popular revolts in Eastern Europe and Russia.

However, a few states controlled by communist parties continue: China, Cuba, Laos, Vietnam, and North Korea. China does not publish death penalty statistics, but Amnesty International reports that as many as 8,000 executions took place in 2006. Arrests, torture and imprisonment of spiritual and religious groups, dissenters and human rights activists continue. More than 3,000 Falun Gong meditation practitioners have died in custody as a result of torture, more than 70 percent of them women. In Tibet, scores of Buddhist nuns and monks remain in prison.[29]

Today, communist revolutionaries are conducting armed insurgencies in India (Naxalites), Colombia (FARC), the Philippines (the New People's Army), Peru (the Shining Path) and Bangladesh. The Unified Communist Party of Nepal (Maoist) fought for ten years before declaring a ceasefire and running for election. Nearly all of these follow the Maoist strategy of waging a protracted people's war, operate in remote wilderness areas, and instill fear.

Prout rejects indiscriminate violence and terrorism. The Proutist approach is to change consciousness through mass education, inspiration and a cultural renaissance, not through fear. Political revolution can never create a just society unless the tendency to exploit others is overcome in the minds of the leaders and people.

Sarkar wrote, "The concepts of dialectical materialism, the materialist conception of history, the withering away of the state, proletariat dictatorship, classless society, etc., are defective ideas which can never be implemented. That is why the post-revolutionary stage in every communist country has suffered from turmoil and oppression."[30]

Atiriktam: Rational Incentives

Prout advocates: "The surplus wealth should be distributed among meritorious people according to the degree of their merit."[31]

This surplus is known in Proutist economics by the Sanskrit word *atiriktam*, and remedies the problem of equal distribution in communism. It is used as an incentive to motivate people to render greater service to society. Atiriktam can, for instance, be given either as increased salary or as other benefits. Its purpose is to encourage people to develop their skills and increase their capacity to assist society. Atiriktam can take the form of task-related privileges. For example, a talented researcher may be given access to expensive laboratory facilities, while an effective and selfless social worker may be offered more support staff.

In an article published shortly before his death in 1990, entitled "Minimum Requirements and Maximum Amenities," Sarkar expanded on the relationship between minimum salary and atiriktam. He stressed that while providing the minimum necessities, people should not be left with a bare-bones existence. Higher salaries should be provided to the meritorious, yet continuous and collective effort will be needed to raise the economic standard of the common people to an appropriate level for that time and place.[32]

The Five Fundamental Principles of Prout

The following five statements direct how resources should be distributed under Prout. Sarkar first gave these in 1959 in the last chapter of his book, *Idea and Ideology*. Together they comprise what is known as the Five Fundamental Principles of Prout.[33] They are fundamental because all Prout policies are based on these, and whereas policies will change over time, these principles do not. A unique aspect of the Prout model is that it recognizes the physical, psychic and spiritual qualities of human beings as well as of natural resources.

1. *"No individual should be allowed to accumulate any physical wealth without the clear permission or approval of the collective body."*

This point recognizes that the physical resources of this planet are limited; hence the hoarding or misuse of any resource would diminish opportunities for others. Hoarding wealth or using it for speculation rather than productive investment directly reduces the opportunities of others in society. Hence, reasonable ceilings must be placed on salaries and inherited wealth, as well as on property and land ownership.

This principle is based on the concept of Cosmic Inheritance mentioned in the previous chapter, which asserts that human beings have the right to utilize and share, but not hoard or abuse, the resources that we have been endowed with by the Creator.

Earnings should be capped at reasonable maximum levels. When evaluating compensation, all components such as performance bonuses and personal expense accounts must be included. The gap between the minimum wage and the maximum salary will have to be gradually decreased; however, it should never be reduced to zero.

There is growing acceptance of the concept of controlling and reducing the income gap in the business world as well. Renowned economist John Kenneth Galbraith wrote, "The most forthright and effective way of enhancing equality within the firm would be to specify the maximum range between average and maximum compensation."[34] Some Japanese and European companies already have such policies. Neoconservatives advocate that no limits should be placed on what they call "economic freedom," but a principle of law is that the freedom of one individual cannot be allowed to infringe on the freedom of others, and the over-accumulation of wealth does infringe on the economic rights of others.

Sarkar used the term "the collective body" to refer to society. He indicated that the government would have to assume responsibility for setting limits to the accumulation of wealth. It would do this by forming economic boards. He insisted that the members of the boards should be "those who are honest, who really want to promote human welfare... [by] rendering social service collectively..."[35] In addition to setting economic policies and standards, Prout economic boards will also hear applications from citizens for exceptions to the ceilings. For example, a paraplegic person would need a sophisticated and expensive computerized wheelchair.

This principle applies to physical wealth. Intellectual knowledge and spiritual wisdom are unlimited, and so their accumulation is not a problem, as long as others are not prevented from using them.

2. *"There should be maximum utilization and rational distribution of all mundane, supramundane, and spiritual potentialities of the universe."*

Maximum utilization means to make the best use of the planet's resources, with maximum economic and mechanical efficiency while protecting the natural environment. Everyone can enjoy a high quality of life if we use our resources wisely. As the American scientist and visionary R. Buckminster Fuller said, "We have enough technological know-how at our disposal to give everyone a decent life, and release humanity to do what it is supposed to be doing–that is, using our minds, accomplishing extraordinary things, not just coping with survival."[36]

Excessive wealth concentration causes deterioration and poor utilization of the earth's resources and human-made material resources. Corporate capitalism focuses on quarterly profits, ignoring externalities and consuming non-renewable resources. When an elite few own vast land holdings, they often leave them sitting idle, or they produce cash crops for export. Poor rural farmers are thus forced onto marginal land, which they clear and cultivate for bare subsistence with dire ecological consequences.

Supramundane potentialities include properties which cannot be perceived by the sense organs, but which would include subtle knowledge and powers, such as ideas, concepts, scientific theories, aesthetic creations, intuition, etc. Spiritual potentialities refer to spiritual philosophy and practices, and the attractive force of the universe, which draws people towards the Supreme Consciousness.

Maximum utilization involves three considerations. First, effectiveness, or doing the right thing, selecting the right policy. Second, efficacy, which means getting things done, meeting targets in a timely manner. Third, efficiency, or doing things in the most economical way, reducing wastage, achieving more with less.

Research and development is a key to finding more effective and efficient uses of our resources, minimizing the harmful effects of production, and discovering alternative ways to harness renewable energy sources.

Rational distribution is also crucial, because without it, the world today has huge stockpiles of food while people die of starvation. The three priorities of Prout regarding rational distribution are to guarantee the basic necessities to everyone, to take care of the special needs of some people (those with disabilities, for example), and to provide incentives for those who make greater contributions to society.

3. *"There should be maximum utilization of the physical, metaphysical and spiritual potentialities of the unit and collective bodies of human society."*

This principle concerns the utilization of all human resources, emphasizing the value of both individual and collective well-being. Healthy individuals contribute to a healthy society, just as a healthy society fosters the development of healthy individuals. According to Prout, there is no inevitable conflict between individual and collective interests. Rather, their true interests are shared.

The results of excessive individualism can be seen in the breakdown of the family and the selfish "me-first" attitude which is sadly all too prevalent throughout the Western world. A materialistic consumer society pressures people to increase their own pleasures and comforts, while remaining indifferent to the needs of others.

This principle, however, does not support submerging all individuality for the intended good of collective society. Society needs to respect human diversity, and to allow people the freedom to think for themselves, to express their creativity, and to form diverse relationships. An important goal of Prout is to encourage individuals to realize their full potential and achieve their dreams and goals. Communism amply demonstrated the danger of excessive collectivism. Most communist governments have been dreadfully inefficient, and made life joyless, dull and mechanical.

A continual process of education and consciousness raising is required to help people realize that true happiness comes from overcoming selfishness and doing good to others, and that we need to balance our individual and collective interests.

Metaphysical or intellectual resources are wasted when people lack education, or are denied opportunities to develop their talents and contribute their ideas because of racial or sexual discrimination or economic exploitation. How wonderful it will be when the creativity of human beings is encouraged and channeled towards improving our world, instead of being wasted or misdirected by advertising that tries to convince us to purchase what we don't need.

The spiritual potentialities which allow humans to develop peace, harmony, wisdom, wholeness, and lasting happiness, remain mostly undiscovered in materialistic societies. Yet throughout history mystics of all cultures have dedicated their lives to practicing spiritual techniques to realize this inner treasure and share it with others.

This principle aims at providing the opportunity for each individual and every group of individuals to develop their full potential. This requires learning and training opportunities, meaningful work, and a culture that is accepting of everyone and which encourages creativity and initiative. These standards will continually rise as social justice improves.

4. *"There should be a proper adjustment amongst these physical, metaphysical, mundane, supramundane and spiritual utilizations."*

This principle concerns how to make the real-life decisions in choosing how to use each resource. The desire for short-term profits must be balanced with the long-term needs of future generations and the planet. Material needs must be considered alongside cultural and spiritual needs.

The traditional economic principle of comparative advantage states that each country and person should do what it, he or she is best at. Sadly, this principle has sometimes been used to argue that Central America is best at producing bananas for North Americans, and that the United States is best at producing everything else! The Food First Institute has demonstrated that every country in the world today has the agricultural potential to feed its entire population.[37] Prout asserts that regional self-sufficiency is the most effective means to increase the living standard of all people. Hence Prout requires that the farmland of every region should first produce food for its people, and only after that requirement is achieved should surplus production be exported.

The central issue here is one of holistic development of both the human being and society. For example, in China during the Cultural Revolution and in Cambodia after the Khmer Rouge took over, all doctors, nurses and other university graduates were forced to the countryside to do farm work on communes. This both harmed society and underutilized their skills. Whereas all who are engaged in honest work possess dignity and deserve society's respect, those with developed intellectual skills should not be employed only for manual labor.

Individuals who have developed spiritually, who embody deep wisdom and compassion, are still more rare. They should be allowed to spend the majority of their time sharing their teachings with others.

Prioritizing the more rare and valuable qualities also pertains to physical resources. A wilderness area with especially inspiring scenic beauty should be preserved as a natural park instead of being mined for iron ore. Similarly, the burning of fossil fuels is destroying our climate and our environment. To re-establish pramá -- dynamic equilibrium -- every effort should be made to develop and utilize alternative energy sources such as sunlight, wind, tides, wave power, magnetism and geo-thermal.

5. *"The methods of utilization should vary in accordance with the changes in time, space, and person, and the utilization should be of a progressive nature."*

This principle acknowledges that change is constant. There are many types of change: natural, seasonal, gradual, sudden, disasters, human-made, technological, etc. Every change requires that we adapt, which means overcoming resistance, fear, traditions, dogmas, and sometimes the government itself.

The Prout model is not set in stone–rather it is a comprehensive set of dynamic principles to be applied considering the many special conditions of the location and culture where they are put into practice.

Technological development has the capacity to both create and destroy. Today, institutions and individuals with great wealth control the direction of scientific research, and use that power for their own interests. Capitalists often use technology to decrease labor costs and control workers, by creating repetitive, boring jobs.

The challenge for a Proutist society is to direct research and development for the long-term welfare of humanity and the planet. We can welcome new technology when it frees human minds and hands for higher pursuits. Every effort should be made to assess technology's impact and minimize its negative repercussions.

Using the Fundamental Principles to Evaluate Social Policies[38]

The Five Fundamental Principles of Prout are a useful tool for activists and policy makers to analyze and compare policies according to how well they benefit people and the planet as a whole. Some questions to consider for each policy:

- Does it help to meet the minimum necessities of everyone: food, clothing, housing, education and health care?
- Does it help to provide jobs with adequate wages?
- Does it promote the maximum utilization of resources for the welfare of all?
- Does it protect and benefit animals, plants and the environment?
- Does it promote both individual expressions of people and their collective welfare, so that no person or group is exploiting another?
- Does it help strengthen the local economy of the community?
- Does it protect human rights and freedoms?
- Does it empower people and communities?
- Does it prevent the personal accumulation of wealth by any individual without the collective approval of society?
- Does it allow people to develop mentally and spiritually?
- Is it flexible enough to change as needs change?

Because Prout's framework is so all-inclusive, many disciplines can and should be used to consider the implications of each policy, including economics, public health, environmental sciences, political science, sociology, administration and law.

For example, to determine if everyone's minimum necessities are being met, social workers and non-governmental organizations need to study indicators of housing, education and health. Ecologists need to monitor air, water, soil, the forests and wildlife; their policy proposals need to be heard and implemented. Economists and cooperative consultants need to study how to create enough jobs that provide goods and services needed by the community. They also need to study the pricing of essential goods and whether or not a person receiving a minimum wage could afford them. Sociologists and psychologists need to explore issues of class, gender, race, age and education.

Factors that Motivate People to Work

It is often argued that wide disparities of income are necessary to encourage the most talented people to be more productive and accept jobs that are more challenging. Prout accepts that some income inequality is beneficial to society because it provides an incentive for greater productivity. However, human motivation is complex–there are many reasons why humans choose to be productive, only one of which is income. There is no need to rely on income alone to raise productivity.

Abraham Maslow explored this theme in detail. He found that healthy, self-actualizing people become devoted to their work because of their interest in the work itself, not because of external rewards. He noted that every child and every adult has the motivation to create and to work, and that most people "are for good workmanship, are against wasting time and inefficiency, and want to do a good job...."[39]

What blocks or inhibits people are negative aspects of the work environment: interpersonal conflicts, intimidation, boring repetitive tasks, confusion, inefficient routines, constant reorganizations and irrational orders. On the other hand, a well-managed, positive work environment enhances the natural desire to do good work. Employing strategies to foster such a positive work force and work environment can benefit the whole society.

Maslow was highly critical of conventional economics, which is based solely on the obsolete motivation theory that people work harder to earn more money to meet their basic needs. Still, he acknowledged the place for healthy competition and monetary incentives, writing, "A boxer needs a good sparring partner or else he will deteriorate... The best product should be bought, the best person should be rewarded more."[40]

Proutist Mark L. Friedman is an Adjunct Professor of Economics at Minnesota State University, USA. He has published a comprehensive evaluation of P. R. Sarkar's system of economic incentives entitled "Living Wage and Optimal Inequality in a Sarkarian Framework."[41] Starting from Maslow's work, and including the analysis of economists Harvey Leibenstein and John Tomer, Friedman presents an economic model to show eight factors that motivate workers to be productive. He states this as an economic formula, where Pr stands for productivity, which is a function (f) of the interaction of the following factors:

$Pr = f$(A, P, DO, Ed, Ex, WE, SC, MI)

A represents individual ability. Friedman assumes some innate differences among people, including inborn talents and acquired abilities.

P stands for personality, including individual drive, maturity, work ethic and mental health.

DO stands for the demands of the organization, along with its accompanying pressure.

Ed stands for education.

Ex stands for work experience.

WE stands for work environment, which includes several components. For example, does the job and organization suit the individual? Is it a solitary job, which some prefer, or does it involve social interaction? Does it use literary or mechanical skills? Are the expectations fair and reasonable? Are meaningful goals part of the work? Are the supervisors and fellow employees fair and supportive? Does the individual perceive the potential to grow and learn in the job?

SC represents service culture, the degree to which service and self-sacrifice are encouraged in the culture. In fact, many people choose to work for a non-profit organization as a volunteer or receiving much less salary than if they worked for commercial companies, simply because they are committed to its noble goals.

This is particularly important because Sarkar asserts that the desire to serve others selflessly is a defining human characteristic. *MI* stands for material incentive or income.

All of the variables interact. For example, those with greater individual ability tend to pursue more education, and more education may enhance ability. Experience would reinforce the benefits of education and enhance ability.

This model asserts that the material incentive or salary of a worker is only one of eight important factors that motivate him or her to be productive, and should not be overemphasized.

Economic Indicators for Setting the Minimum and Maximum Wages

Economists have long wrestled with the question of how to achieve the most efficient output and distribution, in a way that is also equitable and fair. However, economic efficiency and fairness have generally been regarded as two separate issues. Many have argued that economists should not even consider equity at all.

The Prout principle of *atiriktam* (the surplus available to society after the minimum necessities have been supplied to all) resolves this dilemma both logically and morally. Prout asserts that the only justification for granting higher income to a person is to reward him or her for providing a greater benefit to society.

A higher salary may induce an individual to work harder or to improve his or her skills. However, there is a limit to the output any one person can achieve: personal capacity is limited, and there are only 24 hours in a day. Production may increase with material incentive up to a point, but cannot increase indefinitely. Inevitably the production curve levels off. After that peak, additional incentives will not increase the person's productivity. In fact, further increases in income may actually decrease one's productivity, as the individual decides he or she can afford more leisure.

This is based on a central principle of economics known as the Law of Diminishing Marginal Returns. Offering a salary raise that is a hundred times higher cannot induce any individual to work a hundred times harder or become a hundred times more efficient. As was detailed in Chapter 1, some individuals–such as corporation CEOs–are today earning salaries that are hundreds of times that of other employees. This reflects competitive bidding for their services rather than any valuation of their real worth.

Extremely high salaries are also paid to some players in professional sports. This is due to "free agency," the legal right of players to join a different team when their current contract expires. When these rules were established in the United States and then in the European Union, salaries shot up. In the United States, in 2009 the average base salary of a professional National Football League player was about US$990,000,[42] and in 2010 the Major League Baseball player average exceeded US$3 million.[43] The UK Premier League football (soccer) average salary is equivalent to US $940,000.[44] Many sports stars are paid ten million dollars or more per year.

Some economists argue that these astronomical salaries reflect the revenues the stars earn for their teams. Many fans probably prefer that the extra money goes to the players rather than to the owners. Still, it cannot be demonstrated that the quality of play in these sports has improved. In other words, the higher salaries have had no incentive effect. It is unlikely that players would be lured to other careers if their income fell to the level of other professional salaries. From society's standpoint, the higher salaries have little justification.

Prout economist Ravi Batra devised the following system for distributing income, based on the principle of atiriktam (surplus wealth). In the following formula, A stands for atiriktam, NNP for net national product, L for labor force, and w for the real wage required for the minimum standard of living.

$$A = NNP - wL$$

When the real wage–the adequate minimum salary needed to comfortably purchase the minimum necessities of life–is multiplied by everyone in the labor force, and this is subtracted from the total product of a nation or of an enterprise, the excess is the quantity of surplus atiriktam available for distribution as higher wages or incentives.[45]

Continuing from this formula, Mark Friedman has further developed an economic model which demonstrates the optimal level of compensation to achieve the maximum productivity. From society's standpoint, any payment beyond that is wasted, and so society should apply those surplus resources to other purposes. The model provides the theoretical framework for statistical studies; it also allows individual enterprises to pinpoint their optimal individual wages.[46]

Thus Prout ensures an adequate "living wage" for every worker, and that extra amenities are provided for at a level that is fair and appropriate for society. Most importantly, workers are valued and recognized for their unique contributions. Society benefits from the worker's productivity, which is maintained at a high level.

In the case of socio-economic regions, Proutist economic boards will have to calculate the legal minimum salary for an individual and his or her family based on the cost of the minimum necessities in that area. This would be considerably higher than the current minimum wage in virtually every region of the world. Of course, the cost of living is cheaper in economically less developed regions, so the minimum salary can initially be expected to be set lower in those regions than in more developed countries.

The boards will then have to calculate, using Gross Domestic Product and other indicators, the surplus wealth presently produced by the economy–that is, the difference between the total national or regional income and the amount needed to provide the minimum wage. This information would enable the calculation of a maximum legal wage for the local economy. This ratio–between the minimum and maximum salaries–could be expected to be initially set higher in less developed regions, then gradually reduced as the standard of living and the overall quality of life improved.

For example, Norway has one of the highest standards of living (fourth in the world, according to the IMF, with US$52,238 GDP per capita) due in large part to its petroleum reserves and hydroelectric capacity. The United Nations ranked Norway first in the world in its 2010 Human Development Index listing. The country also has one of the lowest wage gaps in the world. The lowest salary for a Norwegian government employee in 2010 was US$36,000 annually (207,900 kroner, wage level 1), and the highest was US$192,000 (1,106,400 kroner, level 98), 5.3 times more.[47] By comparison, U.S. government federal employees have a 10 to 1 gap, starting at US$17,803 (General Schedule grade 1), and the highest is US$179,700 (Senior Executive Service).

Prout economist and historian Edvard Mogstad, together with the think tank *Bevegelsen for Sosialisme*, assert that the egalitarianism of Scandinavia is the secret of its economic success and low unemployment. They propose a policy which ensures that nobody should earn less than half of the average income (which in 2010 was US$70,000), and the maximum wage should not be more than four times the median income. That gives a ratio of 8 to 1, which they feel is the widest acceptable for Europe. They also propose that constant effort should be made to lessen that gap.[48]

The requirement of a livelihood-level minimum wage would eliminate some under-paid, low-productivity jobs. For example, live-in domestic assistants in undeveloped countries are paid so little that most middle-class households have at least one, while in developed countries only the wealthy choose to pay the decent wages required for that service. A Proutist economy would no longer permit the exploitation of underpaid manual workers.

People with physical or mental disabilities, or who for any other reason are unable to do high-productivity work, would have their income subsidized or be employed in a public works project or some type of service cooperative. With the exception of social security for the elderly, a system of full employment would replace most of government's welfare functions.

Keynesian economists will appreciate that raising the minimum wage would stimulate aggregate demand, thereby increasing output and creating more jobs. Several studies have shown that raising the minimum wage in a capitalist economy helps poor people, while causing a decrease in unemployment. The challenge for a Proutist society will be to continually improve people's skills and competence through different types of education. It will also be necessary to encourage productivity through capital investment by making low-interest business loans available for cooperatives and the self-employed.

Comparing Prout with Participatory Economics

One of the very few other alternatives to capitalist market economies and to centrally planned socialism is called Participatory Economics. Activist Michael Albert wrote the definitive work introducing it called *Participatory Economics: Life After Capitalism*.[49] Abbreviated as "parecon", it uses participatory decision-making to guide the production, consumption and allocation of resources in a given society. The author describes parecon as "an anarchistic economic vision" and a form of socialism.

Parecon has a number of similarities with Prout: it strives for decentralized economic democracy, cooperative enterprises, and public management of important resources. It also shares many key values: equity, self-management, diversity and community. Parecon, however, does not have a spiritual perspective–economic justice is the sole aim.

Parecon also differs from Prout in its idea of remuneration. The author states, "Remunerate according to each person's effort or personal sacrifice." Thus he considers it unfair to pay a worker more than everyone else unless their labor includes "longer hours, less pleasant work, or more intense, dangerous, or unhealthy work."[50] The author insists that medical doctors should not receive a higher salary than other workers just because of their long training, during which they would be paid the same salary.

Prout disagrees. Higher income should be given in recognition of people's merit and accomplishments, and to provide them with greater opportunities to serve society. Hence, a certain degree of economic inequality is needed to provide incentives. This will encourage the high volume and quality of human effort needed to produce a level of material abundance consistent with a high standard of human welfare. With the economic model outlined in the previous section, it is possible to determine the exact amount of additional income that could be offered to meritorious individuals to maximize their productivity for the benefit of the world without permitting the over-accumulation of wealth or resources.

Parecon emphasizes a balanced job complex – a way of organizing a workplace or group that is both directly democratic and also creates relative equal empowerment among all people involved. Each worker must do a share of rote tasks (unskilled work) for some time each work day or each week. All workers would also share the more rewarding and empowering tasks in the workplace so it is coordinated with everyone's involvement. It was developed as an alternative to the corporate division of labor.

Prout appreciates this spirit and commends efforts in this direction. All workers should be encouraged to take further training (a general principle of cooperatives), because this is an empowering process. If the strict divisions between manual laborers and intellectuals are downplayed, mutual respect increases and class consciousness shrinks. However, tasks that are more "rewarding and empowering" are not the same for everyone, due to differences in talents, abilities, personality, and individual preferences.

The fourth principle of Prout, explained above, states, "There should be a proper adjustment among these physical, metaphysical, mundane, supramundane and spiritual utilizations." Those with special skills that benefit society should be encouraged to use them, and individuals who have developed spiritually should be allowed to focus their time teaching others.

Another difference is regarding leadership. Parecon is based on self-management, the idea that in each enterprise all persons should have a say in each decision proportionate to the degree to which they are affected by it. Whereas Prout agrees with this principle in cooperative management and economic democracy, Prout also gives importance to the moral leadership of society. Ideal leaders are people valued for their wisdom and experience, often elders, who accordingly provide counsel and hold positions of collective responsibility for the general welfare. (This is explained in Chapter 11.)

Whereas Prout's guarantee of the minimum necessities of life to all is shared by parecon, Marxists and other socialists, the following chapter will further outline its unique economic proposals.

Striving to Achieve Affordable Health Care for All in Kenya

By Didi Ananda Rucira

I arrived in Kenya in 1998 and soon found myself doing a number of free homeopathic clinics in the slums around Nairobi. At first, due to inexperience, I thought I was merely treating flus, colds, and itches; later I realized that these were no ordinary symptoms, rather the patients were suffering from tuberculosis, gonorrhea, AIDS and malaria.

Then a close friend was struck down by malaria and another died of AIDS. I took care of my friend with AIDS until her last breath. The experience was a great shock to me. In 1998 the only treatment was impossibly expensive and wouldn't have significantly extended her life. Hospital doctors told me how frustrated they were because the Kenyan government would not even acknowledge that AIDS was an epidemic. (It finally did so in 2001.)

It became my goal to find an affordable treatment for AIDS and an effective treatment for malaria. On the Internet I found many viable, alternative and affordable treatments for HIV and malaria. When I applied some of these therapies, I found my patients started getting better.

So the Abha Light Foundation opened its first clinic in the year 2000 to promote traditional, natural therapies and health systems that do not need much infrastructure or machinery; yet they can be used to manage or cure a wide variety of diseases. Its Proutist goal is to remove the profit motive from the prescription and extend affordable health care to all.

The benefits of homeopathy and alternative therapies include:

- Even very poor people in the world can afford homeopathy and alternative medicines.
- These therapies are effective in acute, chronic, traumatic, epidemic, and endemic diseases.
- They are safe and free of side effects, so they can be used at all levels, including self-help.
- They can be implemented in situations with very little infrastructure.
- They benefit from, but do not rely on, expensive diagnostic equipment.
- Once established, they continue to grow in popularity.
- In places where a doctor is a two-day walk, a simple homeopathic self-help kit is a lifeline.

We developed effective, natural, drug-free and affordable protocols for treating and managing HIV/AIDS:

1. Homeopathic medicine as the primary therapy to control secondary infections and raise the auto-immune response in the patient.
2. Naturopathic and nutritional support with food supplements to boost the nutritional intake and support the auto-immune system. Some suitable natural sources we have found so far in Kenya are sprouts, neem, honey and wheat grass juice.
3. Self-help groups of people living with HIV/AIDS who support each other to solve their problems, develop a positive outlook, and are there in times of need.

These protocols produce no negative side-effects and have been shown to be effective in controlling opportunistic infections and HIV viral loads as evidenced by better health and improved quality of life, circumventing the high cost of conventional medicines. Later I wrote two books, *Great*

Health, Naturally! – Volume 1: Immune Restoration and Digestive Health and *Volume 2: Nutrition Handbook*, for people living with HIV/AIDS about affordable self-treatment. We continually receive letters from people, thanking us for saving their lives.

The Abha Light College began to train promising Kenyan youth and professionals in the complex art of natural medicine. The two-and-a-half year course includes homeopathy, naturopathy, traditional herbal medicine, massage, acupuncture and nutrition. Together these systems can successfully treat the whole spectrum of human ailments from malaria and HIV to diabetes, hypertension and cancer. The first five graduated in April 2002; ten years later we have trained more than 75 practitioners.

After graduation, ALF has supported them to open their own clinics in their communities and villages in Kenya, Uganda and Congo. The practitioners have been instilled with Neohumanist ethics to treat their patients at affordable prices; most clinics only charge from US$5 to US$20 for their services and medicines combined. ALF also encourages the practitioners to donate some of their time to treat the poorest patients for free when needed.

Our biggest opposition comes from conventional doctors and nurses who see homeopathy and herbal medicine as their competitors. The direction of present day medicine is not so much to treat, but to make money for "Big Pharma," the pharmaceutical conglomerates. Those entities will take any steps to oppose and shut down all avenues of treatment that they can't control or make money from. This opposition results in lack of government support, opposition in the media and lack of funding to support endeavors.

An ideal medical system would integrate alternative and traditional systems with conventional medicine, with practitioners working side-by-side. And it would be free or affordable to everyone.

A second challenge is the tragic cycle of chronic poverty. The people who need health care the most cannot afford it; and the remoteness of their villages makes it expensive for health care workers to get there. The poorest people will either go to a hospital or clinic that offers free medicines, or otherwise delay going for treatment until their suffering has become very acute and often life-threatening. Educating the public on the cost effectiveness of early, alternative treatment is not easy.

The third challenge we face is our dependency on external donors for our projects and programs. Donors have their own ideas about how the funds should be spent without reference to the realities on the ground. Additionally it is very difficult to get large funding for alternative medicine, the underdog of the medical world. When donor funding stops, so does the health care. Lastly, a free clinic funded by overseas donors creates a "beggar" mentality in the minds of the local people, not a feeling of community ownership of the health care services.

The Social Enterprise Solution

A lack of government funding and external donors has pushed us to seek a different model to extend our charitable services and financially support our practitioners. So we chose to convert to a self-reliant social enterprise with a developed business model. Abha Light generates income through the sales of homeopathic and naturopathic medicines that our pharmacy produces.

The practitioners too, need to run their clinics as a small business with careful bookkeeping. Their training includes marketing skills and how to develop and keep their clients. Abha Light Foundation, with funds raised from its own business, subsidizes new practitioners for a short time, but only until they get themselves off the ground and are fully self-reliant and self-employed.

Through the social enterprise model, our Proutist goal of extending quality health services to an increasing number of people in East Africa is being fulfilled, while at the same time creating permanent employment for individual practitioners who serve their communities with effective, affordable health care.[51]

Chapter 4

Economic Democracy

Economic liberation is the birthright of every individual. To achieve it, economic power must be vested in the local people. In economic democracy the local people will have the power to make all economic decisions, to produce commodities on the basis of collective necessity, and to distribute all agricultural and industrial commodities.

— P.R. Sarkar[1]

Humanity needs a clear, compelling vision of an equitable, sustainable economy that brings a high quality of life for everyone–a dynamic economy of the people, by the people and for the people. Rejecting profit-making as the goal of the economy, Prout bases its economic policy on meeting the actual needs of the people.

Political democracy, in which all citizens have the right to elect their government representatives, has serious shortcomings under capitalism, because big money influences elections. Economic democracy, on the other hand, stands for the empowerment of people to make economic decisions that directly shape their lives and communities through locally-owned, small-scale private enterprises, worker-owned cooperatives, and publicly-managed utilities. It decentralizes decision-making and gives citizens the right to choose how their local economy should be run.

Noam Chomsky said, "You can't have meaningful political democracy without functioning economic democracy. I think this is, at some level, understood by working people. It has to be brought to awareness and consciousness, but it's just below the surface."[2]

Economist Richard Wolff writes:

> The 'great' debate between neoclassical and Keynesian econo-
> mists is neither great nor much of a debate. Both sides endorse,
> celebrate and defend capitalism. Their 'debate' between more or
> less government intervention to sustain capitalism… is a side-
> show for the main event: capitalism's weakening battles with its
> own contradictions and with looming demands for transition
> beyond capitalism to economic democracy.[3]

Four Requirements of Economic Democracy

Sarkar identified four requirements for economic democracy to be
successful, and designed the economic structure of Prout to fulfill them.

The first requirement is that the minimum requirements of life and
the basic amenities must be guaranteed to everyone, in order to free all
from the desperation of poverty and want. This was explained at length
in Chapter 3.

The second requirement is that the people should enjoy a gradually
increasing purchasing capacity and quality of life. People need to feel
that the quality of their lives is improving. Measuring purchasing capacity, the ability of people to pay for basic goods and services, is the most
direct and accurate way to assess their standard of living and the true
state of the economy.

This is very different from prevailing consumerism, which manipulates
people through advertising, creating artificial needs, to buy on credit
and to ignore the environmental impact of their purchases.

To increase purchasing capacity, products must be available to meet
local demand. There must be stable prices, periodic increases in wages,
and a steady increase in collective assets and infrastructure, such as
public transportation, energy generating systems, and communication networks. Raw materials, agricultural produce and other assets
of each region should be processed and refined close to their origin.
In this way, improvements in technology and manufacturing benefit
the local inhabitants of every region. Thus Prout promotes sustainable
local economies, rather than the exploitation that floods the world
with cheap goods from China and underdeveloped countries that we
see today.

The third requirement is that local people deserve the right to make the economic decisions which directly affect their lives. It is a basic right of workers to own and manage their enterprises, not being subject to manipulation or exploitation. Whether as small-scale private enterprises or cooperatives or even public-managed utilities, local people and communities need to determine their future. Local economies with sustainable agriculture that grows healthy food, renewable "green" industries, credit unions that offer loans to local people are all elements of a vibrant community. Such a decentralized economy will be discussed in a later section.

The fourth requirement is that we must prevent the outside control of local economies and the drainage of capital. Corporate big box stores and restaurant chains send profits that are earned in the community to outside shareholders. Corporate banks use local deposits to speculate in the global stock market casino. Outside landlords take rent money away, too. Without outside ownership of land and resources, profits earned in the region would not be siphoned off and sent elsewhere or hoarded; rather they would be re-invested locally in productive enterprises. This does not refer to immigrant laborers who are welcome to settle and become part of the community, but rather to landlords and corporations.

Economic democracy is essential to overcome discrimination and marginalization. Poverty and unemployment feed racism, sexism, and anger toward immigrants. Women, people of color, the young and the old tend to suffer lower wages and more joblessness in economic downturns. Decentralized local economies can achieve full employment and financial prosperity, allowing all to develop their full potential as human beings.

We need community-managed institutions based on economic justice to eradicate the causes of inequality, educational programs to overcome discrimination and consciousness raising to change the behavior, attitudes, and ideas that aggravate racism, sexism, ageism and xenophobia.

Industry, Commerce and Service in Three Levels

There are three general ways of owning and managing a business: state-owned, privately-owned or cooperatively-owned. Ownership is important, because whoever owns the enterprise makes the decisions and gets the lion's share of what is produced. Both communism and capitalism tend to be dogmatic about ownership, the first insisting that, as much as possible, everything should be state-controlled, the second that everything should be privatized. Prout, however, recognizes that, depending on circumstances, all three forms of ownership and management have value and are appropriate in different situations. This system is called a three-tiered structure:

Small-scale private enterprises: To encourage creativity and personal initiative, individuals, families and small partnerships should be allowed to open privately owned businesses. They can produce non-essential or luxury goods and services, as well as food to a small extent. Sarkar specified that "enterprises that are either too small, or simultaneously small and complex, to be a co-op, should be private enterprises."[4] For example, home businesses, family restaurants, small retail shops, handicraft producers, artists and private inventors may prefer to manage themselves. All self-employed workers and micro-enterprises will be encouraged to register legally without unnecessary bureaucracy or expense.

Small businesses strive to find niches of willing buyers for their specialty items and are free to set prices as high as the market permits. Actually most small business owners care deeply about what they do and try to continue their enterprise even when they do not earn much profit.

The wisdom of this approach has been demonstrated by the phenomenal success of the Grameen Bank in Bangladesh. Against the advice of banking and government officials, Economics Professor Muhammad Yunus started a bank in 1983 to give loans to the poorest people of his country, those who had nothing. With a focus on providing loans to women, some of whom are illiterate, Grameen requires no collateral but insists that individuals form groups of five to receive loans. Because future loans to other members depend on repayment of outstanding loans, group members have an incentive to encourage and support one another. Every week beneficiaries make a small repayment.

Surprisingly, the bank is owned by the poor borrowers, who hold 94 percent of the total equity. It has maintained a repayment rate of more than 98 percent return on its loans, an extraordinary rate for both local as well as international banks. The Grameen Bank has provided more than US$6.5 billion of micro loans to more than 8.34 million people in rural Bangladesh, with a staff of 22,225 and 2,565 branches. Today other micro-credit programs, modeled on Grameen, are springing up throughout the world.[5] The bank and its founder, Muhammad Yunus, were jointly awarded the Nobel Peace Prize in 2006 "for their efforts to create economic and social development from below."

In contrast to most development programs, the Grameen Bank does not insist on job training before giving loans. On the contrary, it demonstrates that even the poorest rural villagers with no formal education have skills and talents they can market creatively if given a chance. Self-employment in small-scale private enterprises, supported by micro loans from cooperative banks, is an effective means to overcome poverty and achieve full employment.

In a Prout economy, a ceiling will be set on sales volume and number of employees for private enterprises. If a firm reaches one of those limits, it must then choose whether to curtail further expansion or to transform itself into a cooperatively-managed enterprise. This transformation is essential to prevent unlimited concentration of wealth in the hands of individuals, to the detriment of society.

Cooperatives: The cooperative structure is central to the function and organization of a Prout economy. It is a basic right of workers in an economic democracy to own and manage their enterprises through collective management. Industry, trade, agriculture and banking should all be organized through producer and consumer cooperatives. These will produce the minimum necessities and most other products and services, forming the largest sector of a Prout economy. Smaller satellite cooperatives can serve larger cooperatives. For example, an automotive cooperative could produce components that are then shipped to nearby car manufacturing plants for final assembly.

Prout recognizes three requirements needed for cooperatives to be successful. The first is honest, trustworthy management. The second is strict administration with transparent accounting to build confidence amongst the cooperative members and the public. The third requirement is the sincere acceptance of the cooperative system by the local public. This requires popular education and constant promotion to create integrated networks of community cooperatives.

Global capitalism, which wipes out local businesses around the world, also puts unfair pressure on cooperatives. Decentralized economic democracy, however, ensures that everyone in the community has employment and a voice in decision-making processes.

A cooperative market economy has many benefits: it keeps consumer prices low, minimizes inflation, ensures low prices for raw materials, facilitates the equitable distribution of wealth, fosters closer ties among people, and builds community spirit. Chapter 5 focuses on cooperatives.

Large-scale key industries: "Enterprises that are either too large, or simultaneously large and complex, to be a co-op, should be large-scale enterprises."[6] Transportation, energy, telecommunications, defense, mining, petroleum, petrochemicals and steel are all essential parts of an economy. They require large capital investments that lead to natural monopolies and are therefore difficult to decentralize. A Prout economy will manage such industries as publicly owned utilities operated in the public interest.

Key industries will be overseen by the nearest appropriate level of government, what Sarkar called "the immediate government." For example, national airlines would operate under federal legislation, electricity boards under state legislation, and water and sewage management would operate under local government control.

Yet to avoid politicians having direct business control, Prout prescribes that key industries be managed by autonomous bodies set up by the government. Such autonomous bodies will be legally authorized by the state, but afterwards operate independently of government control. The board and not the government appoints the executive officers, who are answerable to the board; the board shall answer to the immediate government representing the people. Autonomous bodies will also manage specialized industries, such as research and development, hospitals and nursing homes, and oversee major infrastructure projects, such as ports and airports. (Essential services are discussed in the next section.)

All types of natural resources, utilities and strategic enterprises collectively belong to the local people. Local governments will monitor operations, ensuring that they are managed in an ecological and sustainable way. Prout opposes pressure by powerful groups like the International Monetary Fund to sell public utilities to private investors.

Key industries will be run on the principle of "no-profit-no-loss." This means that any profits will be reinvested, donated to social programs or paid out as bonuses to the workers to maximize efficiency, quality, and worker satisfaction. A portion of any surplus can be kept in a fund to finance future expansion.

An example of the wisdom of this approach is in telecommunications. City operations are always more lucrative than those in remote rural areas, where installing and maintaining networks is quite costly. Therefore private telecommunications companies have tended to neglect rural community services so that they can pay out more dividends to investors. But by operating key industries as public utilities, essential materials and services can be provided to all individual consumers and cooperatives at affordable prices, stimulating overall economic growth.[7]

Providing Goods and Services to the People

Sarkar created an important field of economics that he termed "people's economy." This analyzes the lives of individuals in relation to the economy as a whole, including their living standard, purchasing capacity, and economic problems. The primary goal of the people's economy is to ensure that everyone receives the minimum requirements. This responsibility includes overseeing the production, distribution, storage, marketing and pricing of consumable goods.

To do this, the federal government will need to classify every type of commodity into three basic categories: essential, semi-essential and non-essential. Essential commodities are those needed to maintain an adequate standard of life: clean water, most foods, most clothing, medicines, housing materials, textbooks and other educational materials, electricity and energy. Semi-essential commodities include some types of food and clothing, books other than textbooks, most electronic goods, various household items, etc. Non-essential commodities include luxury goods.

Cooperatives will produce and sell essential commodities, and will manage semi-essential products wherever possible. Small private enterprises will produce luxury goods and some semi-essential items, or food on a small scale.

As the economy of a region develops, the number of different types of commodities in all three categories will increase. When everyone is able to purchase the minimum necessities, some semi-essential commodities such as household appliances and electronic items will be upgraded from semi-essential to essential status. An item initially considered as a luxury may later be classified to be a semi-essential or essential.

Services will also be classified in the same way. Essential services provide the basic necessities, such as schools (from kindergarten to university), hospitals, water and sanitation utilities, local public transportation, the railway system, the national airlines, energy producers, telecommunications, etc. The local, state and federal government will provide these services through autonomous bodies set up for that purpose.

Some essential services such as health care practices, medical centers and health clinics can be run as service cooperatives, owned and managed by the health care practitioners themselves.

All other services will be classified as semi-essential or non-essential and can be provided by small private enterprises; however, a Prout economy will always favor the development of cooperative enterprises.

Importantly, under Prout, the role of government will always be to coordinate–and not to direct–the production and distribution of goods and services.

One of the revolutionary features of a Prout economy will be to identify productive resources that have previously been invisible and intangible, and to incorporate them into cost calculations. These would include work in the home, child rearing, preservation of environmental diversity and social relations and networks.

The people's economy will have to ensure that everyone who is able to work is employed in some way. Although this is a utopian dream in a world dominated by competitive global capitalism, economic democracy, based on cooperatives, can achieve this. Hence the government will promote and assist the development of cooperatives.

Prout's Housing System

Housing deserves special mention. A housing board in each region will set standards for single-family dwellings in basic terms of size and facilities. The board will ensure that the architectural plan is appropriate for climate and culture, that suitable and safe construction materials are available and used, and that the technology used is appropriate and as ecologically friendly as possible. Design, style and decoration would be left to personal taste.

The cost of monthly payments to rent or to finance the construction or renovation of a house to meet these standards will be included when calculating the just minimum wage for that region. Any person or family without a home, or living in substandard housing, would be entitled to rent with the option to buy such a dwelling, through long-term low-interest loans from cooperative banks. Home-owners would also be allowed to rent a room or two to students or temporary residents.

Owner participation in planning, arranging the loan and, if possible, construction, is recognized as a key factor in successful low-cost community housing programs. The housing board would also set minimum housing standards for individuals, large families and those who wish to live collectively. People who desire it could work harder to buy bigger and better housing, but minimum-quality housing would be guaranteed to all.

Increasing the Purchasing Capacity of the People

Despite nearly three decades of US economic growth, real wages and purchasing capacity of the population have been falling. The US minimum wage, when adjusted for inflation and calculated in 2009 dollars, has fallen from a peak of US$10 per hour in 1969 to less than US$7 in 2010.[8] The average American employee works harder and longer for less. Constant economic growth has been won by exploiting workers.

Prout measures economic health and vitality quite differently: by assessing the actual purchasing capacity of the people and their standard of living. Prout economists will determine a minimum salary sufficient to provide essential goods and services, such as food, clothing, local transportation, health care fund contributions and monthly housing and utilities bills for a family of four.

The government must finance high-quality education at all levels. One way to finance quality medical care for everyone is by a health fund to which all employed workers contribute monthly and which is overseen by the government.

To control inflation, the real wages of people will be regularly reviewed according to the actual cost of all goods and services available. While in capitalist economies the rate of inflation often fluctuates significantly, a cooperative-based economy can keep inflation low for long periods. By guaranteeing the basic requirements of life, capital costs will remain low, allowing capital to be continually reinvested in productive enterprises, and the wealth generated by cooperatives will be spread equitably throughout society.

Another way to stabilize short-term prices is by stockpiling key and essential commodities. When demand exceeds the supply of a particular commodity, tending to push the price up, the government can reduce its stockpile. Similarly, when there is an excess of goods, the government can increase its stockpile. In the long term, economic planners must anticipate demand levels and restructure production accordingly (see next section).

A Proutist economy will guarantee people an increasing purchasing capacity. This means that all workers will have to have their incomes progressively increased at a rate that is higher than the rate of inflation. Thus the minimum wage will have to gradually rise, giving people the opportunity to purchase an increasing range of all types of goods and services.

Another way that wages and salaries could be increased is by increasing their corresponding benefits or by improving conditions. For example, a minimum wage in most countries would probably be set for 40 hours per week, with higher rates paid for overtime work. By introducing improved technology and making cooperatives more efficient, it will eventually be possible to gradually reduce the number of working hours in a week. While maintaining the same level of productivity, all workers can be paid the same amount for, say, 38 or less hours of work each week. This gradual reduction in working time will give everyone more time for cultural pursuits, further education, sports and other hobbies.

Cooperatives would be encouraged to offer their members "flexitime," allowing them to adjust their working hours and schedules to meet family and other commitments, within certain limits.

It will be illegal for children below the age of fourteen to work in the workforce. Young people between the ages of fourteen and sixteen should be limited to working twenty hours a week, and should be paid hourly according to the just minimum wage, unless they are students and the work is part of their apprenticeship training.

Economic Decentralization and Socio-Economic Regions

Prout proposes the formation of economically self-reliant regions, based on common economic and social conditions, common geographic potentialities, common cultural legacy and language. The term "region" here is used in a general sense. Most of the countries of Europe would be considered separate socio-economic regions. Most importantly, regions should be defined so as to promote a spirit of cooperation and self-reliance leading to unity and cultural strength.

For planning purposes, each socio-economic unit would be further divided into districts and "blocks," based upon more local economic, geographic and population considerations. Each block should have a population of up to 100,000 people–less in sparsely populated areas. In Prout's economic planning, the block is the most important unit because it represents the grass roots level.

In a decentralized economy, each country will strive for economic self-reliance, and within each country, each region, district and even block will also strive to be as self-reliant as possible. This is no dreary top-down centralized planning scheme, but a vibrant community process. (At the end of Chapter 6 is a Block Level Planning Exercise.)

The European Union is problematic because it imposes free trade on economically unequal partners and promotes international corporations at the expense of local agriculture and industry–its very constitution promotes global capitalism. Prout promotes fair trade between equally developed regions and countries, and eventually the merging of them into larger and larger confederations.

One of the major defects of uncontrolled capitalism is the appropriation of raw materials and capital from under-developed areas to benefit owners who live elsewhere. Centralized capitalist economies lead to high industrial and urban concentration and the over-accumulation of wealth.

A decentralized economy does the opposite, and by attracting city dwellers towards new job opportunities, creates a higher standard of living and a better quality of life in small towns and rural areas. It also eliminates the need for migrant populations of farm workers to travel from region to region each season harvesting crops. Local economic control is maximized, allowing each locality to develop appropriate plans to achieve economic self-sufficiency and development while protecting the natural environment.

Racism, discrimination and hate crimes have historically plagued movements for local autonomy. Unemployed or underpaid local people often resent foreign workers as well as landowners and capitalists from other countries or regions or with other religious or cultural backgrounds. The major underlying cause for such intolerance, which sometimes leads to violence, has always been economic exploitation. Political leaders seize on the mood of general frustration, bitterness and resentment, and fan the flames of hatred to gain popularity and power.

Prout overcomes this by insisting that anyone may settle in any region, so long as that person merges his or her economic interests with that region's. Profits may not be exported elsewhere. When the minimum necessities of everyone are guaranteed through full employment, and when a reasonable ceiling on salaries and personal wealth is established, anger and intolerance of outsiders will naturally decrease. Schools, popular education and the media will also cooperate to encourage the spirit of universalism.

Comparing the Welfare Economics of Amartya Sen to Prout

Kolkata economist Amartya Sen was awarded the 1998 Nobel Prize in Economics. A former Master of Trinity College, Cambridge, U.K., he is presently a professor at Harvard University. The Royal Swedish Academy of Sciences cited that he had "restored an ethical dimension to the discussion of vital economics problems." He is a major pioneer in what today is known as welfare economics. His wide-ranging work focuses on questions of inequality, the measurement of poverty, and on how societies make choices that are both fair and efficient.

As a child, during the great Bengal famine of 1943 in which five million perished, Sen handed out cigarette tins of rice to starving refugees as they passed his grandfather's house. Thirty years later, still haunted by those images, his research revealed that India's food supplies at that time were not unusually low. Rather, the famine resulted from a run-up in food prices spurred by wartime panic and manipulative speculation. The British colonial rulers, immune to democratic pressures, simply stood by.

In his landmark study on the causes of famine, *Poverty and Famines*, Sen demonstrates that famine is not just a consequence of acts of nature, such as drought or flood, which often precede it; rather it is an avoidable economic and political catastrophe in which the poorest people can no longer afford to buy food because they lose their jobs or because food prices soar. *The New York Times* credits his research with saving many lives. As a result of his study, governments and relief organizations today put less emphasis on directly distributing food to the poor, and instead focus more attention on restoring personal incomes through such programs as public works projects.[9]

Sarkar, a contemporary of Sen who also witnessed that terrible famine, pointed to one of the same causes in 1959 when he wrote, "Throughout history millions of people have died due to artificial famines created by other human beings... By hoarding grains, they cause artificial famines."[10]

In his other works, Sen emphasizes that welfare does not actually depend on material goods, but rather on the activity for which they are acquired. In his view, the importance of income is with respect to the opportunities or capabilities that it creates. Health, he argues, as well as other factors, should also be considered when measuring welfare.

Sarkar goes further than Sen by asserting that excess accumulation of wealth and its lack of circulation in productive investments reduces the ability of the common people to acquire goods, and therefore their purchasing capacity is diminished. Prout includes medical care as a basic necessity which must be available to all people through full employment and adequate purchasing power.

Another of Sen's major ideas is that all well-founded ethical principles assume that human beings are fundamentally equal and therefore should have equal opportunity and equal human rights. He recognizes that different individuals have different capacities to utilize the same opportunities, and concludes that the distribution problem can never be fully solved; equality in some dimensions necessarily implies inequality in others. Sen does not indicate in which dimensions equality is to be advocated and in which dimensions inequality is to be accepted.

Sarkar offers a philosophical perspective to this dilemma with his concept of the Principle of Selfish Pleasure–the basis of capitalism–which he asserts harms the collective interest and eventually leads to the degradation of individual consciousness as well. To avoid this, he urges society to adopt the Principle of Social Equality. Prout achieves this by making the supply of minimum necessities to all the baseline for economic equality, and insisting that no one be denied access to social opportunities. The Principle of Social Equality benefits people both individually and collectively.[11]

Finally, Prout will resolve the inequality question by making special amenities available to meritorious persons who contribute to society. By reducing the gap between minimum necessities and maximum or special amenities, but never closing it completely, a Proutist society will continually raise the standard of living, provide incentives for progressive behavior, and improve the quality of life of everyone.

Barter Trade

Barter is a method of exchange by which goods or services are directly exchanged for other goods or services. When two trading partners agree on exchanging things they both need, it is called by economists a "double coincidence of wants," that is, a reciprocal interest in the other trading partner's product. However such an exact match of needs happens only rarely, so money was introduced, allowing a seller to exchange goods for a widely accepted token. Therefore money is a medium of exchange, in additional to being a store of value, and a unit of account for bookkeeping.

In times of economic recession or turmoil, when money is scarce, barter trade becomes popular. During Russia's transition from a communist-planned economy to a free market during the 1990's, inflation and unemployment soared, and barter was used in half of all industry trade by 1997.[12] When Argentina was plunged into severe recession in 1999 due to the structural adjustment policies of the IMF, "barter clubs" attracted thousands and finally millions of "prosumers" (producers-consumers) who met in neighborhood street markets throughout the country to trade goods. A paper trade unit was created called the "crédito," but as the network grew, it fell victim to counterfeiting and hyperinflation.[13] Still, to this day local barter clubs continue in Argentina and throughout much of Latin America.

Many cooperatives and small businesses today use barter very effectively to increase their efficiency by trading their unused capacity or excess inventory. Empty seats in a restaurant, theater or charter flight can be traded for advertising, accounting or plumbing services. A trade or barter exchange is a commercial organization that provides a trading platform and bookkeeping system for its members or clients. The member companies buy and sell products and services to each other using an internal currency known as barter or trade dollars. There are approximately 600 commercial and corporate barter companies serving all parts of the world.[14] The Wall Street Journal reports that 250,000 US companies traded US$16 billion worth of barter goods in 2008. Globally, the World Trade Organization estimates that US$843 billion, equivalent to 15 percent of all international trade, is conducted on a non-cash basis.[15]

In principle, Prout supports free trade. However, trade among countries should take place when all concerned enjoy economic parity; otherwise the rich and powerful countries tend to exploit the poorer ones. For example, the North American Free Trade Agreement (NAFTA) ratified in 1994 has been quite lucrative for US corporations and investors, but has caused more than 10,000 Canadian companies to be taken over by foreigners,[16] and a net loss of 879,280 U.S. manufacturing jobs to Mexico's *maquiladora* factories where wages are kept low.[17]

Guidelines are needed to ensure that trade is beneficial to all parties concerned. In an economic democracy, resources are considered the common property of the region's population. Refinement and manufacturing should therefore take place as close to the source of raw materials as possible.

Once a local economy is able to meet the basic needs of its people, finished goods or half-finished goods can be imported if they are not available and cannot easily be produced, so long as they do not undermine the market for local goods.

The best form of trade between regions and countries is barter or bilateral trade, because this avoids the need to pay in foreign currency. Both countries benefit, meeting needs by exchanging excess goods. President Hugo Chávez of Venezuela has pioneered barter trade, signing bilateral barter agreements with developing countries, swapping Venezuelan oil for other products or services the country needs, including 50,000 Cuban doctors and dentists who provide free medical care in city slums and remote rural villages. Futurist Hazel Henderson estimates that as much as 25 percent of world trade is actually conducted in barter, but this is overlooked by the Gross Domestic Produce measurement, which counts only monetary transactions.[18]

With increase in trade, a greater variety of goods becomes available to the people. This will develop prosperity and economic parity amongst socio-economic regions. Gradually, neighboring socio-economic regions will merge, and free trade zones can be created that are based on fairness and economic democracy.

Prout's Monetary System

Money is a social tool that facilitates the economic activity of a community. Its value increases with its mobility, because the more often it changes hands, the more people benefit.

An interesting example of a local currency took place in 1931 in Worgl, Austria. At that time the town, like the rest of Europe and North America, was suffering from the Great Depression. There was high unemployment; roads and bridges needed repair; and the treasury was empty because people couldn't pay their taxes. The local burgomaster, realizing that the only problem was a lack of money, decided to issue numbered "labor certificates" backed by an Austrian currency reserve in the local bank. Almost immediately the town's economy responded, and within two years Worgl was the most prosperous town in Austria. So successful was the scheme that more than 300 other towns began to issue their own currencies. At that point, the Austrian National Bank, seeing its monopoly endangered, forced the government to outlaw all such local currencies.[19]

In Canada the Local Enterprise Trading System (LETS) was developed in 1983 as an accounting system to record all transactions of goods and services between participating members without the need for scrip. Today there are over 2,500 different local currency systems operating in countries throughout the world.[20]

The major shortcoming of local trading schemes is the limitations of the currencies used: where they are accepted (usually only within the local community), and the products and services that can be purchased. Hence Prout advocates the need for a convertible national currency with a stable standard value to avoid inflation. This can be achieved by maintaining gold reserves or other stable commodities equivalent to the quantity of money printed.

A Progressive System of Taxation[21]

Tax is government's claim on a portion of the wealth produced by the community. There are three primary reasons governments levy taxes:

1. To provide public goods and services, such as police, courts, schools, roads, garbage collection, etc.
2. To pay for public insurance schemes, such as retirement pensions, health and accident insurance.
3. To promote more equitable distribution, through programs such as unemployment insurance, welfare payments and food stamps.

Some governments, such as those of Scandinavia, are interested in reducing the gap between rich and poor, unlike the United States. In 2001 and 2003, President George W. Bush pushed through legislation that cut personal income tax rates, cut tax rates on capital gains and dividends, and cut the federal estate (inheritance) tax on multi-millionaires. The savings from these cuts, which cost the government US$2.5 trillion by the end of 2010, went to the wealthiest households.[22]

Most government budgets, whether in the United Kingdom, Poland or New Zealand, are equal to about 40 percent of GDP, but half of that is transfer payments to households in pensions and unemployment. Governments should set tax levels sufficient to fund their spending without borrowing, except in extraordinary circumstances, such as recovery from natural disasters.

What is an effective tax? Economists evaluate taxes according to three criteria:

1. Equity or fairness: In fact there are two types of equity, that are not necessarily consistent with one another. First is the benefit principle: those who benefit from the service provided by the tax should pay it. For example, motorists pay taxes to

maintain the highways and airplane passengers pay airport tax. Second is the ability to pay principle, which means those who are wealthier should pay more. So income tax is progressive if the richest pay a higher percentage; whereas most sales taxes are regressive, causing the poor and middle classes to pay a much higher percentage of their income than a rich person who buys the same items.

2. Efficiency: taxes should not cause undesirable behavior or distortion, such as smuggling or black markets controlled by criminals.

3. Simplicity: Simple taxes are inexpensive to collect and administer. An example of one that is *not* simple is the U.S. income tax, which costs the Internal Revenue Service US$12 billion annually to collect, and which causes citizens to spend more than 6 billion hours and US$200 billion per year to comply with it;[23] the instructions of the U.S. federal tax code in 2010 were 71,684 pages in length!

Though Sarkar said little about taxes, and not all Prout economists are in agreement, certain proposals arise from Prout's perspective. Below are eight common types of taxes:

1. Personal Income Tax: In addition to the complexity and high enforcement and compliance costs mentioned above, income tax causes a high percentage of errors, impedes economic decision making, leads to inequitable treatment of citizens, and promotes tax avoidance, evasion and an underground economy. It is bad psychology to give money and then take it back. Rather than abolishing this approach immediately, it might be wiser to gradually raise the tax-free levels, freeing the working classes from this burden, while increasing tax at the highest income levels to promote equity.

2. Corporate Income Tax: Large privately-owned or publicly-traded corporations are not acceptable in a Prout economy. However, what happens if a Prout cooperative becomes very successful and starts earning big profits? This would signal to the rest of the economy that a good business opportunity is available—new cooperatives could jump in to replicate its success in different places. If the co-op becomes too large, it

would have to split or become a public company. Instead of the government taking the excess profits, they could be directed to local charities. For example, all cooperatives in Mondragón, Spain, donate 10 percent of their profits to charities.

3. Personal Consumption Tax (Sales Tax and VAT): Essential goods, such as food and medicine, will be exempt from tax. Semi-essential goods and services should be taxed, and non-essential luxury goods and services would be taxed at the highest rate. A simple sales tax is charged only at the final point of sale, and a Value Added Tax (VAT) appears the same to the buyer. But in fact VAT levies a tax at each stage in a production sequence, so that collections, remittances to the government, and credits for taxes already paid occur each time a business in the supply chain purchases products from another business. Sarkar wrote, "Taxes should be levied at the starting point of production,"[24] and some Prout economists consider VAT as the most logical method to do that, though it does have higher administrative and compliance costs than a simple sales tax.

4. Import Tariffs: Prout recommends setting import tariffs to protect new local businesses and essential goods and services from unfair overseas competition. However, in the long term, import taxes can hide inefficiencies and keep costs high. Sarkar suggested that young cooperatives producing essential goods and services require a "protective armor" in the form of "exemption from sales tax, duties, etc." Such systems of protection "should be withdrawn slowly."[25]

5. Resource Tax: Taxes on various natural resources are an important way for a Prout government to encourage the use of some resources, discourage the use of others and to fund research into alternative technologies. The tax rate on each resource should be adjusted to reflect its reserves, as well as all social and environmental costs. The Netherlands and Scandinavia are pioneering 'eco' or 'green taxes' that promote environmental protection. Resource taxes would cover water, air, forests, mineral ores, ocean resources and satellite bands. These areas require constant monitoring and ongoing scientific and economic research to effectively evaluate and adjust society's impact on the environment.

6. Wealth and Inheritance Tax: A major cause of social injustice is extreme concentration of wealth, the gap between rich and poor. Wealth taxes in Austria, Denmark, Finland, Germany, Luxembourg, the Netherlands, Norway, Spain, Sweden, and Switzerland range from 0.5 to 2.5 percent. Proutist economist Ravi Batra recommends a progressive wealth tax in transition from a capitalist to a cooperative economy to shift wealth ownership. The rich would have to sell some assets to pay the tax. The United States now taxes 35 percent of the wealth that is passed on to descendants.

7. Land Tax: This is very simple and efficient with low administration costs. Land cannot be hidden; ownership is easily established and land tax generates regular revenue. Land tax should be progressive, because wealthy people own more valuable land and thus should pay more tax. (But in the United Kingdom, the top landowners, who own more than 100,000 acres of land each, do not pay any taxes; rather, the British government pays *them* taxpayer money to maintain their lands![26]). Increasing tax on unutilized land in transition from a capitalist to a cooperative economy could shift land ownership and discourage speculation, reducing demand and lowering prices. Farmer's cooperatives should be taxed a fixed percentage of their harvest, to reflect seasonal conditions.

8. Special Purpose Taxes: These target particular kinds of economic behavior. For example, commodities harmful to people's health, such as cigarettes and alcohol, should be taxed at rates significantly higher than normal sales tax. These are sometimes referred to as "sin taxes." Under Prout, neither the producers nor sellers of these items will be allowed to advertise or earn profits from their sales, and the revenue from such taxes will go to finance the health care system.

The collection of taxes should be done by different levels of government. If a national government collects all the tax and distributes money to the regions, the regions would have minimal economic power. Tax sharing between different levels of government must be annually negotiated.

Sarkar wrote:

Prout advocates the abolition of income tax. In India today if income tax is abolished and excise duty on excisable commodities [goods produced within the country] is increased by only ten percent, there will be no loss of government revenue. When there is no income tax, nobody will try to accumulate black money. All money will be white money. As a result there will be economic solidarity, an increase in trade and commerce, more investment, more employment and an improvement in the position of foreign exchange. Intellectuals should demand the abolition of income tax.[27]

An established Proutist government would likely get money from resource taxes, consumption taxes, import tariffs and land taxes. A variety of user taxes, punitive taxes and other special-purpose taxes could be set according to social and economic policy. Finally, Proutist taxation depends on time, place and people, and will always strive for maximum utilization and rational distribution for the welfare of all.

Earth Rights and Land Value Capture

According to the UN Habitat Agenda: "The failure to adopt, at all levels, appropriate rural and urban land policies and land management practices remains a primary cause of inequity and poverty. It is also the cause of increased living costs, the occupation of hazard-prone land, environmental degradation and the increased vulnerability of urban and rural habitats, affecting all people, especially disadvantaged and vulnerable groups, people living in poverty and low-income people."[28]

Proutist Alanna Hartzok, author of *The Earth Belongs to Everyone* and co-director of Earth Rights Institute in Pennsylvania, USA, is helping to lead a progressive tax reform movement based on land use. Inspired by classical economist Henry George (1839-1897) and his book *Progress and Poverty*, she points out that speculation and private profit from land rent are major sources of unearned profit in capitalism–and one of the major causes of poverty.

"Land Value Capture" is a way to build a fair economy via an ethical and practical approach to public finance policy. Simply put, Land Value Capture equitably returns to everyone the value–"land rent"–that attaches to land due to natural opportunities and the contributions of society as a whole. Sometimes called "land value taxation" this is not a tax that burdens productive activities; rather, it is a type of property tax focused solely on the value of land sites and natural resources. Taxes on wage income and productive activities can then be reduced or ideally, entirely eliminated.

When land rent is captured for social purposes and needs, there is no longer profit to be made by holding unproductive land for speculation or real estate investment. Thus land is no longer treated as a for-profit commodity, but rather as a commons, meaning what used to be and should be "held in common", that is, collectively owned or shared by the population.

Property taxes in the United States, India and many other countries include an assessment of both the sale value of the land and the value of whatever buildings are on the land. So tax increases whenever a building is constructed or repaired, thus acting as a disincentive for improvements. However land value tax eliminates taxes on houses and buildings, and shifts taxes to the value of land sites.

Fifteen cities in the state of Pennsylvania, USA, have implemented a partial reform called 'two-rate' or 'split-rate' property tax: lowering taxes on buildings, thereby encouraging improvements and renovations, while raising the tax on land values, thus discouraging land speculation.[29]

"Tax bads, not goods" is the slogan of the Green Tax and Common Assets Project, which works in conjunction with the University of Vermont Masters in Public Administration Program. They report, "If work, income, wages, and investments in productive activities are taxed less, these items will be encouraged. If resource use, land use, and pollution are taxed more, resources will be conserved, land will be used efficiently, and industry will avoid pollution."[30]

Hartzok writes:

> We see this situation all over the world: people working longer and harder and still unable to buy affordable housing, a basic necessity of life. Traditional property taxes penalize small home-owners for improving their properties. High rents and high-interest loans and mortgages put people further behind.
>
> We need to stop taxing labor, in order to increase the purchasing capacity of middle and lower-income people. Land value tax or resource rent should be understood as taxing the unearned billions of dollars of income that a few capitalists reap from

the gifts of Nature. This system is similar to the "polluter pays" taxes that have drastically reduced air and water pollution in countries that have applied them. This unearned income needs to be shared equitably to benefit the community as a whole.[31]

A Proutist Response to Land Value Capture

By John Gross, PhD., Department of Economics,
Duke University

Land value taxes or geo-taxes, based on the ideas of Henry George, have a valuable role when properly applied within a capitalist economy, or in any economic setting in which a small proportion of the population controls most of the land and its resources. Many of the benefits of such a tax system within these settings are explained above.

A Proutist economy, however, is very different from a capitalist economy, and policies that make perfect sense within capitalism can produce poor and even unintended consequences when applied within Prout.

Fundamental to a land value tax are two, usually unstated, assumptions: land and resource holders are profit maximizers, and profit maximization is desirable.

These are so deeply ingrained in neoclassical economic theory that most economists would describe any other behavior as either irrational or untenable. Land value taxes are calculated as a proportion of the profits (often termed surplus or rent) that can be earned on any given piece of property under the assumption that the owner uses the land in its most profitable form of production while acting as a profit maximizer. Thus, any land owner who does anything other than this will face difficulty paying the taxes and will have an incentive to sell the land.

Prout, however, rejects profit maximization in favor of output or consumption maximization. In fact, according to P.R. Sarkar, Prout's system of cooperative production for the purpose of consumption minimizes profit.[32]

Under Prout, production will lead to greater output and lower prices than under capitalism because optimal cooperative output would occur where price equals marginal cost, so long as it is sufficient to cover production costs. Otherwise, price would be set at or just above average cost. In either case, output is greater and prices are lower than if profits are maximized.[33]

If land value taxes are imposed, cooperatives will be required to reduce output and increase price in order to earn sufficient income to pay their taxes. In other words, they would be forced by the tax to become profit maximizers. The increase in price and reduction in output also means increased deadweight loss.[34]

Land value taxes attempt to capture surplus value that exists in capitalist economies due to profit maximization. However, under Prout, rather than maximizing profit, cooperatives use this surplus to produce additional goods and services provided at lower prices. Hence the imposition of such a tax in a Proutist economy would have the unintended and undesirable consequence of raising the prices and reducing the output of goods and services produced by cooperatives, undoing one of the crucial and best features of Prout cooperative production.

Chapter 5

Cooperatives for a Better World

Prout supports the implementation of the cooperative system because its inner spirit is one of coordinated cooperation. Only the cooperative system can ensure the healthy, integrated progress of humanity, and establish complete and everlasting unity among the human race.[1]

—P.R. Sarkar

Is Human Nature Competitive or Cooperative?[2]

English biologist Thomas Henry Huxley (1825-1895), who popularized Charles Darwin's ideas of evolution, stated, "The animal world is about on a level of a gladiator's show... whereby the strongest, the swiftest, and the cunningest (sic) live to fight another day."[3] Another Victorian scientist, Herbert Spencer, coined the term "survival of the fittest", applying it to human society, claiming that competition is our fundamental nature. This belief, known as Social Darwinism, shaped public opinion and policy in Great Britain and the United States for more than a century.

In 1966 Austrian ethnologist Konrad Lorenz published a bestseller called *On Aggression* in which he argued that human beings are innately aggressive, competitive, possessive and violent. His work had significant impact on the social and biological sciences. A decade later evolutionary biologist Richard Dawkins published *The Selfish Gene*, about the human instinct for self-preservation; it sold over a million copies, and was translated into more than 25 languages. These scientists popularized the idea that evolutionary success depends on each person being self-ishly preoccupied with their own self.

Hollywood and the U.S. mass media seized on and simplified these theories, reducing them to the notion that people are fundamentally individualistic, selfish and competitive, driven to get ahead by any means necessary. Popular expressions such as the "law of the jungle", "every man for himself", and "dog eat dog" reinforced this theme, stressing winning at all costs. These ideas of innate aggression and selfish genes helped fuel our individualistic, consumer culture, influencing the way people think throughout the world.

Because leading scientists have declared this is the way we are, econo-mists and government officials create policies that favor the largest, most "efficient" companies to survive. "Too big to fail" was the justification governments made for the big bank bailouts during the financial crisis of 2008, bailouts that they did not extend to small and medium-sized companies in trouble.

People who argue that "you can't change human nature" make the mistake of assuming that because people are led to behave in a certain way in a capitalist society, that behavior reflects the essential nature of human beings. Capitalism rewards selfishness and greed, and winning by any means, fair or foul. Therefore such people conclude that this behavior is natural for all human beings and that it is impossible to establish a society based on anything except a competitive struggle for private profit.

Many new studies, however, point to quite different conclusions. Robert Augros and George Stanciu, in their book *The New Biology: Discovering the Wisdom of Nature*,[4] found that in fact cooperation, not competition, is the norm in nature, because it is energy-efficient and because predators and their prey maintain a kind of balanced coexistence. They found that "nature uses extraordinarily ingenious techniques to avoid conflict and competition, and that cooperation is extraordinarily widespread throughout all of nature."[5]

Today most anthropologists and psychologists assert that the question of nature or nurture is not an either/or issue, but one of interrelation-ship.[6] We are born with certain instincts and tendencies, but through education, upbringing and our own conscious choices, we can transform our conduct, nature and personality.

Research now indicates the existence of "selfless genes"–genetic code that favors cooperation, kindness, generosity, and heroism. It is not uncommon for people to risk their lives for strangers. Firefighters, soldiers, human rights advocates and accidental heroes may endanger themselves or even sacrifice their lives in order to save others. In addition, our world is filled with countless smaller acts of kindness: giving up a seat on the train, returning a wallet with money that was lost. Biologists now say these impulses are just as primal as aggression, lust, and greed. Furthermore, they play a powerful role in the survival of the species and the wellbeing of individuals.[7]

"Mirror neurons", first described in 1992 by neurophysiologists at the University of Parma in Italy, fire not only when we experience something ourselves, but also when we observe the experience of others.[8] For example, witnessing a serious injury will cause traumatic reactions in the observer; seeing laughing, loving people will brighten our day. These are neurological mechanisms that develop empathy for others, which builds trust, a prerequisite for cooperation.

Another biological factor related to cooperation is oxytocin, a neuropeptide that affects social attachment and affiliation. It is key to bonding between mother and child, between lovers, and even among friends. When triggered, it reduces fear and increases trust and empathy–leading to more cooperative behavior.[9]

Alfie Kohn spent seven years reviewing more than 400 research studies dealing with competition and cooperation. In his classic work, *No Contest: The Case Against Competition*, he concluded that, "The ideal amount of competition... in any environment, the classroom, the workplace, the family, the playing field, is none.... [Competition] is always destructive."[10]

Even the selection committee for the Nobel Prize in Economics, after four decades of honoring proponents of free-market capitalism, is starting to recognize the importance of cooperation. In 2009 Elinor Ostrom of Indiana University shared the prize, the first woman ever to receive it, for her work focusing on how well groups of users manage natural resources as common property. The traditional view is that common ownership results in excessive exploitation of resources, such as when fishermen over-fish a common pond; and the only solution lies in government-imposed taxes or quotas. However, Ms. Ostrom's empirical research on collectively-managed natural resources around the world has shown that this explanation is "overly simplistic." There are many cases in which common property is "surprisingly well-managed" cooperatively, often better than under either socialism or privatization.[11]

As part of the science of yoga, relevant to the idea of improving human behavior, Sarkar used the term "biopsychology" to describe how the glands, nerves and brain of the body affect our behaviors, thoughts and feelings. He asserted that every human being has the same basic instincts, both negative ones, such as anger, hatred and greed, and positive ones, such as hope, conscience and repentance. The postures of yoga, a vegetarian diet and meditation are all ancient techniques that are used to overcome selfish, negative instincts and to channel the mind in a positive direction. On the social level, Sarkar encouraged society to promote cooperation for economic success and community growth. He suggested that cooperatives are the enterprises best suited to achieve that.[12]

Successful Cooperatives

Throughout the twentieth century and until today, cooperatives have been mostly invisible, ignored by the mass media and political leaders who are more interested in power, fame and control. Yet more than one billion people, a sixth of our global population, are members of co-ops. The world's largest non-governmental organization is the International Cooperative Alliance (ICA), representing 246 national and international organizations.[13]

The ICA offers this definition: "A cooperative is an autonomous association of persons united voluntarily to meet their common economic, social and cultural needs and aspirations through a jointly-owned and democratically-controlled enterprise."[14]

In Bolivia, Norway, France, Japan, Canada and Honduras, one out of every three people is a member of a cooperative. Co-ops manage 99 percent of Sweden's dairy production, 99 percent of Japan's fish harvest and 95 percent of its rice, 75 percent of western Canada's grain and oil seed output, and 60 percent of Italy's wine production. Some of Europe's major commercial banks are cooperatively owned or organized, including Germany's DZ Bank, Holland's and France's Credit Agricole, Caisse D'Epargne and Confédération Nationale du Crédit Mutuel.[15] In Quebec, Canada, the largest and most successful financial services institution is the Désjardins consumer credit cooperative.

In India, cooperatives have empowered many people who were marginalized or excluded. AMUL is a dairy cooperative which is jointly owned by 2.8 million milk producers in the state of Gujarat. Founded in 1946, its revenue in 2009 was US$1.3 billion (Rs. 6711 *crores*).[16] From 1970 to 1996 the national government ran Operation Flood, to produce, distribute and sell cheaply a "flood of milk" throughout India. It supported 72,000 village milk-producing cooperatives with infrastructure and transportation systems free of exploitation that continue today.[17]

In the Indian state of Andhra Pradesh in the 1980s, *dalits* (so-called low caste), long barred by discrimination from participating in the formal economy, started a consumer food co-op called ASP (Ankuram-Sangaman-Poram). They added banking, weaving and cell phone cooperatives, which now serve a total of 150,000 members.[18] In the state of Kerala, the South Indian Federation of Fisherman Societies (SIFFS) benefits over 50,000 fish workers with their cooperative services. Hired auctioneers systematically sell the daily catch of each boat to the highest bidders, significantly increasing the income. Three percent goes to administration, and two percent to member savings accounts. When the tsunami of 2004 destroyed every single boat on the southern coast of India, SIFFS used these savings to replace its members' boats, motors and nets, while most private and commercial fishermen were unable to do so.[19]

Cooperatives provide over 100 million jobs around the world, 20 percent more than multinational enterprises. Cooperatives are also more likely to succeed than privately-owned enterprises. In the United States, 60-80 percent of companies fail in their first year, while only 10 percent of cooperatives fail during that period. After five years, only three to five percent of new U.S. corporations are still in business, while nearly 90 percent of co-ops remain viable.[20]

In North America the largest co-ops are agricultural service or marketing cooperatives, such as Sunkist (6,000 grower members) and Ocean Spray (750 grower members, 2,000 employees, sales of US$1.4 billion in 2005). Calavo Growers of California formed in 1924 to popularize avocados, becoming so successful by 1990 that its gross sales were more than US$150 million. Unfortunately, because it had expanded into Mexico, the so-called "free trade" tariffs on cooperatives operating internationally were so high that its members voted in 2001 to become a multinational stock corporation instead.[21]

The NAFTA agreement of 1994 caused Mexico to charge co-ops twice the tariffs that they charged private enterprises, requiring them to carry expensive life insurance on every member–in effect tripling their total tax burden. Since then the legal status of cooperatives in Mexico has changed continually, sometimes yearly. NAFTA does not allow Mexico to subsidize coffee or corn growers, even though the U.S. government subsidizes their own corn growers as well as coffee growers in Vietnam.[22] Brazilian law requires a minimum of 25 members to incorporate a cooperative, compared to Venezuela, which requires only five. In countries with discriminatory legal structures, most would-be cooperatives are forced to register as an association, "civil society" or something else, with no legal protections.

Different problems have plagued cooperatives in Africa, Asia, and the Pacific, where many newly independent developing countries tried to establish cooperatives through government policy. Many failed because they were not organized by the communities themselves from the bottom up. Government subsidies were often paid out to save them, further undermining their independent spirit. Too often, dishonest leaders stole the money. Due to these problems, cooperatives unfortunately have gotten a bad name in many countries.

The Mondragón Cooperatives

The Mondragón group of cooperatives in the Basque region of northern Spain is generally considered to be the world's most well-developed co-op model. José María Arizmendiarrieta, a Catholic worker priest, arrived in that region in the 1940s when it was still devastated by the Spanish Civil War. Searching for a way to improve people's lives in a practical way by creating jobs, he studied the cooperative movements in Great Britain and Italy. He saw in them a nonviolent way to unite workers and owners.

In the Catholic school he directed, Arizmendiarrieta passionately immersed his students in the study of cooperatives. In 1956, some of his graduates pioneered the first industrial cooperative in the region, manufacturing high-quality domestic appliances and machine tools. The fiercely nationalistic Basque people, with their profound social consciousness, supported the initiative from its inception. The company grew steadily, branching out into new co-ops.

Arizmendiarrieta realized that an essential key to success would be a cooperative bank. Caja Laboral, a credit union, began funding the movement in 1959. By the 1970s the cooperative Fagor Electrodomésticos had become one of the top ten companies in Spain and the greatest cooperative success story in the world.

Mondragón's greatest challenge came when Spain joined the European Union in 1986. Suddenly Spain's taxes of 18-35 percent on foreign imports disappeared, allowing multinational corporations to flood the market with their products, bankrupting many small industries. In response to this danger, the workers chose to centralize their management and formed to compete aggressively in the global market. The corporation opened factories overseas; by the end of 2009 it employed more than 85,000 people and had total assets of €33.3 billion (US$45.6 billion).[23]

The annual starting salary today in every Mondragón co-op is close to €14,000 (approximately US$19,000). All new workers start with a six-to-twelve month trial period. If they demonstrate their ability and accept the cooperative system, they can become a member by investing about one year's salary–an amount that can be borrowed from the Caja Laboral and repaid over 36 months at 3.7 percent interest.[24]

The benefits of being a cooperative member are impressive. For €30 per month, all members and their families get full health coverage. For €15 per month, members can send their children to the best private school, which is also run as a cooperative. There is subsidized housing, and, most important, members have job security for life. If for any reason their cooperative needs to lay off workers, they will be transferred to another cooperative. Of the 120 cooperatives, only 12 of them lost money in 2005, and a total of 110 workers had to be relocated to other co-ops.

A one-to-three wage differential in worker salaries lasted more than 20 years. However, in order to avoid losing their top management to private companies, Mondragón Corporation raised the highest salaries to 4.5 times more than the minimum in most of the cooperatives, and the Chief Executive Officer gets 9 times more, or €126,000 (US$173,000) per year–a tiny fraction of most corporate CEO salaries.

Education, research and innovation have always been essential to the corporation's growth–more than €140 million (US$193 million) was invested in research and development in 2009; the corporation also funded the University of Mondragón and seven other cooperative schools which together have a total of more than 8,500 students. Eleven research and development cooperatives have earned the cooperative network a reputation for a high level of technological sophistication. Twenty percent of the sales of the hundreds of industrial products made by the cooperatives in 2009 involved new products which did not exist five years before.[25]

There are only four agricultural cooperatives, some of which are very small. Women comprise 43.7 percent of the total cooperative members of Mondragón.

Every cooperative has a general assembly of all members which decides the general policies and strategies of the cooperative and appoints and removes by secret vote the members of its Governing Council and the Auditing Body. The Governing Council in turn appoints the managing director and other staff.

The Mondragón cooperatives have had very few problems with dishonesty or corruption. Mikel Lezamiz, Director of Cooperative Dissemination, said, "Each cooperative has both internal and external audits. In addition there is strong social control, meaning our Basque culture and the cooperative spirit that has developed for 50 years encourages group trust and solidarity. To my knowledge there have only been three cases of members stealing from a cooperative. None of them were top managers; all of them were discovered relatively quickly. All three were dismissed by the general assembly of their respective cooperatives."[26]

Unfortunately the negative aspects of consumerism and materialism have started to affect cooperative workers, just as they affect workers in the rest of the world. Corporate Chairman Jose María Aldecoa wrote in the 2009 annual report that there is "a fairly profound crisis of values, with some clearly appearing to be in decline, such as responsibility, work well done, endeavor, solidarity, collective advancement, being replaced by more material ones that have taken hold amongst us."

Sadly, Mondragón's expansion abroad does not reflect its cooperative principles. None of its 75 overseas factories and facilities in other countries, which employ 13,400 workers, are run as cooperatives.

In March, 2007, the Mundukide Foundation and the Lanki Institute of Cooperative Studies selected 11 South American cooperative activists, including José Albarrán, then president of the Prout Research Institute of Venezuela, to study intensively the Mondragón cooperatives for one month. He wrote:

> We interviewed leaders at the university, the technical colleges, the research centers and the cooperatives, including some that are not part of the corporation. I observed seven aspects that I consider to be keys to the success of both the Mondragón cooperative experience as well as the cooperatives in Venezuela and the rest of Latin America. These are: a deeply-felt need for

change, strong commitment and determination, clear ethical values, openness to constructive criticism, practical management and development, social commitment intercooperation amongst the co-ops and community.[27]

In a letter to the author, Lezamiz wrote:

I believe that a lot of similarities exist between the philosophy of our Mondragón Cooperative Experience and that of Prout. For example, the importance of economic decentralization (each cooperative is independent and maintains its own autonomy), participatory democracy, the balance between the social and the economic, etc.... Perhaps the biggest difference that exists between you and us is that we have always avoided being too belligerent with the nearby economic systems (capitalist and communist) to avoid arousing suspicions and to make our own road.... Another significant difference could be that our cooperativism is more directed at the level of labor. Outside of the company we are not too sensitive with spiritual life (although we do strive for social transformation toward a more fair, equal and united society). I believe that you are more spiritual than us and your philosophy of life and your practice of it is very consistent with the values that you propagate. I would say that you demonstrate cooperativism 24 hours a day, while we do so only during the eight working hours.[28]

Worker Cooperatives

Of the three levels of a Proutist economy–small-scale private enterprises, cooperatives, and large-scale key industries–co-ops will employ the largest percentage of the population. These cooperative enterprises–industrial, agricultural, service, consumer and credit–form the core of economic democracy. They encourage human beings to work together, a key aspiration of Prout.

One requirement vital to the success of cooperatives is moral leadership. A high degree of integrity is essential to the administration's effectiveness. Strict accounting and organizational standards applied by honest managers will build confidence among the cooperative members and the community.

Sarkar asserts:

> Human society is one and indivisible. A human being cannot live alone... In society human beings have to work jointly with others so that everyone can move forward collectively... Where individuality dominates human life, the environment, the welfare of different groups and even the continued existence of humanity may be adversely affected.[29]

Successful cooperatives grow from the energy and commitment of local people. The foundation of the cooperative system lies in "coordinated cooperation", in which free human beings with equal rights and mutual respect work together to fulfill a common need, for their mutual benefit.

Co-ops are different than both traditional capitalist enterprises and socialist communes formed through forced collectivization. Both of these systems are administered through "subordinated cooperation," in which managers supervise and give orders to the workers. Cooperatives, on the other hand, integrate economic and social objectives, spreading wealth and power to each member equally.

Cooperatives hold a competitive advantage over both private and public enterprises because members have a personal interest in their co-op's success. The members own the co-op, so are more likely to buy its goods and use its services. Shares in cooperatives are not publicly traded because the members own the shares. They themselves decide how to spend the co-op's profits.

Today many cooperatives in capitalist countries involve pooling investment money and then sharing the profit; in Prout, only cooperative banks and consumer co-ops function like this. In all other cooperatives, every member actively works for the enterprise. This leads to a better working environment and enhanced productivity. In such cooperatives, labor employs capital instead of the reverse, as in capitalism. With labor at the helm and no longer subject to the dictates of capital, a sense of self-worth is restored to people and the community is strengthened.

Also in contrast to capitalism, cooperative productivity is measured not only in terms of output and income, but also in terms of job security and happiness.

How Worker Cooperatives Function

Membership in a worker cooperative is open only to those who work there. New workers enter the cooperative on a trial basis before they become full members. The control of the firm and the right to any residual assets and profits are based on labor contribution rather than the value of capital or property holdings.

Control rests on the principle of one member, one vote, and not on the number of shares or amount of a person's investment in the cooperative. If non-worker shareholders were allowed to become members, it would introduce conflicts of interest that could dilute the worker incentive system. Capital financing can be accepted only if it does not have the power to influence decision-making.

The incentive system for pay and profit-sharing must be both fair and attractive, so that competent people will join. Prout advocates rewarding workers' performances according to their skill and contribution, but within a minimum and maximum income range. In a Prout economy, the ratio between the lowest-paid and highest-paid workers is determined according to the time and place, but the difference will naturally decrease as the overall standard of living rises. Rewards may also be given in other forms that boost productivity and worker satisfaction, such as better equipment, education and training, assigning more workers to a unit, and work-related travel subsidies.

In traditional private enterprise, financial incentives are used to demand high standards of personnel training and development. Yet in cooperatives, even higher levels of resourcefulness, communication skills and interpersonal discipline are needed. The importance of investing in continual worker education to foster interpersonal skills as well as business management expertise cannot be overemphasized. Each member should be encouraged to further his or her education, keep abreast of technological developments in the field, and share knowledge with others. The members' ability to contribute to the enterprise will increase, and along with it, their self-esteem. In this way cooperation and working conditions will improve for everyone.

Sharing of cooperative values and the sincere attempt to practice them allows people to integrate their social and economic lives with their beliefs. This can lead to a deeper sense of worker satisfaction, loyalty, and commitment to economic democracy.

The degree of collective decision-making depends on the size of the cooperative. In small collectives, all members jointly make key decisions. Larger cooperatives generally elect boards to make policy decisions. Boards select a manager who is a member of the cooperative to be in charge of day-to-day operations. Each cooperative, according to the realities of its business, must decide which decisions the manager, the board, and the entire membership respectively will make. Guidelines are based on other cooperatives' experience.

Coordinated cooperation requires members and management to have mutual respect and trust for one another. Experience has shown the importance of teaching cooperative ethics to workers so that they can develop their ability to participate in and manage their firms. Where cooperatives have been most successful, the managers are also teachers, awakening in the workers an understanding of the cooperative and how it functions.

Experience shows that in addition to wages, workers must participate in the growth or decline of the firm itself in order to have sufficient incentive for long-term investment. They do not necessarily need total ownership or control over the assets.

Mondragón's model of collective ownership relies on a balance of incentives. The innovative system of internal capital accounts spreads gains or losses in the net worth of the cooperative to individual workers' accounts. The cooperative restricts workers from taking out their balances at will, so that it can use the assets for reinvestment in the cooperative. Yearly interest is paid on each account. The balances on each member's account are eventually paid out after a designated period of time, such as five years, or when a worker leaves the cooperative.

Without good leadership and a wise cooperative structure, workers sometimes choose poorly. For example, in the Vakhrusheva coal mine in the Khabarovsk region of the Russian Far East, workers preferred immediate dividends, high wages and access to imported goods as opposed to reinvesting their profits back into the development and long-term future of the cooperative. Today this mine is being worked by a privately-owned company.[30]

Cooperatives provide greater job security than do private enterprises, which are not answerable to the community and whose boards might choose to relocate to where labor costs are lower. Cooperatives consider labor a fixed rather than a variable cost over the short run. This means that workers are not immediately laid off if production is cut back. Viable alternatives to layoffs include decreasing the work hours of all members, opening new lines of production or services, retraining workers, and transferring members to other cooperatives.

A Supportive Infrastructure

It is difficult in a capitalist economy for a cooperative to survive as an isolated enterprise. As Sarkar has noted, sincere acceptance of the cooperative system by the public is a requirement for success.

The vast majority of cooperatives are relatively small. The only way they can afford certain services is through mutual support. Together, several cooperatives may form a supportive infrastructure to provide financing, technical and management assistance, joint marketing and purchasing of supplies and services, research and development of new products, cooperative education and training, and lobbying and public relations services. When co-ops have access to these types of support, they often outperform conventional private firms.

Access to funding from a sympathetic credit union or bank is crucial to success. In the Mondragón group of cooperatives, the Caja Laboral cooperative bank has provided the capital financing needed to grow and overcome various difficulties. The Stiga independent consulting report for 2009 rated Caja Laboral first among 105 financial institutions in Spain in terms of excellence of service.[31]

Credit unions are cooperative banks, owned and democratically-managed by their members, which give loans at lower interest rates than commercial banks. In the United States, there are 7,339 federally insured credit unions, with 90.5 million members and total assets of $914.5 billion. Credit unions have fared far better than other financial institutions in recent years, with only 1.74 percent delinquency ratio on US$564 billion in loans. In 2010, only 28 retail credit unions failed, resulting in US$221 million in NCUSIF losses, but no loss to any deposit holder.[32]

There are several reasons why credit unions are more successful than corporate banks. First, because they are legally incorporated as not-for-profit cooperatives, earnings are not given away to stockholder investors. Second, credit unions do not speculate with their money on risky financial investments because their goal is not amassing profits. Third, credit unions in the United States have been exempt from taxes since 1937, because they are member-owned, democratically operated, with the specific mission of meeting the credit and savings needs of consumers of modest means. Fourth, the members of the board of directors of each credit union are volunteers. Finally, credit unions are people helping people, working hard through education and community service to benefit everyone.

Worker and community takeovers of failed capitalist enterprises have tremendous potential, as Noam Chomsky explains in Chapter 13. Argentina has the largest number of these takeovers; in response to the country's 2001 economic crisis, workers occupied bankrupt factories and collectively managed them. Called the *Fábricas Recuperadas* Movement, which means "reclaimed or recovered factories", this tactic expanded to other enterprises, such as the Hotel Bauen in Buenos Aires. The communities came out to defend these initiatives whenever the police tried to evict the workers.

The reclaimed businesses are run cooperatively, with important management decisions taken democratically by a general assembly of the workers; in most, all workers receive the same wage. By 2005, about 13,000 Argentine workers were running 250 recovered businesses[33]– amazingly, only two of the recovered enterprises have failed.[34] By 2011 the movement had brought about the signing of a new bankruptcy law that facilitates takeovers by the workers.[35] In Brazil in 2005, there were a total of 174 enterprises that had been taken over and were being managed by the workers as part of the solidarity economy.[36]

The benefits of worker-management include a higher level of loyalty and commitment by the workers, greater support from the community and less financial responsibility and stress on the shoulders of a single owner or CEO. The greatest obstacles faced are sometimes internal disagreements and often difficulty getting credit for operations, because commercial banks are wary of lending to new cooperatively-managed enterprises, especially those with a history of financial troubles. In Argentina, recovered factories found it easier to collaborate with other worker-managed enterprises to reach a critical size and power enabling them to negotiate successfully with the banks.

Cooperatives have tremendous potential to expand economic opportunity and wealth building for impoverished communities. In 2008 a group of community organizers in predominantly Afro-American neighborhoods of Cleveland, Ohio, started the Evergreen Cooperative Initiative to create jobs and wealth building through a network of ecologically-friendly, community-based co-ops. In an area known as Greater University Circle where 43,000 residents have a median household income below US$18,500 and where over 25 percent of the working population are unemployed, they used the Mondragón Cooperative Experience to create a network of worker-owned enterprises. A non-profit corporation ties them together, with a revolving fund so that 10 percent of the income generated is used to start new cooperatives.

The Green City Growers Cooperative is a year-round, hydroponic food production greenhouse. On just two hectares of land (5.5 acres), 40 employee-owners are producing three million heads of healthy, organic lettuce per year, and 300,000 pounds of herbs annually for local markets. The Evergreen Cooperative Laundry is an industrial-scale, high-tech laundry with 50 workers that uses only a third of the water and heat of traditional laundries to service the hospitals and the nursing homes in the area. Ohio Cooperative Solar employs workers who "face barriers to employment" to install solar panels on Cleveland-area institutional, governmental, and commercial buildings. The enterprise became profit-able within its first five months in operation; in the off-season the co-op helps weatherize low-income housing in the area. These and many other small, quickly-growing cooperatives focus on economic inclusion and building a local economy from the ground up.[37]

Laws concerning cooperatives are different in every country; in fact some laws were written to hinder and block cooperatives. Those who wish to start a cooperative should first consult their national association of cooperatives and visit successful co-ops, ideally those which operate in the same sector, to learn as much as possible from the experience of others. These experienced cooperative workers can also advise about psychological ways to win the support of the local people.

Cooperatives benefit the community at large by creating jobs, retaining wealth and increasing social connections among the inhabitants. The practice of economic democracy in co-ops raises awareness of democratic issues among the workers as well as in the wider community.

What Makes Cooperatives Successful?

R.M. Baseman, an associate researcher and advisor to the Prout Research Institute of Venezuela conducted a passive Internet survey to find worldwide consensus on the question of co-op success. First he found primary-source articles and publications in which authors expressed opinions and conclusions about the success and failure of co-ops. The sources reflected experience from all continents and more than 10 countries, including ones by the International Labor Organization, the International Cooperative Alliance and the United Nations. Studying these, he located 175 factors for success that he grouped into 13 categories and prioritized according to the number of similar responses:

1. supportive environment
2. sound advance planning
3. real economic benefits for members
4. skilled management
5. belief in co-op concepts
6. grassroots development and leadership
7. financially self-sustaining
8. innovation and adaptation
9. effective structure and operations
10. networking with other co-ops
11. communications
12. common member interests
13. education

Co-ops, much more than corporations, closely reflect the lives and thoughts of the member-owners. If the common interests of the members and the interests of the co-op move apart, the co-op dies.

All the basic factors for success in any business also apply to co-ops, as would be expected: there has to be a real demand for the product; planning has to be thorough and realistic; and the enterprise has to make money. There are also clear differences between consumer and producer co-ops, making their factors for success also somewhat different. For example, widespread community support of a consumer food co-op is essential, because without thousands of regular customers it will have to close. On the other hand, a co-op that manufactures custom automation solutions for industry is much less dependent on community support.[38]

Examples of Small-scale Cooperatives in Maleny[39]

Maleny is a small town of 5,000 people situated 100 kilometers north of Brisbane on the Sunshine Coast of Australia. Twenty successful cooperatives function there, linking every aspect of community life: a cooperative bank, a consumers' food co-op, a cooperative club, an artists' co-op, a cashless trading co-op, a cooperative radio station, a cooperative film society, four environmental co-ops, and several community settlement co-ops.

MCU Sustainable Banking (Maleny Credit Union)

The Maleny Credit Union was started in 1984 with the objective of creating an ethical financial institution which would foster regional financial autonomy by lending exclusively to local people and projects. Initially it was staffed by volunteers, who worked from rented rooms and entered deposits manually into a journal. On the first day of operations, local people deposited more than US$25,000.

Today MCU has grown to more than 5,500 owner members, and US$52 million in assets, including its own building. People from all over Australia invest their money with the Credit Union; about half its deposits come from outside the community.

The services MCU offers include savings, checks, loans, credit cards, term deposit accounts, ethical superannuation and insurance. Since its inception, the Credit Union has made many small loans to local people who would have been ineligible to borrow from major banks. These loans have helped them to buy land, build their own homes, and start more than 100 new businesses that create jobs. Despite some initial difficulties, today MCU is extremely successful, principally because it developed the right balance of financial expertise and cooperative spirit.[40]

Consumers' Food Cooperative

In 1979 a small group of people, who wanted whole foods and produce grown by local farmers, formed the Maple Street Co-op. Today it operates an organic health food retail outlet on the main street of Maleny, open seven days a week, with 1,700 active members. It has 40 employees and stocks more than 4,500 health products. Although it functions as a consumers' cooperative, it also sells to the public.[41]

The co-op's first priority is to provide organic food. It focuses on locally-produced food; if that is not possible, on Australian-grown products. It refuses to stock anything that contains genetically modified material, nor does it stock products from companies that it considers to be exploitive of people or of the environment. It operates on the principle of consensus decision-making.

At first, labor in the co-op was voluntary, but as it prospered, the number of paid workers slowly increased. During its 32 years of operation, it has overcome several major hurdles. At various times in its existence, the co-op dealt with problems such as lacking a viable business plan, operating at a loss, making poor investment decisions, lacking experienced financial management, and spending a lot of time resolving differences of opinion among its members.

Learning from experience, the co-op gradually evolved a sound strategic and financial plan. For the last decade, the co-op has made a profit. However, it is structured as a non-profit enterprise, so the profits are either reinvested to expand the co-op's services and develop its infrastructure, or are donated to community activities.

In 2006, the Maple Street Co-op chose to share management with the Upfront Club, a cooperative restaurant, bar and entertainment venue located in the shop next door. The club is still operating as a welcoming and friendly "social heart" for Maleny. It regularly hosts film nights, open microphones, art exhibitions, fundraisers and game evenings along with a great variety of live music. Volunteers help in many areas of the Club, from washing dishes, to planning events and beautifying the grounds. The two co-ops together produce over US$2 million in cash flow yearly.

Other Maleny cooperatives

Maleny has one of Australia's most successful Local Energy Transfer System (LETS) schemes. It functions as a cashless trading co-op whose members trade their products and provide services to each other without the use of money. Instead, they use a local currency: the Bunya, named after the local native pine nut. This allows people with little or no cash to participate in the local economy.[42]

The Maleny Community Kindergarten was built by a group of community volunteers in 1939. Today it still operates in the same premises with a beautifully-landscaped garden out front. The kindergarten is run by an elected board.

Maleny has three environmental co-ops. Barung Landcare is one of several hundred community-based landcare groups throughout Australia; it runs a successful nursery, provides environmental education, and promotes the sustainable harvesting of native timber. Booroobin Bush Magic runs a rainforest nursery, while the Green Hills Fund works to reforest the Maleny hinterland.

There are four community settlement cooperatives in Maleny, including the Crystal Waters Permaculture Village. Crystal Waters houses 200 residents on private one-acre lots. Two community lots that are owned by a cooperative of residents include buildings for community events, small businesses and a monthly market. The Prout Community Settlement Co-op has ten families and uses half of their land for the River Primary School, with more than 200 students on 25 hectares of beautiful rainforest land.[43]

The Venezuelan Cooperative Experience

The first legal cooperative in Venezuela was a savings and loan association formed in 1960. By the end of 1998 there were 813 registered cooperatives with 230,000 members. Most of these are still active, tough and resilient because they were created by the members with no government support or funding. For example, the Cooperatives of Social Services of Lara State (Cecosesola), founded in 1967, now includes producer and consumer food co-ops that serve 60,000 people each week, credit unions, health clinics and a network of cooperative funeral homes that is number one in the western region.[44]

When President Hugo Chávez took office at the beginning of 1999, he began to emphasize cooperatives in order to transform property into collective forms of ownership and management as a key to the Bolivarian Revolution. In 2005 he called for a "Socialism for the Twenty-first Century". His job-training program for the unemployed, Mission *Vuelvan Caras* ("About Face"), included cooperative education and encouraged all graduates to form one. Co-op registration was made free of charge; they were exempted from income tax; micro-credit was made available; and laws were passed directing the government to give preference to cooperatives when awarding contracts.

The goal was to transform the profit-oriented capitalist economy into one oriented towards endogenous and sustainable social development by involving those who had been marginalized or excluded. The result was a phenomenal creation of 262,904 registered cooperatives by the end of 2008, but many of these never became active or collapsed. The national cooperative supervision institute, SUNACOOP, recognized about 70,000 as functioning,[45] which is still the highest total for any country after China.

The majority of cooperatives have only a few members; most of these workers are unskilled. Because of the high rate of failure among the registered cooperatives, in 2005 the president shifted the government's approach from cooperatives to socialist enterprises and worker takeovers of factories. In this way, the government pays the salaries, but keeps the ownership. Prout on the other hand supports worker ownership as well as worker management.

The Prout Research Institute of Venezuela designed two surveys, in 2007 and a follow-up one in 2010, to understand the problems and needs of 40 cooperatives in the rural district of Barlovento, a two-hour drive east from Caracas. More than 90 percent of the population there are Afro-Venezuelans, descendants of former slaves, who have historically suffered racism and discrimination. The district has high levels of poverty and unemployment, economic disparity and emigration to the cities.

The objective was to diagnose the problems and challenges that worker-owned enterprises are facing. The results show that:

Eighty-five percent of the cooperatives were still functioning three years after the first study, with little or no government support.

Those that closed as well as a few that survived were robbed by corrupt co-op managers.

Sixty percent of cooperative members have not had training in cooperatives.

The majority of workers believe they are receiving the same or lower wages than if they were working for private enterprises.

There is little inter-cooperation among cooperatives, and little support from the community in Barlovento.

The most stable co-ops are those in which the members provided at least part of the initial capital.

Clearly the cooperatives of Venezuela need practical training and professional consultants responsive to their needs.

Guidelines for Successful Cooperatives

The successes of the Maleny cooperatives have been achieved through great struggles over the last two decades. Proutists there, in consensus with other members of the management committees, have drawn up guidelines they consider important in building successful cooperative enterprises:

1. Fulfill a need. People have to come together in order to fulfill a genuine need in the community. No matter how good the idea, if there is not a community need, the enterprise will not succeed.

2. Establish a founding group. A few committed people have to take on the responsibility of developing the initial idea through to inception. Usually, however, one person will need to provide the leadership.

3. Commit to a vision. Commit to the ideals and values implicit in cooperative enterprises, and try to ensure that both the members and the management are honest, dedicated and competent.

4. Conduct a feasibility study. Objectively evaluate the perceived need, and determine whether the proposed enterprise can fulfill that need by conducting a feasibility study.

5. Set out clear aims and objectives. The members of each enterprise must formulate clear aims and objectives through consensus. These will help direct everything from the founding group's initial focus to promotional strategies and budgetary processes in the years to come.

6. Develop a sound business plan. The enterprise will require capital, have to manage its finances efficiently, and at some point will have to make effective decisions about loan repayments and profit allocation.

7. Ensure the support and involvement of the members. The members own the enterprise–at every step their support and involvement are essential.

8. Establish a location. Secure adequate operational premises for the enterprise, in the best possible location in the community.

9. Get skilled management. From within the community, bring into the enterprise people who have the necessary management, business, financial, legal and accounting skills.

10. Continue education and training. Ideally, the members will have the skills–particularly the communication and interpersonal skills–necessary to run the enterprise successfully. If not, they will either have to develop such skills or bring in new members who have them.

Golden Rules for a Community Economic Strategy

- Start small, with the skills and resources available within the community.
- Make use of role models, those with experience in community development, whenever possible.
- Make sure the enterprise involves as many people as possible.

Community Benefits

Cooperative enterprises benefit a community in many ways. They bring people together, encourage them to use their diverse skills and talents, and provide them with an opportunity to develop new capabilities. They strengthen the community by creating a sense of belonging, fostering close relationships amongst different types of people, and empowering people to make decisions to develop their community.

All this fosters community spirit. Working together, a community is able to accomplish much more than when individuals go their separate ways.

On an economic level, cooperatives foster regional economic self-reliance and independence from outside control, empowering local people. They create employment, circulate money within the community, and offer a wide range of goods and services. Because cooperative enterprises are owned by the members themselves, profits stay in the local area. Cooperatives thus increase the wealth and build the strength of the community.

In essence, successful cooperative enterprises transform a community by establishing economic democracy.

Cooperative enterprise is the socio-economic system of the future. With global capitalism terminally ill, developing cooperatives as independent alternatives makes a lot of sense. In Mondragón, in Maleny, and in Venezuela, that future is unfolding now.

Chapter 6

An Agrarian Revolution and Environmental Protection

The cooperative system is the best system of agricultural and industrial production... It will help a country to become self-sufficient in food production and other commercial crops, and free from shortages in the supply of food.[1]

— P.R. Sarkar

A Deepening Crisis in Agriculture

For about 10,000 years, human societies have been practicing various types of agriculture, manipulating ecosystems to gain their basic needs: food, fiber for clothing, medicine and raw materials for industry. Agriculture is considered a primary activity because it draws energy and resources from the environment. The greater the value of the agriculture, natural resources and energy produced in any region, the greater is the economic potential of the rest of that economy.

Planet Earth already has a number of wastelands which are memorials to shortsighted agricultural practices. The inhabitants of the Roman city of Timgad in Tunisia abandoned it when the soil became depleted and could grow no more food. Magzalial in northern Iraq was once a hardwood forest; on that land are the earliest traces of agriculture yet discovered–today the place is a total desert.

The Sumerian civilization on the lower Euphrates River began forming at least 9,000 years ago, but that society collapsed due to salinization of the soil. Intensive irrigation of marginal lands carries salts from underground up to the surface topsoil, where it is deposited and accumulates. The amazing truth is that the Sumerians knew all about this danger and even how to avert it.[2] Yet the greed and shortsightedness of the farmers caused them to neglect doing what was needed. The same thing is happening in the Indus Valley of Pakistan, and in Australia where 2.5 million hectares of land have become salinized since the introduction of European farming methods.[3] Then, as now, if farmers can make a good profit for ten or twenty years by growing a crop in a certain way, many will do so, not caring that their actions are gradually depleting the soil and will affect coming generations.

During the last century, non-sustainable agricultural techniques have been introduced on a large scale. Modern corporate farming is based on high inputs of chemical fertilizers, herbicides and pesticides. Though high yields can be produced in the short-term, this gradually deteriorates the humus and structure of the soil. The burning of fossil fuels in agriculture and the enormous quantities of methane gas produced by breeding animals for slaughter in concentrated feedlots are factors considered by scientists to be main contributors to the global warming of the planet, as well as to the poisoning of ground water.

Unfortunately, the cultivation of monocrops is an over-simplification of the ecosystems of nature. Large plantations of monocrops are, by their very nature, more vulnerable to pests and diseases than those planted with mixed crops. The continued application of chemical nitrate fertilizers poisons groundwater and pollutes adjacent ecosystems. For example, the Great Barrier Reef of Australia is gradually being damaged by nutrient and sediment runoff from sugar cane farming. In the Gulf of Mexico, marine habitat is destroyed as a consequence of the nitrate fertilizers used in the American Midwest.

Certain scientific principles, which are very effective in engineering, create serious problems when applied to agriculture. For example, in inorganic and synthetic production, the laws of measurement, stress, balance, force and counterforce all hold good. It is possible to produce valuable and reliable standardized products according to specification– from structural steel and pre-stressed concrete to bricks and plywood.

In agriculture, however, this type of reductionist, input-output approach, commoditizing and separating the components, creates serious problems over time. Much of the fertility, range and resilience of farmland depend precisely upon its biological complexity and lack of uniformity. Trying to standardize farming in monocultures endangers fertility.

Corporate agriculture also threatens biological diversity. The GATT trade agreement granted plant-breeding companies the right to patent seeds. The Pioneer Hi-Bred Corporation, for example, is now protected by patent rights when it mass-produces seed varieties. But local farmers the world over who have saved some seeds while rejecting others, thus modifying plant species for thousands of years, are not protected or compensated. Today biotechnology and genetic engineering have begun to penetrate into agricultural systems, and scientists are unsure about the long-term effects of this.

During the 1990s, the World Bank and the International Monetary Fund convinced India to adopt trade liberalization, structural adjustment, and privatization. The Indian government abolished farm subsidies and opened their markets to multinational corporations, encouraging farmers to switch from subsistence agriculture to export crops, especially cotton. Farmers bought genetically-modified seeds and pesticides from Monsanto, but then found themselves imprisoned by debt and at the mercy of global price fluctuations. More than a quarter of a million Indian farmers are estimated to have committed suicide from 1995 to 2011; in 2009 alone, 17,638 farmers committed suicide—one farmer every 30 minutes.[4]

Corporate farming is bankrupting small farmers and driving people off the land. Since 1935, the number of family farms in the United States has decreased by more than two thirds, and today less than one percent of the US population works on the land.[5] This pattern is occurring throughout the world, and as farmers lose their land and move to the city, many rural places where they lived are also becoming ghost towns.

Agricultural subsidies are direct payments to farmers by rich governments to supplement their income and to protect the country's food supply. Whereas this is a noble goal, in fact agricultural subsidies go mostly to the biggest corporate farms, encouraging overproduction and exportation of the excess.

This leads to "international dumping", in which subsidized farmers "dump" commodities on foreign markets at prices that are sometimes below the actual cost of production. Dumping encourages developing countries to buy food cheaply from wealthy countries instead of from local farmers, weakening the agricultural sector and even forcing many small growers to go bankrupt and lose their land.

In 2010, the European Union spent €57 billion (US$74 billion) on agricultural development, of which €39 billion was spent on direct subsidies.[6] Along with fisheries subsidies, this represents over 40 percent of the EU budget. The United States government currently pays farmers approximately US$20 billion per year in direct subsidies.[7]

Food Sovereignty

Via Campesina is an international peasant movement that unites the landless, rural women, peasants, farmers, small producers and indigenous people in 56 countries to defend food sovereignty, decentralized production and indigenous land rights.[8] In 1996 this alliance coined the term "food sovereignty" to refer to the right of peoples to define their own food, agriculture, livestock and fisheries systems, in direct confrontation with agribusiness control and corporate manipulation for profit.

Via Campesina's seven principles of food sovereignty are inter-related and form a good base from which to achieve economic democracy and Prout's goal that every region should produce the food its population needs:

1. Food is a Basic Human Right: Everyone must have access to safe, nutritious and culturally appropriate food in sufficient quantity and quality to sustain a healthy life with full human dignity. Each nation should declare that access to food is a constitutional right and guarantee the development of the primary sector to ensure the concrete realization of this fundamental right.

2. Agrarian Reform: A genuine agrarian reform is necessary which gives landless and farming people–especially women–ownership and control of the land they work and returns territories to indigenous peoples. The right to land must be free of discrimination on the basis of gender, religion, race, social class or ideology; the land belongs to those who work it.

3. Protecting Natural Resources: Food Sovereignty entails the sustainable care and use of natural resources, especially land, water, seeds and livestock breeds. The people who work the land must have the right to practice sustainable management of natural resources and to conserve biodiversity free of restrictive

intellectual property rights. This can only be done from a sound economic basis with security of tenure, healthy soils and reduced use of agro-chemicals.

4. Reorganizing Food Trade: Food is first and foremost a source of nutrition and only secondarily an item of trade. National agricultural policies must prioritize production for domestic consumption and food self-sufficiency. Food imports must not displace local production nor depress prices.

5. Ending the Globalization of Hunger: Food Sovereignty is undermined by multilateral institutions and by speculative capital. The growing control of multinational corporations over agricultural policies has been facilitated by the economic policies of multilateral organizations such as the WTO, World Bank and the IMF.

6. Social Peace: Everyone has the right to be free from violence. Food must not be used as a weapon. Increasing levels of poverty and marginalization in the countryside, along with the growing oppression of ethnic minorities and indigenous populations, aggravate situations of injustice and hopelessness. The ongoing displacement, forced urbanization, oppression and increasing incidence of racism against smallholder farmers cannot be tolerated.

7. Democratic Control: Smallholder farmers must have direct input into formulating agricultural policies at all levels. Everyone has the right to honest, accurate information and open and democratic decision-making. These rights form the basis of good governance, accountability and equal participation in economic, political and social life, free from all forms of discrimination. Rural women, in particular, must be granted direct and active decision-making on food and rural issues.

Prout's Agrarian Revolution

One of Prout's goals is to restore Pramá–dynamic equilibrium and dynamic equipoise (explained in Chapter 2)–in the environment. This concept is similar to what David Suzuki calls "the sacred balance."[9] Prout advocates that we utilize Nature's gifts in a balanced and renewable way, while preserving the planet's forests and other wild places and restoring degraded areas. The difference between "utilizing" and "exploiting" the environment can be compared to "using" or "abusing" something.

Sarkar called for an "agrarian revolution", regarding agriculture as the most important sector of the economy. He emphasized that every region should strive to produce the food its population needs. This simple idea of regional food supply is radically different from the corporate agriculture of today. Food in the United States travels an average of 3000 kilometers (2000 miles) before it reaches one's plate![10]

Prout asserts that farming practices should be sustainable to preserve the planet's future. These techniques include organic farming, biological farming, permaculture, holistic management, natural pest control, composting, crop rotation schemes, inter-cropping and other similar practices.

A Proutist economy will also tackle the division of land. According to land type, soil fertility and the availability of water for irrigation, a minimum size will be determined for an economic land holding according to the local technology and farming practices. Such a farm would be economically viable, that is the market price of the produce would be more than the cost of production after including the costs of all inputs. Thus the same accounting standards that are normally used in industry should also be applied to agriculture. Often everyone in farm families works, but their labor is not included in food pricing.

Proper accounting in the pricing of farm products will ensure stability in the lives of farmers and rural communities. Although at the beginning, the price of some products might rise, they will later stabilize. This will not cause hardship, because the guaranteed minimum wage will account for this.

Many small farmers in the world have insufficient land to provide a reasonable living standard or even subsistence. On the other hand, very large farms often have lower yields per acre and leave much land poorly utilized. Therefore, an economic holding should be neither too large nor too small.

Agricultural Cooperatives

Prout recognizes agricultural cooperatives as the ideal form of farm management for many reasons. Cooperatives enable farmers to pool their resources, purchase inputs, and store and transport their market produce more easily. Most importantly, they eliminate intermediaries–traders who buy produce very cheaply from the farmers and then sell it for a high price to city retailers. Instead in a Prout economy farmers' cooperatives would sell directly to consumers' cooperatives, benefiting both. Finally, agricultural cooperatives promote economic democracy, empowering farm families to decide their own future.

The cooperatives envisioned by Prout are radically different from the state-run communes of the former Soviet Union, China and other communist countries which have, for the most part, been a failure. In these communes, very low rates of production often resulted in drastic food shortages. By denying private ownership and incentives, they failed to create a sense of worker involvement. Central authorities issued plans and quotas, and the local people had no say over their work. Coercion, and sometimes violence, was used to implement the commune system.

Prout does not advocate the seizing of agricultural land or forcing farmers to join cooperatives. Traditional farmers have an intensely strong attachment to the land that has been held by their ancestors–some would rather die than lose it.

After carefully evaluating what the minimum size of economic land holdings in a particular area should be, small farmers with insufficient or deficient properties (uneconomic holdings) would be encouraged to join cooperatives, while still retaining ownership of their land. Compensation would be paid by the cooperative for both land and labor, with roughly equal shares paid for work done and for the percentage of land owned within the cooperative. There would also be a bonus system based on profits. Hence the inherent desire of people for ownership and self-determination would not be violated. There would also be a system of elected management, with remuneration paid for special skills as an incentive for further education, good management and innovation.

A major benefit of this system is the potential for the collective purchasing of farm equipment that is beyond the means of most individual farmers. Moreover, in countries where agricultural land is limited and population density is high, a good amount of land is wasted on borders and boundary fences that the cooperative could immediately utilize. By selling collectively, farmers will get higher prices for their produce.

Very large land holdings which are unproductive would be handed over to cooperatives. After the success and benefits of agricultural cooperatives have been adequately demonstrated to the public, all owners of farmland would be requested to join cooperatives on a voluntary basis.

In a Proutist society with all-round human development, ownership of land will become less and less important as a true collective spirit develops.

Ideal Farming

The maximum utilization of land is one of the main objectives of Prout. To help achieve this, Sarkar advocated three alternative crop systems: mixed cropping, supplementary cropping, and crop rotation. Mixed cropping involves planting complementary crops in the same field, for example in alternating rows. This technique can improve space utilization, reduce erosion, and conserve water. It also utilizes natural complementary plant relationships, for example where one plant uses nitrogen while another replenishes it.

In supplementary cropping, a secondary crop can be planted to utilize extra space around the main crop. For example, eggplant can be planted beneath peach trees in an orchard. In warm and temperate climates, crop rotation is the alternate planting of crops with different growing seasons so that land can be productive almost year round.

Integrated farming incorporates all types of sustainable agricultural production including apiculture (bee-keeping), horticulture (fruit and vegetable gardening), floriculture (flowers), sericulture (silk), dairy farming, animal husbandry, and pisciculture (fish). Prout advocates that seeds of different varieties should be collected and disseminated to preserve our planet's biodiversity.

Renewable energy sources can also be developed on agricultural cooperatives through the use of bio-gas (a byproduct produced in a tank of decomposing organic matter), solar power and wind power.

Water conservation is a key issue in sustainability. Underground water reserves are crucial to a region's ecological balance; hence preference should be given to using surface water over well water for irrigation and other purposes. Reforestation to increase rainfall, and the construction of many lakes and small ponds to capture rainwater, are important. Planting certain trees that retain water in their roots along rivers and around lakes and ponds will help to prevent evaporation and maintain water levels.[11]

When the spirit of Neohumanism is applied to agriculture, a shift will take place in animal husbandry. Whereas domestic animals have contributed to agriculture for thousands of years–fertilizing the soil and turning grass into milk, for example–the present cattle, sheep and poultry industries are causing great ecological destruction. Since 1950, the number of farm animals on the planet has risen 500 percent; now they outnumber humans by three to one and consume half the world's grain.[12]

Raising animals for slaughter is cruel and, from a food perspective, inefficient. The vast lands and enormous quantities of water used to raise livestock could feed many more people if planted with grains, beans and other crops for human consumption.[13] Furthermore, the cattle industry is a major cause of greenhouse gases and groundwater pollution.[14]

Awareness is growing of the ill effects on health of high meat consumption. Prout supports the current trend towards lower meat consumption for both health and ecological reasons. This initiative should be encouraged through regular campaigns of popular education.

The Benefits of Growing Your Own Food

1. Improve your family's health. Eating fresh fruits and vegetables, with their high vitamin content, is one of the most important things you can do to stay healthy. The fewer chemicals on your food, the healthier it is. Kids who grow up eating home-grown produce usually continue their healthy diet when they become adults.

2. Save money. Learn how to feed your family well on very little. Your food bill will shrink as you begin to stock your kitchen with fresh produce from your backyard. If you learn to dry, can, or otherwise preserve your harvest, you'll be able to feed yourself even when the growing season is over.

3. Reduce your environmental impact. By growing your food organically, you reduce pesticide and herbicide pollution of the air and water. You'll also reduce your dependence on corporate agriculture with its burning of fossil fuels to grow and transport food across the planet to your supermarket. When you inspire others to follow your example, you contribute to making a better world.

4. Exercise. Planting, weeding, watering, and harvesting add meaningful physical activity to your routine. Children can join in, too, and they like to eat the food they grow. Gardening is also a way to relax, de-stress, center your mind, and get fresh air and sunshine. Being connected to nature is medicine for the soul.

5. Enjoy better-tasting food. Freshly-picked food has a much better flavor than supermarket produce which has been traveling a long time to reach your supermarket.

6. Develop a sense of accomplishment. Planting a seed, caring for it, and later harvesting its fruits are very gratifying, some of the most purposeful tasks that humans have done for 10,000 years.

7. Avoid waste. You can compost all your kitchen scraps and garden trash to make wonderful fertilizer and reduce the garbage going to the landfill.

8. Enjoy shade. Planting fruit and nut trees around your house and garden will eventually provide lovely shade as well as annual harvests for your family. Planting trees is investing in the future of our planet.

9. Appreciate variety. You will soon be growing more different types and flavors of vegetables. Instead of running to the store because you forgot to buy a vegetable, you can just stroll out to the garden and help yourself to whatever you like.

10. Grow community. When you start growing your own food, you can share the extra with your family and friends. There's nothing in the world better than something produced by your own sweat. Often people are so grateful to receive "real", tasty and wholesome fresh food, they reciprocate by offering you return favors, so the hard work gets shared around and friendships strengthen. Perhaps you can inspire others to join you in making a community garden.

Rural Development: Agro- and Agrico-Industries

Rural poverty is a very serious problem facing most countries of the world. Free-market capitalism has shown little interest in the development of rural economies. If one drives just one or two hours away from a large city in a wealthy country, one often finds areas of poverty. Industrialization has usually taken place in urban centers where there is good infrastructure, transportation, and access to cheap labor. This tends to drain rural areas of their population and creates ever-expanding mega-cities, especially in the economically undeveloped countries of the Global South.

The primary sources of income in impoverished rural economies are farming and the extraction of raw materials such as timber and minerals.

Prout proposes that industries be set up in rural areas to produce what agricultural workers need, and to process the crops that are harvested. These rural industries are an important part of economic democracy, in creating jobs and raising the living standard of the rural people.

The term agrico-industry refers to pre-harvest industries that produce what farmers require, such as hand tools, animal and tractor-drawn implements, seeds, fertilizers, greenhouses and pest-control products. Agro-industry is post-harvest, processing raw agricultural products. These industries include flour, oil, textile and paper mills, fruit and vegetable preservation and processing, dairy plants, and medicinal herb laboratories.

Combined with agricultural cooperatives, improved education, advanced communication, and the introduction of cottage industries, such industries will diversify and revitalize depressed rural economies. This is in line with Prout's goal to create counter-magnets to attract urban populations away from the overcrowded cities into smaller, more sustainable and humane settings.

A Balanced Economy

Economic over-development and economic under-development both create economic and political imbalances. This disruption blocks the progress of the people and often has catastrophic effects on the environment.

In many parts of the developing world, including India, Africa and China, the proportion of people working in agriculture is very high. When more than 40 percent of the population depends directly on agriculture for their livelihood, subsistence farming exerts excess pressure on the land. Overly industrialized countries, on the other hand, usually try to bring agricultural countries under their influence, using them as sources of cheap agricultural products and as markets for their consumer goods.

Prout advocates that to reduce trade friction and to establish balance, each region needs to have a steady and reliable source of nutritious food, as well as a developed industrial sector. To achieve this, the working population of a region should ideally be divided in the following way: 20 to 40 percent of the population should be employed in agriculture (including the preservation and extraction of natural resources); 10 to 20 percent in agro-industries; 10 to 20 percent in agrico-industries; 10

percent in general trade and commerce; 10 percent in the service sector, administration, management and public service; and 20 to 30 percent in non-agricultural manufacturing.

These percentages are strikingly different to present levels in most countries. In the United States, less than 1 percent of the population works in agriculture, 26 percent in industry of all types and 72 percent in services and trade. In Brazil, 26 percent works in agriculture, 23 percent in industry, 13 percent in commerce, and 36 percent in service.[15]

Sarkar warns that if the number of people engaged in agriculture falls below 20 percent, that important sector of the economy will be neglected. This is taking place today in Japan, where only four percent of the population works in agriculture, and national self-sufficiency in food is estimated at less than 30 percent and declining.

Apart from the threat to the security of a region's food supply, human beings need to maintain a link with Nature. When so many people are removed from the land and the experience of living and working in Nature, a collective disruption and alienation takes place. Indigenous peoples as well as eco-psychologists suggest that many of industrialized society's ills are caused by this alienation from Mother Earth. Sarkar warned, "The harmful internal consequences of over-industrialization not only affect the personal, social and national health of the people, they also precipitate gradual individual and collective psychic degeneration."[16]

In the developed countries of the world, there is an ever-growing demand for organic food which local farmers are unable to meet. Surprisingly, in many undeveloped tropical countries, even in rural areas people often complain that fruits and vegetables are too expensive for them, because fresh produce is not grown locally. Agricultural cooperatives in both developed and undeveloped countries can help to solve these problems by offering training, support and efficient working conditions and benefits to the unemployed.

There is historical precedence for such a shift. In Japan, at the end of the Second World War, the government mobilized a great effort towards agricultural development. The country successfully absorbed the labor of thousands of unemployed soldiers and migrants returning from overseas.

Most small-scale farming is backbreaking work, which nearly everyone finds unattractive. This is another reason why young people have abandoned rural areas. To attract people back to rural life, the same zeal that has been applied to making industrial manufacturing more efficient needs to be applied to agriculture. Combined with the revitalization of rural industries, reduction in working hours, and vital research and development, agricultural cooperatives can utilize all the technical, managerial and intellectual skills presently focused on industry to make rural life more interesting and attractive.

Benefits of a Shift Towards a Balanced Economy[17]

There are a number of benefits a country would gain by launching an agrarian revolution based on Prout:

- Reducing trade friction by becoming less dependent on both exports and imports.
- Creating new and more secure employment based on local demand.
- Safeguarding national security by increasing food self-sufficiency.
- Freeing the country from pressures of international financial institutions, and enabling local people to make decisions on the basis of local needs.
- Decreasing vulnerability to international economic fluctuations and other unforeseen events through greater reliance on domestic consumption.
- Decreasing overcrowding in major cities by attracting urban dwellers to move to the countryside for employment in agricultural cooperatives and agro- and agrico-industries.
- Stimulating economic and cultural revival in rural areas, permitting a lifestyle that is more connected to nature for the whole population.
- Rural migration will encourage the building and renovation of more and bigger homes. This in turn will stimulate the construction, furniture and home appliance industries.
- Improving the environment by a shift towards organic agriculture, a shift away from factory farming, and a reduction of industrial and urban pollution.

Prout Master Units

Sarkar gave great importance to the need to establish "model rural multi-purpose development centers," examples of Prout that he called Master Units. He directed them to extend all possible services, particularly in the fields of education, culture, economics and spiritual upliftment, saying they should be the "nerve centers of the society." He prescribed only three hectares (five acres) as the minimum size for a Master Unit, however he envisioned they would gradually expand and involve an ever greater part of the population. They should be economically self-sufficient in all respects.[18]

Sarkar listed the primary requisites of an ideal Master Unit to "correspond to the five minimum necessities of Prout":

1. To organically grow food and raw materials for agro-industries.
2. To produce fibers and fabrics for clothing.
3. To open primary and secondary schools.
4. To open medical units that emphasize alternative treatments.
5. To construct houses for extremely poor people.[19]

Sarkar prescribed intensive farming with great diversity with all the varieties of ideal integrated farming (that were listed in the earlier section). He also recommended that Master Units should have, if possible, renewable energy, a seed bank, nursery, an agricultural training center, a wildlife sanctuary, and agro-industries to buy and process the produce of the neighbor farmers, such as a mill, bakery or dairy farm.

An ideal Master Unit is a community, an ecovillage, so the more people who come to live or participate in some way, the healthier the project will be. The more genuine service that the Master Unit provides, the more good will it will create. There are three categories of Master Unit service projects:

1. Service to neighbors: These might include treating illnesses with homeopathic medicines, opening a school, organizing cooperatives, providing employment, sharing farm equipment, organizing community activities and festivals and teaching yoga and meditation.
2. Residential service programs: The clients of residential programs stay at the Master Unit for several months or longer. In the Anandanagar Master Unit in India, for example, there is a degree college and an engineering institute with hostels for students who come from far away. Other residential programs could include: homes for pregnant women, the physically or mentally impaired, those who are undergoing alcohol or drug rehabilitation and newly-released prisoners.

3. Special health and educational services for visitors: The clients of these programs come from some distance to attend special courses and stay for a weekend or longer. Examples could include courses in biopsychology, wellness, naturopathy, ayurveda, yoga and meditation, fasting and vegetarian cooking. Another excellent service is to host day visits by school groups, allowing students to see and experience the farm.

Community Supported Agriculture (CSA)

There is a growing initiative in Japan, Europe and North America called *Community Supported Agriculture* or CSA farms in the US, while in Japan they call it "Farming with a face on it." Consumers join with farmers to produce locally-grown, pesticide-free seasonal foods. Each spring, consumers pay a share to help meet the farmer's operating expenses, thus helping him or her avoid taking high interest bank loans. In return for their investment, they receive a weekly supply of fresh produce throughout the growing season. CSA farms support local sustainable farming, and also encourage consumers from the city to visit and help during harvest time. Thousands of these types of farms exist today, a wonderful example of the mutual economic benefit of producer cooperatives selling to consumer cooperatives, and at the same time encouraging city dwellers to spend more time on farms.[20]

CSA has become a popular way for consumers to buy local, seasonal food directly from the farmer. It can also be seen as combining a producer cooperative and a consumer cooperative into one. The idea behind CSA is that farmland becomes the community's farm. Growers and consumers mutually support each other and share the risks and the benefits of food production. This arrangement extends "vegetable box schemes", where consumers can register with a farm for a weekly delivered assortment of seasonal vegetables or other farm products.

CSA is not a rigid system, so local variations exist. A CSA organization would normally entail that there is a transparent budget for the CSA farm for the coming year. Consumers pay upfront for the coming productivity period and in return receive seasonal produce. Thus they participate in a holistic cycle of a year's worth of agricultural production.

CSA schemes can potentially catapult food production into thoroughly sustainable practices. Although not compulsory, CSA organizations mostly adopt organic agriculture. They foster local supply of healthy food and tend to preserve soil fertility and biodiversity. By avoiding intermediaries, producers receive a higher income, while consumers pay less. Farmers get paid upfront, ensuring a guaranteed outlet and a fair return; consumers share the risk and as a consequence get connected to the cycles and uncertainties of nature. Also, the money paid for food remains in the local community, in contrast to money spent in supermarkets which generally is drained towards headquarters and global markets.

Furthermore, a core feature of CSA is that it also serves a social purpose in bringing consumers closer in contact with producers. Often, CSA farms organize events and fairs; some farms offer to consumers possibilities for educational and recreational engagement by inviting kids and people of all ages to tours, working holidays or courses on the farm, strengthening bonds of the members. Some farms even offer consumers to pay in labor instead of cash. North America now has more than 13,000 CSA farms. CSA farms can contribute to economic democracy by uniting urban and rural spaces, culture and people and create an ecosystem of mutual support, understanding and interdependence.

Food, Farms and Jobs

Illinois in the American Midwest is an agricultural state that produces so much soybeans and corn for livestock feed, further processing and export, that it often ranks first or second highest in production in the country. Yet despite the enormous quantities of cereals and livestock grown, more than 95 percent of the US$48 billion that people of Illinois spend annually on food buys imported food and leaves the state.[21] Because most of the agriculture is very large scale, only a tiny percentage of the population is employed in the sector, and in March 2010, the official unemployment rate in the state was 11.5 percent.[22]

In 2007 the Illinois Local Food, Farms and Jobs Task Force was created to facilitate mechanisms by which the vast unmet consumer demand for locally grown food could be met by Illinois farmers growing food on the state's rich and productive agricultural soils. Long-time Proutist Charles Paprocki, who himself grows many tons of fresh produce in a small community garden, joined this body just as the Global Financial Crisis began to break. The seriousness of its impact on the state economy caused the group to be more receptive to some of the radical proposals of Prout that he suggested.

The motto they chose was "Growing the Illinois Economy", and their mission statement was:

> To facilitate the growth of an Illinois-based local farm and food product economy that revitalizes rural and urban communities, promotes healthy eating with access to fresh foods, creates jobs, ensures a readily available supply of safe food in an emergency event, and supports economic growth through making local farm or food products available to all Illinois citizens.[23]

In 2009 the Task Force convinced both political parties in the state legislature to pass the bill they proposed. It recommends that by 2020 all state institutions that serve food, including universities, schools, hospitals and prisons, should purchase 20 percent of their food from farmers within the state. It also created a 35-member Council appointed by the governor.

The demand for local food is growing every year. The state has the second highest number of farmers' markets in the nation, and there would be more if there were more farmers to supply them. Because of this demand for local food, the Illinois legislature is fully behind this initiative. Many other state government agencies also support it, including the largest one, the Department of Human Services. They are very concerned, because they realize that the type of food they have been supplying to welfare and food stamps recipients in poor communities has contributed to the rising levels of obesity and diabetes.

Officials of the state Emergency Management Agency are also interested in local food. Most analysts nationwide estimate that there is only a 3 to 5-day supply of food in home shelves, grocery shelves and distributor shelves collectively. If any natural or human-caused disaster disrupted long distance transportation, people would go hungry very quickly. Illinois is the first state in the country to include local food in its emergency preparedness plan. Other states have not yet seen how precarious their food supply is.

Jim Braun, another member of the Illinois Food, Farms and Jobs Council that was established, explained the considerable obstacles this initiative faces:

The average age of the Illinois farmer today is nearly 60. Most Illinois farmers today are reluctant to leave their tractor cabs and do the hard physical labor required to grow table food....

Illinois rural communities are very close-knit, and anyone who grows anything other than corn and soybeans is considered a fool, a radical, an oddball, or worse. Years of delicate education are required to change rural communal norms so local food farmers are accepted. Simultaneously, new farmers must learn how to grow table food, a support system must be built that helps farmers overcome problems unique to local food production, new types of farm equipment must be developed or imported, and sources of capital must be obtained. This type of cultivation is so "foreign" to the culture that banks are hesitant to lend money to farmers who want to grow table food.

A commodity farmer friend of mine back in Iowa made the decision two years ago to convert 160 acres from growing number two yellow corn (for livestock, processing, and export) into sweet corn for local human consumption. He made verbal agreements with local grocers to purchase it. However when the crop matured, the grocers refused to buy due to a glut of inexpensive imported sweet corn. He found a market 200 miles away that would purchase his crop, but he could not afford to transport it that distance. He eventually plowed his crop under without harvesting a single ear of sweet corn!

My friend had a great idea, but he did not have the firm foundations required to achieve success. We must not allow this to occur in Illinois, because not only the farmer but all his neighbors will also be reticent to grow local food for a long time out of fear that the same economic disaster might happen to them.

The "Illinois-grown" label and certification program, also created by the 2009 bill, is now encountering great resistance. While consumers desire to know the source of their food, existing business interests that profit from the great distance import/export model do not want people to be concerned with or know the true source of their food. I encountered this same fight on the federal level while trying to enact "country of origin labeling".

The Illinois model can be studied, built upon, and modified to create what is needed elsewhere if people find value in this model. The principles that will apply within every state in the nation are:

1. Local food means economic development, job creation, rural urban revitalization, public health, and homeland security.
2. People must desire to build a local food system for it to be successful.
3. Government must be engaged in and support the process for it to grow and flourish.
4. Government and citizenry must learn to work together to accomplish the goal.
5. Problems must be responsibly analyzed and solved as they arise.
6. People must learn that vibrant lives and communities are created by people unselfishly working collectively to create healthy lives and communities.[24]

Another obstacle this initiative faces is the Farm Credit System, the largest federal agricultural lending program in the nation, which was established by Congress in 1916 to facilitate the special needs of farmers. A percentage of their lending portfolio is mandated to meet the needs of beginning farmers. Despite this mandate, the Farm Credit System and the Federal Land Bank are quite reluctant to loan to beginning local food farmers.

Sadly, the Council was sabotaged by a few state political leaders in a backroom deal. They slandered its members, took away grant money that was approved and secretly gave it to another entity.

However, so much work has been done by individuals, community organizations and the Council that this noble dream continues to grow. See: www.foodfarmsjobs.org.

Endangered Rainforests

Global capitalism places tremendous pressure on all natural resources, but perhaps its most insidious effect is the continued destruction of the world's rainforests, which endangers our very planet.

The Amazon Rainforest is the largest forest in the world, stretching from Brazil into eight other countries, covering an area almost as large as the continental United States. The incredible variety of animal and plant life in the Amazon is difficult to comprehend. Just one Amazonian river has more varieties of fish than are found in all the rivers of Europe combined. In just one reserve–the Manu National Park of Peru–there are more species of birds than can be found in the entire United States. One in ten known species in the world lives in the Amazon Rainforest.[25]

Scientists estimate that the Amazon has 20 percent of all available freshwater in the world.[26] When this evaporates, clouds form that move throughout South America and elsewhere, determining the amount of precipitation even in other continents. This is fundamental for Brazil, which relies almost exclusively on the energy generated by hydroelectric plants, which require large reservoirs filled by rain. Moreover, it is known that the climatic conditions of the entire continent, which affects food production, is heavily influenced by the Amazon. It is believed that the Amazon biomass is the most important regarding the production of oxygen, filtering air pollutants, and absorbing carbon dioxide, the main gas that causes global warming. It is estimated that Amazon Rainforest stores between 80 and 120 billion tons of carbon, equivalent to a decade of greenhouse gas emissions by humanity at today's standards.[27]

Scientists estimate that the Amazon Rainforest is responsible for 20 percent of the world's oxygen turnover through photosynthesis and respiration.[28] Sarkar called the Amazon "the lungs of the planet" and urged Proutists to fight to save it.

During the Brazilian military dictatorship (1964-1986), the government initiated grand schemes to develop the Amazon and attract migration. Since that period, numerous individuals and companies have moved in to acquire land and money, many of them driven by intense materialism and corruption.

Most of the soils in the Amazon are of medium to low fertility. In the name of so-called "land reform", the government allots properties to small farmers there. After clearing and burning the forest cover, these farmers plant coffee or other crops. Within just a few years the thin, fragile soils are completely depleted, forcing the farmers to move on to find new land to clear. Cattle farmers then purchase and combine the abandoned lands to create vast pasturelands. According to statistics from the Ministry of Agriculture, in 2005 there were a total of 74.5 million head of cattle in the nine Amazonian states, half the total number in Brazil, and about 23 million people.[29]

Timber is the most coveted raw material in the Amazon. The constant stream of heavy trucks bearing out huge logs is a very common sight in the region. Satellite photos show that 20 percent of the area–700,000 square kilometers, greater than the size of France–has been deforested, most of that substituted for pastureland.[30] Timber companies cut in legally permitted areas, which are nearly exhausted, and illegally in protected reserves. The indigenous populations and the extractive communities who tap the rubber trees and gather nuts and fruits are endangered. To support these communities and stop the deforestation of the Amazon Rainforest is the greatest contribution that Brazil can give to the stability of the planet.

Forest Preservation Strategies

There are various types of protected forest areas in Brazil today. Permanent preservation areas are those that should never be deforested because of their fragile ecosystems or social importance. These include biological research reserves, and federal and state parks that promote eco-tourism. The rainforest is very rich in springs, brooks, streams, rivers and islands, and the Brazilian Forestry Code protects 30 to 100 meters of forest on every side of these watershed areas, which are fragile ecosystems that have great importance.

Indigenous tribal reservations are also protected. Unfortunately, in Brazil–contrary to international law–indigenous people are considered minors, and their communities have no right to own the land they live on. Each reservation is owned by the government, and can be diminished or revoked at any time.

Another type of protected area is the extraction reserves, where people are allowed to live and harvest rubber sap, nuts, fruits, medicinal plants, etc., and to hunt and fish, without cutting down the trees. Vested interests often try to drive the people out of the extraction reserves, and in 1988 ecologist Chico Mendes was assassinated defending them. By fostering cooperation with the forest people, the government has found that they become skillful protectors of the land. Unfortunately, due to the low prices their products fetch, many forest communities are suffering; those that have organized cooperatives to market their products are faring better.

Some local governments are helping, as in the state of Acre, where factories were established to process latex, chestnut, and other forest products. These actions represent a hope in the search for "sustainability". However, there is also a well-known paradox in the concept of "sustainable development". Amazon's recent history has shown that the "development" follows an opposite direction to what is sought in the "sustainability", making it a very fragile concept that approaches utopia.

Unscrupulous capitalists create enormous stress on all these types of forest reserves. Illegal loggers and miners constantly encroach on the borders.

Other exploiters weave elaborate legal strategies to clear the land. Corrupt government officials and dishonest forestry specialists write elaborate project proposals which appear to be legally correct, but which actually authorize timber companies to log protected areas. Some state politicians themselves own vast tracts of cattle pasture, and are so powerful that they can violate environmental laws with impunity. All this is done in the spirit of "development."

Fully aware that the forest resources deserve the highest guaranteed market price, some forest extraction communities and indigenous tribes, with the support of national and international organizations, have begun to invest in an alternative called Sustainable Forestry Management. In this approach, forest engineering techniques are applied to harvest selected timber without degrading the forest. This strategy prioritizes the maximum utilization of forestry resources in a sustainable way with minimum harmful impact. It also decreases illegal logging.

Brazilian law demands that every landowner in the Amazon maintain up to 80 percent of their property as forest. Forestry consultants are advising small farmers to combine their forest areas and apply Sustainable Forestry Management. The income that they gain is then invested in cooperatively-owned machines, implements and agro-industries.

Edemilson Santos, a Proutist and forest conservation engineer, has been working in the Amazon Rainforest since 1999. He says: "The main challenge to protecting the Amazon is the need to awaken humanity's consciousness about the importance of forest conservation for the future of Planet Earth. And this awakening is happening, from small actions being done by the forest inhabitants, and by those who are engaged in changing the world."[31]

Tribal Knowledge of Medicinal Plants

About 60,000 plant species grow in the Amazon. The indigenous peoples of the forest, through trial and error over millennia, have developed a vast knowledge base of the thousands of plants which have medicinal qualities. Yet forest habitats are being destroyed, and tribal cultures are fast disappearing.

It has been well documented that some American evangelist missionaries contribute to tribal extinction. Predicting the imminent second coming of Christ and the destruction of the planet, they try to baptize and save souls before that fateful day arrives–they have no interest in helping the community in its transition to the modern world. During the last four decades, dozens of remote tribes in Central and South America have disappeared due to the New Tribes Mission and the Summer Institute of Linguistics. These groups first offer the Indians material possessions, and then teach that the tribal ways are sinful. They intentionally divide the community in order to weaken the influence of the elders. As a result, the people suffer depression, malnutrition, sickness and thoughts of suicide.[32]

Because of these missionaries and the allure of Western materialism, young people in most tribes are no longer interested in learning forest knowledge. It has been said that whenever a shaman dies with no one trained to replace him or her, an entire encyclopedia of knowledge is lost forever to humanity.

Pharmaceutical corporations earn hundreds of millions of dollars from the many wonder medicines derived from forest plants–yet they pay nothing back to the indigenous peoples who first showed them these plants.

Slowly this bio-piracy is beginning to change. Ethnobotanist Mark J. Plotkin spent years living with various Amazon tribes, including the Tiriós in southern Suriname, learning about their medicinal plants. He then helped start the Amazon Conservation Team (ACT),[33] a nonprofit organization that works in partnership with indigenous people of tropical America in conserving the biodiversity of the Amazon Rainforest as well as the culture and land of its indigenous people. Plotkin also translated his findings into the Tirió language and published the *Tirió Plant Medicine Handbook*–prior to this, the people had only one book written in their own language: the Bible.[34] ACT works with tribal groups in the Colombian Eastern Andes and the interior of Suriname in an attempt to preserve, strengthen and perpetuate their ethnobotanical knowledge and to inspire young people of each tribe to study under the elder shamans.

This type of collaboration and sharing the material benefits of their knowledge between Western and indigenous cultures has demonstrated to the people of these tribes the great value and potential global importance of their culture.

These initiatives share Prout's ecological vision: to preserve the rainforests, to reforest degraded areas, to respect every culture and language, to share knowledge with forest people, and to set up cooperatives to benefit their communities. However, until global capitalism ends, the destruction continues.

The Future Vision Ecological Park

The exodus of people from the countryside to urban centers seeking jobs and educational opportunities is creating a profound imbalance in both economically developed and developing countries. Brazil is an extreme case: in 1960, 55 percent of the population lived in rural areas, but by 2005, only 15 percent remained.[35] Bankruptcy, alcoholism and suicide plague the poor rural population, while those who moved to the city slums face high unemployment, drug abuse, crime and violence.

In 1992, Dr. Susan Andrews moved to a small property near the village of Porangaba, in the state of Sao Paulo, Brazil. A world-renowned speaker and author of more than 12 books on education, psychology, health, yoga, meditation, nutrition and ecology that have been translated into many languages, her goal was to create an ecological village that would show how this situation could be reversed. A former Fulbright scholar from Harvard University, Andrews met P. R. Sarkar in 1969 and was inspired to dedicate her life to developing and sharing his ideas with the world. She founded the Future Vision Ecological Park as a model of integrated rural development based on Sarkar's vision. With the help of many supporters, financial grants and the tireless work of dozens of volunteers from all over the world, the dream has become reality.

A two-hour drive from the city of Sao Paulo, the center's 100 hectares of land now provide the basic needs of the community's members with little outside input and without creating waste, "closing the cycles" of natural systems. The entire project is based on the concept of "bio-economy", applying the operating principles of natural biological systems to both society and the economy. The goal is to provide the basic necessities of life (food, clothing, education, health care, housing and energy) through self-organizing and self-sufficient cooperatives, generating minimal entropy and seeking the maximum utilization of human and natural resources.

At Future Vision, solar panels provide electricity and solar water heaters provide warm water. Wind and solar-powered pumps draw water for both irrigation and household use, while ponds catch rainwater to restore the natural hydrological cycles. Waterside trees and plants around the ponds prevent erosion and reduce evaporation. "Managed wetlands"–biological water treatment systems of aquatic plants–catch nutrients in waste water and return them to the soil. This system even purifies the sewage from the toilets for reuse in irrigation, so that not a single drop of water is lost. Organic waste is composted to produce fertilizer for the gardens.

Extensive organic agriculture provides most of the community's food needs, including rice, beans, corn, vegetables, fruits, spices and teas. Produce is also sold in nearby markets, generating income for the rural population. Medicinal herbs from the garden, planted in the form of mandalas, sacred geometry, are processed in a laboratory to produce natural medicines, shampoos, soaps, and cosmetics, creating more jobs and contributing to medical self-sufficiency for the community. An ayurvedic center provides alternative health care including naturopathy, herbal medicines and yogic treatments.

Delicious whole grain breads, pies and cakes are baked on-site for the community and for sale.

The Ecological Park reaches out to its neighbors in other ways. A pre-school offers children a culturally and artistically rich learning environment based on Neohumanist Education, designed to develop self-esteem, dignity, ethical values, creativity and an attitude of love toward all beings.

The most popular programs at the Ecological Park are the courses in biopsychology led by Dr. Andrews. Over 100 participants arrive every weekend, a total of 9,000 each year, to discover how the ancient knowledge of Tantra Yoga combines with the latest research in Mind-Body Medicine to promote the integrated physical, mental and spiritual development of the human being. Introductory, intermediate and advanced courses include visualization, deep breathing, group dynamics, yoga postures, art therapy, psychodrama, meditation and nutrition. Biopsychology teaches the conscious control of negative emotions that harm our health and life. Practical techniques harmonize the endocrine glands and their hormones, which correspond to the subtle psychic chakra centers.

Extensive guest rooms, dormitories, theaters, cafeterias, and meeting rooms comfortably accommodate the guests, immersing them in nature, art, health and peace. Situated 700 meters above sea level with sweeping views of the surrounding fields, visitors are encircled by beautiful gardens and the gentle sound of flowing water and chirping birds. Everything in the ecovillage was carefully designed to be in harmony with nature: creative architecture in the form of sacred geometry, beautiful murals on the walls, flower gardens, the meditation room, lakes, forest trails, art and music centers–and especially the delicious cuisine, prepared with love.

In fact, consciousness and love are the fundamental principles guiding all aspects of the center, including the focus on art. Plays, rituals and art workshops for children and young people in the neighborhood are based on Sarkar's theme: "Art for service and blessedness."

The Ecological Park is also a catalyst center for activists, designed to inspire personal transformation and cultivate the energy to put into practice a new paradigm of ethics, environmental awareness and cooperation. By depending more on local products to meet local needs, the center reduces the importance of money, reconstructing the social fabric of communities where deep and lasting relationships are defined by love, generosity and fellowship.

Gross National Happiness (GNH) is an indicator originally developed in Bhutan to measure the progress of a community or nation; it is based on the premise that the calculation of "wealth" should consider other aspects besides economic development. GNH is the focus of international conferences and programs organized by the Ecological Park and a goal of the community there, seeking to integrate material development with psychological, cultural, and spiritual aspects–all in harmony with the Earth. The four pillars of GNH are:

1. the promotion of equitable and sustainable socio-economic development
2. the preservation and promotion of cultural values
3. the conservation of the natural environment, and
4. the establishment of good governance.[36]

At Future Vision Ecological Park, plans are made cooperatively, decisions taken collectively and financial resources maximally utilized, with a fair and equitable distribution of income for everyone. It is a holistic model for rural development that can be replicated not only throughout Brazil, but throughout the world.[37]

Block-Level Planning Exercise

The imaginary "Republic of Inflatonia" is a capitalist country with high inflation and stagnant growth. Gross National Product per capita is US$750. Half of the country's exports are agricultural commodities. Most industry is owned by foreign companies, using cheap labor to assemble electronic goods for export. The government is heavily indebted and forced by the International Monetary Fund to liberalize trade and open up their markets. Most local industries have been destroyed by cheap imports, and cheap imported food grown in the United States with government subsidies hurts the local farmers. This exercise will focus on the imaginary block of "Keyyan":

The population is 120,000 people, with a growth rate of 1.8 percent per year.

The infant mortality rate is 57 per 1,000 live births (45 is the national average). One-third of all children are malnourished.

The literacy rate of the adult population is 85 percent. There are no available education statistics, but interviews indicate that not all children are in primary school, and the quality of secondary and higher education is generally poor.

Employment: Nearly 75 percent of the population works in agriculture, of which 5 to 10 percent are fishermen. Official unemployment is only 5.3 percent, but the percentage of those with insufficient income or no regular salary is much higher. Families spend an average of 50 to 60 percent of their income on food, 25 percent on rent and utilities, and the last 15 to 25 percent on health, clothes, education, transport, recreation, and all other expenses. (In Great Britain, an average family spends 12 percent on food, 17 percent on rent and utilities, 71 percent for other purposes.) Eighty percent live below the poverty line. There are few employment opportunities for high school and college graduates, so most leave the area to find jobs in the big cities.

Agriculture: Seventy-two percent of arable land is under cultivation. There are 5,322 farms in Keyyan, of which 83 percent are rice farms. Most farms are between one to three hectares, but only one-third are fully owned by the farmer working it. Other farmers are sharecroppers or they lease the land. Most farmers raise poultry for their own consumption. Corn and coconuts are also grown, and some cattle. There is no forestry or mining.

Geography: Keyyan has 250 square kilometers, with a population density of 480 persons per kilometer. With a tropical climate, it has good fertile clay soil that can grow almost anything. It is situated on the coast, with most of the area flat or with low slopes. Nearby mountains feed three rivers that dry up in the dry season. Usually two rice crops can be grown each year. There is no major industry, only home-made foods, auto mechanics, furniture making, etc. There is no tourism. The major imports are food, manufactured goods and petrol. Keyyan has good deposits of limestone (for making cement). There are no other known mineral deposits.

Housing, water and electricity: The majority of these rural people live in their own houses built from locally available materials. Most get their drinking water from wells, streams or springs. Fifty percent of houses have electricity.

Problems: Since the "Green Revolution" introduced new hybrid seeds that need massive amounts of fertilizers and pesticides, planting a hectare of rice is expensive. Most farmers are heavily indebted and need to borrow from money lenders at planting time at 10 percent interest per month. At harvest time, the price of rice drops 30 percent, but farmers are usually forced to sell all their rice to pay off their loans. All the members of farming families work without pay to save costs. Two successful crops a year on two-and-a-half hectares will earn an annual income of US$1,667, or US$139 per month. Yet many families don't own their land, or own less than two-and-a-half hectares, and hence cannot support their families. Without transport and access to bigger markets, farmers are unable to sell perishable fruits and vegetables. Fishing yields have dropped by 40 percent over the last ten years due to outside factory ships trawling too close to shore, and illegal dynamite fishing which damages the coral reefs where the fish spawn.

Transport and communication are also problems, because roads, shipping, telephones, and basic infrastructure are inadequate. The municipal government spends 80 percent of its revenue to pay salaries for teachers, clerks, and other employees, so there is very little money for development.

Objective: Formulate a realistic, detailed plan how to increase the purchasing capacity and quality of life of the people of Keyyan. After noting down all your ideas, see the solutions in Appendix D.

Chapter 7

A New Perspective on Class, Class Struggle and Revolution

Ever since the beginning of this world the power to rule has been in the hands of one class or another. Long, long ago... mere brute force determined the capacity of a group to rule... Even after the advent of early civilization, rajas, kings and maharajas depended on and ruled with the help of their physical strength... With the passage of time, as the mental faculties developed, physical force was replaced by mental capacity (the capacity of planning and forethought, etc.) as the essential requirement of ruling over others. With further economic development, money became important. Those in possession of money controlled the knowledge of the learned and the courage and strength of the brave. Hence the authority to rule passed on to the moneyed class–the capitalists.[1]

— P.R. Sarkar

Classes Based on Social Psychology

Social classes are forms of 'social stratification'. Sociologists usually denote three main classifications: the upper class or elite, the middle class, and lower class. The main determinants of class are a person's hereditary family, wealth, income, influence, power, educational attainment and occupational prestige. In Latin America, for example, race and ethnicity have been and still are prime determinants of class, with white-skinned colonial elites claiming privilege, and the various mixed-race, indigenous and African descendants having much less privilege.

In Marxist theory, only two classes exist: the bourgeoisie, who own the means of production, and the proletariat, who only have their own labor power which they sell for a wage or salary.

P. R. Sarkar presents a radically different perspective on social classes. Basing his model on how humans relate to their natural and social environments, he identifies four basic types. In Sanskrit, these groups are known as *varnas*, or "mental colors." The concept of varnas is a valuable model for analysis of class dynamics. Like archetypes, these classifications are useful in identifying the powerful forces which influence societies, more so than for understanding individual psychology, where other complex factors apply.[2]

This concept of varnas generates a model of social dynamics and historical analysis unique to Prout. The theory holds that at any given time a society is dominated by the psychology and administration of a particular varna. It further proposes that social change occurs in cycles. Together these ideas are referred to as the Theory of the Social Cycle, which describes the changes that take place in society as dominant values and power bases shift from one varna to the next in a cyclic manner.

The four varnas are: *shudras*, workers; *ksattriyas*, warriors; *vipras*, intellectuals; and *vaeshyas*, merchants.

Prout's theory of class is quite different than the caste system of India, which uses the same terms, but locks people into a rigid system of stratification and discrimination by birth. Sarkar vehemently opposed the caste system. Instead he viewed varna as a psychological tendency which manifests in a particular style of survival and development in a given environment.

On an individual level, every person possesses a mixture of and potential for all the four varnas, although usually one psychology tends to be dominant. Through education, training and social environment, a person can develop any of these tendencies, or even all four simultaneously. Each varna has both positive and negative qualities.

Shudra (Worker)

The first class displays the characteristics of a human mind that is simpler than that of the other classes, guided by basic instincts and by the material and social environment. These people often work hard to

154 AFTER CAPITALISM

survive and to obtain mundane pleasures, for example to relax with a beer in front of a TV. The shudra mind seeks safety, security and reasonable creature comforts, and lacks higher aspirations and dynamism. They are followers, not leaders. Of course, the shudras of today are much more developed than those of the past. Shudras live according to the trends of the dominant collective psychology. This class essentially reflects mass psychology.

In general, common people who have not been politicized and who have not entered a struggle for social justice, exhibit these characteristics. However the mentality of working and unemployed people changes when their consciousness is raised, when they begin to fight for their rights and the rights of others. As their minds expand and they acquire new skills and perspectives, their varna begins to shift.

Ksattriya (Warrior)

The second varna is composed of those with a warrior mentality, who bravely confront the environment with physical strength and fighting spirit. Such people who embrace challenge and struggle gravitate towards athletics and martial arts, the military, police, firefighting, seafaring and rescue work. They strive for self-mastery through will, patience and hard work. They are willing to take calculated risks to achieve a noble goal, and are ready to die to keep a promise or oath. Usually stoic, they give great importance to loyalty, honor, integrity, courtesy, discipline, and self-sacrifice for others, to protect the weak.

However on the negative side, they may also choose violent aggression, blind obedience, machismo, cruelty, and ruthless competition. They can be trained to kill, to torture, to commit war crimes and crimes against humanity. The Nazi and Japanese empires that committed crimes against humanity were ksattriya societies gone amok.

Vipra (Intellectual)

Those with a developed intellect, who seek to influence society by virtue of their mental faculties, constitute this third class. Their positive qualities include critical thinking, intellectual curiosity and skepticism. They can think independently, impart knowledge and communicate ideas, concepts, arguments and explanations. Vipras push scientific, religious and cultural boundaries, questioning assumptions and doing original, creative research. They can use their gifted minds to inspire and empower others, ideally developing humility, intuition and wisdom.

But vipras can also allow their dark side to develop. Theoretical, impractical and irrelevant intellectuals can waste their time on projects that benefit no one. They can be arrogant, cynical and argumentative. They can criticize, insult and condemn opponents. Hiding their ugly nature through hypocrisy and clever lies, they may impose dogmas, fear and inferiority complex in simple-minded people. Creating divisive rules and policies for their own selfish desires, they can manipulate, dominate and verbally torture others.

Vaeshya (Merchants)

The fourth varna or social class is that of the vaeshyas, a mercantile or entrepreneurial class which excels in the administration and accumulation of resources. An entrepreneur is a risk taker and opportunity seeker who always looks for new ideas and money-making opportunities and then makes a plan to get them to market. Results-oriented, these people are efficient and effective, strategically organizing and managing large numbers of people to accomplish the task. Imaginative, ambitious and innovative, they are persistent and refuse to accept the idea that something is impossible. Creating wealth, they have the capacity to enrich communities and benefit thousands of individuals with creative products, services and employment.

Unfortunately, people with a capitalist mentality can also be ruthless exploiters. Greedy to own everything, they can mercilessly bankrupt competitors. The craving for more wealth can propel them to degeneration, exploiting the markets of pornography, prostitution, drugs and organized crime.

History and the Social Cycle

The social cycle progresses in a natural sequence of historical eras from shudra (laborer) society to ksattriya (warrior), followed by vipra (intellectual) and then vaeshya (merchant). Subsequently, a new cycle begins. This cyclical view of history does not imply that society moves in circles, retracing its steps. Rather, the social cycle is like a spiral gradually progressing toward greater human consciousness.

The beginning of each era is characterized by great dynamism on all levels: political, cultural, and economic. This occurs as new leaders arise and free people from the oppressive institutions of the old order. This optimistic trend eventually peaks as the new class solidifies its control over society. Eventually social decline occurs as the dominant class strives to extend its power at the expense of the basic needs of the people. Social unrest builds.

From the time of the first human beings, who lived together in clans or tribes for mutual protection, shudras struggled to survive amidst the inimical forces of nature. Through clashes with the hostile environment and inter-group conflicts over food and other resources, the human mind slowly grew in complexity and strength. In this way, some humans developed confidence, bravery, and the capacity to rule and dominate over others as well as their environment. Thus the ksattriya psychology appeared.

These Stone Age warriors gradually won acceptance as symbols of the unity of the tribe in the true beginning of human society in its most basic form. Unity, discipline and a sense of social responsibility slowly developed in these clans. The fight for prestige and supremacy raged between different clans during the Ksattriya Era, and people developed strong feelings of loyalty and pride regarding their clan. The early ksattriya societies were matriarchal (detailed later in this chapter).

The golden era of the ksattriyas was one of expansion and conquests, dating from the prehistoric era through the great empires of ancient history until the end of the Roman Empire, the Chin Dynasty and the Indo-Aryan expansion. Ksattriyas placed great importance on the qualities of courage, honor, discipline and responsibility, making ksattriya societies well-organized and united.

In the struggle of warrior societies against one another, human intellectual power began to develop. The ingenuity of the emergent vipras resulted in the earliest scientific achievements. As warfare became more complex, superior weapons, strategy and logistics became as important as strength and skill. Without sharp minds to devise tactics, victory in warfare became impossible. Society gradually became more sophisticated; its administration by skilled ministers also became essential. Hence vipras gradually became the most valued assets of the ksattriya leaders.

Over time the intellectual ministers acquired more actual power than the warrior kings. At the same time, organized religion assumed the role formerly held by tribal shamans. The Hindu and Buddhist societies of Asia were vipra-led, as was the Catholic Church, which gained greater power than all the royalty of Europe. At the same time Islam swept across the Middle East, Northern Africa and Asia. In Tibet, the monks and lamas assumed both political and religious power. With the coming of the Vipra Age the personal authority of the warrior kings became less important as social administration based on scriptures and laws developed. Through different social, religious and scriptural injunctions, intellectuals in the roles of minister, priest, lawmaker and advisor began to rule society and shape its development.

The vipra stage of the social cycle saw a flourishing of education and culture. Human beings attained new heights of mental development and awareness. Cultural, religious and governmental institutions grew in strength during the golden age of the vipra era. Under the auspices of these institutions, science, art, and the other branches of knowledge flourished. The early Buddhist ages of India, China, and Southeast Asia all illustrate this trend, as do the monastic centers of learning in the European Middle Ages. Some rulers, such as King Frederick the Great, became great proponents of science and learning in such periods of human development.

In time, of course, the vipra class also became oppressive, focusing on the perpetuation of its own material and social privileges. To maintain their dominance, they resorted to ever-greater hypocrisy, injecting superstitions, dogmas and psychic complexes into the minds of the other classes.

Gradually, their preoccupation with comfort and privilege caused the vipras to become subservient to those possessing the wealth, the vaeshyas, who in turn developed the capacity to buy the vipras' land and employ them in their service. In this way, the merchant class slowly grew in size and influence, infusing new dynamism into societies that had been suffering under a corrupt vipra class. The skillful and practical vaeshyas (who directed the great maritime voyages of discovery around the Earth in that age) gradually overcame the superstitions and decadence of the late vipra era. As they gained power, they created new financial, political and social systems.

When the conquistadors and colonizers first arrived in the Americas, Spain, Portugal, France and England were in transition from a vipra society–dominated by the royal family, court ministers and the Church– to a vaeshya one. They employed the warrior class with their superior weapons to invade and colonize the world in an effort to extract resources, including slaves. Most indigenous tribes of the Americas and Africa that they encountered were led by warriors (ksattriyas), though it is possible that a few were led by intellectual "shamans" (vipras). The vast fortunes that were made in the colonies and through slavery helped to establish the wealthy elites as the new power brokers.

In Latin America, Africa and elsewhere, European capitalists also encouraged priests and ministers simultaneously to try to convert the people to Christianity. Wherever they were successful, inferiority complexes were imposed and the populations became more compliant. Leonardo Boff and others have argued that there have, in effect, always been two Catholic Churches in Latin America: one of the rich and one of the poor. The Catholic Church of the rich and the military have served the financial interests of capitalists.

Democratic movements led to the creation of the House of Commons in Great Britain, the American and French revolutions, and a gradual increase in gender equality. Great advances in the arts and sciences were also stimulated under the patronage of the commercial class.

Capitalists tend to view all things, even human beings, as potential sources of profit. The merchant class built industrialized nations by exploiting the labor and resources of the rest of the world. In capitalist eras, business leaders and corporate directors are depicted as heroes. Wealth and power are considered qualities of human greatness.

Political rule is also determined by capitalists behind the scenes who buy and sell politicians and hold true power. All capitalist societies are in this condition now, as illustrated by the dependency of political leaders in most countries on "big money" to finance their election campaigns. Though constitutional democracy was a positive development in the merchant age, as practiced today it has largely become a tool of the financially powerful to control national economies.

Intellectuals and warriors are also bought by capitalists to do their bidding. Most scientific research that is funded benefits corporations. The United States military establishes bases in other countries and goes to war to protect US corporate interests.

Today, the capitalist age is declining. Hunger, poverty and unemployment generate greater misery and affect more people than ever before. Decadence and degradation of the human spirit have become extreme. The gap between the rich and poor is greatly increasing. Money is accumulated and hoarded by the rich, therefore circulating less in the economy. Most intellectuals and warriors are reduced to the economic condition of shudras. Fewer and fewer people are benefiting from capitalism. These are clear indicators of the extreme exploitation of the other classes by the capitalists.

Shudra Revolution and a New Cycle Begins

According to the Social Cycle of Prout, due to increasing exploitation and eventual market failures, the common people–under the leadership of disgruntled intellectuals and warriors–will eventually rise up in a popular revolt and take economic and social power into their own hands. This shudra revolution marks the end of the merchant era and the beginning of a new cycle. Sarkar wrote:

> A day comes when some intelligent people emerge from the exploited masses having detected the exploiters' techniques to dupe the people, even though the media is controlled. At this stage the exploiters become active intellectually to prevent the germination of the seed of liberation. They take control of the education system, the printing presses and the propaganda agencies in a last and desperate attempt to raise high embankments to contain the surging tide of public discontent. But soon after comes the day of change when the viksubdha shudras (disgruntled masses) rise up in revolt and the high sand embankments get washed away by the floods of revolution.[3]

Although technically speaking shudras should lead society in the wake of the overthrow of the vaeshya order, this shudra period is essentially a very brief time of anarchy, lasting only as long as it takes the ksattriya-dominated leadership of the revolution to solidify their power. The workers' revolutions of the communist countries, beginning with Russia in 1917, qualify: vaeshya rule ended through shudra revolution, resulting in a new, ksattriya-dominated society.

The Social Cycle moves in perpetual rotation. Based on the psychological characteristics of the different classes (varnas), we can detect distinct ages in the history of different societies. The social and administrative domination of one of the classes characterizes each age and determines the dominant values and social psychology of the society. As a rule, at any given time in the past of a certain society, only one class was dominant.

The four ages of shudra, ksattriya, vipra and vaeshya together constitute one complete spiral of the Social Cycle.

Within each spiral there is also a dialectical movement that accounts for the birth, maturity and death of an age, leading to the birth, maturity and death of the next age.

Actually, the Social Cycle does not always move smoothly forward, but rather moves with expansion, then pause, followed by contraction. There are periods of intense social movement followed by periods of relative pause.

When a new idea inspires a movement to change society, it is called an "antithesis." As it develops dynamism and strength, it creates a "manifestative motion." When it finally succeeds, it fundamentally changes the existing social structure and creates a new synthesis. This is called the state of "manifestative pause." This pause is the apex of social movement, the period of its greatest vitality. The strength of this synthesis rests upon the strength of the ideas upon which it is founded.

Eventually, however, the new order begins to deteriorate and contract because the dominant class oppresses and exploits the other classes. When society finally degenerates to a state of stagnation, with little vitality or dynamism, it is termed "systolic pause." In this stage, due to the increasing suffering of the people, new inspiration and ideas emerge–a new "antithesis" in opposition to the now stagnant order.

Thus, every age of the Social Cycle begins with a formative dynamic phase, in which new vitality is infused into the social structure. Society then attains a sustained peak subsequently followed by decline and staticity, usually accompanied by rampant exploitation. The antithesis of the stage of systolic pause then emerges from the varna that will lead the next phase of the Social Cycle.

Types of Social Movement

Within this general pattern, there are several types of movement. Normal movement includes changes and conflicts that do not substantially alter the power base of society.

Evolution refers to dynamic periods of progressive social change, following the flow of the Social Cycle. The collapse of communism in Eastern Europe and the former Soviet Union illustrate social evolution.

Counter-evolution is a force of regressive backlash, which moves the Social Cycle backwards.

Revolution is a period of dramatic change characterized by the application of tremendous force which pushes the Social Cycle forward. The communist workers' revolutions, in Russia in 1917, in China in 1947, and in Cuba in 1959, are examples of shudra revolutions that overthrew the exploitative vaeshya class and radically changed society in every sense.

Counter-revolution is when tremendous force is applied to revert the Social Cycle to the rule of a previous varna. An attempted counter-revolution was the Bay of Pigs Invasion in April 1961, when a force of 1,500 Cuban exiles, trained and armed by the CIA, attacked southern Cuba in an attempt to overthrow the Communist government and re-establish capitalist rule. They failed, and within three days all survivors surrendered.

Counter-evolutions and counter-revolutions can only be short-lived; the natural movement of the Social Cycle cannot be checked indefinitely. Counter motions are always regressive, as they revert society to a stage of the Social Cycle that had already reached the point of stagnation or degeneration.

In 1964 in Brazil, leftist grassroots movements were gaining strength and moving in the direction of a shudra revolution. This development was repressed brutally by the military–the ksattriyas–who seized control of the government and imposed martial law. According to Social Cycle theory, if this were a counter-evolution or counter-revolution, the dictatorship should have lasted only a short time before the masses won power back. In actual fact, military rule lasted 22 years in Brazil, and when it ended, capitalist-controlled democracy was re-established. In fact, in every Latin American dictatorship of that period, the ruling capitalist elite continued to finance and control the generals from behind the scenes

The Mutual Influence of Civilizations: Various nations, states and communities are in different stages of development at different times, and their mutual contact affects the movement of their Social Cycles. For instance, many ksattriya and vipra societies rapidly moved into vaeshya eras under the influence of colonialism. Today, global capitalism has forced virtually every nation, even the former communist countries, into the vaeshya era.

Bloodless Revolution and Armed Struggle

In his book *The Liberation of Intellect: Neohumanism*, Sarkar explains that reactionaries support exploitation because they personally benefit from the injustice. Reformists want change, but believe that it should be gradual, and so they support some patchwork improvements. Sarkar criticizes reformists who are afraid of radical change that might cost them their personal comforts. Their sluggishness delays revolution that would benefit everyone.

According to Sarkar, the structural death of a social system does not necessarily require armed struggle. It is possible to have a bloodless revolution in which an entirely new system rises from the fall of the old order. This could happen if there are a sufficient number of dedicated intellectuals who are not afraid of the tremendous force of a revolution. They can inspire and guide the people to use the overwhelming strength of numbers to overthrow the corrupt capitalist class and install a new society. Their participation and leadership can minimize the level of bloodshed.

It should be remembered that the use of nonviolent tactics, such as in the "people power" movements that mobilize thousands of people in the streets to protest injustice, does not mean that no violence occurs. Global capitalism causes unnecessary suffering, hunger and death, which is called structural or institutional violence, every day. It is also true that when popular movements against exploitation begin, the government often directs its police and military forces to suppress them violently.

The ruling powers determine whether or not a revolutionary movement will have to use arms or not. In the early years of the South African civil rights movement against apartheid, Nelson Mandela's contribution was as lawyer and a leader of the African National Congress. But when the violent racist regime outlawed every type of protest and imprisoned or exiled every known member of the movement, he finally accepted the role of chief of the armed wing of the liberation movement.

In the words of Brazilian activist Frei Betto, "It is curious that the ones who decide the methods of struggle we use are not us, but rather the elite that governs Brazil. We can and should struggle legally and legitimately, and we should exhaust all those forms of struggle. But what determines if, at a certain moment, these forms of struggle are no longer possible? It is the government and the elite who control this country."[4]

A New Vision Of History

While the theory of Social Cycle shows great promise in articulating the movement of human society, it still requires much research. Social phenomena and historical trends are diverse and complex in their expression. Art, politics, economics, religion, philosophy, science, technology, music, dress, and customs should all be integrated into a holistic vision and understood as expressions of the prevalent social psychology.

Disagreements may arise among Prout historians in this process, partly because there is not always harmony and consonance in these different human expressions. Usually a new social psychology appears first in the subtler fields of art, culture or science while in the fields of economics and politics an older psychology may linger on, dominating the social structure until the transformation is complete.

Hence in transitional periods it is not easy to identify whether a certain era is dominated by the former social psychology or by a new one. The expressions that characterize the psychology of a certain social class (varna) may also be quite different in the beginning of its age, during its youth, at the time of maturity, and in its old age or a period of degeneration.

Our historical records are also lopsided, eulogizing ruling kings, ministers, and political leaders, while giving little attention to the way of life as experienced by common people. The internal dynamics of the ruling class may also be only partially understood.

It is important to remember that all four classes exist in each society. For example, in the United States, if one reads *Soldier of Fortune* magazine (for military people), *Police Magazine*, *Field & Stream* (for hunters and fishers), or martial arts magazines, one would be immersed in a world of aggressive ksattriya values and adventure. In the same country there are hundreds of academic journals that influence the thinking of intellectuals; *The Wall Street Journal*, *Forbes Magazine* and others inspire capitalist investors. There are also millions of poor working class, unemployed and homeless people who are just trying to survive. All four classes live in the same country, but have little contact with one another. Which varna is greater in number? The shudras are. Yet the ones who pull the strings, who buy the politicians, who control media and advertising, who pay the military and the universities (with tax-payer money) are the capitalists. They are probably fewest in total number, yet they control the society, successfully imposing capitalist values and a consumer mentality on almost everyone.

A Tool for Understanding Social Change

Notwithstanding the complications involved in historical analysis, the the Social Cycle theory is a powerful tool in comprehending conflicting forces in current societies and understanding how best to work for their eventual resolution. For example, for more than 70 years the United States, and with the help of the NATO alliance after it formed, applied its military, economic and political power to break the Soviet Union, without success. It was the Russian intellectual dissidents and students who rose up and overthrew the Communist Party military dictatorship in only three days. The same dynamic had taken place a few months earlier in all the Eastern European nations.

The People's Republic of China is a fascinating example of how different varnas interact. Many of the ksattriya soldiers who survived the epic Long March and the Civil War became Communist Party leaders under Mao Zedong, ruling the country with an iron hand. When the student democracy movement blossomed in Tiananmen Square in Beijing in 1989, the tanks and soldiers of the People's Liberation Army were ordered to attack it.

In 2012 there were 95 billionaires in China, according to *Forbes Magazine*, each with an estimated wealth of from 1 to 10.2 billion dollars.[5] There is tremendous energy in the economy, the world's second largest, showing a six-fold increase of gross domestic product since 1978. The economy functions almost like a decentralized multinational corporation, or a "socialist syndicate". Yet the Chinese capitalists do not control the society as they do in capitalist countries.

Political scientist and China specialist Dr. Szu-chien Hsu explained this dynamic:

> The Communist Party is very centralized and controlling. Its leaders believe in Communism, historical materialism, nationalism and material power–these are the only things they trust. It is a great honor to be a member of the Party, so capitalists try to buy membership to win influence and bribe Party bosses. This type of corruption is common. But it is said, becoming rich attracts the 'red eye illness'–the jealousy of others. The Party can decide to bankrupt or execute anyone, because they control the courts, the media, everything. If injustice is done to you, who will you tell your story to? So the very rich are also very scared. They can influence people as long as the Party allows them to do it, but they can never have their own voice.[6]

Clearly the ksattriya military leaders are still firmly in charge in China. They have allowed capitalist vaeshyas to develop the economy and to gain significant wealth, but not to control the society. We can predict that one day communism will collapse in China, North Korea, Vietnam, Laos and Cuba due to a revolt by vipra students and intellectuals.

Venezuela is an example of a country that seems to have undergone a change of varna through a nonviolent electoral process. Lieutenant-Colonel Hugo Chávez, a career military officer, organized 130 officers and nearly 900 soldiers, approximately ten percent of the Venezuelan military, to attempt a coup d'état in 1992 to overthrow dictator President Carlos Andrés Pérez and end his reign of corruption, censorship and abuse of human rights.[7] Though they failed, Chávez became a popular hero.[8] After two years in prison he received amnesty and started an electoral campaign among the poor that won him the presidency at the end of 1998. As of December 2012, his coalition has won 16 out of 17 national elections due to his successful consciousness raising and politicization among the masses.[9]

The capitalist-led opposition attempted a military overthrow of Chávez in 2002 with U.S. government knowledge and support; two days later the masses and the military united and brought him back from the island naval base where he was held prisoner. After that, Chávez has become much more strident in his rhetoric about class warfare against the oligarchy, calling them "squalids." Socialist and military values have influenced the masses to a great extent in terms of participatory democracy, grassroots communal councils, frequent military parades, the new national police force and other initiatives.

The heads of the Venezuelan Central Bank and economic ministry are not bankers, but revolutionaries, orchestrating government buyouts of key industries at an accelerating rate, with more than 200 expropriations of private enterprises in 2010 alone. Chávez has announced that he is committed to "the elimination of capitalism". Government-owned and community media influence the masses with values of solidarity, people's power and socialism for the twenty-first century. Many capitalists have fled to Miami and elsewhere, and while others remain, they are frustrated and nervous because they are no longer in power.

An unprecedented revolutionary wave of protests has swept the Middle East and North Africa, beginning on December 18, 2010 with Mohamed Bouazizi's self-immolation in Tunisia to protest police corruption and ill-treatment. Within two months, Tunisia, Egypt, and Libya had undergone revolutions of historical consequence, while major protests also rocked Algeria, Bahrain, Djibouti, Iran, Iraq, Jordan, Morocco, Oman, Syria and Yemen. Called the "Arab Spring" by many journalists, the heads of state in Tunisia, Egypt, Libya and Yemen have been overthrown, and three heads of state have announced they would not stand for re-election. These are spontaneous mass democratic uprisings, using social media such as Facebook and Twitter to organize, communicate, and raise awareness in the face of state repression and Internet censorship.

The 1994 Zapatista rebellion in Chiapas, Mexico, was a ksattriya-led shudra (peasant) revolution. Though checked by the strength of the vaeshya status quo, its popularity continues to grow in strength. Revolts against vaeshya dominance usually occur first in the less developed countries due to greater exploitation and greater disparities in wealth.

The Occupy Wall Street movement began in New York City on September 17, 2011, but within a month had multiplied into an international protest movement against social and economic inequality in 951 cities in 82 countries.[10] Taking inspiration from Egypt's Tahrir Square protests and the Spanish *Indignados*, the movement has morphed into hundreds of different forms. Proutists predict that sooner or later it will reach the point of revolution.

The Sarkar Game

This is an action learning process that introduces participants to the Social Cycle and its holistic perspective of social change. It was created in 2004 by Peter Hayward and Joseph Voros of the Strategic Foresight Institute at Swinburne University of Technology in Australia. Their colleague, Sohail Inayatullah, has successfully used this technique in hundreds of workshops with professionals. In an article, "Creating the experience of social change", they wrote:

> Sarkar's theory of the Social Cycle is concerned with the ways that humans, and their social organizations, have dealt with the existential problems of how their physical and social environments relate to one another. His theory of macrohistory proposes that civilization has cycled through four major 'states'... [that are] both material power structures and epistemic or paradigmatic forms of individual and collective psychology. Further, each state has a beneficial phase (*vidya*) and a perverse phase (*avidya*); thus, even though each state is successful in managing existential problems, it also contains the seeds of its ultimate decline.

P.R. Sarkar's Social Cycle elegantly demonstrates how easily 'social roles' are adopted and how these roles bring forth partial and limited understandings of change and change processes. Both as a macrohistorical model of social change and the embodiment of the process of social construction, it is a pivotal learning element in the subject.... By 'creating' the experience of the Social Cycle in the classroom, the students learn of their own social constructions and roles. They experience the frustration of how these roles and constructions limit the effectiveness of their actions. They can also recognize the qualitative difference in the potential of actions that arise from adopting an 'integral' stance in participating in social change.[11]

University students and other groups tend to enjoy this activity very much. The facilitator divides the participants into four groups; each group is given a simple script explaining the varna that they will represent. While a good amount of laughter often accompanies the impromptu acting, the debriefing and deconstruction of the roles that follows awakens many questions and insights. The creators note:

The Sarkar game experience taps into the 'deep' scripts that we all have, scripts that cover role, power and relationship. Our societal processes have programmed those scripts into us and they continue to operate unconsciously until an experience draws them into consciousness, thereby making them accessible to inquiry and examination... The game, therefore, is a serious one. While we 'play' at learning, the consequences of not learning are serious indeed. Sarkar's social cycle at its heart is revolutionary...[12]

Below are written instructions to be handed to each group, as well as instructions for the facilitator:

SCRIPTS:

Group 1, Workers:
You are guided by basic instincts.
You are preoccupied with survival and mundane pleasures.
You want safety, security and reasonable comforts.

You want inspiration and faith to alleviate suffering and the fear of death.

TV, a cold beer, sex, watching sports are common pastimes.

You usually leave complicated political and economic decisions to leaders you trust.

When inspired, you loyally follow leaders of the other classes.

But if your needs are not met, you can disrupt, create chaos or even bring the system down.

Your group will begin the game. So prepare a simple skit lasting a couple of minutes or so demonstrating your nature until the other groups enter and interact with you. Remember there are both positive and negative aspects of your archetype. Use your imagination and speak loudly and clearly.

Group 2, Warriors:

Your physical strength and courage are your greatest assets.

You embrace challenge and struggle.

You value honor, discipline, and self-sacrifice.

Your will, patience and hard work are your strengths.

You protect society from danger and chaos, by enforcing order.

Sports and martial arts are your hobbies.

You obey and expect others to obey authority and follow orders, no matter what.

Your group will be the second group to enter the game. Decide how you will interact with the first group of workers. Remember there are both positive and negative aspects of your archetype. Use your imagination and speak loudly and clearly.

Group 3, Intellectuals:

Your developed mind is your greatest asset.

The search for truth, removing errors and confusion, is your purpose.

Some of you have knowledge of science, while others have knowledge of spiritual reality.

You protect everyone by making rules and laws and ordering the warriors to enforce them.

You debate hard so that the best ideas win.

You create enlightenment. The arts are your hobbies.

You lead others by establishing your religion, your science or your political system as the Truth.

Your group will be the third group to enter the game. Decide how you will interact with the groups of workers and warriors. Remember there are both positive and negative aspects of your archetype. Use your imagination and speak loudly and clearly.

Group 4, Entrepreneurs:

You make money easily and invest it wisely.

You excel in administration and organization.

Efficient and effective, you manage large numbers of people to produce new products and accomplish difficult tasks.

Through wealth and power, you can help everyone.

You reward loyal service with higher salaries.

Efficiency is very important.

Your group will be the last group to enter the game. Decide how you will interact with the groups of workers, warriors and intellectuals. Remember there are both positive and negative aspects of your archetype. Use your imagination and speak loudly and clearly.

FACILITATOR INSTRUCTIONS:

Split the room into four equal groups and give each group their script, and props if you can: tools to the first group, toy guns and/or kitchen knives to the second, books to the third, and credit cards and play money to the fourth.

Stand in the middle of the room and explain the game:

"Read your script and play just that role. Do not show your script to the other groups. Please remember that there are both positive and negative aspects of your archetype. Be aware of both potentials as you interact with others. Take a few minutes to discuss in your group what you want to do."

Invite the workers to begin. After a couple of minutes, invite the warriors to respond. The other two groups observe until called in.

When you feel that perverse behaviors are present or the game is going flat, stop the play (with a bell, whistle, red flag, whatever) and ask the intellectuals to enter.

The tripartite dynamic continues until the behavior becomes perverse and the entrepreneurs are invited in.

The game runs until you are satisfied that the dynamic is sufficient.

Ask the groups to take their seats but stay in their groups. Debrief each group in turn, with everyone listening. Ask one member to read their script aloud. Then ask the group to describe how they tried to act out their role, and ask the other groups for their opinions. Build a dynamic picture of each group. Highlight the healthy form of each type of organization, how each group wins power, and the inherent suffering that each group eventually creates.

Once the nature of social change is clear, you can then introduce the idea of an invisible fifth force in the room. Conscious of the strengths and weaknesses of each group, one can choose another path, that of the spiritual revolutionary (see Chapter 8).

The Exploitation of Women Throughout History

Sarkar viewed the domination of women in society as a gradual historical process. Prehistoric human societies were matriarchal (led by females). Brave and spirited women were recognized as clan mothers to preserve the identity and lineage of each tribe. Following the matrilineal system, both men and women used to bear the name of their clan mother.[13] Many ancient societies also worshiped a female goddess who represented both agricultural and reproductive fertility, in the form of the Universal Mother.[14]

Warrior societies generally prohibited the killing of women, protected the weak and, for the most part, respected the rights of both women and men. Marriage, which evolved in all cultures prior to reliable recorded history, awakened in men a sense of responsibility and duty to wife, children and family relationships. Women surrendered their independence for security so that they could care for and educate their children. Society progressed as children got more attention and education. Since patrilineal families became the norm, with the inheritance of names, property and sometimes titles through the male line, clan mothers slowly lost their authority. Male rule and privilege, and female subordination gradually became institutionalized. The ancient Greek, Roman, Hebrew, Germanic and Arabian cultures all exemplify the transition from the worship of female goddesses to male gods, from matriarchal to patriarchal societies.[15]

Later, when the vipras gained control of society, they increased their power by creating religious edicts and so-called "divine" commandments to strip women of their rights, crippling them in every sphere and turning them into wageless slaves. Many societies prohibited women from getting an education and from all positions of influence or power. During the Inquisition, which began in the twelfth century and continued into the eighteenth century, the Catholic Church tortured, tried and executed women healers and mystics, accusing them of being witches or heretics. Approximately 60,000 were burned to death in Europe.[16] Unrecorded lynchings of suspected witches have happened throughout history in different countries. Many religions taught that women were somehow spiritually inferior to men and prohibited the ordination of women. Divorce was generally forbidden to women, but it was often socially acceptable for husbands and even priests to be promiscuous.

The exploitation of women intensified even more in the vaeshya age. The slave trade from Africa made women the legal property of their male owners, to rape or sell at will. With no guaranteed income, most women were compelled to marry just to survive. When democracy was established in Western countries, women were excluded from the process. Women's struggles for equal rights intensified during the nineteenth and twentieth centuries.

Yet during all these centuries, great women overcame discrimination and obstructions to contribute to human progress. Countless inventors, scientists, doctors, artists, writers, social reformers and revolutionaries have redefined our world. However intelligent, independent women were often ignored, belittled and even erased from history by patriarchal societies. Throughout the centuries and even today, each woman who chose to enter a traditionally-male occupation faced discrimination, ridicule and condemnation. Their stories of struggle and perseverance are seldom told.

The Exploitation of Women Today

Under global capitalism, the degradation of women has actually worsened, because the advertising industry and the media use sexy women to increase the sales of almost any product. Because profit, or "the bottom line", is the major goal of a society dominated by vaeshyas, norms of what is appropriate and permissible are continually falling, and people are bombarded with graphic images of sex in the media and popular culture. Women are taught at a very young age that their value depends on how beautiful, thin and sexy they look, and that buying the right clothes and beauty products are the key to success in relationships as well as in life. Eating disorders, low self-esteem and depression plague many women who are unable to achieve a perfect image of beauty.[17]

Tragically, greed for material wealth propels some women to become willing partners in their own exploitation. Yet fear, poverty and emotional vulnerability are more common underlying causes that trap the vast majority of victims into participating. Just as the Bible's creation story that Eve was created from Adam's rib places women in a subordinate role, many women have been socialized from an early age to believe that they are incomplete and should rely on men for emotional, financial, and intellectual validation. Psychologically, many women get their identity first through their fathers, then from their boyfriends or husbands, and feel they must please men and be subordinate to them in order to survive.[18]

In a landmark five-year longitudinal study, Harvard psychology professors Lyn Mikel Brown and Carol Gilligan listened to the stories of 100 adolescent girls. They found that when young girls in the United States reach adolescence, they start to receive contradictory expectations from parents, teachers, peers, the media, and themselves.[19] Girls struggle with these conflicting messages, trying to figure out how to act, when to speak up, and who to please in their everyday lives. There are strong pressures from society for them to be beautiful, likable, passive and self-sacrificing. Many adolescents respond by falling into silence and disconnection.[20]

Unfortunately, all this means that many women are taught to distrust and compete with other women for the attention of men. In many cultures single women are anathema, with a social stigma attached to older, unmarried women or spinsters.[21] Other women are often more critical of a woman's appearance, for example, than are men. Some women even learn to hate each other.

Poet Robert Bly points out why so many men become abusive towards women. The industrial revolution and modern capitalism have caused fathers to be increasingly absent from the house, so that young males have not received the teachings that they need to mature. Feelings of abandonment and rejection lead to destructive patterns of competition, aggression and juvenile delinquency.[22] Equating sensitivity to weakness, many men develop sexist attitudes towards girls and women, judging them on how closely they meet an artificial, impossible, and shallow ideal. In addition, pornography is freely available, filled with images of sex without emotions, commitment, or consequences. Because both sex and violence make a lot of profit for films, television and video games, all too often images of sex are linked to violence.

What are the results of sexism and exploitation today?

Violence against women: Up to 70 per cent of women experience violence in their lifetime. World Bank research shows that women aged 15-44 are more at risk from rape and domestic violence than from cancer, car accidents, war and malaria. The most common form of violence experienced by women globally is physical violence inflicted by an intimate partner, with women beaten, coerced into sex or otherwise abused. In Australia, Canada, Israel, South Africa and the United States, 40 to 70 per cent of female murder victims were killed by their partners, according to the World Health Organization. Psychological or emotional harm by intimate partners is also widespread.[23]

Trafficking: Between 500,000 to two million people are trafficked annually into situations including prostitution, forced labor, slavery or servitude–women and girls account for about 80 per cent of the detected victims. Throughout Latin America, poor girls and women are tricked into national and international sex slavery, lured by false newspaper advertisements, beauty pageants, boyfriends and "false husbands".[24]

Missing women: Nobel laureate Amartya Sen studied the statistical demographics of the relation between genders in different populations. He convincingly demonstrated that abortions of female fetuses, infanticide of baby girls, and the reduced food and medical care that many girls and women have access to in families compared to boys and men, have resulted in 100 million "missing" women, most of them in India and China, killed as it were by discrimination.[25] In South Asia, a woman is sometimes killed by her husband or in-laws because her family cannot meet their demands for dowry — a payment made to a woman's in-laws upon her marriage as a gift to her new family.

Gender Disparity in Education: The majority of the world's 100 million out-of-school children are girls.[26] To eliminate this disparity is one of the unmet Millenium Goals of the United Nations. Unfortunately, even those girls who attend primary and secondary school do not necessarily receive gender-equitable education that is empowering.

Economic Exploitation: Studies in most countries show that men continue to earn more than women at every level of education. The gender wage gap for women with the same qualifications doing the same job as men is 15 per cent on average in the European Union, 17 per cent in the UK, 23 per cent in the US, 35 per cent in Asia, 46 per cent in Africa and 51 per cent in Latin America.[27] When the gender wealth gap is measured, it is often much greater: in Germany, 30,000 euros (US$42,000),[28] and in the United States, nearly half of all single black and Hispanic women have zero or negative wealth, meaning their debts exceed all of their assets.[29]

With the globalization of manufacturing, international businesses seek inexpensive labor pools that can be controlled in undeveloped countries. Hence it is usually women who are exploited in sweatshops. Similarly, women are disproportionately affected by structural adjustment policies that limit access to education and health care.

The Awakening of Women

Throughout his life, Sarkar was deeply concerned about the conditions of women in society.[30] He supported their emancipation from violence and dogmas, and he recognized that one of their greatest obstacles is an inferiority complex that has been imposed on them over centuries. He urged women to reclaim their self-respect as equals in society. He called on men to join their struggle for human rights and equal opportunities.

Sarkar outlined three steps for the liberation of women:

1. Quality education for all girls and women
2. Economic democracy and self reliance
3. Social Justice

Quality Education for All Girls and Women:

-   To teach women how to care for and strengthen their bodies, their minds and their spirits.
-   To learn the hidden history of women's great contributions to every aspect of society.
-   To see through the imposed veils of superstition and dogmas.
-   To value diversity and view gender, racial and cultural differences among people as enhancements of our human family.
-   To achieve the necessary self-confidence to apply their talents and knowledge for the benefit of society.

These goals should not be limited to school, but should also be encompassed in lifelong campaigns led by nongovernmental organizations and the media.

Economic Democracy and Self-reliance:

- Financial independence gains women a voice both in the household as well as in society. Men will no longer be able to impose their whims on women who are not economically chained to them.
- Cooperatives empower women to decide how their local economy will be run.
- Women who choose to live at home with their children can start cottage industries, such as home services, handicrafts, gardening, food services, tailoring, computer businesses, and consultancies.
- Economic statistics must include the value of women's work in the home. Caregivers should be supported by the government.

Social Justice for Women:

- A healthy society must protect women from both physical and psychic abuse and exploitation.
- The judicial system must guarantee equal treatment for women.
- Every job should be open to women, because with modern technology virtually no job still relies on brute strength.
- Parity representation in government.

Men and women each possess unique physical, intellectual and emotional qualities. The domination by men and subordination of women must end. Sarkar encourages "coordinated cooperation" between the sexes, recognizing the importance of both male and female contributions and visions to the effort to create a universal society based on equality and collective welfare. He wrote, "There is no chance for the welfare of the world unless the condition of women is improved. It is not possible for a bird to fly with one wing."[31] He also said, "Let women be the vanguard of a new revolution which humanity must achieve for a glorious tomorrow."[32]

Comparing the Class Analysis of Marx and Sarkar[33]

By Dr. Ravi Batra

Dr. Ravi Batra, born in India, is a world-renowned economist and the author of more than a dozen books, including The New Golden Age: The Coming Revolution against Political Corruption and Economic Chaos *and* Greenspan's Fraud. *He has been a student of Sarkar and Prout since the 1960s.*

Marx's philosophy has been subjected by critics to careful and minute dissection, but its beauty lies in the fact that, even after all its weak links are severed, its fundamental point is undeniable, namely that capitalism suffers from severe contradictions. The profit-seeking, wealth-accumulating propensities of the wealthy must shoulder blame for the recurrence of business cycles, which, quite often in the last two centuries, have shaken the very foundations of Western civilization. Even today the threat of recessions looms like a Sword of Damocles over the shaky capitalistic economies...

Both Marx and Sarkar use a historical method of analysis. Both believe in the inevitability of historical patterns of societal evolution, though not in the repetition of events themselves. Both agree that capitalism will be brought to an end by some sort of revolution, though for Sarkar this revolution may be bloody or peaceful, whereas Marx believed it would always be violent. Marx calls it the revolution of the proletariat, whereas to Sarkar it is the social revolution of the laborers. Both agree that the workers are victims of the capitalists' unbridled rapacity and penchant for more and more wealth, although for Sarkar, the laborers are vulnerable to exploitation in every facet of civilization. One might say that as far as the description of capitalism is concerned, Sarkar echoes Marx in several respects.

In a rare reference, Sarkar looks at Marx in an unconventional light: "A group of exploiters loudly object to a remark that was made by the great Karl Marx concerning religion [that it is the opiate of the people]. It should be remembered that Karl Marx never opposed spirituality, morality and proper conduct. What he said was directed against the religion of his time, because he perceived, understood and realized that religion had paralyzed the people and reduced them to impotence by persuading them to surrender to a group of sinners."[34]

Sarkar himself, while sharply distinguishing between true spirituality and blind faith in religious dogmas, believes that emissaries of religion have in the past exploited humanity in every civilization and continue to do so even today.

Prout's Social Cycle[35]

By Dr. Johan Galtung

Dr. Johan Galtung, winner of the Right Livelihood Award, is Professor of Peace Studies at the European Peace University and several others, Director of TRANSCEND (a peace and development network: www.transcend.org) and is author of more than 70 books and hundreds of articles.

P. R. Sarkar was a great thinker and a great practitioner. I have chosen to honor him as a great macrohistorian, focusing on his theory of Social Cycles and their implications for world unity and peace… But, given the ethnocentrism of the USA and Europe, Sarkar will not easily make it into textbooks or courses about civilization.

For one thing, the West quotes itself on matters concerning the West, and Sarkar gets straight to the core of our history with a scheme so simple, unashamedly universal and so evidently inspired more by Indian society and history than by our own. He turns the world upside down: whereas India is supposed to be captured, dissected and understood in our paradigms, instead he understands us in his. In Sarkar's work, the West is no longer intellectually in command.

Second, Sarkar draws very concrete implications from his macrohistory and the philosophical underpinnings: Prout, the Progressive Utilization Theory. This is the theory of a self-reliant economic and political system that is spiritually rather than materialistically inspired . . . . In this system money is no longer in command, nor are economists. The goal is not "economic growth" and the accumulation of wealth, but true human growth that satisfies basic needs, and unlimited spiritual growth topping that. This alone disqualifies Sarkar as a utopian, a person to be marginalized. There is more to come…

History is then viewed as a spiral, with history telling the incumbent "time is up," and the next in line "it is your turn." When any group comes back into power, society is not entirely the same; hence a spiral, not a circle.

Of course, this is a reflection of the reincarnation cycles for individuals. Non-Western views tend to be cyclical; only the West builds its project on linearity and the promise of an, even imminent, end-state. This is also what makes the West so dangerous, because some people get the idea that the end-state is around the corner, and the utopian tradition is born. The result is Stalin and Hitler and their fight over that end-state in the twentieth century. That fight was won by somebody else also claiming "the end of history," with globalized markets and "free and fair elections." It will soon prove equally delusionary...

However, recent world history has produced phenomena with great synchronizing potential, in addition to communication. One of them is colonialism... The colonies were supposed to accept being suppressed, brainwashed and exploited, both by colonial powers and by their cooperating elites. In fact, the people reacted, with a vengeance, and in most colonies (as Sarkar would predict) the military took over, also to tame their own populist forces...

To the merchants, "freedom" is the freedom–as the Americans, with their permanent over/under-layer of merchant mentality, say–"to use private property to make more private property." They demand their slice of the cycle, the Westerners among them, with the usual lack of realism, forever. There are only two economic systems, they proclaimed: capitalism and socialism; and socialism collapsed, hence capitalism will prevail forever.

Sarkar's theory would predict otherwise: a popular revolt when the exploitation has come sufficiently far. Moreover, given the global synchronization of the phases, the revolt–violent or not–might also be fairly global. Who lives will see, but Sarkar's theory evidently has some explanatory power. In a sense this is not so strange: Indian understanding of the world is so much older...

Sarkar's message is very clear: elites cannot sit on top of people without the people sooner or later reacting, and they see elections in a democracy mainly as elite rotation.

Are there exits from the Sarkar cycle? Of course there are. Sarkar has one formula: combine the courage of the warriors, the creativity of the intellectuals, the industriousness of the merchants and the down-to-earth common sense of the people in one person. The sadvipras see to it that each elite is used by this process for its positive contributions... and yields the ground to its successors when the negative aspects become dominant, like repression (warriors), ritualism (intellectuals) and exploitation (capitalists). And [the destructive expression] of all elite groups:

arrogance. The sadvipras, similar to the bodhisatvas [spiritualists who renounce their liberation in order to reincarnate to serve humanity] in some branches of Buddhism, serve this function. [See Chapter 8.]

Chapter 8

Spiritual Revolutionaries

In many countries a well-knit and prosperous society could not be built in the post-revolutionary phase due to the defective leadership. Concepts such as Plato's philosopher king, Confucius' sage, Nietzsche's superman, Marx's proletariat dictatorship, etc., were propounded to develop ideal leadership, but all these concepts have failed. There is a vast difference between a theory of leadership and the practical, human qualities of a leader.... Sadvipra leadership is the ideal form of leadership. Such leaders will be physically fit, mentally developed and spiritually elevated. With their help and guidance, revolution will be materialized.[1]

— P. R. Sarkar

Sarkar's Vision of Spiritual Revolutionaries: *Sadvipras*

During different epochs, various classes led society and passed from a progressive, dynamic phase into an exploitative, degenerate one, due to their selfish class interests. Because of this reality, the movement of the Social Cycle has not been smooth. Class conflicts ignite revolutions and counter-revolutions between progressive and reactionary forces. This erratic, turbulent movement causes great suffering and confusion, and often brings society to the brink of disaster. Is humanity doomed to be continually dominated by opposing class interests?

While Prout takes a macro view of class struggles, it also accepts that strong individuals have the ability to influence and offer hope to society. Prout envisions the formation of intellectually developed spiritual leaders called *sadvipras*, which literally means those with subtle minds. Sadvipras are those who by virtue of their physical, mental and spiritual efforts have developed the positive qualities of all classes combined. They also possess the moral force and courage to fight injustice and exploitation and to protect the weak.

The qualities of a sadvipra include honesty, courage, dedication and sacrificing spirit for humanity. They are firmly established in the universal ethical principles that are outlined in the following chapter. They are leaders devoted to the welfare of society. By personal example they can inspire and guide society forward in a holistic and progressive way.

During his lifetime, Sarkar always spoke of this concept with the highest respect, saying that sadvipras represent the greatest ideal that one could aspire to be. We can understand that as society progresses, an ever-higher ethical standard will be expected of these spiritual revolutionaries.

Anyone can become a sadvipra by humbly learning the positive traits of all four classes and setting a personal example of self-discipline and service. Sarkar writes:

> Our approach is not to call these classes bad, ... [but rather to encourage everyone to] practice and develop the qualities of all these classes. For instance, the developed mind required by vipras for an intellectual is necessary for everyone.... . Even if one is a shudra or a vaeshya, or a member of any other class, every person ... has to work to have a developed and strong mind. Every person has to work to build a strong and healthy body. Every person has to work for a living.... . The work of a sweeper–the lowest form of work–is far more respectable than depending upon others for one's daily needs. Not only has earning money and having a balanced and dependable economic life been given importance, ... but even the lowest of these classes, in whom people usually do not see any good, has been given equal importance. Everyone... has to serve others physically. This is the work of the shudras, or the workers. [Sadvipras] cannot develop themselves completely unless they can also perform this work efficiently. In short, all the requirements of the four classes have to be mastered by each individual.... .

It is not only the mastery of these trades which is necessary; the regular practice of these trades is an essential duty.... . Every individual thus becomes universally fit. One makes as good a vipra as a shudra. Thus, no scope is left for an individual to leave others behind and form a special group.

A classless society is not aimed at ... but is evolved by practice. This approach, to break a society full of classes and sects, was never thought of before. The very classes which appeared as a logical development and evolution can be broken up by an even more logical method to form only one classless society.... .

[Prout] has not been formed as a result of cyclic changes in the economic sphere of the world like the evolution of communism, rather it is a radical departure from all existing economic practices or theories conceived so far. It is a revolution in the economic sphere of the world's life.[2]

While Sarkar sees the rotation of the Social Cycle as inevitable, he believes these socio-spiritual visionaries who have struggled to rise above their class interests can smooth society's progress. Because they have risen above their class identity, they feel allegiance to everyone, not to any group or party or nation. They are magnanimous, multicultural, dedicated to justice for all. Without personal ambition, with a universal spiritual outlook, their thoughts are clear. Sarkar describes their role as one of working in the "nucleus" of the Social Cycle, assisting each group to develop and lead society in turn. As soon as signs of social decay or exploitation appear, sadvipras will apply sufficient force by mobilizing the people to accelerate the transition to the next varna, thereby decreasing periods of turmoil.

Prout's model of sadvipra leadership seeks to harness the dynamic forces of humanity in a positive way. Prout utilizes the individual and collective potentials on all levels–physical, psychic, social and spiritual– and synthesizes them in an effort to create an ever more progressive and vibrant society.

How Sadvipras Develop: Spiritual Activism

Sarkar wrote, "It becomes the prime duty of all people to make themselves and others sadvipras."[3]

Sarkar emphasized that there is a perennial conflict going on everywhere between good and evil, light and darkness, virtue and vice. Humanity progresses through this conflict. Through this struggle for justice, through this churning, sadvipras are created.

However, spiritual revolutionaries also develop through another struggle, the inner one. To continually expand the mind through meditation and spiritual practice, to accept the Supreme as one's goal, must take place simultaneously with the struggle for social justice. Both are essential.

"Sacred activism" is a term coined by theologian Andrew Harvey which expresses the spirit of the sadvipra. He writes, "From the heart of the sacred activist flows a golden, ecstatic torrent of passion to change all things out of love for all things."[4]

Sarkar indicated that in addition to one's conduct, morality and fighting spirit, one's universal outlook is also a way to judge whether a person is a sadvipra. "Due to their benevolent idealism and mental development they naturally look upon all with love and affection. They can never do any injustice in any particular era or to any particular individual."[5]

This is interesting, because conversely, a person's sentiment for a particular group would be a way to recognize that a person is not yet qualified to lead society. Some activists still hold an unconscious feeling of superiority of their nation, family, language, race or class. Some men have a distrust of women in leadership positions, and some women feel resentment against men because of this and so many wrongs committed.

Even among activists, it is very easy to get attached to one's own plans. Yet if we refuse to listen to others and discuss other positions, then our rationality becomes of less concern than being "right".

All of these feelings have developed due to our upbringing and our life's experiences. They are a natural result of what has happened, and yet they prevent us from "looking upon all with love and affection." Can we honestly say that we feel love and affection for every person we know? To strive for that highest spiritual outlook and to develop compassion for all is the personal goal of a spiritual revolutionary.

True leaders empower others to be great. They sincerely listen to the opinions of others, and they encourage and praise the accomplishments of others. Such leaders know that "who I am" does not depend on titles or positions. As loving parents are proud of the accomplishments of their children, these leaders show joy when others become great too. Because economic democracy is about empowering people and communities, sadvipras are uniquely suited to facilitate this process.

One of the best examples of this in my own life was my trainer, Dada Vicitrananda, who guided me when I was studying to become a monk in 1978. He encouraged and inspired me, gave me self-confidence, and empowered me to develop my own identity.

Facing Our Shadows

A position of leadership gives one an unusual degree of influence over others, but that influence may be either positive or negative. Studies in capitalist enterprises show that the actions of the leader account for up to 70 percent of employees' perceptions of the climate of their organization.[6]

Great leaders are forged through great struggle. Oppression and imprisonment have helped mold some modern leaders, such as Martin Luther King and Malcolm X in the United States, Andrei Sakharov in Russia, Anwar Sadat in Egypt, Vaclav Havel in the Czech Republic, Aung San Suu Kyi in Burma, Rigoberta Menchú in Guatemala, Xanana Gusmão in East Timor, Luiz Inácio Lula da Silva in Brazil, Hugo Chávez in Venezuela and Nelson Mandela in South Africa.

The path of revolution is the most difficult path of all, and all those who choose to walk that path will encounter greater and greater risks and challenges. However, the greatest enemies to be faced are one's inner enemies and bondages: one's complexes, weaknesses and fears. For example, many people are afraid of failure and looking bad in front of others. Organizers will eventually find themselves confronted with whatever it is they fear. The key is to face these fears courageously and overcome them.

The inner work of leaders is very important. As human beings, we all long for love, for approval, for certainty, for belonging. If we are unconscious, then we tend to blame others for our unmet needs, usually those who are around us.

The process of self-analysis is essential to inner progress: evaluating one's mistakes each day–indeed, each moment–and struggling to overcome each defect as it arises.

The downfall of many revolutionaries has been the desire for small comforts and security. The powerful spirit of spiritual struggle, as embodied in the ancient science of Tantra Yoga (explained in Chapter 2), can help to overcome such desires. Rather than avoiding physical and psychic clashes, one needs to confront and embrace these clashes for personal transformation and development.

It is true that what we despise in others–the qualities that we hate–are actually within us. Every human being has the same basket of mental propensities; we express them according to our individual tendency. People are inclined to project what they dislike within themselves onto others, seeing those who disagree with them as enemies, and getting into heated arguments and bitter conflicts. Projection is a trick the mind plays to avoid facing the enemies within.

There is a way to identify this tendency. Think of someone with whom you have the greatest difference of opinion. This person may have done something wrong; you or others may have been hurt by their actions. But if you experience feelings of hatred, anger or superiority in relation to this person, then that is a problem that you must confront and overcome. While you may disagree with someone's actions, and while you should fight against immorality and injustice, you should not confuse behavior with the person.

Sarkar counseled, "Even while dealing with persons of inimical nature, one must keep oneself free from hatred, anger and vanity."[7] The feeling of jealousy should be overcome by super-imposing the idea of friendliness towards that person. Hatred should be overcome by compassion and forgiveness, envy by praise and encouragement. This is certainly not easy, but with continued effort each propensity can eventually be brought under firm control. It is a life-long practice of continued self-improvement. This endeavor is vital to the ethical fundamentals of social responsibility.

Goodness, Evil and How to Train Heroes

We like to think that we are very different from those who commit terrible crimes of torture and violence. However Sarkar's discourses on biopsychology and extensive scientific research support the opposite view: the potential for good and evil lies within all of us.

A series of famous psychological experiments were conducted in the early 1960s to examine the question of whether ordinary people could be coerced into contributing to evil, such as the Holocaust. Yale University psychologist Stanley Milgram tested whether normal volunteers would be willing to obey an authority figure who instructed them to perform acts that conflicted with their personal conscience.

Participants were asked to play the role of a "teacher," responsible for administering electric shocks to a "learner" who sat behind a wall in the next room when the learner failed to answer test questions correctly. The participants were not aware that the learner was secretly working with the experimenters and did not actually receive any shocks. As the learner failed more and more, the teacher was instructed to increase the voltage of the shocks—even when the learner started screaming, pleading to have the shocks stop, and eventually stopped responding altogether. Ordered by a serious-looking man in a lab coat who said he would assume responsibility for the consequences, most participants continued to administer ever higher shocks until they reached 300 volts or above, described on the control panel as a potentially lethal shock. The majority delivered the maximum shock of 450 volts.[8]

Why would normal people do such a thing? A high school friend of Milgram was Philip Zimbardo, who in 1971 designed an experiment at Stanford University to answer that question. A group of 24 normal male college students were randomly assigned to be prisoners or guards in a mock prison located in the basement of the psychology building. The two-week planned study into the psychology of prison life ended after only six days due to the emotional trauma being experienced by the participants. The students quickly began acting out their roles, with guards becoming sadistic and prisoners becoming traumatized and depressed.[9]

In 2004, when the terrible story became known about the torture, rape, humiliation and murder by United States soldiers and contractors at Abu Ghraib prison in Iraq, the military tried some of the perpetrators, calling them "a few bad apples." Whereas hundreds of guards knew at least some of what was going on, only one, Sergeant Joseph Darby, courageously reported it. Zimbardo testified for the defense, explaining that few individuals can resist the powerful social pressures of a prison, particularly without proper training and supervision. He said:

> When you put that set of horrendous work conditions and external factors together, it creates an evil barrel. You could put virtually anybody in it and you're going to get this kind of evil behavior. The Pentagon and the military say that the Abu Ghraib scandal is the result of a few bad apples in an otherwise good barrel. That's the dispositional analysis. The social psychologist in me, and the consensus among many of my colleagues in experimental social psychology, says that's the wrong analysis. It's not the bad apples, it's the bad barrels that corrupt good people.[10]

Psychology recognizes a trap that discourages people from acting, known as the "bystander effect." When a lot of people witness an emergency, there is a common tendency to think, "Surely someone else will do something." This is like "good guards" who keep silent when they observe misconduct: most of us keep silent when we should speak out. We have to resist the urge to excuse inaction and justify that evil deeds are acceptable means to supposedly righteous ends. Whistleblowers who report crimes or corruption in government or business often face ostracism, physical threats, and the loss of their jobs. A hero is one who speaks out, and even disobeys authority when it starts to act inhumanely.

In the same way that people commonly believe that they could not do evil, it is also common to think that heroes are somehow superhuman, practically beyond comparison to the rest of us. In fact, heroic deeds are nearly always done by ordinary people in extraordinary situations. Zimbardo believes that we are all potential heroes waiting for a moment in life when we are called on to perform a heroic deed. If we can make people aware of this, through education at all levels and ages, more of us may answer that call when it comes.

By studying heroic deeds from ancient times until today, Zimbardo observes that a code of conduct invariably served as the framework from which heroic action emerged. These principles serve as a litmus test for right and wrong and remind us, even when we would prefer to forget, that something is wrong and we must attempt to set it right (see Chapter 9).

Emotionally Intelligent Leaders

Effective leaders must develop what Daniel Goleman calls "emotional intelligence." This concept explains how some people may be brilliant intellectuals, with vast knowledge and skills, yet still be unable to understand or be sensitive to the impact of their actions on others. Those who lack emotional intelligence are unaware of how others feel. Ideal leaders are "visionary," "coaching" and "democratic," and rarely use the less effective "pace-setting" and "commanding" styles.[11]

Most people communicate more easily with others from the same cultural background. Yet in the struggle to change the world, activists will have to live and work with people from different races, cultures and nations. Cultural clashes, translation difficulties, misunderstandings, disagreements about values, and different ways of seeing the world, are very real phenomena that leaders must confront every day. Neohumanism teaches that one must overcome false superiority and groupism based on geo-sentiments and socio-sentiments (explained in Chapter 2). Ideal leaders treat all people as their brothers and sisters, dealing fairly with everyone based on universal principles and individual merit.

Another important principle for all leaders is to set an example by individual conduct before asking others to do the same.

Some leaders unfortunately become arrogant. They believe that because their cause is great, they are also great. This is not necessarily so. Arrogant leaders lack sensitivity and care little for the feelings and values of others.

True leaders, instead of developing ego, develop humility. A leader who is humble gives joy and inspiration to others.

Insecure leaders feel threatened by the success of others. Some men feel threatened by the achievements of women and may even create obstacles in their paths to diminish their success. Insecure leaders, both men and women, often become fiercely competitive, viewing the success of another's project as a humiliation of them. Although healthy internal competition can inspire people to work harder, the spirit of coordinated cooperation is also needed.

Insecure leaders are also afraid of losing control. They are afraid to hear complaints or criticism, of doing things a new way, of challenge and change. They are afraid of failure. They do not realize that they can learn from every failure, that every unsuccessful effort is an opportunity for personal and collective growth. They fear that admitting a mistake and apologizing for it will mean a loss of face. On the contrary, an honest apology for an error along with a willingness to make up for it, whether it was done knowingly or not, heals hurt feelings and often increases one's esteem in the eyes of one's peers and the public.

How to Inspire Others and Yourself

Inspiration is vital for activists who receive no material compensation. The only fuel they get for serving others and sacrificing for a noble cause is inspiration. Without it, they may feel like giving up.

Common questions that activists have include "How can I inspire new people to join this struggle? How can I inspire my fellow activists to carry on? And, most important, how can I inspire myself?"

There are several ingredients for inspiration:

1. *Spiritual practices*: Daily meditation strengthens the mind and opens one to the source of all inspiration and wisdom. The more time one devotes to it, the more one will experience peace and joy. The company of other spiritualists also helps immensely to keep the mind inspired and growing.

2. *Positive outlook*: From a spiritual perspective, all obstacles and difficulties help one to develop. Both individually and organizationally, one can learn much when things go wrong. Rather than become discouraged when a loss is suffered, by redoubling one's efforts one can often make it up. Hidden in every crisis lies an opportunity.

3. *Enthusiasm*: To inspire, one must be dynamic, cheerful and full of energy. By speaking to others in an exciting and dramatic way, one can transfer some of the thrill and exhilaration of the global movement to create another world. There is an old French saying, "Miracles happen to those who believe in them." We all need to open our eyes to the marvelous adventure that is taking place all around us every day.

4. *Actively collect and communicate good news from around the world*: From the dawn of our species, human beings have desired to belong to a large group. Being part of a popular movement gives a feeling of success and security. Yet one's humble efforts sometimes seem too insignificant to have much effect on the local community or the wider world.

   It is only by expanding one's vision to see all the efforts and projects in every country of the world that one can realize how strong the global effort to make a better world is growing. Hearing and telling others of the successes of this movement inspires everyone.

5. *Invite Creative Expression*: The collective struggle needs everyone's help. Recognizing that people have diverse experiences and abilities, leaders should invite them to express their talents in a constructive way. When people discuss freely and frankly, and ask sincere questions to their heart's content, they can learn and develop more in the spirit of Neohumanism.

   New ideas and new ways of doing things, if carefully planned, breathe fresh life into tired activists and generate enthusiasm. And the resultant new experiences will challenge and empower people to take risks and overcome their fears.

6. *Laugh Together*: There is an old proverb, "If you take yourself too seriously, no one else will." A good sense of humor is one of the loveliest qualities that leaders can have. Those who spent time with Sarkar remember well how often he lightened their feelings with a funny story or joke. Sometimes he made everyone laugh so hard that their sides hurt and tears came to their eyes. His jokes were always an invitation for everyone to relax and laugh together as a family.

To be a positive example and a continual source of inspiration for those around should be the goal of every activist.

Becoming Sadvipras

By Satya Tanner

Rather unconventionally, Satya Tanner combined her vegetarian and yoga lifestyle with a 16-year career as a pilot and aerospace engineer in the Royal Australian Air Force, reaching the rank of Squadron Leader. During that time she was among the first 15 women to become an Air Force pilot; she supported humanitarian operations after the Bali bombings of 2002; she organized national competitions and led teams in military sporting events; and she studied and used empowering, holistic leadership principles to guide individuals, teams and organizations through personal and collective change. She now works as a leadership development trainer for organizations and communities that are in search of liberating leadership and healthy cultures. www.revolutionaryfutures.com

The Arab Spring and Occupy movements of 2011 highlighted the power of collective revolution and the facilitative role of the sadvipra. When the oppression and exploitation of a dominating class reaches a critical breaking point, the floodgates open due to a wave of courageous efforts aimed at restoring balance.

As a volunteer yoga and meditation teacher, I have started many of my courses by asking, "What do you want out of life?" Some people answer that they want something material, such as a house, car or food, while others desire something emotional and psychological, such as healthy relationships, a sense of security, or to be respected. The responses tend to confirm Maslow's hierarchy of needs. We then ask each other: "Why, and what do those things give you?" The answer is, without fail, personal happiness.

Turning to Sarkar's Social Cycle, if we were to plot society's happiness, such as the Gross National Happiness, against time, with each era of the Social Cycle, happiness would rise and fall with the beneficial and exploitative phases.

At first glance, Sarkar's Social Cycle may seem a little too predictable and defeatist–not another exploitative phase! But herein lies the beauty of the sadvipra concept.

Sadvipras become aware of exploitation as soon as it begins and are ready to act against it, facilitating the revolutionary change of power from one class to the next. They ought not to be confused with unnecessarily destabilizing groups, though their wisdom in knowing when to act and when not to act evolves over time.

As sadvipras develop, the level of exploitation that society tolerates will become less and less. Therefore the duration of each exploitative phase will shorten, and the total happiness will continue to increase in both a cyclical and linear fashion. This gives humanity a sense of control over our collective happiness, freeing us from fatalistic notions of helplessness.

Where do we find these sadvipras? Perhaps surprisingly, we don't need to look elsewhere, because they are inside us. Each of us has the capacity and duty to become one. The more we engage in spiritual practice (e.g. meditation and other inner wisdom practices), the more connection we feel with our deepest self and those around us. The more connection we feel, the less we can tolerate exploitation and the faster we will want to act and inspire others to act.

Inner work through spiritual practice isn't the only criterion of a sad-vipra and a clear shortage of them in the world today might make one wonder if this is an overly-idealistic endeavor. However, this pragmatic idealist doesn't believe so. The qualities of sadvipras can be found in many individuals, though perhaps not all together in one person at this point in history. Some individuals have a tremendous revolutionary spirit which we can learn from. Some teach us how to liberate the disempowered. Some demonstrate unwavering moral courage and selfless service. Others have great compassion, love and spiritual wisdom. The sadvipra self is a collection of the best components of leadership and moral courage, and our movement along the path to becoming a sadvipra is a natural evolutionary step.

Here are some tips to start you on your evolutionary (and revolution-ary) way:

Develop your shudra self by doing selfless volunteer service with the homeless, prisoners, mental health patients, addicts, etc. By listening to and working with those who are suffering, you will learn to broaden your compassion, develop humility and realize the importance of human values.

Develop your ksattriya self by joining a sports team, doing martial arts, learning first aid and rescue skills, or anything else involving teamwork, action and overcoming challenges/fear. This will help you to develop courage and become a team player.

Develop your vipra self by refining your intellect, creativity and intuition through study, artistic endeavors and meditation. This will help you to be more innovative and wise in an increasingly complex world.

Develop your vaeshya self by starting a small business or cooperative, joining a fundraising effort, or taking on some managerial/organizational roles in paid or volunteer positions. This will help you learn how to mobilize resources and ideas, necessary for achieving all kinds of goals.

Practice ethical behavior and moral courage by standing up for what is right. However, choose your battles wisely to avoid burnout.

Develop a Neohumanist mindset by challenging your worldview and removing your "isms." Look for opportunities to meet, dialogue and work with people from other races and cultures.

Become a 'less-ego'[12] leader through the principles of servant leadership, collective leadership and facilitative/coaching leadership. Rarely are the best leaders single-handed visionary heroes using their charisma to seduce us towards their goal. Rather they are the ones who facilitate growth and learning by empowering others to be part of a revolutionary process–no matter how big or small.

Avoid the pitfalls of leadership stereotypes (e.g., the savior, the superhero, the emotionless manager) by breaking with tradition and developing a style that works for both you and those around you.

Build your emotional intelligence by developing dialogue, conflict resolution and active listening skills. Build your spiritual intelligence by developing your existential and transcendental awareness, conscious state expansion, and personal meaning/life purpose.[13]

Develop critical thinking skills and commit to being a life-long learner by engaging in reflective-action learning and self-analysis.

As more people commit to the journey of becoming a sadvipra (whether consciously or otherwise), the greater is our collective capacity to develop a society that promotes collective happiness and fulfillment. Everybody has the capacity to become a sadvipra–all you have to do is start.

Prout Lessons from Development Work in West Africa

by Dada Daneshananda

In June 2000 I arrived in West Africa to coordinate AMURT development projects. These last twelve years have been an incredible adventure for me, giving me the special privilege to work closely with the people in villages in Ghana, Burkina Faso and Nigeria. I am very grateful for having had this opportunity to expand my mind and open my heart to the beauty of the human spirit that, in spite of the continuous struggle for survival, shines brightly in the African village.

Lesson 1: Seva Clinic–The community must initiate and own their projects.

In February 2002, a group of community leaders in the Mafi-Zongo District of Ghana requested us to help them start a primary health clinic. We called a big meeting in April, and 150 women and men from ten villages attended. The discussion was long and lively with many different opinions about where to locate the clinic and how it should be managed. We made it clear from the beginning that the community would own and manage the clinic, not AMURT.

At the end of the meeting, the communities agreed to complete a half-constructed building in the village of Seva, to send candidates to be health-care workers to the Domeabra AMURTEL clinic for training, and to obtain official permission from the government health department to open the clinic. Everyone agreed to finish all this by September.

It was not until April 2003 that the building was completed, all affairs with the health department were sorted out, and the local health-care workers were ready. We spent April arranging furniture, equipment, supplies and medicines. The clinic opened quietly on May 1, 2003. From the first month, the clinic has been financially self-sufficient in operating expenses and staff salaries. AMURT has played a supporting role to help improve the facilities and services available to the community.

AMURT helped train women health promoters and Traditional Birth Attendants to educate and assist births in the villages. The women named themselves "*Kekeli* Women." *Kekeli* means "brightness" or "light". In 2012 we started a new program for teenagers called "Kekeli Girls." In Burkina Faso, AMURT's presence in Deou Department goes back to 1986, when we began construction of a hospital. The safe motherhood initiative there has trained midwives in 37 desert villages. Today AMURT works with the communities on surface water harvesting schemes to make it possible to grow more vegetables in the arid semi-desert region.

These projects are self-reliant and supported by the communities due to three crucial factors:

1. The community identified their own needs and priorities.
2. They took the initiative and made the commitment to make it a reality.
3. And crucially, the community provided the leadership.

In my experience these are the most important factors for a successful community development project. Even with good intentions, clever planning and enough funding, if the communities are not empowered from the beginning, we are not likely to achieve true development and the projects will not last.

AMURT is a partner and a catalyst. Relief workers can play an important role, but we must never consider ourselves to be more important than the community. If we do, we will create financial and psychological dependency. We will perpetuate the debilitating neo-colonial attitude which is exactly what we wish to break down. If we are not careful, our presence could even cause more harm than good.

Lesson 2: Mafi-Zongo Water Project–Set aside western notions of timelines and efficiency.

In Ghana we helped start a big water project in Mafi-Zongo. The sources of drinking water the people were using were not safe, were often shared by animals and they dried up in the dry season, forcing the women and girls to trek long distances to fetch water. A local assembly member from Mafi-Zongo invited AMURT to come in. A medium-sized reservoir was planned with a slow sand filtration system to purify the water. This simple technology is affordable to maintain, and the people can learn to operate it themselves. It is also ecologically sound, because it doesn't deplete the underground water reserves, which are already scarce in this part of Ghana.

The design called for a reservoir to be constructed on top of Kpokope Hill, from where the treated water would flow by gravity to all the villages. The hill is very steep and to bring cement and other construction materials up was a huge logistical challenge. We called a meeting with representatives from all the communities and explained the situation. The communities agreed to collect the sand, transport it to the foot of the mountain and carry it up the hill in three weeks.

It took three months, with men and women from a dozen communities working hard, to bring enough sand to the foot of the mountain. Then we called an emergency day of communal labor for all the communities. That day the hill was alive and swarming with dozens of men, women and children, carrying pans of sand, making the difficult climb to the top.

This delay would have been avoided if we had bought the sand and paid workers to carry it up. But that would have been a mistake. Community development projects are not about meeting deadlines of international donors, but about bringing the whole community along together.

After that the people of each community dug the trenches and laid the pipes connecting them to the dam. In total, a network of 61 kilometers of pipes was laid that now provides safe drinking water to 10,000 people in 30 villages.

AMURT was first invited to Mafi-Zongo in 1993. The work started in 1994. It was not until 2005 that the first ten villages got piped water, and it was not until 2011, 18 years after it began, that the project was completed.

The sense of pride and accomplishment felt throughout the villages when the project was completed created a sense of ownership and tied the populations of the 30 villages together. That pride and unity remains today and has been essential to the sustainability of the project.

In African villages, people are not bound by clocks and calendars. They are patient, because they perceive time as moving in cycles. Time is vast, like the sky. People have enough time. Westerners, on the other hand, see time as linear–we are always in a hurry, we lose patience and lament if we "lose time". We could learn a lot from African villagers.

Lesson 3: Ebonyi Maternal Health Program–The emergence of new leadership.

Nigeria has the ninth-highest maternal death rate in the world. In 2010 AMURT chose to work in Ebonyi state, the poorest and least developed state in southern Nigeria. In partnership with the communities, local NGOs and the government, we have set up three primary health care centers with outreach programs to serve the people of Ekumenyi, in the Abakaliki Local Government Area, where the maternal mortality rate is double that of Nigeria's national rate. Our special focus is to reduce infant and maternal mortality, saving lives. We also work with water sanitation and hygiene committees elected by each village, to drill and manage boreholes.

We needed a baseline survey at the beginning. We trained a dozen health workers to go from compound to compound. They registered 5,000 women of child-bearing age, 15-49, in 36 villages. We were shocked by the results, because the surveys reported there had been 31 maternal deaths in the last three years.

We decided to verify each one. The unenviable task fell to Paulinus, an unemployed health worker from one of the villages in the project area. Visiting the different compounds and asking about the mother who had died in childbirth, he met suspicion, and at times hostility. One man who had lost his young wife threatened Paulinus with a machete! Often his questions brought anguish. The father-in-law of a woman who died started weeping openly, and as a result all the men, women and children also started weeping. Paulinus verified all the heartbreaking details of 31 maternal deaths from 2009 to 2011 from a population of just over 20,000.

Our outreach health education program includes home visits to all pregnant women in the area. Only by maintaining staff on duty 24 hours a day in the clinics, can the maternal health program work. All the planning and investment would come to naught if we had failed to recruit dedicated staff from the nearby communities. They communicate well with the people, and so there is a high level of trust and understanding. As the women's confidence in the health centers grows, the numbers coming for prenatal care and delivery is steadily increasing. The health centers are owned and managed by the local committees, and the communities feel that the health care centers are their own.

Blessing was only 17 when she first volunteered on immunization days at her local health post. Since then she has trained and worked at a number of clinics and health centers. Because she came from a poor family, she never had the chance to go to nursing school. When the AMURT clinic at Offia Oji opened, Blessing was 23, but the government health department did not pick her to work there. Still, she came and worked as a volunteer.

It was impossible not to notice Blessing's dedication. She has helped at the clinic almost every day, always volunteering for weekend and holiday shifts. Of the 150 deliveries at the clinic, she has assisted in more than 100. In community meetings, local traditional leaders and the women leaders sing her praises. It's moving to see how this young woman, without formal education or position, has earned such respect through her dedication, sacrifice and positive attitude.

The success of the maternal health program can be directly traced to the emergence of new local leaders, such as Paulinus and Blessing. In West Africa I have found that genuine leaders, who have the welfare of their people at heart, can be found in every village. They are like scattered jewels. Our challenge is to invite these dynamic people to come forward and take charge. Community development projects are opportunities to serve for those who truly have the welfare of their people at heart. The best hope for the future of the neglected communities lies with the new leadership. They are more important than us, more important than any money or technology or clever concepts we have to offer.

Lesson 4: Thinking in terms of all-round growth.

Community development is the micro-view of Prout and can play an important role in social change. By working at the grassroots level, from the bottom up, keeping Prout's key principles at the front, work for the poor takes on a revolutionary character. In one's spiritual life, a meditation mantra leads to self-realization and helps to morally guide our choices. In a similar way, I believe that before undertaking any new project, we should think Proutistically and decide whether or not this action will promote the good and happiness of all. Ask yourself:

Does it increase the living standard, quality of life and security of the people?
Does it promote moral leadership?
Does it train sadvipras?
Does it promote the economic self-reliance of the community?
Is it environmentally sustainable?
Is it practical and replicable?
Is it based on cooperative principles and collective decision-making?
Does it provide everyone with the chance to develop their full potential?

If the answer to the above questions is "yes", then, as is done with certification for organic agriculture or fair trade projects, we can declare that an undertaking is a "Certified Prout Project."

Ideally every action we undertake should have these goals. Continue your life's work, but for each choice, ask yourself whether the action directly or indirectly promotes these aims of Prout. If the answer is yes, do it. If the answer is no, don't do it. If you don't know, then study until you find the answer!

P. R. Sarkar urged everyone to accept this challenge:

In every age the dominant class first governs, then starts to exploit, after which evolution or revolution takes place. Due to the lack of sadvipras to lend their help, the foundations of human society fail to become strong. Today I earnestly request all rational, spiritual, moral fighting people to build a sadvipra society without any further delay. Sadvipras will have to work for all countries, for the all-round liberation of all human beings.[14]

Chapter 9
A New Concept of Ethics And Justice

All the clashes, all the doubts and all the violence that shake human society, are the result of one defect: misguided intellect, that is, the intellect which disconnected from the Supreme Benevolence does not proceed along the virtuous path... Unless there is a change in the human mind, no permanent solution to any problem can be found. By exerting circumstantial pressure we can discipline immoralists, exploiters and anti-social elements, but this is not the permanent solution. Collective efforts in this regard will always continue, but simultaneously we must strive to arouse benevolent thoughts in the human mind so that people are encouraged to move along the right path, uniting their intellect with the spirit of benevolence. Only one approach will not do - both are required. One is temporary, the other permanent.[1]

— P.R. Sarkar

A Moral Wilderness

Our modern world is every day more confusing. Rapid technological transformations, the mass media, and forced encounters with other civilizations having different value systems create increasingly complex ethical dilemmas: doctor-assisted suicide, genetic engineering, cloning, bio-piracy, the death penalty, war, abortion, pornography, drug abuse, nuclear waste, insider trading, animal rights, and many others.

In 1995 the American Psychiatric Association published a study on criminal psychology. The research report concluded that the most common factor among habitual offenders was the tendency to lie.[2] This character defect they share with some of the richest and most powerful people on the planet! Political leaders lie to their citizens, corporation directors cheat on their accounts and tax statements, lawyers lie for (and to) their clients, advertisers falsely exaggerate the benefits of their products, and the world's most sophisticated military forces demonstrate the maxim that: "In war, truth is the first casualty."

A common theme which pervades TV and film today is that of cheating on one's spouse. Popularizing this idea contributes to deceit, betrayal of trust and broken promises. Family members, especially children, suffer as a result.

In the West, Judeo-Christian values–introduced between two to three thousand years ago–are breaking down, in part because of their inability to provide clear answers to new moral dilemmas. Global capitalism offers the whole world a new model of individualism, greed and indifference in the face of poverty and suffering of members of our human family. Price tags determine the value of everything and everyone, without considering the moral character of the person.

This materialistic outlook breeds corruption and dishonesty at every level of society, draining economic resources and breaking apart communities.

To find answers to the ever-more complex moral questions that are being thrust upon us requires deep reflection and strength of character. Sadly, these qualities are now more rare in our hectic world than ever before.

Why is Violent Crime Increasing?

Violence is escalating dramatically in the economically developed countries of the world. In the United States, the rate of aggravated assaults, where human beings are attempting to kill one another, combined with robbery, stealing with violence or the threat of violence, rose more than six times from around 60 per 100,000 in 1957[3] to 395 per 100,000 by 2009.[4] This rate would be even higher were it not for the high numbers of violent offenders that are imprisoned in the United States. In Canada, per capita assaults increased almost fivefold between 1964 and 1993. According to Interpol, between 1977 and 1993 the per capita assault rate increased nearly fivefold in Norway and Greece, and in Australia and New Zealand it increased approximately fourfold. During the same period it tripled in Sweden, and approximately doubled in Belgium, Denmark, England, Wales, France, Hungary, Netherlands, and Scotland. In India during this period the per capita murder rate doubled. In Japan juvenile violent crime went up 30 percent in 1997 alone.[5]

The United States military knows exactly why this is happening. Human beings, like the healthy members of most species, have a powerful, natural resistance to killing their own kind. Studies during the Second World War and the Korean War revealed that in actual combat, 75 percent of U.S. soldiers never fired their personal weapons at the enemy for the purpose of killing, even though they were under direct threat.[6] Though the results of this study have been contested, the U.S. military took it very seriously and designed all their training since then to increase the willingness of soldiers to kill under orders. They were so successful that in the Vietnam War, the non-firing rate had dropped to only 5 percent.[7]

The military designed three psychological processes to enable adolescents to kill. All three have now become commonplace in Western society.

Desensitization and classical conditioning: During basic training for decades, soldiers were ordered to shout, "Kill! Kill!" and other violent chants until killing started to feel normal. Today's violent films are much better at this. Numerous studies have demonstrated that regularly watching violence and sex on television and in films, usually portrayed as powerful and exciting, desensitizes people to violence.[8] In two surveys of young male felons imprisoned for committing violent crimes (murder, rape, and assault), 22 to 34 percent reported that they consciously imitated crime techniques learned from television programs.[9]

Operant conditioning: To develop a "quick shoot" response, the military stopped training soldiers to lie down and shoot at bulls-eye targets. Instead modern soldiers stand in a foxhole and watch a natural terrain until realistic human-sized figures pop up periodically in different places. Police training courses alternate figures with weapons and innocent bystanders to train officers in what they call "shoot-no shoot."

Violent video games have much more realistic environments in which the player shoots at enemy figures; a hit is rewarded with splattering blood and flesh.

Role models: All soldiers are trained by a drill sergeant, a decorated veteran, who rewards the troops for obedience and is very harsh for indiscipline. Whereas sanctioned violence is praised, pointing a weapon at another service member, for example, is severely punished.

In the early years of film, heroes, such as a cowboy or detective, usually fought bad guys to uphold the law and justice. Later came films with vigilante or criminal heroes who fought for revenge or greed. More recently Hollywood has produced countless horror films with normal-looking psychopaths who torture and murder innocent men, women and children in revolting detail; instead of being killed in the end, they return again and again in sequels. While watching such gore, viewers are rewarded with popcorn, candy, and companionship–a powerful group process humiliates or belittles viewers who walk out or even close their eyes during violent scenes. This is a very sophisticated level of desensitizing a generation to the point at which inflicting pain and suffering has become entertainment.

"The conclusion of the public health community, based on over 30 years of research, is that viewing entertainment violence can lead to increases in aggressive attitudes, values and behavior, particularly in children." This Joint Statement was signed on July 26, 2000 by representatives of the American Medical Association, the American Academy of Pediatrics, the American Psychological Association, the American Academy of Child and Adolescent Psychiatry, the American Psychiatric Association and the American Academy of Family Physicians.[10]

The advice of the six largest public health bodies in the United States to reduce entertainment violence has not been followed. Under capitalism, unethical profit-maximization by the entertainment industry is more important than public health.

Ethics for Personal and Social Transformation

Sarkar believed that morality is the foundation upon which a better society and economic democracy must be built. He pointed out that traditional rules-based morality, expressed in terms of absolutes, is inadequate to the task of solving most moral questions in the relative world. If a deranged gunman is shooting innocent people, the Biblical commandment, "Thou shalt not kill," is inappropriate to the immediate need to stop him as fast as possible at any cost, in order to save other lives.

It is natural that people may react if morality is imposed on them. When people are coerced to obey dogmatic rules, some respond by rejecting all morality whatsoever.

Sarkar appealed for a moral framework based on "practical wisdom." He drew a subtle distinction between what he termed "simple morality" and "spiritual morality." He pointed out that throughout history, most moral values have reflected the interests of the rich and powerful. Each ruling class has exploited other classes through force and cunning, creating rules and justifications for those rules to suit their interest. Human history is a chronicle of exclusion and power.

Instead of simple do's and don'ts, Sarkar insisted that in choosing the correct way to act in different situations, the intention behind each deed is of great importance. Spiritual morality is based on Neohumanism and cardinal human values, which include kindness, honesty, courage, mercy, humility, self-restraint and compassion. These qualities are considered virtues in every society and religious tradition because they give meaning and enhance the beauty of life, transforming people and society. Cardinal human values challenge us to protect the weak, avoid harming others, overcome selfishness and denounce the lies of those who abuse their power.

Prout recognizes the existential value of every being; this value supersedes the social value or utilitarian value of a being. Hence every life has spiritual potential and should be preserved and encouraged as far as possible.

Throughout history, a gradual trend has emerged to establish a more permanent set of moral values based on the intrinsic value of human life. The struggles against slavery, tyranny, injustice and poverty reflect this. Ultimately, all cardinal human values arise from the evolution of consciousness and the spiritual urge to discover oneself.

One important contribution Sarkar has made to the ethical debate is his emphasis on balancing individual and collective interests. He proposed ethics and the sense of justice as the basis of idealism and inspiration in spiritual life, and that they are indispensable for the creation of a better society. Sarkar emphasized that while morality is the beginning of both the individual and collective movement, in itself it is not worthy of being the goal of life:

> The morality of a moralist may disappear at any moment. It cannot be said with any certainty that the moralist who has resisted the temptation of a bribe of two rupees [Indian currency] would also be able to resist the temptation of an offer of two hundred thousand rupees... It cannot be said that the

ultimate aim of human life is not to commit theft; what is desirable is that the tendency to commit theft should be eliminated.[11]

To restore pramá (dynamic equipoise) in our communities and in our personal lives, we need a clear code of moral conduct. We need to broaden our sense of right and wrong to include "right living" in the world.

Ten Universal Principles

Sarkar adopted ten ancient ethical principles of yoga. The first five are called *Yama*, which means, "controlled contact with others"–they show us how to live in peace with others. The second five principles are called *Niyama*, which means "controlled conduct for self purification"–guidelines for how to be at peace with oneself. These two sets are complementary, and they are both constructive and positive. Because Sarkar viewed ethics as tools for liberation and not for suppression, he re-interpreted these principles, discarding old dogmatic interpretations. Universal in nature, they can be an effective guide to choose wisely one's actions in any time, in any place, and with any group of people.

The first five principles of Yama, or social values, are:

Ahim'sá: Not to intentionally harm others with one's actions, words or thoughts.

Daily life involves struggle and the use of force–the mere acts of breathing and walking result in the unintentional deaths of thousands of microorganisms. Sarkar differs with some fundamentalist religious interpretations of ahim'sá by teaching that this principle does not preclude the use of force for survival, for self-defense or to defend others.

Prout insists that ahim'sá includes a people's right to resist foreign invasion as well as structural or institutional violence. It does not mean literal nonviolence at all times (as some, including Mahatma Gandhi, have interpreted it) because that is both impossible and impractical.[12]

The most important part of ahim'sá is one's intention. Individually, it means striving to avoid hurtful thoughts, words and actions. In fact, every violent act begins with a thought, so if thoughts of anger or hatred arise, one should intentionally substitute positive thoughts until the angry ones fade away.

Ahim'sá recognizes certain actions as so inimical they must be stopped at any cost. Individuals or organizations that threaten murder with a weapon, kidnap someone, steal or burn another's property, or poison someone are "human enemies." So in the example mentioned above of a deranged gunman killing innocent people, in order to save lives the killer must be stopped as quickly as possible. Ahim'sá would not preclude killing the gunman in this case if it was the only way to save others.

A nation needs an armed police force and military for its security. Appropriate training and discipline are important to instill this principle of ahim'sá in protectors of the peace. They must resist the temptation to use their authority or their weapons to punish or kill someone out of anger, hatred or a lust for power; rather, their intent should be to protect everyone.

Satya: To use one's words and one's mind for the welfare of others; benevolent truthfulness.

Prout is based on this spirit of benevolence; encouraging the physical, mental and spiritual development of everyone. This collective outlook is considered the most important of all the ten principles, because it directs one's life for the goal of others. Satya directly opposes the lies of convenience and hypocrisy of those in power.

However, situations do arise when the truth can hurt others: for example, if a fugitive from a violent mob seeks your help, benevolent truthfulness would probably indicate hiding the victim and lying to the mob when they come hunting for that person. In other words, instead of simple truth, this principle aspires to a higher sense of morality based on benevolence.

One who continually thinks for the welfare of others will develop great inner strength and mental clarity that will enable that person to inspire others and realize his or her hopes and dreams. In interpersonal relations, the truth should be communicated with gentle and loving words.

Asteya: Not to take what rightfully belongs to others, and not to deprive others of what is their due.

In all societies, human beings have created systems of ownership and laws to avoid conflicts. Prout recognizes the need to question and collectively struggle to redesign unjust laws for the welfare of everyone. Yet when one breaks the law or steals for self-interest, the mind becomes crude–greed, lust and habitual lying bring about one's downfall.

This principle rejects corruption and cheating, which are especially destructive in economically undeveloped countries. From the very inception of the Ananda Marga and Prout movements in India, their members have maintained strict honesty in their personal lives. Sadly, this has often resulted in persecution. For example, when a member who was an employee of the police, customs or tax department informed fellow officers that he or she would not accept bribe money, this moral stand was commonly viewed as a threat to the rest of the department, and punitive recourses against the moralist were often taken.

The mental desire to steal must also be overcome, otherwise greed, jealousy and anger can poison the mind and cause constant frustration and disappointment.

Personal integrity and trustworthiness are essential qualities of an activist. One with ideal character is respected by all good people.

Brahmacarya: To respect and treat everyone and everything as an expression of the Supreme Consciousness.

Our welfare is entwined together. This is an attitude that is both spiritual and ecological, accepting that every being has profound physical, mental and spiritual potential. We are each a part of the whole. We are each consciousness. Thus we have the right to object to one's actions, but we do not have the right to hate that person.

At the end of a yoga class in a prison in Great Britain, the instructor announced a homework assignment: "To everyone you see this week, think, 'I love you.'" One prisoner thought it ridiculous, but decided to try it anyway, as no one would know, it was all in his head. It was hard for him not to laugh when he thought 'I love you' as the meanest prisoners and toughest guards passed by. Within hours people were asking him why he was grinning all the time. By the end of the week, both convicts and guards asked him what had happened, because he wasn't getting into arguments or fights anymore, and he always seemed cheerful and friendly. He wisely decided to continue the exercise. What worked for him can work for anyone.

Aparigraha: Not to accumulate wealth or indulge in comforts which are unnecessary for the preservation of life.

This is a principle of ecology, living simply with only as many material belongings as is necessary. It is a mistake to run after worldly objects in one's search for happiness. A materialistic lifestyle restricts one's love and concern to a very limited circle of friends and family, and causes feelings of jealousy, envy, and vanity to increase. Everyone longs for inner peace and love; no physical object can provide that.

This tenet echoes the words of British economist E.F. Schumacher, author of *Small is Beautiful: Economics as if People Mattered*: "An attitude of life which seeks fulfillment in the single-minded pursuit of wealth—in short, in materialism—doesn't fit into this world, because it contains within itself no limiting principle, while the environment in which it is placed is strictly limited."[13]

Aparigraha is based on the idea of Cosmic inheritance, that we do not own the wealth of this planet. Instead we are its caretakers, and only have the right to use and share resources for the welfare of all. Unfortunately, in North America 5 percent of the world's population is consuming 30 percent of the world's resources and creating 30 percent of the world's waste; if everyone in the world copied this lifestyle, we would need five planets![14] Ecologists prescribe personal recycling, home energy conservation, reducing automobile use and changing one's diet to consume organisms lower on the food chain.

Each of these steps requires some amount of personal sacrifice, inconvenience and time. Education is the best way to awaken consciousness about the need to reduce our consumption to help restore ecological balance.

The five principles of Niyama are about positive self-control, which lead to personal strength:

Shaoca: To maintain the cleanliness of one's body and the environment, as well as mental purity.

The cleanliness of our body and our environment is critical to our physical and mental health. Likewise, our social environment—family and society—also has a positive or negative effect on us. Unfortunately, modern society bombards us with messages about violence and sex that have a very disturbing effect on our minds. Pornography pollutes our thoughts and corrupts our behavior.

This principle also refers to internal cleanliness. For example, eating excessively leads to indigestion, mental dullness, obesity, and, in most cases, unhappiness. Self-restraint is important for mental purity and peace of mind.

Santosa: To maintain a state of mental contentment and peace.

The dominant modern lifestyle in developed countries is extremely hectic, stressful and often superficial. Materialism and consumerism stimulate greed, causing even wealthy people to feel frustrated and unhappy. People often shop to escape boredom or loneliness. Investigative journalist Duncan Campbell observed, "Americans have more time-saving devices and less time than any other group of people in the world."[15]

It is profoundly important to stop and spend time with children, family and friends. Despite all the problems we encounter each day, we should keep our patience and sense of humor. This is the attitude of an optimist, who always sees the bright side of everything, without closing one's eyes to the pains and sufferings of others. This principle instills a profound sense of gratitude for all the blessings of life, and instills hope in others.

Mental peace also comes from the deeper understanding that, spiritually, everything has a purpose. This is articulated by Reinhold Niebuhr's famous prayer: "God, grant me the serenity to accept the things I cannot change; courage to change the things I can; and wisdom to know the difference."

Tapah: To alleviate the suffering of the needy through personal service and sacrifice.

Giving one's personal time to help those who are less fortunate, perceiving them as members of our human family, profoundly enriches one's own life. Volunteering in this way is only considered tapah when it is done without the thought of reward or publicity. This type of true service develops mutual respect and instills humility.

Fear and ignorance prevent many people from serving others. By confronting our fears and reaching out to others in need, we overcome artificial barriers that divide people and learn to listen and identify with the problems of others. Service is essential for activists who want to change the world, because it creates a bond of friendship with the common people we want to help.

Albert Schweitzer, the Nobel Peace Prize laureate, said, "You must give some time to your fellow men. Even if it's a little thing, do something for others–something for which you get no pay but the privilege of doing it."

Svádhyáya: To read and endeavor to gain a clear understanding of spiritual books and scriptures, and listen to wise teachings.

To gain such a clear understanding, it is imperative that we use our rational, questioning minds. This practice gives the reader contact with great personalities and daily inspiration to begin and continue the personal path to self-realization.

While it is important to respect the spiritual traditions and paths of others, it is also important to oppose irrational and superstitious practices which cause harm to others. Blind obedience to religious dogmas results in fanaticism, a socio-sentiment. An example of this is the outlook: "Only the followers of my religion are the chosen children of God. Only we will go to heaven when we die, while everyone else will be condemned to eternal hell." This type of intolerant attitude has led to the Crusades, the Inquisition, the justification of slavery and untold religious wars and persecution throughout history. The principle of svádhyáya asks us to question internally what we read and hear as we search for truth and wisdom.

Iishvara Pran'idhána: To accept the Cosmic Consciousness as one's shelter and goal.

This principle offers an answer to the ancient mystical question, "Who am I?" We are more than our physical body, more than our mind, we are pure consciousness, a drop in the infinite ocean of the Cosmic Mind.

This is also an attitude of surrender to a higher purpose. The famous Prayer of Saint Francis, which begins, "O Lord, make me an instrument of Your peace," is an example of this spiritual tenet.

The late Jennifer Fitzgerald, in her extensive analysis of Sarkar's ethics, wrote:

> Sarkar straddles the absolute and the relative with a powerful combination of love and wisdom. He builds his ethical discourse on the simple, homegrown and sustainable base of wisdom. He has a deep understanding of the interconnectedness of all things in the world, of the essential forces which drive all those things, of basic needs, of essential nature, and of aspirations.[16]

Cardinal Human Values as the Basis for Legal Justice

Crime and violence are increasing steadily in both so-called "developed" and "undeveloped" countries, despite tougher laws, longer sentences, more prisons and increased spending on police. The inmate population in the United States has risen 19 times from 119,000 in 1970 to nearly 2.3 million by the end of 2011;[17] one out of every fifty children in the country now has a parent in prison. More young Afro-American males are now in prison than in college.[18] Yet the incidence of crime and violence continues to rise.

To translate ethics into action, the laws of each land need to be rewritten to reflect cardinal human values. For example, the principle of Brahmacarya–seeing everyone as an expression of the Supreme Consciousness–leads us to realize that human beings have the capacity for change and transformation.

The message of transformation is fundamental to virtually all religions and spiritual paths. The Bible includes the stories of a number of people who committed serious errors and even crimes, and then reformed themselves: Noah, Abraham, Esau, Jacob, Rebecca, Moses, David, Solomon, Mary Magdalene, Peter and Paul. A notorious killer of ancient India was Angula Mala–Buddha transformed him. The first person that Sarkar initiated in meditation was Kalicharan, an infamous thief who later became a great saint. This possibility runs counter to what is politically popular today in the United States: punishments of death or life imprisonment without parole.

Society should make every effort to rehabilitate an individual. If it is unable to do so, it does not have the right to kill him or her. It is like a doctor who, unable to rid a patient of a disease, prescribes death as the final cure. Or as the popular saying goes, "Why do we kill people who kill people to show people that killing is wrong?" Both capital punishment, which is practiced in the United States, and unofficial executions, carried out by members of the police or secret death squads throughout Latin America and much of the undeveloped world, should be condemned as barbaric and stopped.

Sarkar wrote, "Assassins and murderers must be brought within a penal code based on Neohumanism so that their thirst for blood is permanently eliminated."[19] Because execution is meted out in most cases to prisoners who are poor, a group of young Proutists once wrote on their courthouse wall:

Capital punishment = those with the capital give the punishment!
From the social point of view, nearly every executed criminal leaves
behind a husband or wife, sons and daughters, parents and friends, who
are alienated and bitter at the killing. Their resentment and pain (with
or without any wrongdoing on their part) undermines society. Hence
the abolition of capital punishment, both legal and illegal, is needed to
build social unity and solidarity.

Sarkar insists that judicial systems must be corrective, not penal. "The
divine system (the law of cause and effect) that controls every pulsation
of human existence, alone has the right to penalize humans, and no
other."[20] While society has an obligation to protect itself from anti-social
elements, the purpose of its judicial system must be to reform, not punish.

Great importance should be given to the selection of judges. Judges
need to be learned and possess penetrating intellects. They should also
have indisputably good character, and, ideally, wisdom.

Restorative Justice

For economic democracy to be successful, criminal offenses must be
reduced and prevented from taking place in the community; whatever
violations do occur need to be resolved peacefully. Reforming offenders
is an essential part of this process which includes a full admission of
one's wrongdoing, acknowledgment of the victims, families and friends
who were hurt physically or emotionally, and restitution when possible.

The restorative justice movement, which has successful model programs in various countries, is a great step forward in this change of
consciousness from punishment to correction. Instead of treating the
crime as a breach of the state's peace, this approach is aimed at restoring balance in the community and bringing about healing. When an
offender admits guilt (perhaps caught in the act), a facilitated meeting
takes place with all affected parties: the offender, the victim, their families, friends and co-workers. This meeting has great value in showing
the offender the effects, both physical and emotional, that the crime had
on the victims. It is also an opportunity for the victims to see and hear
the offender as a human being too.

Restorative justice conferences often have a profound impact on
offenders, awakening in them feelings of great remorse because of the
suffering their thoughtless acts caused. Many criminals never experience
this in traditional trials and sentencing. Instead, they deny personal

responsibility for what happened, and pass their sentences filled with anger and bitterness at society. In the United States, 67.5 percent of convicts return to crime and are back in jail within three years of their release,[21] and in Finland, more than half return within five years.[22]

The facilitators of restorative justice conferences attempt to reach a consensus with all parties on what type of restoration should be recommended to the court. The goal is two-fold: to change the offender, and to help the victim become re-empowered and heal. By involving families, friends and co-workers, the community strives to find a mutually acceptable solution that usually involves service and restitution.

Even prison directors believe that many inmates would do better if they were able to remain in their communities: U.S. Senator Paul Simon surveyed prison wardens across the nation and found that 65 percent of them advocate more prevention programs and increased use of alternatives to prison.[23]

Archbishop Desmond Tutu, recipient of the Nobel Peace Prize, strove to realize these goals of correction and healing when he headed the Truth and Reconciliation Commission of South Africa after the racist apartheid regime ended.

A metastudy review of research on restorative justice in the United Kingdom and elsewhere shows that across 36 direct comparisons to conventional criminal justice, restorative justice has, in at least two tests each:

substantially reduced repeat offending for some offenders;

doubled (or more) the offenses brought to justice as diversion from conventional criminal justice;

reduced crime victims' post-traumatic stress symptoms and related costs;

provided both victims and offenders with more satisfaction with justice than conventional criminal justice;

reduced crime victims' desire for violent revenge against their offenders;

reduced the costs of criminal justice, when used as diversion from conventional criminal justice;

reduced recidivism more than prison (adults) or as well as prison (youths).[24]

Re-Education Centers for Personal Transformation

Protecting society from violent criminals is another task that the justice system must undertake. Just as doctors quarantine an infectious patient to prevent the spread of the disease, it is necessary to segregate those whose actions are a danger to others. Unfortunately, most prisons systems do not adequately control the violence behind their walls. Bo Lozoff writes:

> More than 70 percent of prisoners are doing time for nonviolent offenses. Without building a single new prison, we have plenty of room for truly dangerous offenders. But by throwing in 70 nonviolent offenders–most of them scared to death, just wanting to get out alive–with 30 violent ones, what percentage do you suppose will be nonviolent by the time they are released? I know many young men and women who have been encouraged by older prisoners to attack and/or kill a fellow prisoner the first week after they arrive, so that they can earn a reputation that will keep them reasonably safe from predation.[25]

High walls are needed for violent criminals; however, a totally different approach from that of traditional prisons needs to take place behind those walls. Sarkar urged Proutists to:

> Knock down the prisons and build reform schools, rectification camps. Those who are inborn criminals, in other words, those who perpetrate crimes because of some organic defects, ought to be offered treatment so that they may humanize themselves. And regarding those who commit crimes out of poverty, their poverty must be removed.[26]

In order to re-educate offenders, it is important to understand some of the different causes of criminal behavior. Sarkar emphasized that criminals differ from one another, and there are varying reasons why they commit crimes, such as sudden passion, poverty, the bad influence of others, drug or alcohol intoxication, psychiatric disorders, etc.

Sarkar lamented that science has not yet developed satisfactory methods to rectify criminal behavior psychologically, sociologically, or, in certain cases, neurologically. He prescribed that re-education centers should be "more pure, more human," and should create "a congenial environment" for transformation.[27]

The staff of the institution should be made up of professionals who possess compassion and high moral character. Psychologists, psychiatrists, sociologists and teachers should work together as a team to help prisoners change. The guards should also be compassionate. Prisoners the world over know that even the most modern and progressively designed prisons are only as good as their guards. If the guards are petty and invective, creating unnecessary rules and punishing slight infractions with loss of privileges, they make life hell for prisoners.

In many countries, there is great disparity among the sentences that different prisoners have received. Prout would suggest that all sentences should be reviewed. When the entire team of experts reaches consensus that the offender no longer poses a threat to society, prisoners should be released into halfway houses and reintegration programs.

Education is a key to personal transformation, and the institution should encourage every inmate to further his or her education through classes or correspondence courses. In his autobiography, Nelson Mandela describes how he and his fellow political prisoners on notorious Robbin Island in South Africa eventually earned the place the nickname, "The University." They did this through their constant struggle for study privileges and correspondence courses; they even held small classes and tutorials in groups while doing hard labor in the limestone quarry.[28] Education is a never-ending process of self-improvement that instills self-respect. Every inmate should be continuously encouraged and assisted to learn at his or her own level.

Nature has a very therapeutic effect on the mind, so within the high walls of every institution large gardens should be created. Animals and pets should be included to foster compassion. An essential therapy for those with any type of mental illness is to be kept active in meaningful work, so garden work should be part of every inmate's daily routine. All types of sports and games should also be organized to build physical health and fitness.

A nutritious, balanced diet should be served to everyone. One reason for the surprisingly low level of violence in Indian prisons, despite the severe overcrowding, is that almost no meat, fish or eggs are fed prisoners due to budget restrictions and cultural tradition. Smoking should also be banned, as it is in Korean prisons.

Music has the capacity to raise one's consciousness. Elevating classical and spiritual music should be played regularly on the institution's sound system.

By controlling the environment, imposing a disciplined routine, and preventing negative and distracting influences, life inside a corrective

institution can become ideal for reflection, deep thought, and meditation. Some of humanity's greatest writers and thinkers, including Sarkar,
evolved their philosophy during periods of unjust imprisonment.

Sarkar's final word on corrective institutions is the most demanding
of all. The environment must be so congenial, pure and human that
"even if a person be innocent, he or she will be as much benefited by
the corrective measure as will the real culprit... Even if this system of
impartial justice be faulty, there is no possibility of harming anybody."[29]

The nature of these institutions would differ fundamentally from the
current judicial system. The task of the judge is to determine whether
any type of intentional wrongdoing was done. The penal code can then
be greatly simplified and rewritten according to cardinal human values.
One day in the future, a universal penal system should be developed
that will be binding on all the people of the world.

Transforming Prisoners Through Yoga and Meditation

After emphasizing the importance of regarding prisoners "with
benevolent, humanistic sentiments," Sarkar then made the following
remarkable statement: "[Criminals] can of course be cured quite quickly
through spiritual practices, and in a slightly longer period through yogic
methods, but for this a congenial environment is essential."[30]

Many yoga and meditation teachers are working in prisons. One of
the most famous organizations behind this work is the "Prison-Ashram
Project" of Human Kindness Foundation, started in 1973. They teach
prisoners to treat their cell like a yoga ashram where they can train for
their physical, mental and spiritual development. Bo Lozoff's famous
book for prisoners, *We're All Doing Time: A Guide for Getting Free*, has
over 385,000 copies in print.[31] And the teachers of The Prison Phoenix
Trust in Great Britain and Ireland now give yoga and meditation courses
in more than half of the prisons in those countries.[32]

Proutist Dr. Steven Landau has been teaching Ananda Marga yoga
and meditation at Wake Correctional Center in Raleigh, North Carolina,
USA since 2002. A five-year study of 190 inmates who took the course
found that those who attended more than four classes were significantly
less likely to be reincarcerated upon release, only 8.5 percent compared
to 25 percent who attended less often.[33] The media picked up the story,
and now there are seven prisons in the state with regular yoga training
programs.

There are two main obstacles encountered by yoga and meditation teachers who want to give courses in prisons. First, some prison administrators refuse to give permission, citing security issues. Second is the lack of motivation most prisoners feel due to the depression and despair they suffer in their harsh environment.

I have personally been inspired, along with other Proutists, to offer lectures on yoga and meditation and start weekly classes to help prisoners transform their lives in several prisons of Brazil, Portugal and Venezuela. In each session, we usually do some yoga postures together, chant mantras and meditate in silence. Then we share a spiritual story from one of the wisdom traditions and ask some thoughtful questions of all the participants. By listening carefully and respectfully to each reply, we can gradually demonstrate that their thoughts and ideas are important. We always emphasize that they are important people with great potential to become positive examples in the prison, in their communities and in the world. The personal transformation which different participants undergo makes this humble work deeply gratifying.

Some prison directors have been impressed by this work. Colonel Carlos Roberto de Paula, warden of José Maria Alkmim Penitentiary in Belo Horizonte, told a reporter from the *Jornal do Brasil* newspaper, "Great changes among the prisoners that do meditation have been noticed. The most important is the decrease of aggression."[34] Carmen Lucia dos Santos, the warden of Carandiru Women's Prison in São Paulo, wrote in a letter of appreciation, "The prisoners who participated were greatly benefited, and are now more happy and calm, and they are less agitated, aggressive and stressed. We believe that it is helping us transform their lives and making the environment a little better for everyone. We hope that you will continue this work with the other inmates of our institution."[35]

Drug Abuse Is A Health Issue

The illegal drug trade results in both organized and petty crime that cause terrible violence, destroying lives and exacting a terrible toll on communities. However, statistics in the United States show that the drug which is related to the greatest amount of violence is actually alcohol.[36]

A study in the British medical journal, *Lancet*, determined that alcohol is a more dangerous drug than both crack and heroin when the combined harms to the user and to others are assessed. The scientists rated alcohol the most harmful overall and almost three times as harmful as cocaine or tobacco. The World Health Organization estimates that risks linked to alcohol cause 2.5 million deaths a year from heart and liver disease, road accidents, suicides and cancer. The scientists assessed damage according to nine criteria on harm to the user and seven criteria on harm to others. Drugs were then scored out of 100, with 100 given to the most harmful drug and zero indicating no harm at all. The scientists found alcohol was most harmful, with a score of 72, followed by heroin with 55 and crack with 54. Marijuana was given a score of 20.[37]

A billboard stands in the black ghetto of Harlem, New York, with an advertisement for whiskey. A young black man in expensive, flashy clothes lounges on a sofa surrounded by three beautiful black women. The message was clear to any child on the street: The only young black men who can afford those clothes and that apartment are drug pushers and pimps, and the three beautiful, well-dressed girlfriends holding onto him can only be prostitutes. The alcohol company specially designed this ad for black Americans, yet it promotes the destruction of family and community values.

In 1971, President Richard Nixon declared a "War on Drugs". Since then, the United States has spent more than US$1 trillion on drug arrests, and yet drugs are cheaper, purer and more available today than ever.[38]

At least 500 economists, including Nobel Laureate Milton Friedman, signed an open letter explaining why.[39] They noted that according to the principle of supply and demand, reducing the supply of marijuana (or any illegal drug) without reducing the demand causes the price, and hence the profits of marijuana sellers, to go up. The increased profits encourage the producers to produce more drugs despite the risks. So even as the prisons of the world fill up with dealers and smugglers, the chance to get rich quick lures more and more people to try it.

To end this vicious cycle, Prout suggests that both drug and alcohol dependence should be viewed as health problems, not criminal offenses. All drugs should be legalized and those in prison for only drug offenses should have their sentences reevaluated. However, the purpose of this legalization is not to encourage drug use–far from it. The goals are:

1. To remove the huge profits from the illegal drug trade;
2. To eliminate the need for drug users to turn to crime to support their habits; and
3. To discourage drug abuse.

The government should legally regulate the cultivation, production and sale of all currently illicit drugs. This will automatically stop their illegal production and smuggling.

All psychoactive substances should be rated and categorized by medical experts based on their addictive potential, health risks and social risks. Each category of substances will be given different conditions for cultivation, manufacture, distribution and sale based on their associated risk factor. For example:

Low addictive potential, low health and social risks (such as caffeine): Freely available through retail outlets.

Medium addictive potential, moderate health and social risks (such as cannabis): Sale restricted for licensed vendors only, age-limits, ID proof required, no advertisement.

High addictive potential, high health risks but low social risks (such as tobacco): Sale restricted for licensed vendors only, age-limits, ID-proof required, no advertisement, no display of product.

High addictive potential, high health risks and high social risks (such as alcohol): Sale restricted to licensed vendors or government outlets only, age-limits, ID-proof required, no advertisement, no display of product, standard limits for serving portion size and substance strength.

Very high addictive potential, high or moderate health and social risks (such as heroin, cocaine, methamphetamine): Medical prescription only, sale only from pharmacy with prescription, ID-proof required, no advertisement, no display of products, standards for serving size and substance strength and purity.

Education campaigns to discourage drug use should be based on these findings. Ending prohibition will take the profits and power out of the hands of criminals. Sales profits and taxes should be invested in education campaigns and rehabilitation programs that actually reduce consumption.

We should stop considering the tragedy of drug abuse as a criminal question, and treat it as a public health crisis. Greed, the yearning for happiness, alienation and depression all contribute to this disaster; the entire community must resolve to overcome it together, with courage and compassion.

Chapter 10

"Our Culture is Our Strength!" Cultural Identity and Education

Prout's socio-economic units will not only have to fulfill people's social and economic needs, but also their cultural aspirations. Culture denotes all sorts of human expressions. Culture is the same for all humanity, though there are differences in cultural expression. The best means of communicating human expressions is through one's mother tongue, as this is most natural. If people's natural expression through their mother tongue is suppressed, inferiority complexes will grow in their minds, encouraging a defeatist mentality and ultimately leading to psycho-economic exploitation. Thus, no mother tongue should be suppressed... To arouse the cultural legacy of the people and raise their socio-economic consciousness, they must be made aware of who the exploiters are and the nature of psycho-economic exploitation so that they become imbued with fighting spirit.[1]

— P.R. Sarkar

Psychic Exploitation

When Sarkar first introduced Prout in 1959, he focused on the need for cultural recovery following colonial domination of India and the rest of the so-called Third World. In addition to political and economic exploitation, the cultural identity of colonized people had been harmed.

He pointed out the need to reclaim local traditions, knowledge, memory and identity.

Sarkar explained how exploitation takes place in the intellectual sphere in three ways. First, in both developed and undeveloped countries, public education is neglected. Little money is allotted to public schools, and most elites send their children to expensive private schools. Because of lack of proper financing, public schools have difficulty attracting the most qualified people to teach, and to afford other curricular and extra-curricular programs that stimulate and enrich the lives of the students. This neglect causes academic standards to fall, teachers and students to lose their motivation, and rising levels of school dropouts.

Secondly, there is a lack of development of social and economic awareness, a factor which maintains the cycle of exploitation. The great Brazilian educator Paulo Freire condemned this lack of critical awareness:

> Fundamentally I think that one of the things that is lacking in us in the learning experience, in both teachers and students, is an experience of critical reflection about our presence in the world. What is generally emphasized in most schools is the transfer of content, transferring information of biology, geography, history and mathematics that minimizes the importance of your presence in the world.[2]

Freire revolutionized the teaching of literacy through dialogue, recognizing and respecting the knowledge that poor people already have. He also helped them to question the reasons for their poverty in a process of *"conscientization."*

A third type of psychic exploitation is imposed by encouraging fear and inferiority complexes in people in order to keep them passive. For example, the capitalist media promotes the idea that anyone can become rich. It can be logically inferred, therefore, by anyone who is not rich, that it is somehow their fault that they are not. Unemployed people often suffer depression, a low self-esteem, and sometimes a bitterness and anger at society which can tragically explode in violent acts of crime.

The dominant message in the educational system, the mass media and advertising is individualistic and competitive: "First get an education; then get a job; make as much money as you can; and buy as much as you can." These institutions rarely convey a message of responsibility towards others in our human family. Many governments and private corporations advertise lotteries and gambling casinos to poor people, encouraging them to dream of getting rich. This selfish, materialistic attitude is expressed as, "I win, you lose," or more correctly, "I win, and it doesn't matter to me what happens to anyone else." This individualistic outlook is destroying human relations, communities and the planet itself.

Culture, Civilization and Pseudo-culture

Collective life is characterized by a people's culture and civilization. Sarkar defines culture as a variety of human expressions, including traditions, customs, art, language, dress and diet. In every community of the world, culture has matured naturally along with the development of the human intellect.

Civilization, on the other hand, pertains to the level of humanity and rationality present in a culture. Some traditional cultures have been plagued with superstitions, intolerance and violence. Other societies may represent a high degree of culture, but if they embody discrimination, exploitation or a sentiment of superiority, Prout would consider them uncivilized.

Prout's universal outlook recognizes unity in human diversity. It accepts that human culture is essentially one, with many local variations that enhance the beauty of humanity. The fundamental tendencies of the human mind are the same everywhere, but they are expressed in various ways and proportions in different places. In order for true unity to develop, we must honor this diversity while recognizing our inherent humanity.

Throughout history, some cultures have tried to destroy others. In the past, imperialists used superior weapons to invade and conquer other lands. They told the defeated people, "Your culture is primitive; your religion is defective; your language is unsophisticated." Colonialists used both violence and the imposition of an inferiority complex to break people's will to resist.

When colonialism gradually collapsed during the twentieth century, capitalists developed clever techniques to continue their exploitation of the newly independent countries. One of their most powerful techniques has been to impose pseudo-culture.

Pseudo-culture means that which is fake, imposed, which does not uplift a people. Pseudo-culture refers to ideas and products that paralyze the collective outlook of a people and prepare them for economic exploitation. They offer to make life more pleasurable than was the case under their own culture, but in fact they undermine the resolve of the people. The widespread dissemination of consumer culture, with its appeal to material pleasures, ultimately has a debilitating effect psychologically and spiritually. It also lowers the resistance of those who try to maintain their cultural heritage.

Many of the television programs broadcast around the world promote a U.S.-based materialistic pseudo-culture. The powerful impact that this has was demonstrated in a study done by Professor Maria Doronilla of the University of the Philippines. She interviewed several hundred Filipino elementary students at different schools. One question that she asked them was: What nationality would you like to be? The majority of the children answered American, while others wanted to be Japanese or European. Less than 15 percent wanted to be Filipino.[3]

Psychologically, this has a damaging effect on one's personality. Advertisements portray a life that is seemingly more pleasurable than one's real life. Such ads make people want to be rich and white–to enjoy the glamorous clothes, cars and houses that everyone in Hollywood TV shows and films seems to have. Most Filipino children see their parents struggling, living with much less income and fewer material goods, and so start to feel that they are backward and primitive. If children want to be someone else, it means they don't want to be themselves. Even young children begin to develop a low self-image and inferiority complex because of pseudo-culture.

The corporate-owned mass media continually promotes the desire to get rich quick; it does not broadcast revolutionary music, theater or news. Pseudo-culture paralyzes people and breaks their will to resist exploitation.

In 1981, a cable television network was created in the United States for pop music. Called MTV, today it beams its programs to more than 250 million households in 71 countries. The owner is Sumner Redstone, who became one of the wealthiest people in the world, with assets of over US$8 billion.[4] He is also the most influential "educator" in the world. However, his only message to hundreds of millions of young people on every continent is to consume. The global entertainment industry creates superstars who only ask their fans to enjoy themselves and continue buying. Parents and teachers have a hard time competing with this for the attention of their children.

Shortly before his death in 1997, I interviewed Paulo Freire. I asked him about cultural invasion, which he had first written about in his famous book, *Pedagogy of the Oppressed.* I pointed out that in the Philippines, India, Indonesia and the other countries of Southeast Asia where I had worked, it was clear that American pseudo-culture was being imposed on those ancient cultures by capitalists, so radical students and progressives were able to mobilize resistance against it. In Brazil, however, things are different. TV networks like "Globo," the fourth-largest network in the world, owned by the family of Roberto Marinho, produce Brazilian-made pseudo-culture, so the average Brazilian does not perceive this as a refined form of capitalist domination. Freire replied, "Today domination through the economy and politics must necessarily take the form of very refined control or a cultural invasion. At times the invaded do not perceive that they are exploited! The development of our critical capacity is always very necessary, but also more and more difficult."[5]

Pseudo-culture exerts a very negative and divisive influence, confusing people as to who the real enemy is and weakening the people's will to unite and resist.

An Educational Revolution

Sarkar indicates that teaching is one of the most important professions. "The salaries of teachers in every country should be on par with, if not higher than, the salaries of public servants in the judiciary and the executive."[6] Education, both formal and informal, should be society's highest priority, available to all free of charge. Whereas the government should fund education, schools and universities should be administered by educators, free from political control.

Prout proposes that the media should be taken from the control of the capitalists and run by cooperatives of journalists, artists and educators with the goal of promoting popular education for all ages. It should be inspiring, with uplifting culture, cardinal human values and universalism.

The goal of education should be liberation, to free people from mental bondages and limitations and to promote solidarity. Teaching cardinal human values is very important, awakening in the students a sense of responsibility for the welfare of others. Paulo Freire said, "There is no such thing as a stupid question, and no such thing as a definitive answer."[7] Our education should begin with mutual respect for different outlooks and ideas, and strive to increase awareness and awaken consciousness.

One technique of popular experiential education that I find personally fulfilling, is leading workshops of cooperative games. These activities promote kindness, honesty, trust and teamwork. Full of surprises and initiative challenges, cooperative games require creative problem solving which helps us to overcome our fears. In the process, we lighten up, have fun, and realize that the best things in life are not for sale. These experiences help people to realize the difference between a cooperative paradigm and the traditional competitive one. Luckily there is no copyright on games, and there are many sources of cooperative games in most languages.[8]

Neohumanist Schools

Inspired by the teachings of P. R. Sarkar, in 1982 the members of the Ananda Marga Universal Relief Team (AMURT) of Porto Alegre, Brazil opened a kindergarten in a poor neighborhood. A philanthropic non-profit association, AMURT's objective is "promoting the individual, the child, the family and the community, in all of their dimensions, based on the universal ideas of Neohumanism."

Today, AMURT projects in that city include five kindergartens attended by 270 children aged two to six and a primary school with 290 students. The community actively supports these Neohumanist projects; in fact, the city departments of Education and Health support the schools financially and by donating education materials. The city government and other public and private institutions often invite the schools' directors and teachers to give lectures and workshops about the principles of Neohumanism to teachers, university students and parents.[9]

Neohumanist education strives to develop in children a sense of their own dignity and worth, to free them from inferiority complexes, and to create in them an awareness of their potential for contributing to society. The schools offer a holistic curriculum, infusing knowledge with ecological consciousness. Every element in the Neohumanist program aims to develop all levels of a child's existence: physical, mental, emotional and spiritual. The curriculum goes beyond common disciplines and includes group dynamics, cultural diversity, morality, meditation, relaxation, visualization, fantasy and cooperative games.

Worldwide, Neohumanist Education is practiced in a network of schools and institutes that span over fifty countries with more than 1,000 kindergartens, primary schools, secondary schools, colleges and children's homes. Called *Gurukula*, which means an institution which helps students dispel the darkness of the mind and leads to total emancipation of the individual and society at large. Gurukula Network is creating an international chain of Neohumanist schools and institutes in order to hasten the advent of a society in which there are love, peace, understanding, inspiration, justice and health for all beings.

At Gurukula, all aspects of the human personality are developed using an integrated curriculum that empowers the student to know him or herself, and to use this knowledge in order to serve society. The Gurukula curriculum focuses on intellectual ability, but also includes the development of intuition, aesthetics and an ecological perspective. The main campus for Ananda Marga Gurukula is in Anandanagar, West Bengal, India, where an educational township on a 550 square kilometer rural campus is being built. Current institutes include those for Composite Medical Studies, Acupuncture, Sanskrit, Tantra, Fine Arts and Music, Veterinary Science, Agriculture and the Institute of Technology. A global network of Centers for Neohumanist Studies (CNS), which includes educational and research institutes, conference centers, colleges and universities, is starting in Asheville (North Carolina, USA), Ydrefors (Sweden), and Croatia. These offer adult courses in holistic sustainable communities, holistic health practices, green architecture, biopsychology and futures studies. In addition, Gurukula offers a unique distance learning program by email for Neohumanist Education early childhood teachers.[10]

Local and Global Languages

People express their thoughts and feelings through language. Most people feel more comfortable and communicate more clearly when they use their mother tongue, rather than languages learned later in life. Those who were colonized in the past or compelled by circumstances to emigrate, then forced to speak in an unfamiliar language, often develop shyness or an inferiority complex.

Today there are 6,800 languages spoken in the world, yet 50 to 90 percent are in danger of disappearing by the end of the 21st century. The reasons for this demise are the small numbers of people who speak more than one or two languages, the adoption of more dominant languages such as Chinese and Russian, and government bans on language.

Sarkar pointed out the need for a common *lingua franca* to facilitate global communication. For historical reasons, English today is best suited for this because it has become the most widely spoken. He explained that it is easily understood, it is capable of powerful expression, and it has the facility of easily adopting words from other languages. However, another language may take its place in the future, just as in the past French was more widely spoken. In large countries where many languages or dialects are spoken, national languages serve to unite the population and the nation, such as Swahili throughout East Africa and Portuguese in Brazil.

Eight countries account for more than half of all languages. They are, in order of the number of languages: Papua New Guinea, Indonesia, Nigeria, India, Mexico, Cameroon, Australia, and Brazil. Though languages have died out in the past, what is shocking is that now they are disappearing at such an alarming rate.

However, there are success stories. For example, Hebrew was extinct as a spoken language for 2,000 years, though it was respected and preserved as the holy language of Judaism. At the beginning of the 19th century a revival began, and now Hebrew is spoken by more than seven million people, most of whom live in Israel, where it is the official and most commonly-spoken language.

A 1983 survey estimated that only 1,500 people could speak the Hawaiian language, most of them elderly. However Hawaiian language immersion schools have increased the number of speakers to approximately 8,000 throughout the state, most of them under the age of 30.

Wampanoag (Massachusett) is the first Native American language to be revived in the United States after its last speakers had died. Jessie Little Doe Baird started in 1993 the Wampanoag Language Reclamation Project more than a century after it was last spoken, compiling a 10,000-word dictionary and grammar for the Wampanoag Nation.[11] Maori, Belarusian, Cornish and many other languages are being revived today.

Prout asserts that every language should be given equal rights and recognition. All people should be encouraged to learn and speak their mother tongue, as well as other languages. Prout asserts that the local language should be taught in schools and used in the workplace and government offices of every community, thus encouraging full employment of the local people and a sense of community pride. All schools should also teach the lingua franca and the roman script (which the English language uses) so that students develop the feeling that they are citizens of the world, able to communicate with any other citizen.

The People's Movements: *Samaja*

Sarkar's strategy to end capitalist exploitation centers on the creation of popular revolutionary movements against economic exploitation. He called this kind of movement "*samaja*," a Sanskrit term which means "society," or, more literally, a group of people working together for the common goal of all-round development. Proutists also use this term to indicate a self-sufficient economic region, formed on the basis of common economic and social problems, common geographic potentialities, and common cultural legacy and language.

A samaja is a socio-economic community with a natural cultural vibrancy and cohesiveness. Samaja movements, led by moral leaders, struggle to achieve economic democracy. They are social, economic and cultural movements for the all-round welfare of the people.

Prout places great importance on indigenous cultural expression and on promoting pride in one's heritage and way of life. Virtually every successful revolutionary movement throughout history has had a cultural component. Music, art, theater and literature can stir people's spirits to struggle and sacrifice for the welfare of their country or region. Today there are many popular movements for regional economic and cultural independence: the Free Tibet movement, the Zapatistas of Chiapas (Mexico), the Irish Republican movement of Northern Ireland, Scottish independence, Welsh nationalism, the Kurds (in Turkey, Syria and Iraq), Tamils in Sri Lanka, Basque separatists in Spain and many others. If these movements can be infused with cardinal human values, they can benefit everyone.

When the British Empire conquered India, Bengal was the largest and most prosperous region. It had an ancient spiritual culture and a language, rooted in Sanskrit, that is today the mother tongue of more than 207 million people. With a strategy of "divide and rule," the British divided Bengal into different states, and when independence was granted in 1947, they partitioned Bengal, one half is in India and the other formed East Pakistan, which later became Bangladesh. Today the region is one of the most exploited in South Asia. In the Indian state of West Bengal, the three main industries of tea, coal and jute are monopolized by non-Bengalis who have brought 60 percent of the labor force in from other states.[12]

In 1968, Proutists formed *Amra Bengali*, a samaja movement whose name means "We are Bengalis." Their newspaper, *Notun Prithivi* ("The New Earth") from Kolkata has been published weekly from then until now. The movement has since become a political party in West Bengal, as well as in other states with large Bengali populations: Tripura, Bihar, Odisha, Assam and Jharkhand. The party platform is based on uniting the Bengali-speaking states and districts to form a Greater Bengal ("Bengalistan"), ending the domination of the economy by outsiders, giving preference to local people in employment, and using the Bengali language in official work. In the small eastern-most state of Tripura, Amra Bengali has led protest rallies of up to 100,000 people against politically-motivated violence directed against Bengali people. In Assam the organization has protested destructive mining. In Darjeeling and Siliguri, Amra Bengali is agitating against a conspiracy to once again divide Bengal by creating a "homeland" for Gorkha immigrants from Nepal. Throughout Bengal, the movement is raising consciousness against the imposition of Hindi-language pseudo-culture.

Prout advocates that the existing state boundaries of India should be scrapped, and the country reconstituted as a federation of 46 samajas which already exist but do not yet have economic or political status. Proutist people's movements in half of these are becoming strong, publishing samaja newspapers, running candidates in local elections and mobilizing mass marches against exploitation. The Chatisgarhi and Nagpuri samaja movements have grown so politically strong that they were able to force the Indian national government to create two new autonomous states out of their regions.

Likewise, many of the national boundaries in Africa and the Middle East were fixed by colonizers or former conquerors, often splitting ethnic communities into different countries. Uniting these communities and helping them become economically self-reliant will contribute to political and social stability.

In the Philippines, nine major regional samaja movements are active, each with a different language and flag; together they have formed a Proutist coalition called *Ang Kasama*, which means "united companions" in Tagalog. With 5,000 activists and 200 Proutist leaders, they have adopted the slogan "Our culture is our strength!" Comprised of 18 organizations and many more affiliated associations, they are campaigning to change the country's colonial name (which means the land of former Spanish King Philip) to its original Sanskrit name, *Maharlika*–"small in size but great in spirit."

Ang Kasama's work includes promoting local languages and cultures, starting cooperatives, encouraging solidarity among all Filipinos, and fighting against pseudo-culture and psycho-economic exploitation. Their youth empowerment and leadership training camps recruit massive numbers of young people to join and participate in the struggle for Maharlikan liberation. They organize tree plantings, river cleanups, consciousness-raising seminars, social service projects and relief work after natural disasters. They promote organic sustainable agriculture throughout the country.

With other progressive organizations Ang Kasama successfully defended indigenous people and forced the government to revoke Presidential Executive Order 364 that undermined their ancestral lands and future.

The Maharlika Writers and Artists Association organizes festivals, concerts and recordings of progressive artists performing in the local languages. Their gender sensitivity workshops and protests against pornography and the sex industry have helped raise public awareness about the exploitation of women.[13]

Sarkar never advocated cheap provincialism or nationalism; rather he viewed samaja movements as a way to mobilize the people around a common sentimental cause, while at the same time maintaining a universal vision. Throughout his life, Sarkar promoted inter-cultural and inter-racial marriages and the learning of different languages to transcend cultural boundaries and unite people.

Guerrilla Street Theater for Prout

Guerrilla Theater is a term coined in 1965 by the San Francisco Mime Troupe to describe its performances committed to "revolutionary socio-political change."[14] In unlikely outdoor public spaces where large numbers of people congregate, guerrilla theater's tactic of surprise performances disrupts normal thinking and shifts the perspectives of unsuspecting passersby through the use of satire, protest, and carnivalesque techniques.

The Theater of the Oppressed and Forum Theater are powerful, revolutionary art forms created and developed by Augusto Boal in Brazil that use theater to promote social and political change. The audience becomes active as "spect-actors" who explore, express, analyze and transform the reality in which they are living.

Storytelling, as used by the great Italian playwright and satirist Dario Fo, is another popular style of theater that can powerfully express social issues. Some critics call his works "angry farce". When Fo received the

1997 Nobel Prize in Literature, the committee highlighted him as a writer "who emulates the jesters of the Middle Ages in scourging authority and upholding the dignity of the downtrodden."[15]

Melodrama is also suitable because it plays to the emotions of the audience using recognizable villains, victims and heroes that the public can identify with. The masks of *Commedia Del'Arte* deal with the folly of human passions pushed to the extreme, such as longing, desire, envy, lust, pride, greed, arrogance, avarice and vainglory. Each theater style carries a slightly different message to the public, moving them in unique ways.

Street performances need to be highly visible, loud and simple to follow in order to attract a crowd. In a park or street where everyone is moving, you have to first catch the people's attention in just a few seconds, so it must be done in a spectacular way. Good drummers, huge colorful banners and giant three-meter-high puppets (manipulated by three people) that can be seen above the crowd are useful. A more sophisticated technique is the use of wireless microphones and a sound system. Masked figures can talk with and touch people, an interaction which often radically changes their perception.

Proutist Ole Brekke, director of the Commedia School in Copenhagen, Denmark,[16] created the Nordic Buffoons in the year 2000. Buffoons are a pack of grotesque, deformed and scarred bodies, the opposite of modern people who desire a perfect body while filled with internal complexes and inhibitions. The buffoons are externally ugly but totally happy, spontaneous and free. Inspired by the fools of the Middle Ages, the buffoons at play turn things upside down. Being outsiders allows them to ridicule the public directly, mocking what society holds sacred.

The Nordic Buffoons parade through the streets with drumming, chanting and dancing in a continuous festival of celebration. They are a close-knit pack dependent on one another and held together with their rituals, unlike our modern lives where we are alienated and lacking in meaningful ritual. The buffoons illuminate human follies in comic yet touching ways, mocking the public directly in an "in-your-face" though not hurtful manner. They challenge normal perceptions and ridicule the values of the materialist age.[17]

One play performed by the Nordic Buffoons was "The Fantastic Voyage of the Danish Crown," about the mystery of where the country's money had gone. The buffoons played different currencies, showing how the money was earned by a laborer, paid in taxes, borrowed from abroad, paid off in interest, and finally ended up relaxing on a sunny beach in the Caribbean in offshore banks. A Nordic Buffoon tour of "Who's Bad?" to the Balkan countries was very well received, especially in places that directly experienced the genocidal wars. The buffoons give a voice to outsiders, those left out of normal social discourse.

In economically developed countries, most people will not stop to watch a performance about political or social issues, and they do not want to feel they are being manipulated by "agit-prop" theater. People are too focused on their own activities. Their curiosity can be aroused, however, by playful, mysterious and attractive things. In the example above, the topic of economic exploitation was expressed with comedy and funny, well-acted satire. It's important to build up peoples' trust. If they feel that they are in the hands of skilled performers, many will stay and watch.

Some things to remember:

Look for a drama coach who can train your group in acting skills.

Designate someone to pass out leaflets describing the issue your group is focusing on as well as information about any related events that your group has planned.

Designate several people to answer questions from passersby.

To reach more people, make the skit short and act it out several times, with short breaks in between. The breaks will also give viewers an opportunity to ask questions.

Make sure the message is moving, yet simple. If it is not compelling and concise, passersby might easily walk by without stopping.

Be careful to avoid anything that might cause passersby to mistakenly think that real violence is occurring.

Be sure to get permission in advance from the owners or administrators of the location, if necessary.

Provide passersby with a way to take some specific action right away and have a sign-up sheet for those interested in future activities.

Ole Brekke says:

> A severe problem everywhere today is the lack of community, the spirit of moving together. I encourage activist groups to utilize physical theater techniques to analyze the problems they face and identify useful interventions. Theater involves everyone in a joyful yet profound way, satisfying social needs, as well as creative and intellectual demands. And it's a lot of fun![18]

Future Tasmania

by Liila Hass

Liila Hass is the founder of Future Tasmania, a non-profit dedicated to the development of progressive socio-economic futures for Tasmania. She is a trained presenter with Al Gore's Climate Reality Project, a graduate of the Tasmanian Leaders Program and is currently studying medicine at the University of Tasmania. She has been working with Proutist economics since the mid-1980s and proudly brings its concepts to all her work.

What remarkable and confrontational times we live in! Climate change, fragile ecosystems, drinking water shortages, social unrest and the downturn of the economy mean that all of us are facing unprecedented change in our individual as well as collective lives.

What we do to face up to these challenges, and the tools we use to help move through this era, will have a huge impact on the society of tomorrow. We have a choice to opt for a more harmonious future or to continue on the path we are on—one of narrow sentiments, divisiveness and exploitative capitalism.

The philosophy of Prout, propounded by the late Prabhat Ranjan Sarkar, offers a new way to move forward that is based on progressive ideals and Neohumanism. Its central theme is the idea that all are from one common progenitor and have a right to an equal share in the bounty of the planet. It is a philosophy whose time has come.

Here in Tasmania, a few of us started Future Tasmania, a non-profit organization based on social, economic and environmental change. We hold a conference every year, with the goal of promoting the ideals of Prout, as well as other progressive modes of thought, to the mainstream. Our annual conference brings together people from all walks of life to look at a topic that is both timely and of interest to the local people.

We focus generally on some aspect of environmental and social change. Conferences until now have focused on economic futures, agriculture and food production, sustainable living and the built environment. We recently hosted the Dalai Lama's visit to Tasmania and have been recognized by Hobart City Council, through an environmental award, for our contribution to the Tasmanian community. In 2012 we were acknowledged for our role in creating a better future for Australia with the placement of a photo on the cover of the telephone directory for Southern Tasmania.

Upcoming plans include an economic forum tied in with the United Nation's "Year of the Cooperative" for 2012, a film event for emerging Tasmanian filmmakers called "Future Screen" and the development of the Tasmanian Social Enterprise Network, originally housed under the Department of Economic Development, but now under our care. We continue to generate good media interest with local and national news coverage and to play a role in generating progressive ideas and forums, creating networks throughout Tasmania and right across Australia based on the concepts of Prout.

My advice to activists developing movements in other places:

Start small, and it will grow. Gather together like-minded people and progressive thinkers. Think, talk and brainstorm. Take a challenge.

Commit, commit, commit! Be the example. Be the change you want to see.

Be patient. Accept everyone's help, but make no demands! Our job is to inspire people and bring them together.

Be *loving*. People need a lot of support and love, and if we give others a hard time, surely they will go somewhere else.

Remember our *mantra*!! Sing lots of *kiirtan* and...

Believe in magic.

Using Prout to Evaluate and Support a Community Samaja Movement: The Maya of Panimatzalam, Guatemala

By Matt Oppenheim, Ph.D.

Matt Oppenheim, has his Ph.D in Transformative Studies from the California Institute of Integral Studies. A Fellow with the Society for Applied Anthropology, he teaches at colleges, works to develop service learning, and focuses on indigenous research. This article is dedicated to the goal of inspiring all to bring to life the Prout vision of P.R. Sarkar.

How does Prout come about in a real community? This was on my mind when I learned about the community of Panimatzalam; a village of seven-hundred Quiche and Kachiquel-speaking Mayans in the highlands of Guatemala. The village was part of the region of Solola, some two hours from the capital.

In the course of fifty years Panimatzalam had emerged from a brutal civil war, and evolved an intertwined system of extensive economic cooperatives with a movement for indigenous education. This community could be evaluated by its effectiveness in achieving many Prout goals, including Samaja, Neohumanism, cooperatives and local economy, saving linguistic and cultural heritage, land reform, spiritual perspective, the development of sadvipras and decentralizing population by creating economic opportunities in the countryside.

Finally, it provides an example of an indigenous research and inquiry process that itself emerges from this Samaja, based upon spiritual and cultural processes and challenging the oppressive forces of physical, psychic and spiritual oppression.

In the following story, the village comes together through suffering to bring to life its culture, heritage and spirituality. People work from a deeply shared sense of community, and then inspire other villages in the region to work collectively, not giving in to foreign entities or business-like religions. Over time, organizations flower and cooperatives become larger and more complex. Spirituality is their universal legacy, remembering their ancestors and the creative force behind the universe. Teachings are passed down and future leaders are ignited from a common history of struggle and triumph. It is what P.R. Sarkar has termed samaja.

This village is the center of a regional movement that emulates the cooperative paradigm of P.R. Sarkar. From committees for road construction, to corn mills for women, to sports teams, youth leadership, committees to provide water, festival committees to school committees, to non-profit organizations for health care, preservation of the environment and independent radio stations and its own cooperative bank, this is a truly autonomous village. All these projects were led by inspired young people supported by their elders.

They also have become nearly self-sufficient in food, producing all the fruits, vegetables, grains and meat that they need. They also consider corn to be their sacred food, granted by the Creator to the indigenous people of North and Central America, and used in many dishes each day. They also produce much of their clothing and medicinal herbs; they dig wells for all their water needs; they use sustainable forestry for building materials and furniture.

In Guatemala, I discovered that a great deal of activism had developed in the wake of the brutal 36-year civil war. A particularly dynamic group, the Association of Mayan Middle Schools (ACEM) creates indigenous-based schools for youth. Soon I was hitching a ride with the director, visiting schools in the Guatemalan highlands. Finally we ended up in his home community of Panimatzalam.

I was introduced to Mayan shaman Domingo Quino-Solis and invited to stay in his house. We quickly bonded by sharing our personal stories of transformation. As a young man he was a devout Catholic catechist. However when he married, the aunt of his new wife, herself a shaman, foretold that he would also become a shaman. He rejected the idea, believing shamanism to be the work of the devil. One evening he was kidnapped by a large group of shamans in the hope that he would give in to what they believed was his "calling." He eventually escaped, but while travelling home met a horrible accident. A kind elderly shaman nursed him back to health, and soon after he embraced these ancient spiritual practices.

Across the land deadly battles were taking place between Catholics, Evangelicals and followers of indigenous spirituality. Quino-Solis formed a local movement of all three denominations for greater understanding. As a shaman with a background in the Catholic Church, he was able to inspire Christians to embrace their common Mayan heritage and spirituality. This reminded me of how Sarkar gave great importance to the psychological, cultural and linguistic characteristics of the people, calling this their *"prana dharma"*.

With his renewed faith, Quino-Solis envisioned a regional movement of agricultural cooperatives free from the control of any NGO, government agency or church. He was inspired, as I had been, by the work of Paulo Freire, the Brazilian activist that helped liberate people from their own internalized oppression. Freire's message was that social transformation begins with rigorous self-searching, self-awakening and a process of social change founded on a deep love for all. This is very similar to what Sarkar called Neohumanism.

Quino-Solis was eager to inspire the youth of the village and region through a book for middle school students. Many young Mayans were leaving for the capital or the United States in search of jobs, and losing their culture, language and spirituality along the way. The goal of this book was to tell the story of how former generations had developed their own cooperative economy to provide meaningful work for everyone, while sustaining the strength of their language, community and culture at the same time.

Together we decided to form a research collective to write the book with two female teacher/activists and a male mechanic who was a member of the village council. We applied a process called "indigenous research" based on the work of Linda Tuhiwai Smith,[19] replacing an inappropriate academic style of research with one that reflected indigenous rituals, worldview, storytelling and imagery, and that emerged from the community itself.

The book used Paulo Freire's "critical pedagogy", challenging readers to both reflect and act on what they were learning to create new futures. It would be written in Spanish, and used in bilingual Mayan/Spanish classes.

Before starting, the five of us walked up to Quino-Solis' personal shrine. The following stanza began our ceremony:

In the name of the Heart of the Creator of the Wind,
In the name of the Heart of the Creator of Fire,
In the name of the Heart of the Creator of the Earth,
We give thanks to You for working with us.
You, Creator, planted us, raised us, and make us...

Afterwards we brainstormed ideas for the book. They decided to interview elders about each stage of the project.

The first consumer cooperative started in 1965, and grew in the course of a few years, constructing its own building which still stands today. Afterwards villagers formed the first village council, and started the first primary school. Then they arranged a loan from an international organization to buy the surrounding farmland, 40 percent of which was owned by Europeans. This was similar to Sarkar's call for the local cooperative ownership of agricultural land. Then they arranged a loan to build strong houses after many were destroyed in an earthquake.

Many youth became educators, accountants, project managers, mechanics, artisans, or full-time farmers and craftspeople. The village sponsored two radio stations to spread local music and news, and soon two women's economic cooperatives began, focusing on milling corn and traditional weaving.

Reviewing the Curriculum Book

The book was designed to engage students in the development of their village. In the introduction students are challenged to action through the text, and this is emulated at the end of each chapter through a section titled *Manos de Obra*, "Take Action," which includes problems to solve.

Next is the defining story of how four brothers who won a small card game in 1965 used their winnings to start the first consumer cooperative which they later named Bella Vista. They sold soap, light bulbs, toilet paper, and sweets, and their income quickly grew. Two years later, the civil war reached their village and soldiers stole everything from the cooperative, closing it down. The war, partly funded by the CIA under George Bush Sr., lasted for 36 years and left no family untouched by its violence and oppression. Over 250,000 Mayans fled the country, mostly to Southern Mexico, and nearly the same number was killed.

At the end of this chapter students are asked: "What touched your heart the most?" They are then asked to form groups and begin critical reflection by addressing: "What was the cause of the war? Who *really* benefitted from the Peace Accords?"

The next chapter tells the story of the first inhabitants of the village in the middle of the 18th century leading up to the legalization of Panimaztalam as a municipality of the Region of Solola in the 20th century. Thus begins the intentional development of the village with the early stages of community organization, to the first cooperative and ending with the founding of *Chilam Balam*, the indigenous technical institute.

Quino-Solis and Juan Morales Quino, two original members of the movement for young professionals, then came up with a collective vision for the community: "The goal would be to expand our cooperative in the coming years to generate jobs for the members and leave in inheritance a better future for our sons and daughters."

Together with other young educated Mayans, they returned to Panimatzalam to create a cooperative movement. Soon, they formed the Association for the Integral Development of Mayan Youth (ADJIMA), and were adamant about starting a training school for professionals.

Readers are then given the community's comprehensive vision–a set of values and principals, a respect for Mayan spirituality, and a plan of action that defines integral development. Readers will find many similarities with Prout's concept of Samaja:

> When, in a given community, there is sufficient food, land for cultivation, a decent house to live in, schools for children to study in and other basic diversified educational centers; when there are higher education schools, educational centers with practical and productive workshops, sports fields, community assembly halls, health dispensaries and low-cost medicines available to the people, potable water for consumption, respect for the rights of people, equality for all, and where every man, woman, youth and child is organized, we refer to that as integral community development. In addition, if we can count on a modern education which includes the different cultures of the region, which is all inclusive, free from class, religious or any other discrimination, an education that fosters unity, respect of mother nature and the harmonious practice amongst all as brothers and sisters within a cosmographic horizon, that is called integral development.[20]

Important processes to reach success in integral development include: *Communities are changing, they are not static.* As in Sarkar's Social Cycle, leaders must adapt to changes in the flow of history.

Break the paradigm of silence, which reflects the oppression of religion that taught the Maya to reject their own spirituality. Also to work for liberation, both from social oppression and to awaken the desire for spiritual liberation.

Hold conscientization meetings. This is Freire's concept, "To invite, convince, encourage and make people understand the importance of their participation."

El Cholq'ij' - The Mayan Sacred Calendar

Finally, there is an explanation of the Mayan calendar, called the Cholq'ij'. Considering that the sun, moon, stars, planets and people are all interconnected, the calendar elaborates the vital energies that pervade life. The final section of the book calls readers to "Take Action":

Do something so that you may become a better leader and a better professional.

Demonstrate to humanity that you have the capacity.

Investigate why and for which purpose there is so much talk about community development.

As you know, everything has a beginning and an end. These are the experiences and knowledge that have been achieved through the year, which we hope may be of much use for you to share with your parents, friends and associates, from the Heart of Heaven and the Heart of Earth.[21]

Final Reflection

In addition to writing the book, the research collective developed a fruit-tree cooperative with a large group of students from ACEM schools. Finally, the group reflected upon what they had accomplished and what they had learned through the inquiry.

One teacher/activist wrote:

As a former student of a Mayan educational center, it has raised my consciousness to value our culture, because it is unique due to its values, customs and traditions that have produced great per-sonalities. I am inspired to contribute a little so that other young people may find satisfaction with their identity and be proud wherever they go.[22]

Conclusion

In this project, my role as a Proutist was to assist and support the existing movement in Guatemala, not to lead. However I was able to help inspire the research collective to some degree by showing them some of the similarities between Prout's global vision and their local struggles.

Prout is a synergistic movement; it can best be understood by how its features are mutually supportive and dynamic.

Coming into a movement with a consciousness of discovery is much more effective than coming in with preconceived projects and processes.

The style and paradigm of Prout research can evolve with the people worked with. It is the best way to work with people towards their own method of social change. In this case, indigenous research, or research embedded in indigenous culture evolved with the research team.

I want to warn the reader not to try to see this story as a model or template to follow in achieving Prout or a "Prout-like" movement. In 1989 P.R. Sarkar warned me to discern the differences between Prout and simulations that may appear like Prout.

To learn more about the book created by the research collective, *From a Game of Cards to the Development of Regional Cooperatives*, and the project of Panimatzalam, see www.proutresearchinst.org.

Chapter 11

Prout's Governance

The greatest social welfare for the human race will be accomplished if those who aspire to establish the world government or Ánanda Parivára (the universal family) engage themselves only in constructive activities and selfless service... They will have to go on rendering social service with steadfast commitment, without any ulterior motive in their minds.[1]

— P.R. Sarkar

Different Views on Governance[2]

Most indigenous and tribal societies were and are led by a group of elders: people who had earned their community's respect because of their wisdom and knowledge. Their deep understanding and comprehension of truth and their ability to perceive and choose the best courses of action earned them the right to lead their people. Most elders were known for their spiritual perspective and intuition, and tribes trusted their elders to make wise decisions for their common future.

In the ancient Chinese view of governance, it was wise leaders, not political systems, that defined society. According to the classical Chinese political historian, Ssu-ma Chien (ca. 145 BC–86 BC), who wrote an authoritative history of more than two thousand years of Chinese government, Chinese society was once characterized by the rule of wise philosopher kings, Taoist sages under whose reign everyone benefited. Eventually, a shift occurred and tyrants captured power until, in another cyclical shift of history, a new sage king rose to prominence to rescue the people.[3]

The Western view of representative democracy is defined in part by the 18th-century French philosopher Montesquieu with his call for the separation of the executive, legislative and judicial powers. This form of checks and balances and limits to the accumulation of power, which is taken for granted in all Western democracies today, is an answer to Sir John Dalberg-Acton's famous warning, "Power tends to corrupt, and absolute power corrupts absolutely."[4]

Participatory democracy is another style of popular governance with the broad participation of citizens in meaningful decision-making. Examples of this include New England town hall meetings, the participatory budgeting that was pioneered in Brazil, the general assemblies of the Occupy Movement, the self-organized communal councils of Venezuela, work-place democracy in cooperatives and constitutional assemblies. Local and face-to-face, these forms of participatory democracy empower people to make the decisions that directly affect their lives.

These various paradigms of government, as well as others, are based on different opinions about the nature of the human being. For example, in the West, neither secularism nor traditional Western religions offer much hope that individuals can systematically improve their character and virtue. The Judeo-Christian idea that "we are all sinners" is, in fact, a rather negative outlook, tending to discourage trusting others. In 1651, English political philosopher Thomas Hobbes wrote that since we are all sinners, including our leaders, we must set up safeguards against the accumulation of power.[5] As a result, political life is commonly viewed as continual compromise with the making of power deals among mediocre politicians and financiers.

Another great difference among political systems of governance has to do with whether individual rights or collective responsibility are considered most important. Sarkar pointed out that the U.S. form of government gives excessive importance to individual rights, so much so that capitalists are without controls.[6] At the opposite end of the spectrum are Communist Party governments in which minimum needs are usually met, but human rights are often ignored for the sake of the collective.

Prout's form of governance incorporates *all* of these different approaches. Sarkar accepts that democracy, as it has gradually developed, is the best system of governance available today; however, he warns us that it has serious defects. There is a great need for good leaders and wise elders, persons of the highest moral character and universal outlook who choose the best path for society. Combining the personal with the social, he calls on all of us to strive to develop such qualities in ourselves while also cultivating them in others. At the same time, he prescribes specific reforms to improve democracy by taking money out of politics, and creating safeguards to check leaders who fail to demonstrate the virtues expected of them, or who become corrupted by power. Direct participation is fundamental to economic democracy, where all workers are empowered to own and manage their enterprises, making the economic decisions which directly affect their lives. Finally, Prout also balances individual needs with collective responsibility.

Sarkar proposed:

- specific reforms to improve political democracy,
- an outline for an ideal constitution,
- a model for world government,
- a plan for a more radical and ideal form of sadvipra governance for the future.

Prout's Proposals for Democratic Reforms

Political democracy today contains significant flaws: money, party politics and the mass media have more to do with the success or failure of a candidate at the polls than does his or her moral character and position on current issues. In many of the poorer countries, corruption is rampant; votes are even bought and sold.

In the United States, money wins elections. In the 2004 elections, the candidate who spent the most money won in 98 percent of House of Representatives races and 88 percent of Senate races. The average cost of winning a House race in 2010 was about US$1.4 million, and US$9.7 million for a Senate seat.[7] "The depressing thing about American democracy is I can check the fund-raising balances at the Federal Election Commission and tell you what the election results will be before the election," said Larry Makinson, executive director of the Center for Responsive Politics, a nonpartisan group that studies money and campaigns.[8]

Once elected, most representatives continue to cater to the interests of their rich and well-connected supporters. Party politics usually entails bargaining–trading favors for influence. This means that decisions made by leaders in democratic countries do not necessarily reflect the interests of society as a whole. The cry of the Occupy Wall Street Movement, "We are the 99 Percent!" is an accurate portrayal of the problem–political leaders are paid to represent the selfish interests of the richest one percent, not of the many.

As explained in previous chapters, economic democracy based on cooperatives is crucial for raising the standard of living and empowering local communities. In a Prout society, the role of government would be to stimulate this balanced economic growth, rather than engage in direct management of the economy. Some of the government's important responsibilities would include: ensuring the defense and security of the nation, guaranteeing a universal bill of rights, implementing policies that guarantee increasing purchasing capacity for everyone, paying for public education at all levels, providing essential services, maintaining the health care system, promoting cooperatives, establishing autonomous bodies to manage various key industries and essential services, protecting the environment, initiating research and development programs, funding all political election campaigns, and building and supporting various infrastructure projects.

The powers of the judicial, legislative and executive branches need to be clearly defined and separated from each other. In addition, Prout proposes that a fourth branch should be added: an audit department, headed by an auditor general, with the power to monitor government spending and audit the accounts of the other three branches, including all government departments and autonomous bodies. If the audit department finds evidence of financial mismanagement, it would initiate criminal proceedings.

Every effort should be made to ensure that those who run for public office are ethical leaders. Candidates ought to pass an exam verifying their education and their socio-political and economic consciousness. They should also be active in social service, and possess proven expertise and administrative skills. Finally, they should demonstrate in their daily lives and work the highest ethical standards.

An electoral commission can be responsible for creating guidelines for election manifestos. All candidates would be required to publish and sign their manifestos in the form of a statutory declaration. Any elected officials who then contravened their written promises without due cause, would be charged with breach of contract and made to answer for their actions in a court of law. If found guilty, they would be removed from office.

Government funding of elections would ensure fairness for all candidates. Equal quantities of election literature would be printed for each candidate by the government. The media, managed by cooperatives of journalists, should be required to give equal media coverage to each candidate to present his or her platform and to debate the issues. No candidate would be allowed to spend any personal money or to accept donations from any source. In this way, voters would be able to compare objectively the stand of each candidate.

Political parties are often another big obstacle to real democracy. Hypocritical party bosses control the nomination of candidates, fund elections, manipulate the actions and votes of elected officials, and force policy decisions. Sarkar wrote, "Proutists have to fight against today's party politics. Proutists are not against politics or political science, but they have to fight against professional politicians."⁹ Of course, there are some small parties in the world that are progressive, including a Prout political party, which registered in India as a tactic to spread its message. But it is almost impossible to compete with the biggest parties with all their money and power. Hence, Prout's proposal is to disband all political parties, allowing individual candidates to stand on their own merits, experience and written proposals.

Prout supports a continual process of political education in ethics, logic and civics to raise the consciousness of all voters. Ethics is needed to understand the moral implications of new developments. Logic is needed to understand confusing and sentimental arguments made by politicians. Civics is needed to understand the rights, duties and powers of citizens to choose and oversee their government. The media's role will be to explain the campaign issues in a clear and balanced way. In this way, voters may be better equipped to decide who are the most worthy candidates.

In this process of popular education, an examination of voters could be set up to encourage everyone to achieve a minimum understanding of the issues, just as all motorists are required to pass a driver's examination to get a license. Driver education courses and preparation manuals assist everyone in achieving a basic level of skill, which in turn ensures a certain level of safety for society. In the same way, educational materials and courses to help prepare every citizen for voter exams would achieve a basic level of voter awareness.

We should remember that all Western democracies place some restrictions on participation in the electoral process. For example, most countries prohibit those under 18 and those serving time in prison for criminal offenses from voting. Prout would lower the age restriction, but add the voter examination.

It is true that voter examinations have been misused in the past; for example, in the southern part of the United States they were used to discourage black people from voting. Minorities and women in most countries have struggled for decades to achieve universal suffrage. Yet despite these historical injustices, the system of voter exams has many advantages, as long as voter education is aimed at every person. Educated voters are less likely to be fooled by the false claims of politicians.

Finally, with Prout's ceiling on the accumulation of wealth and the restriction on private contributions to electoral campaigns, money will no longer be a factor in the outcome of elections, nor will it unduly influence the conduct of elected representatives.

Constitutional Proposals Based on Prout

Sarkar realized the need to use constitutional structures to ensure political and economic rights for the people. Hence his work included an analysis of the constitution of India and listed many constitutional reforms. Whereas a number of very progressive constitutions already exist in the world, especially in Latin America, Sarkar went further, advocating that individuals should have the right to sue the government to force it to provide access to the minimum necessities.

In September, 1999, when Venezuela was drafting a new constitution, a group of Proutists drafted proposals for how such reforms should be worded, and presented them to Comandante Wilmar Castro, chief of the National Constitutional Assembly Subcommission for Economics.

Universal Bill of Rights:

1. Every person is guaranteed the five minimum necessities of life: food, clothing, shelter, education and medical care.
2. Every adult has the right to a job with adequate purchasing power.
3. Cultural expressions and indigenous languages must be protected.
4. The country's bio-diversity and endangered species must be protected. Strict pollution controls must be enacted and enforced,

and vigorous efforts must be made in applying technologies to continually reduce pollution and waste.

5. Spiritual and religious practices for self-realization must be protected.

6. No expression of these above rights can be allowed to violate cardinal human values.[10]

7. Three socio-political principles must be guaranteed: 1) people should not lose their jobs until and unless alternative employment can be arranged for them; 2) people should never be forced to convert from one religion to another; 3) no one's mother (native) tongue should be suppressed.

8. The penal code must be based on universally accepted cardinal human values such as the right to a decent life. Capital punishment is banned.

9. Quality education must be guaranteed to all and be free of political interference. Education is more than simply acquiring objective knowledge, and should include ethics, character building and creativity. It should instill a spirit of cooperation, service and self-knowledge.

10. We are all members of one human family without divisions. No person can be discriminated against because of race, sex, color, language, beliefs, sexual orientation, origin, or health status.

Constitutional Proposals for the Economy

Economic democracy is a prerequisite to the task of eliminating poverty and elevating the standard of living. For this reason, the following policies should be implemented:

1. Private enterprise will be permitted and encouraged for small-scale businesses that produce non-essential items and services.

2. Most enterprises should be run as cooperatives. Industrial, agricultural, producer and consumer co-ops will produce essential items.

3. Key industries will be administered by autonomous boards set up by the government.

4. A ceiling on income and wealth will be established to prevent super-accumulation and economic exploitation.

5. As far as possible, raw materials should not be exported out of the country. Rather they should be processed or refined in the local region and then sold for local consumption. The excess can then be traded or sold abroad.

6. Banks should be run as cooperatives, while the government will set up an autonomous body to control the Central Bank. The currency printed by the government and put into circulation in the economy should be based on a proportional quantity of gold bullion stored in the national treasury.

7. In addition to the executive, legislative, and judicial branches of the government, there should be an independent audit department. This will monitor government spending and publicize the strengths and weaknesses of its programs. This department will audit the accounts of the other three branches and prevent corruption. All four of these powers should function independently.

8. The first priority of the government shall be to guarantee the production of the five minimum necessities to all people at affordable prices. As far as possible, each region of the country should be made self-sufficient in these five necessities.

9. Impoverished regions will be developed especially through the media of agricultural cooperatives, agro-industries and agrico-industries.[11] The resultant decentralization of the economy will create economic democracy, in which the local people make all economic planning decisions. Non-citizens may not interfere in economic planning. Profits may not be exported abroad, but rather should be re-invested for the development of the country.

10. Income tax should be abolished; instead, tax should be placed on the production of goods.

Beyond Nationalism to a World Government[12]

To address the root problems of war, to guarantee human rights to all, and to ensure social justice, Prout proposes that a world government be established. World consciousness is certainly moving in this direction. Every year there are more requests made by governments, organizations and the media to the United Nations to resolve injustices and conflicts, and find common solutions to global problems. Information networks, citizens' associations and cosmopolitanism are opening people's minds to the ideas of universalism and global consciousness.

The world government should be composed of two houses of legislature: a lower house and an upper house. Representatives should be seated in the lower house according to population, while the upper house will be composed of one representative from each country. Proposals for new laws should be made in the lower house. If accepted, they should then be discussed and finally approved or vetoed in the upper house. In this system, small countries which cannot send a single representative to the lower house will have the opportunity to discuss the merits and demerits of proposed acts with other countries in the upper house.

The world government should create a world constitution guaranteeing human rights, the minimum necessities of life and a common penal code for all. The constitutional proposals listed above could also serve as the basis for a future world constitution.

To overcome resistance and fear, Sarkar proposed setting up the world government in gradual stages. Initially, the world government's role should be to settle disputes and frame a number of world laws while national governments continue their administration. It should also have the right to judge whether the existing laws of any country are detrimental to any minority group. A world militia will also be needed, ready to go anywhere in the defense of human rights; its numerical strength, however, may gradually be reduced as growing economic prosperity and security leads to a reduction in the number of conflicts worldwide. Over time, the world government's powers would be expanded until it carries out a full range of legislative, executive, judicial and audit functions.

The main obstacle to forming a world government would seem to be the fear of national leaders that they will lose their power. However, once this hurdle is overcome, such a government would have many benefits: There will be a reduction in violent wars and conflicts. People will consequently feel less fear as the danger of war decreases, and be able to focus their energies in a more productive manner. The tremendous amount of resources currently spent on arms will be made available for social development. And, everyone will have the freedom to travel wherever they like.

As with many other distinguished thinkers who have called for a world federation, Sarkar's goal is to unify humanity. Interestingly, he emphasized selfless social service as the key to raising consciousness. As the Proutists in many countries are demonstrating, service work mobilizes communities, empowers people and is a catalyst for social change.

Sadvipra Governance: The Rule of the Wise[13]

Sarkar indicated that over time the moral standard of reformed democracy would continue to gradually rise towards a higher, ideal form of Prout governance led by sadvipras. As explained in Chapter 8, sadvipras are spiritual leaders who possess moral force, courage and a sacrificing spirit. They are visionaries who have struggled to rise above their class interests, who have no personal ambition, and who cultivate a universal spiritual outlook.

This model of governance reaches back to the tradition of governance by elders. Sarkar points out that whereas human rights, including the right to share the physical, mental and spiritual wealth of the planet, belong to all, "...it does not follow that everybody has the individual right to run the administration of a country. For the good and the welfare of the people in general, it is not fitting to leave the onus of the administration in the hands of all."[14]

This system will emerge gradually and spontaneously from the grassroots as individuals become more inclined to think in terms of their collective welfare. Because a Prout government would invest heavily in Neohumanist education and economic justice, as well as promote media with a socially conscious perspective, a collective spiritual consciousness will gradually spread throughout society, and the general public will develop an ability to recognize and appreciate spiritually elevated leaders.

This in turn will increase the number of spiritually-minded people, so that the electoral college of ethical voters will slowly transform into an electoral college of sadvipras. The minimum requirements for the electoral college of ethical voters in a reformed democracy would eventually grow to include a demonstrated record of social service and moral integrity. Sadvipra governance will emerge from the bottom up, from blocks and socio-economic regions, and not from the top down.

Sarkar proposed that economic democracy should always be decentralized and participatory, so that workers and communities decide their own destiny. This empowerment of all people will continue to spread and strengthen from the grassroots of each community. Yet the most important policy decisions which determine our collective future should be made in a centralized way by wise representatives who have demonstrated their selfless work for universal welfare.

Still a number of checks and balances have been prescribed. The first is term limits, probably five years, after which all sadvipras will have to stand for re-election. Second, sadvipra governance is not a form of individual leadership, but a collective one through boards and sub-boards. Such boards will set policy and select qualified people to administer this policy. Whenever a leader, whether an elected member of a board or one appointed by a board, is found to be unfit for whatever reason, he or she will be replaced by the board. Their collective rule should promote universal well-being.

Sarkar was opposed to theocracy in which religious leaders govern a state. First, many religious leaders are dogmatic, believing, for example, that they and their followers are going to heaven while everyone else will go to hell. Sadvipras, on the other hand, must have a universal outlook and be magnanimous, treating all as sisters and brothers in one human family. Second, Sarkar insisted that any system of governance that goes against human psychology or human welfare cannot last. So the acceptance of sadvipra governance will rest with the people, and sadvipras will always remain accountable to the masses of people whom they lead.

According to Prout, there are three kinds of potential in the universe: physical, intellectual and spiritual. When harnessed, these become three types of power, and hence three ways to administer a society.

1. *The rule of brute force*: A dictator uses police and military might to instill fear in the people to obey, and rewards with wealth and power those who serve the dictator's ends, which are self-interest and the amassment of power.

2. *The rule of reason*: A strong mind is more powerful than brute force. An intelligent leader detects the weaknesses in an adversary's argument, formulates a convincing counter argument and presents very clear views. Success in debate, however, does not necessarily mean the leader is not motivated by self-interest and ambition, and hence should not be the deciding factor in choosing a leader. When such leaders lose power, their reputation often falls, too.

3. *Spiritual leadership*: Spiritual strength, such as intuition, wisdom, compassion and unconditional love, is more powerful than intellect. Sadvipras use all three types of power, but their physical strength is always controlled by their strong mind, and their mind is always focused towards connectedness, compassion, altruism and a higher purpose. To

them, no one is high and no one is low. This means that sadvipras will always be stronger than normal politicians or others with self-interest. Even an uneducated person who is spiritually wise and humble and truly motivated for the welfare of all can become great and inspire millions.

Transformative Strategies and the Futures of the Prout Movement[15]

By Dr. Sohail Inayatullah

For more than 30 years, Sohail Inayatullah from Pakistan has been writing on P.R. Sarkar and Prout. A political scientist, he is a professor at Tamkang University, Taiwan and at the University of the Sunshine Coast, Australia. In 1990, he completed his PhD on the intellectual contributions of P.R. Sarkar. The doctorate led to a series of books on Sarkar including: Understanding Sarkar, Situating Sarkar, Transcending Boundaries *and* Neohumanist Educational Futures. *His encyclopedia entries on Sarkar include contributions to the* Routledge Encyclopedia of Philosophy, *the* Oxford Encyclopedia of Peace *and the* UNESCO Encyclopedia of Life Support Systems.

Understanding the futures of any movement is by definition problematic. The future, for one, does not yet exist (except from perhaps an absolute spiritual perspective wherein past, present and future exist simultaneously). Yet it is possible to identify certain patterns within all movements. Charles Paprocki has analyzed the rise and fall of social movements based on Sarkar's Wave Theory. He argues that new movements appear once old movements (cosmologies, ideologies and the institutions that support them) cannot sustain legitimacy. The old movement dies because of its own internal contradictions; that is, its inability to maintain agreement or belief. By providing a more coherent analysis and explanation of reality, the new movement challenges the past and, if it is successful, becomes the new thesis.[16]

Worldview/Paradigm Change

Thomas Kuhn has echoed this approach in his classic, *The Structure of Scientific Revolutions.*[17] However, he adds a demographic dimension.

Knowledge revolutions occur when a particular age-cohort retires or dies off, thus allowing a new batch of scientists with different assumptions of reality to gain hegemony. What is studied, what is considered the norm, then shifts.

Leading educationist Richard Slaughter sees this through the lenses of the "Transformative Cycle." In phase one of this cycle, traditional meanings break down and are referred to as problems. In phase two, new ideas emerge that reconceptualize or renew meanings. In phase three, there is conflict between the new and old meanings. Out of this conflict, a few proposals, new ideas, and new movements gain legitimization. This is the fourth phase. These new ideas then become the paradigm through which we view the world.[18]

Prout asserts that we are at a transition from an old paradigm to a new one. Recent intellectual history has attempted to explain the world from the position of mechanistic Newtonian physics and materialistic liberal capitalism. While the world has numerous specific problems, many of these are a result of the larger paradigms that we use to explain empirical reality. For example, the breakdown of the family, crime, desertification, global warming, and the global financial crisis appear to be unrelated problems, a litany of unconnected events and trends. But, in fact, they are outcomes of a materialistic worldview that places the individual first and society second, that disowns nature as it focuses solely on technological progress. Moreover, social divisions are blamed on the individual and the family instead of the inequitable structure of the economy. This worldview is also short-term oriented, mortgaging the future for present gains.

Emerging Issues

Many of the ideas of Sarkar and the Prout movement can be considered as emerging issues.[19] Emerging issues are at the bottom of the s-curve of events. They have a small following, their frequency of mention in journal articles is low and the issues are not considered urgent for world leaders to attend to. Over time, some of these issues become trends–there is more and more data to confirm their reality and importance and eventually a few become global problems. At this stage, the window of opportunity to make foundational or deep changes has decreased since the issue has now become politicized via the tar-pit of party politics. It is earlier, in the emerging issues phase, where transformative possibilities abound.

Emerging Issues Analysis

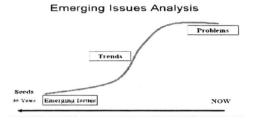

From a Proutist viewpoint, many of Sarkar's ideas–vegetarianism, the rights of animals and plants, meditation as part of daily practice, world government, the theory of microvita, cooperatives as a model for a national economy–will move up the s-curve eventually moving from fantasy to reality.

In this sense, the Prout movement may be at the same stage in many parts of the world as the ecological movement was a generation ago. From Rachel Carson's *Silent Spring* to Earth Day to electoral victories in a few nations to Al Gore's Nobel Peace Prize for his documentary "An Inconvenient Truth", environmentalism has become normalized. Seen with this perspective, Prout and its core ideas is an emerging intellectual force. Like the ecological movement, its ideas are likely to become quickly popular. It will then possibly become a trend and eventually a movement that will have to be grappled with by academia, civil society, business and government.

At present, in any discussion of the future of humanity, the Green alternative is always brought up. In the near future, through publications, movements and social service, Prout too may be in that position. Once Sarkar's movement enters the mainstream press, it will challenge old movements. Then there will be a debate for legitimacy. Proutists, like the Greens, or the socialists of the past, will argue that their image of the world and future is more compelling, elegant and realizable in the real world of material and emotional suffering. At this stage, the strength of Prout will be tested. Can it provide a new paradigm surpassing liberal capitalism or environmentalism? Can its image of the world provide new meaning to individuals?

Alternative Futures

Several alternative futures are possible.

First, Prout succeeds because it meets foundational needs for survival, growth, identity and purpose. Like other successful social and economic movements, Prout and its core ideas becomes the dominant framework. This occurs because (1) through its alternative economic framework (focus on guaranteeing basic needs) issues of survival for the global population are resolved; (2) issues of growth are realized through increased productivity, healthier lifestyle and higher quality of life (work becomes more efficient and meaningful, higher equity leading to stronger and healthier communities and more social and economic integration); (3) issues of identity are resolved as every language and culture is honored even as more and more humans become truly planetary, accepting that as the only way forward (other identity formations–patriarchy, dogmatic religion, and conflicting nation-states–point the way to civilizational collapse); and, (4) issues of purpose and direction are served through Prout's focus on consciousness raising, integrating the spiritual and material, personal growth and collective welfare, nature and technology.

Second, Prout as a movement remains marginal but its ideas succeed. Prout's main contribution is in helping create a new worldview which leads to foundational shifts in survival, growth, identity and purpose. Prout organizations do not become a global political player (for example, a world Prout political party does not eventuate). Another group that has had an impact disproportionate to their small number are the Quakers (Religious Society of Friends), whose total number in the United States is 250,000 or just 0.0008% of the population, yet they have significantly influenced many social justice changes, including the abolition of slavery, educational reform, women's suffrage, the civil rights movement, penal reform, environmental protection and the peace movement.

Third, Prout is unable to play a social or political role and its ideas do not captivate leading thinkers, policy think-tanks and decision-makers. Instead, world capitalism continues moving forward, purchasing and co-opting dissenters every step of the way, and at every bottleneck of accumulation, every world crisis, it adapts. World capitalism appropriates a few slogans and ideas from Prout and other movements, making the capitalist system even stronger and more durable.

Of course Proutist thinkers and activists prefer the first two but not the third. The first assumes a strong hierarchical organizational structure with clear lines of discipline, thus allowing political-institutional success. In the second scenario, it is the replicability of Prout projects that is crucial. Instead of a strong organizational structure, it is the peer-to-peer inspiration and the decentralization of projects and ideas that creates a wave of transformational change.

Finally, which will become reality depends on individual and collective images of the future. What individuals and groups prefer to happen and believe will happen, is likely to happen. Our future reality will also depend on decisions humans will make over the next decades.

Using Prout's theory of the Social Cycle, a change in the system of capitalism, the worldview underneath it (individualism, linear theory

of progress, nature and the Other as externalized) and the deep defining story (greed is good), is likely to occur. Because, whereas capitalism
has been able to adapt and reinvent itself, the current economic crisis
is so overwhelming, impacting almost every issue (global governance,
climate change, terrorism, change in the images of what it means to be
human), that the system is likely to either collapse or transform, with
the continuation of business as usual very unlikely.

To contribute to global transformation, Prout requires a successful
strategy.

Strategic Success

The success of Prout's challenge requires strategy at four levels, moving
from the most visible, the empirical litany to the least visible, the realm
of myths and metaphors.

The first level of change is empirical litany, repeating the daily head-
lines over and over until we see them as official reality. Changing these
measurable indicators means that Prout must offer new measurements
that better reflect its vision of the future. These would measure core areas:

- neohumanism (equal opportunity, no discrimination, rights of nature
  and animals, movement towards a vegetarian society);
- political economy (movement of money, ratio of maximum to minimum income);
- spirituality (seen as not only a legitimate way of organizing society
  but a preferred measurement, the percentage of individuals who
  adopt a spiritual practice);
- coordinated cooperation (between genders, different nationalities,
  workers and management); and,
- governance (a legal contract between political leaders and citizens,
  constitutional guarantees of purchasing power, increased movement
  - conferences, binding treaties, laws - towards regionalism and world
  federalism).

The second level of change is systemic change. Systemic change ensures
that new ideas prosper. Each state creates systems that support its values.
For example, governments can change energy use by choosing to subsidize
alternatives like wind and solar power instead of oil consumption. They
can provide house loans for first-time home owners that require solar
energy to be used to access the grant. For a new system such as Prout
to become the norm, numerous systemic changes are required. First, in
schooling, a space and time for quiet meditation would slowly change
the nature of what students value. Given the relationship between regular

meditation and enhanced IQ as well as decreased illness, we can expect to see productivity gains and decreased health care costs. Second, in economic structure, governments can create legislation that favors the cooperative model instead of the corporatist model. This would allow a flourishing of new types of enterprises. Governments can also promote employee-managed and employee-owned businesses by changing taxation strategy as well as pension-superannuation funding. Third, creating new global organizations and programs to solve problems that states are unable to handle (a global tax on speculation, a world peace insurance scheme to reduce the military costs of nations, a world currency), as well as reform of the United Nations, would enhance federalism.

The third level of change is worldview. We are currently in a transition where the modernist worldview focused on shopping (I shop, therefore I am), the nation-state (my nation is better than yours), patriarchy (rule of the strongest male or nation-state) and externalizing all costs (to nature in particular), is giving way to a new worldview. What this new worldview will be is still up for grabs. Will it be transmodern, that is, going beyond the modern (by including other ways of knowing) but keeping the progressive nature of rights that modernity brought? Will it be postmodern, with new core values allowing all perspectives? Or will it be a return to the fundamentalism of the nation-state or religion? For Prout, not only are new indicators and systemic changes crucial, but so is being part of the debate of creating a new worldview. This debate is not just intellectual but part of our unconscious–essentially how we see the self, others, and the transcendent. Prout views this as essentially a spiritual transition, an awakening of the self linked to a new planetary ethical framework. Currently, the emerging image is ahead of current reality (which is still defined by the narrow boundaries of nation-statism and economic short-termism). Many individuals believe that a new spiritual future is possible but they are unable to reconcile the desired future with the often brutal realities of the present. However, more and more there is evidence that current reality itself is undergoing a transition.[20]

The final level of change is the mythic and metaphorical. This is about reframing issues at the deepest level. Instead of debating which system is truer or better, this is telling a new compelling story about what it means to be human. Sarkar offers the analogy of humanity being on a journey together, moving forward like a family and ensuring no one falls behind. This is very different from the modern capitalist story of technological progress and survival of the fittest. For Prout, the new story includes the worldview of evolution that is not only about physical survival, but also an intellectual struggle, a battle of memes, and, most importantly, with a spiritual direction. Life is more than just the economy or society, it is about individually and collectively moving towards ananda, bliss.

As Joseph Campbell said, "Follow your bliss."[21] Prout offers this new mythology as well as a practical way to achieve it. But ultimately this is not a path to bliss - Prout *is* the path, bliss *is* the path.

The way will certainly be very difficult and full of struggles, as Sarkar often reminded us. Humans can always quit, choosing the easier downhill path that moves away from our bliss. For this reason, it is crucial to imagine and feel that the future has already arrived, it is not distant, we are living it today.

As Sarkar said, "Even a half-hour before your success, you will not know it."

Chapter 12

A Call to Action: Strategies for Implementing Prout

Despite its advent onto this earth many thousands of years ago, humanity is not yet capable of building a well-integrated and universal human society. This is in no way indicative of the glory of human intellect and erudition. You, who have understood the predicament, realized the urgency, seen the naked dance of evil and heard the hypocritical and raucous laughter of the divisive forces, should throw yourself into this noble task without further delay. When the ends are just and noble, success is inevitable.[1]

— P. R. Sarkar

The purpose of economic democracy and the Prout movement is to construct a society for "the welfare of all." This includes all those who have traditionally been abandoned by the present exploitative system, including women, minorities, indigenous peoples, laborers, the unemployed, the landless, the homeless, the uneducated, prisoners and those without legal documents.

To change a society is difficult. To create a total transformation benefiting all humanity as well as the planet, requires much more effort. However, the greatest things are achieved with great effort and struggle.

Once in 1990, Sarkar informally told a small group of people, "Prout will not be established by mantra, muscle, sword, bloodshed or military might. It will be established by the efforts of many intellectuals and spiritualists." He went on to say that it was their duty to inform everyone about Prout, and that in time the intellectuals and spiritualists would make it happen.[2]

"Another World is Possible!"

In 2001, the first World Social Forum was organized in Porto Alegre, Brazil, in opposition to the World Economic Forum of the rich nations held in Davos, Switzerland, at the same time. The forums have been growing exponentially: more than 100,000 people representing 6,000 different organizations from more than 150 countries have participated in most of the subsequent World Social Forums.[3] The power of these events is the shared dream: that it is possible to construct another world with justice for all.

The same dream–that we can change the world–filled Occupy Wall Street in September 2011, which spontaneously blossomed in more than a thousand places and forms of the Occupy Movement, with its open general assemblies, participatory decision making, and community building.

Whenever I give public talks about Prout, I usually begin by saying, "The slogan, 'Another world is possible' invites the question, 'What kind of world do we want?' So I would like to begin by asking each person to say just one sentence expressing one aspect of the kind of world you would like to see." If there are more than 40 people, then I just invite people to call out responses at random. Afterwards I say, "Responses from groups around the world are invariably the same: a world without wars, without hunger and poverty, with human rights, democracy, environmental protection, in other words, peace and justice on earth! Now I would like to present an alternative model that I believe can achieve peace and justice on earth...."

Awareness is a key factor in social change. Whenever exploitation occurs, it is the moral duty of good people to raise the consciousness of everyone about it. At the same time, practical alternatives such as economic democracy and Prout need to be publicized. Many economists believe that the world capitalist system suffers from fundamental flaws, that it is dangerously unstable and volatile because all financial markets are hopelessly interdependent. When capitalism collapses, every country will desperately seek alternatives to survive.

Prout's principles are being tested and developed each day in different countries. Significant policies have been elaborated about many aspects of society including the economy, regional development, health care, education, the arts, the media, the environment, social justice, agriculture, the judicial system, the political system and more. Taken together they offer the world the basis for an alternative society.

Be a Spokesperson for Prout

To talk to people about Prout and the relationship between the social and the personal, you should first be able to briefly explain what it is. This type of brief explanation is sometimes called an "elevator speech" because it lasts no more than 90 seconds, the time it might take to ride an elevator. Try out your simple explanation on friends, family and strangers.

The best part of doing this is the questions you receive, because they teach you what you need to improve in your presentation. You learn more with every question about Prout you try to answer. Don't be afraid about questions you cannot answer–nobody knows everything. Once Sarkar smilingly advised a group of Proutists that if they were asked a question when giving a public talk and they didn't know the answer, they could say, "That's a very good question! But it will take some time to answer it. Come back tomorrow and I'll reply." Then, he said, they would have 24 hours to study or ask someone until they found out what the right answer was!

If you go to a talk on a social or economic subject, or you meet an important person, these are good opportunities to ask a question about Prout. A question such as: "The Progressive Utilization Theory or Prout is a socio-economic model that supports regional economic self-reliance, cooperatives and an ecological and spiritual perspective. Do you think that economic democracy, based on a local economy with cooperatives, could provide jobs for everyone?"

Learning more about Prout is essential to becoming better qualified to teach it. Appendix A includes discussion questions for a group that wants to use this book as a resource, and Appendices B and C explain how to design an exciting Prout Study/Action Circle.

The Electronic Edition of the Works of P. R. Sarkar (Version 7.5) CD contains all his books originally in English or translated into English as of 2009: 1272 articles from 138 books, all in the latest editions. With an excellent Search Engine and tools for locating and displaying text, it is an ideal tool for writers, translators, teachers and those who wish to study the philosophy of P.R. Sarkar.[4]

The Prout College online course from Australia is also an excellent resource for higher studies of Prout. It is designed as a one-year postgraduate diploma course. Anyone can take it, but the course load of readings and written essays that are required are at a postgraduate level and require a fair amount of self-discipline to keep up. The eight subjects are:

1. Introduction to Prout Studies
2. Tantra, Spirituality and Social Change
3. Macrohistory and World Futures
4. Transformative Economics
5. Neohumanism, Policy Making and Contemporary Issues
6. Frontiers of Science
7. Gender, Spirituality and Coordinated Cooperation
8. Education for Liberation

Learn more at www.proutcollege.org.

Silent meditation is at the spiritual base of Prout and a powerful tool for generating hope both individually and collectively. Meditation gradually transforms people, making them courageous and instilling in them a fighting spirit. It infuses awareness of one's infinite potential, of the divine force that is always with us. It fills one with a sense of purpose and a mystical connection with the highest assets of humanity. Proutists teach meditation free of charge and encourage activists to practice it for their personal spiritual growth. Personal daily self-analysis is also invaluable for realizing and overcoming our defects as much as possible.

Inform the Public

An important goal of Prout work is to inform the public that a socio-economic alternative to capitalism exists, and that it is called Prout. Marketing consultants and political candidates call this "name recognition"–blitzing the message out until everyone is familiar with the name and knows what it means.

The most powerful means to do this is through the media: TV, radio, newspapers, and magazines. Of course, nearly all large communication systems are owned and controlled by profit-making corporations–for the most part they avoid airing material critical of the capitalist system.

Still, the media will sometimes broadcast or publish progressive messages if offered interesting interviews or press releases about radical events. There are also thousands of smaller newspapers, magazines, radio and even TV stations that are not owned by large corporations, most often in areas of lesser population, and they are usually more accessible and open to new ideas.

Another interesting way to get the large newspapers and magazines to publish the ideas of Prout is in one of the most widely read sections, the letters to the editor. Many readers can be reached by a short message explaining how a key concept of Prout could solve a current problem.

A different way to inform the public about Prout is by putting up posters in the area. For example, before a symposium at the State University of Rio de Janeiro in 1998, the organizers printed 500 full color posters that read, "Searching for Solutions to the Global Crisis: The Progressive Utilization Theory". Whereas 300 people attended the program, tens of thousands of people saw the inspiring posters that hung in all the metro stations, universities and the downtown area. During election campaigns in India, Proutist candidates have put up thousands of posters detailing their radical platform, such as regional autonomy (samaja) informing the public about Prout's proposals.

Popular cultural expressions create a very positive impact. Street theater, giant puppets, songs and dance are all powerful media to convey new concepts to many people in a beautiful and unforgettable way. Kevin Danaher notes that the young people from all countries who are protesting against global capitalism, "have redefined the term political party, to mean a real party, with giant puppets, drum circles, chanting and dancing!"[5]

Key Thinkers and Moralists

Another goal of Prout work is to persuade intellectuals, students and others that Prout is viable. This process takes more time, because it involves explaining the principles and responding to questions and doubts.

P. R. Sarkar advised Proutists to "unite the moralists". By moralist, he meant not only honest people, but all those who fight against injustice. Such "moralists" are often leaders and activists in non-governmental organizations (NGOs) and social movements. They work long hours for little or no pay to feed the poor, fight for human rights, protect the environment or expose corruption. Most NGOs are highly participatory, and most of their leaders would agree that a new moral discourse is needed to create a brighter future.

Opening up a dialogue with NGO leaders and other activists is a vital strategy for success. It is a process of mutual learning. By joining progressive coalitions such as the Occupy Movement or the World Social Forum, we can share resources and unite around common causes. Every Proutist should become an active participant in this global exchange of ideas by joining at least one other progressive coalition or organization.

Prout lectures, debates and symposiums should be organized in every city and town. Newsletters, magazines, newspapers and leaflets are important, as are more comprehensive books and study guides. These materials can be distributed at tables and exhibits set up at universities and at progressive conferences. Prout materials can also be personally presented to community leaders, writers and thinkers by making appointments and sharing ideas with them.

Organizing progressive conferences is an excellent way to share Prout. Prout conferences in Kolkata, India (annually),[6] Caracas, Venezuela ("Economic Solidarity" 2011),[7] Lisbon, Portugal ("(R)evolution Portugal" March 2012)[8] and Madison, Wisconsin, USA ("Economic Democracy" October 2012)[9] have united many organizations and forward-looking thinkers around key themes on a common platform.

"Thought Exhibition" is a term that Sarkar used to describe a series of posters with ideas and graphics that explain Prout. One can think of it like an art gallery or museum, in which visitors wander freely to view both the illustrations and learn new concepts. The simplest way to do this is by pasting two or three paragraphs of text in large font on poster board, and cutting out photographs from magazines to illustrate the ideas. If you cover it with transparent plastic, the posters will last longer for future events. If they are attractive, many people will stop to look and read them when they are hung on walls at a university or a progressive conference. Often I have observed up to three times more people studying a Prout Thought Exhibition outside an auditorium than the number of people who actually entered to listen to a Prout talk.

Before the 2011 Prout conference in Caracas, Venezuela, Spencer Bailey and Darlin Pino digitally prepared a Thought Exhibition of 10 large banners with clear text, images and colorful designs to illustrate the following subjects: Introduction to Prout, Prout's Economic Democracy, Prout

Cooperatives, Prout and Ecology, Neohumanism, Spiritual Practices of Prout, Prabhat Ranjan Sarkar, the Prout Research Institute of Venezuela, the Centro Madre Master Unit, and the Neohumanist Kindergarten. These can be downloaded in English, Spanish, Portuguese or French from www.priven.org/publications/.

Internet resources such as the Prout web pages (for example www.proutglobe.org and www.proutwomen.org) with links to other progressive web pages are vital tools to reach the growing number of people with computer access. Electronic mailing lists in various languages and regions that discuss Prout ideas and programs should also be developed and expanded. Italy,[10] Argentina,[11] Portugal[12] and Germany[13] are a few countries with developed Prout web pages in their own languages. Social media blogs, Facebook, Twitter, etc. are also very powerful communication tools. The scope of the Internet to reach people is extraordinary and constantly growing.

Dedicated Activists

> Our world needs a great change in order to move forward and progress. A new order, a new wave, will have to take the place of the old to remedy all the physical, social, intellectual and spiritual ills of the world. As the vanguard of this new movement, the youth are indispensable. It is the youth, and the youth only, who have the vigor to bring about the necessary change. It is the youth who have the resilience to change and adapt and implement the vision of a new society.[14] P.R. Sarkar

The vital energy, enthusiasm and idealism of young people must be harnessed to change the world. The fact that many of the thousands attending the World Social Forum and participating in the Occupy movements are young is reason to believe that another world is not only possible, it is inevitable.

At the same time many young people have been fooled into believing that they are powerless in the face of the all-mighty steamroller of global capitalism. Disillusioned, with little hope of finding meaningful and rewarding work, and with a poor sense of self-esteem, many become cynical and nihilistic, escaping reality through entertainment, drugs and sex.

The hope and confidence of young people must be restored. They should also be shown how to struggle for justice.

Proutist Universal encourages young people to dedicate their lives as full-time activists and offers a wide range of opportunities for this. Training in character development, spiritual practices, the social reality and Prout's practical alternatives is available in many countries.

An organization's strength depends not on its financial resources, but on the dedication, training, diversity and adaptability of its cadres. Regular communication between activists is essential for education, inspiration and constructive feedback. Finally, one of the most essential ways to inspire activists is by encouraging their creativity and personal expressions in their work and struggle.

Leadership cannot be imposed from above. True leaders must have the qualities of dedication, sincerity, ideological zeal, fighting spirit and all-round capacity. They are not born with these qualities, rather they gradually acquire them–step by step. They need to develop a foundation of integrity and unity with the oppressed. This means that their integrity must be impeccable; they must work in solidarity with the exploited people.

Organizing Marginalized Farmers

The rural Bilaspur District in Chhattisgarh, India had been torn apart by communal violence, forced religious conversions and human trafficking. With limited water sources and poor crops, most young people migrated away for jobs. There was huge mistrust among the different communities due to unequal land distribution and ownership of resources. Alcoholism and domestic strife were common.

Pradeep Sharma and 15 young Proutists started meetings in different villages, listening to the problems of the people. Then they invited all the different groups to meet; together they resolved to construct an earthen check dam with volunteer labor. With local materials and indigenous techniques, they created a reservoir of six million liters of water which irrigated 43 hectares. This has raised the underground water table as well.

Several agricultural cooperatives were also formed that shared the income generated so that both landowners and landless farmers benefited from their contributions. This was all accomplished without any outside funding or donation, greatly raising the spirits of the people.

Next Pradeep started an organic farming technique that is very successful and which is now implemented in more than 100 villages of the district. First the men of the village dug an *Akshay Chakra*, which means a non-depleting energy center, a large hole that is two meters deep, two meters wide and two meters long, with canals and branching canals leading away from it in all directions. Then the men filled it with a mixture of cow dung, cow urine and rice water, creating a very fertile area of land in which the women intensively plant a wide variety of vegetables. Every day a truck from the cooperative collects the organic harvest and pays each woman the equivalent of about US$4 for the produce, which forms new additional income for thousands of families. Malnutrition among women and children is falling. The purchasing capacity and quality of life of the people is increasing.[15]

In the state of Odisha, India, Kanhu Behura has built a strong organization of many ideological, full-time Prout workers. They have organized agricultural producer and consumer cooperatives with tribal people and very poor farmers. A successful cooperative credit union was also formed. Now they are starting to organize poor miners in another part of the state. They are also working with non-governmental organizations and building a grassroots Proutist political organization that is putting pressure on the government to effect real change.[16]

In Hualien, Taiwan, Proutist Yie-Ru Chiu (Jiivandeva) has organized a local permaculture association based on a weekly salon with featured progressive speakers. The salon is funded by a small organic farmers' market that uses 10 percent of the income to fund projects. In order to publicize the ideas as widely as possible, videos of most of the presentations have been posted on their blog in Chinese. This movement also assists marginalized tribal people, the original inhabitants of the island, to adopt sustainable farming, increasing their income by organizing them into a cooperative. Chiu teaches at the local university, and expresses that he is much happier doing this practical work than the "theoretical" Prout work he did in the past.[17]

Prout Research Institutes

In 1988, Sarkar gave a plan for a Prout Research Institute to be set up in every country to encourage the study and planning of Prout's implementation. Though no physical building or full-time staff was created, extensive studies were done for the Togo government in West

Africa and for the Khabarovsk Krai region of the Russian Far East. Proutists reviewed the economic situations, analyzed the nature and cause of current problems, proposed specific Proutist solutions and recommended political reforms and economic policies to resolve the region's economic difficulties.

Proutists around the world are committed to future consultations for other countries and communities that are interested in pursuing sustainable development for the welfare of all.

An excellent resource is the 72-page manual for PRI staff, *An Introduction to Block Level Planning*. It explains why Prout economic planning always must begin at the local level, working up from the grassroots. There are so many local differences in terms of geography, climate, natural resources, infrastructure, communities and other factors that it is impossible to create just one effective plan for an entire large or medium-sized country. The Block Level Planning Exercise at the end of Chapter 6 and Appendix D are drawn from this source.

The manual clearly shows how to study the actual problems that a particular community is undergoing. Then it explains how to collect economic and social data from existing sources as well as through direct interviews, how to analyze the data, and finally how to formulate a workable development plan.

In this way it is possible to craft practical and realistic proposals that will actually benefit the lives of people and strengthen the community as a whole. Anyone who is seriously interested in local economic development and planning is encouraged to read the manual, which is available free from www.priven.org/publications/.

The bibliography of this book includes a few significant books about Prout, but many more are needed. It is important that people with fresh ideas and experiences write articles or books about how to apply Prout in their areas. The monthly magazine published in Delhi, *Prout: A Journal of Proutistic Views and Neohumanistic Analysis*, is an excellent source of new articles; copies are sent to subscribers around the world.[18] Only by sharing can we learn from each other. Translating Prout books, especially the original works of Sarkar, into the different major languages of the world is also of great importance in making the ideas accessible to all.

The Prout Research Institute of Venezuela

In May 2003, the Spanish edition of my book, *After Capitalism: Prout's Vision for a New World*, was published in Venezuela. A few months later Leopoldo Cook of the national petroleum company of Venezuela (PDVSA) invited Proutist author Dr. Michael Towsey from Australia and myself to come and give a three-day training course called "Proutist Economic Development: Constructing a New Future for Venezuela" to two groups of supervisors. Two years later PDVSA again contracted a team of three Proutists and me to give a series of lectures and workshops.

I returned in 2006 with the first volunteers, and in 2007 the Prout Research Institute of Venezuela was officially registered as a not-for-profit independent foundation.[19] Its mission is: "to empower all people to improve their quality of life and live in a more just society by fostering the development of worker cooperatives, self-reliant communities, environmental protection, universal ethics and spiritual values."[20]

Our goal is to raise consciousness, support cooperatives and promote a balanced economy. We strive to transform lives and strengthen communities for the welfare of all, through research, education and outreach. One of our aims is to make a model institute that can be replicated in every country, and for this reason everything we publish or produce is available for free download from the Resources section of our web site.

We designed a survey of 80 questions to help us to determine how closely Venezuelan cooperatives resemble a "model" cooperative. We then interviewed workers in 50 co-ops in the rural region of Barlovento to diagnose the problems and needs those enterprises have.[21] In 2007, Proutist documentary filmmaker Paul Alister from Australia helped the Institute produce a half-hour documentary called "Another Life is Possible: Cooperatives in Barlovento, Venezuela" about how cooperatives are transforming the lives of common people.[22]

In 2011 the Institute organized a three-day public conference in Caracas, "Building a Solidarity Economy based on Ethics and Ecology." About 300 people came to listen to five morning panels with a total of 21 expert presentations about the solidarity economy, ecology, cooperatives, ethics and community. There were simultaneous workshops each afternoon where participants could interact with and question the speakers. Half of the presenters and facilitators were women, and one-fourth talked about Prout. Afterwards the Institute staff dedicated two months of their time to transcribing all the talks, translating them all to English, and then uploading all the text, audio and video files to our web site. This has allowed our ideas to reach far beyond the auditorium, to thousands of people around the world who have since read, listened to or watched the presentations on the Internet.[23]

The Institute has been given the permanent use of a large, beautiful house in Caracas with lovely gardens. About ten people normally live here, half Venezuelans and half from other parts of the world. The house was renovated to accommodate up to 40 visitors at a time, and we serve delicious vegetarian meals.

The Prout Research Institute of Venezuela supports Centro Madre, a sister Master Unit project in San José de Barlovento, a two-hour drive east of Caracas. This community project was founded in 2000 by Didi Ananda Sadhana to encourage self-sufficiency through education, sustainable agriculture, integrated development and ethical leadership. Centro Madre is located on three and a half hectares of land. Three times the project has received an evaluation of excellence from CIARA, the government institute of agriculture, certifying it as a national model for small-scale sustainable agriculture. Over 100 visitors are coming to Centro Madre each month, mostly agricultural students and professors and local farmers, to see and learn how so much food can be grown intensively on such a small plot of land. Centro Madre reading program volunteers lend children's books each week to families in the villages to read together, and also create programs in schools.[24]

Both the Institute and Centro Madre need volunteers who are flexible, self-motivated and ready to work 40 hours a week as positive team members in a collaborative environment. We seek individuals of all ages and ethnicities with enthusiasm and an open mind, to grow, learn and experience the beauty and challenges of Venezuela.

The Prout Institute (Eugene, Oregon, USA)

In Eugene, Oregon, USA, the Prout Institute organizes research, policy and education initiatives. In 2002, construction of a physical campus was begun. Known as *Dharmalaya* ('abode of dharma'), it has become a model of sustainable living practices. Its features include rainwater catchment, organic gardening, permaculture landscaping, photovoltaic electricity, a solar hot water system, greywater-constructed wetlands, a barrel oven, composting, and straw bale and cob natural building practices. The mission of Dharmalaya is to promote *dharma* (the path of spirituality and righteousness) holistically in personal, social, and ecological spheres of life.

The President of the Prout Institute's Board of Directors is Jason Schreiner, who has also served as an adjunct instructor in environmental studies at the University of Oregon. The founder and Executive Director is Ravi Logan, who has written and lectured on Prout extensively since 1974.

An increasing focus of the Institute is offering trainings in personal development and in solution-oriented design that presently include: Dharma Training, Urban Permaculture Design Course, Prout Summer Academy, Prout Design Practicum, and Prout Institute Yoga Life Training. Intern positions are often available, college service learning and practicum opportunities can be accommodated, and hostel-type accommodations are available for visitors.[25]

Model Cooperatives and Service Projects

Cooperatives contribute to social change through the valuable process of education and consciousness raising. One of the requirements for the success of a cooperative is its popular acceptance by the surrounding community. Every cooperative helps to educate both its own members and the public at large about cooperative principles.

All Proutists should carry out social service, and in this way connect with the common people, experiencing their hardships firsthand. Serving the dispossessed is an unforgettable experience that fundamentally changes one. P.R. Sarkar, in his children's book, *The Golden Lotus and the Blue Sea*, describes this process, telling how the hero was deeply touched by the misery he saw: "The beautiful eyes of the prince were deprived of sleep that night. He was thinking continuously, 'If I cannot free humanity from such meanness, what is the use of my education, my intellect? My coming to this earth as a human being bears no value.'"[26]

Hence cooperatives, Neohumanist schools, children's homes, and feeding programs are invaluable projects to link Proutists with the common people. These projects begin the crucial process of people working together. Such collaborative efforts will take on great importance when the global economy shifts. At that point, people's attention will focus on finding practical alternatives to the status quo.

How to Introduce Prout in a Community Service Project

Volunteers can turn local social service projects into educational centers for Prout and models of Prout in practice. Here are some ideas:

Cultivate leaders: Search for moral leaders in the community, and ask them collectively to set priorities and plan the project. Offer training courses and mentor young leaders, by giving them increasing responsibility as they become empowered. Ideally, they can take over your role.

Teach ethics: Post the ethical principles of Prout (Yama and Niyama), so that volunteers and visitors can see them. Also post moral dilemmas that your community faces and schedule a discussion to talk about them. In small groups, develop a collective answer to a question, explaining your reasons. Here are some sample questions relevant for Venezuela. Readers will understand that while the questions appear simple, they are designed to elicit complex moral thinking:

Is it all right to kill people?
Is it all right to kill animals?
Is it all right to fight for social justice?
Is it all right, if someone does wrong to you, to get revenge?
Is it all right to lie to avoid personal problems?
Is it all right to lie if it will help someone else?
Is it all right to criticize someone when they are not present?
Is it all right to cheat in school?
Is it all right to cheat on your spouse?
Is it all right to accept a bribe?
Is it all right to give a bribe?
Is it all right to accept a gift if it was stolen?
Is it all right to make as much money as you can?
Is it all right to spend a lot of money to throw a big party?
Is it all right to watch pornography?

Form a board of directors for the project: Invite community representatives to meet regularly to collectively decide the future of the project. Ideally these representatives should be elected by the community.

Form an income-generating cooperative: Find a product or service needed by the community and form a cooperative to provide it. The goal is to make your project self-reliant, increase the purchasing capacity of the local people and reinvest earnings in the community. Cooperatives make the workers and members more independent.

Make your project replicable: As much as possible, learn from other projects and NGOs in the region. Write down the story of how your project started and explain how others could start a similar project. Include the mistakes you made and how to avoid them. Share your knowledge on the Internet. Offer free consultation to those who want to start a similar project elsewhere.

Make your project environmentally sustainable: Grow your own food. Reduce, reuse and recycle as much as possible. Post signs to educate visitors about your garden, your compost, and your recycling. Use posters to raise consciousness about avoiding pollution.

Teach Prout: Form a Prout Study/Action Circle. Schedule monthly Prout talks. Hang banners at your project center explaining what Prout is. Choose Prout topics and language that are appropriate for the people of your area.

Promote holistic health: Grow and educate others about medicinal plants. Teach hygiene. Promote a vegetarian diet. Share the benefits of yoga with others.

Inspire the staff to commit to personal growth: Every human being has some negative tendencies, emotional blocks and conflicts with others. Dedicate time to exploring and sharing these interpersonal obstacles individually and collectively. Invite qualified therapists to facilitate this process.

Teach spirituality: It is very important to be sensitive to the religious sentiments of communities. Promote and demonstrate the spiritual values of Prout. Explain the significance of the *"Baba Nam Kevalam"* universal mantra (which means "Love is all there is"), and why it benefits those who hear it. Make available a list of the benefits of meditation along with a brief explanation of how to meditate.

A Popular Youth Movement in Hungary

After finishing a one-year internship at the Prout Research Institute of Venezuela, Istvánffy András and Szakmáry Donát returned to Hungary in 2007 with a determination to change the Hungarian approach to politics and public life. Like the other former Eastern-bloc countries, 20 years had passed since the collapse of the Communist regime. Economically the region had become a dumping ground for Western consumer products and a cheap pool of well-qualified labor. There was little consciousness about democracy; consumer rights and public affairs campaigns were in their infancy; there was silence on serious issues; and most of the country's wealth was in private hands. The people either blamed one of the political parties for the country's problems, or remained disillusioned and alienated.

Twice Donát helped lead 3,000 people to form a Peace Symbol with candlelight in the historic Heroes Square,[27] and András participated in a squatter's movement.

Together with other friends, the two started a popular youth movement called the 4K!-Fourth Republic. Its name indicates the need for an alternative to the present Third Hungarian Republic which followed the fall of communism. The movement represents the Y-generation (youth) and focuses on emotions and culture, showing people that mainstream politics is a joke. It offers a powerful feeling of participation when people move together.

Mass games and irony are the popular weapons of the 4K!-Fourth Republic. From 2007 to 2011 they organized 60 events, many of which have drawn more than 500 participants to the streets of downtown Budapest. These include:

Capture the Flag: Following an afternoon mass picnic on the bank of the Danube River, this two-hour game involved lots of running and shouting.[28]

Pillow Fight: Hundreds of people gleefully hitting each other with feather pillows for hours![29]

Water Fight: The only goal was not to leave any shirts dry.[30]

Poster-hacking: Putting funny but honest stickers on the political posters of different candidates, such as, "I'm very good in real estate!" or "Would you trust your money with me?"

Mp3 Flashmob: A 36-minute voice recording with music and funny instructions was downloaded from their website. Several hundred people then gathered in a central mall and a horn signaled everyone to start the playing, dancing and laughing.[31]

These events were fun celebrations that danced on the edge of illegality. Many times the organizers argued with security guards and the police. The group's rebellious character is cool, on the cutting edge of the social and intellectual changes in Hungary. The movement promotes a more cooperative, united and conscious society, and has allowed any player to become an organizer. As the movement grew, it formed branches in the capital and other cities.

A group of young singers and rap artists recorded a music video calling for mass political protests on October 23, 2010, the anniversary of the 1956 Revolution. The lyrics of *Nem tetszik a rendszer* ("I don't like the system") include:

> I don't like it that I'm feeling shittier and shittier in my country.
> I don't like it that all my friends and relatives are about to leave this place.
> I don't like it that no one is feeling whole and everyone is scared.
> I don't like it that the poor pay for everything.
> I don't like it, I really don't, that autumn leaves start to fall.
> I don't like it that my degree is worth nothing at all.
> I don't like it that every single day is gloomy, not just Sundays.
> I don't like it that they make stupid mistakes in my name.
> I don't like, I don't like, I don't like the system.
> I don't like, I don't like, I don't like the whole thing.
> I like it when everyone does what they are supposed to do.
> I like it when everyone takes their own responsibility.
> I like it when politicians don't blame others for their own mistakes.
> I like it when they give us a chance to make a living.
> I like it when there is hope, there is intention and we act.
> I like it when no one takes to the streets, cos' there's no need.
> I like it when I enjoy life with all of you.
> I like it when we leave all our fears behind.[32]

More than 30,000 people showed up for the protest at which András announced 4K!-Fourth Republic was going to transform into a political party.[33]

Then began a slow and deliberative six-month consultation process on the Internet by all members who wanted to decide its future. Hundreds of proposals were received and considered. The result? The 4K!-Fourth Republic Mission supports social justice, equality and self-determination. The party is patriotic and leftist, representing working people and protective of the local economy so that young people and professionals will no longer have to move to Western Europe to find work.

Finally on April 28, 2012, the first congress of the 4K!-Fourth Republic Movement was held and legal registration as a political party began. Now the party is preparing for the parliamentary elections in 2014.

Discussions have started with the new alternative party and the main opposition party, and the Hungarian media has given tremendous coverage to this.[34]

Mass Movements

All popular movements are rooted in a sentiment, because an emotional appeal is always stronger than logic. Negative sentiments, such as those directed against another race, nation or class, divide humanity and eventually cause great suffering. Instead, leaders should arouse positive sentiments based on the cultural legacy of the people. The spirit of the people can be rallied against exploitation, against immorality, and in support of their traditional cultural identity. This is the way to generate a positive revolution. Though regional in approach, these strong, positive sentiments can unite society and elevate humanity.

Proutists should start and cooperate with other movements against specific issues of exploitation. By organizing a demonstration, march or protest rally, the public can be mobilized. João Pedro Stedile, a dynamic leader of Brazil's Landless People's Movement (MST), says, "Popular rallies are part of the life of the people... The spirit of marches has been present in the entire history of humanity."[35] The effort to create a popular samaja regional mass movement is based on all of these factors.

Good, brief slogans, about 5-12 words each, inspire people and awaken their curiosity about Prout—see Appendix E. A banner three or four meters long of cloth or canvas can be stretched in front of your group. Additional people can hold a high stick with two signs back-to-back with different slogans, so by turning the stick, people in every direction can see your messages. The more signs, the better. Every banner and sign should say in small letters at the bottom, "The Progressive Utilization Theory (Prout)" with the web page, so that those who are nearby can read it.

Invite those who will march to come for a sign-making party. Give them the list of slogans, and invite them to choose the ones they like best or make up their own. Some slogans translate well into other languages. If the signs are large and well made, they will get media coverage and will be seen and read by both the protesters and the public. The same banners and signs can be saved and used again in other demonstrations and rallies in the future.

Whereas the signs and banners of other groups protest against what is wrong (such as war, exploitation and corruption), Prout's messages are mostly positive and inspiring, offering hope to the people.

How can a revolutionary movement hope to succeed against seemingly impossible odds? The powers that be hold tremendous financial and military power. During the dictatorship of President Ferdinand Marcos in the Philippines, people said that he had "the three G's: all the guns, all the gold and all the goons (criminal assassins)." Yet in 1986 the people took to the streets and united against him, and the tactic they called "people power" had to be added to political science textbooks as a successful strategy for social change. Popular citizens' movements have also toppled dictators in Haiti (Duvalier, 1988), all the Communist countries of Eastern Europe, Thailand (Suchinda, 1992), Indonesia (Suharto, 1998), Yugoslavia (Milošević, 2000), the Philippines again (Estrada, 2001), Georgia (Shevardnadze, 2003), Bolivia (Sánchez de Lozada, 2003), Ukraine (Yanukovych, 2004-5), Kyrgyzstan (Akayev, 2005), Tunisia (Ben Ali, 2010), Egypt (Mubarak, 2011) and Yemen (Saleh, 2012).

P. R. Sarkar explained this type of strength when he wrote: "The forces opposed to revolution possess immense military power. In spite of this, the revolutionaries will achieve victory... because moral and spiritual power is infinitely stronger than physical force."[36]

Protests Against Global Capitalism

Prout states unequivocally that the first priority of any economic and political system must be the welfare of all. Any society that allows a human being to suffer for lack of the minimum necessities of life must be changed. Sarkar put it bluntly when he said, "Considering the collective interests of all living beings, it is essential that capitalism be eradicated."[37]

Proutists have actively participated in the growing wave of protests against global capitalism that have taken place in the last two decades around the world, starting in Seattle against the World Trade Organization in 1990, and later against the World Bank, International Monetary Fund, the G8 Summits, Wall Street, etc. In most of the protests, three different tactics take place. First, there is a process of education and consciousness raising. In the weeks leading up to the event, leaflets, posters and community radio interviews inform the city's population of the protests. Lectures and symposiums are organized in universities, high schools, churches and community centers in which experts explain exactly why these institutions are so problematic. There is a great need for debate about future alternatives to capitalism. Every activist and protester is encouraged to learn about global capitalism and to be able to explain to others what are its flaws.

The second common tactic is a legal march and rally. Organizers negotiate with the municipal authorities and police for permission to assemble in a large park and march through selected city streets. The goal is to attract the largest possible numbers from every section of society to emphasize to the world via the media how widespread is the discontent. These are opportunities for Proutists, along with other organizations, to organize a stand and distribute leaflets, posters, books and magazines and display a Thought Exhibition that detail how the Prout model works.

The third tactic is not a legal one. Nonviolent direct action, also known as civil disobedience, is a revolutionary tactic that creates pressure on the powers that be. While global economic institutions make economic and political decisions in an undemocratic manner, protesters occupy common spaces and physically obstruct the global capitalist meetings from taking place. This can be an incredibly powerful action by people who risk arrest because of their beliefs.

Nonviolent direct action puts the financial institutions on the defensive. It forces bank officials to defend their policies to the press.

Lessons from the Protests

These protests are not led by superstars, nor do the activists follow instructions from any one organization. Instead, most of the organizing coalitions are democratic, making decisions by consensus.

The riot gear that police use in front of protesters is intimidating at first sight and their tear gas, pepper spray, water cannons, batons and rubber bullets are all extremely painful.

The organizing committees offer nonviolent training workshops to help prepare new participants in conflict resolution. It is important to remember that the police are not the enemy; we are fighting to change the capitalist system. In every protest we should refrain from verbally or physically abusing the police.

Before the Washington protests against the World Bank and IMF in 2000, members of the Training Subcommittee asked me if I would be willing to lead yoga and meditation sessions at the convergence site. So we chose the first period in the morning and during the evening dinner hour to schedule 90-minute sessions of yoga and meditation for activists. These became popular with up to 50 people attending each session. The activists felt better after yoga stretching, and they loved chanting and meditating in silence. At the end of each session, we each shared why we had come–a common dream to make a better world. Later, during the protests in the streets, many of the participants came up to me and expressed how grateful they were for those calming experiences, and how they felt it had helped them stay centered in the face of potential violence.

Nonviolent direct action radicalizes those who participate. Direct action protests are unforgettable experiences. Those who take part are forever changed. Just as living a radically healthy yoga lifestyle is personally transformative, by engaging in direct action, people become social revolutionaries.

"When Will Hunger, Poverty and War End?"

This is an exercise in futures thinking, as well as a tool to involve participants. It works well even with large numbers of people as an interval during a class or training session about Prout. Before the participants arrive, lay a strip of adhesive masking tape across the floor of the room. (If the room is carpeted, you can use a string instead; the exercise works even with an imaginary line.) Write "Now" at one end, "100+" at the other end, and "50" in the middle. Then write "10," "20," etc. so the tape becomes a timeline between now and 100+ years.

I would then say to the group, "I would like to ask each of you, 'When do you think hunger, poverty and war will end?' I believe none of us *really* knows the answer to that question. However, I believe there is value in considering this question and our beliefs about the possibility to change the world for the better. So I would like each of you to stand near the point of the timeline that represents your guess as to when you think it might happen. When you are all standing where you want to be, on behalf of 'Prout Radio' I will begin asking people where you are standing, meaning when you think it will happen, and why you believe that. Of course every answer is correct, meaning you are expressing your honest opinion."

Then holding either a real microphone or an imaginary one, I start at the far end, 100+ years, and ask the first person in a loud voice so everyone can hear, "Where are you standing, madam, and why?" If there are less than 20 people, I ask everyone their opinion. If there are more than 20, I randomly interview some people at each point, slowly moving my way down the line toward the present.

After finishing, I say, "Next I would like to ask each of you to stand by the point on the timeline when you *want* hunger, poverty and war to end." There will no doubt be some laughter as everyone moves down to "Now." Then I say, "All right, it's good to know we are all in agreement that we want hunger, poverty and war to end a soon as possible. My next question is, 'What could we do to make that beautiful day come sooner?'" Then I call on some of those who raise their hands. To conclude, remind the group that thinking about the future is very valuable, because it helps us understand what we want for the world, what might be possible and what we should do to help create our ideal future.

Hope for the Future

Most NGOs and social movements are focused on a single issue to achieve clear, short-term goals. The Prout movement differs in that it is comprehensive, working for a total transformation of society. In addition, the emphasis on leadership training, holistic lifestyles and encouraging activists to spend an hour or more a day in meditation can be seen as long-term investments in the future.

We live at a moment of great transition. The exploitative system of global capitalism is terminally ill. P. R. Sarkar said that at this time, "Your actions now are equal to a hundred years."[38] Many scientists would concur, because our present industrial economy is altering and endangering the life-support systems of the planet with a speed that was unheard of in the past. A tremendous urgency exists to offer humanity a practical, ecological alternative to reverse our self-destructive course. The survival and security of our future generations are at stake.

It's easy to get frustrated and depressed because although we care about the whole world, our ability to influence it is extremely small. In fact, the only real control we have is over our own actions, words and thoughts. However, the environmental slogan, "Think globally, act locally" has great significance. By keeping a universal perspective for the welfare of our community and all humanity, we realize that if we do something positive wherever we are, we actively contribute to the healing of the planet. In this way, our circle of influence can also expand, because positive examples inspire others to help as well. Many small efforts, when coordinated, resonate, create synergy and achieve concrete results.

The French writer Víctor Hugo wrote, "Nothing is as powerful as an idea whose time has come."[39] Economic democracy, cooperatives, and Prout are ideas whose time has come.

Can we change the world? Of course we can! The anthropologist Margaret Mead said, "Never doubt that a small group of thoughtful, committed citizens can change the world. Indeed, it is the only thing that ever has."[40]

> Now humanity bleeds. The future is dark. So we have come here to do something. I have come here to do something, and you have also come here to do something. My coming is significant, and your coming is not less significant. We have come with a mission; and our lives, singularly and collectively, are a mission. Not missions—ours is a collective mission. Here we all are one. We have come to do something. And that is the causal factor.

> And what will be the effect? The effect will be that the world will realize that humanity is one and indivisible, and no power in heaven or on earth can destroy this glorious humanity. We have come here to save humanity, and we will save humanity.[41]

> — Prabhat Ranjan Sarkar

Chapter 13

A Conversation with Noam Chomsky, February 21, 2012

A video conversation with Noam Chomsky, recorded by the Occupy Wall Street film crew, about:

The Occupy Movement
Economic democracy and cooperatives
Limiting the accumulation of wealth
Consciousness raising
Latin America.[1]

Dada Maheshvarananda: The viral growth of the Occupy Movement, and the public support of it, is testament to the tremendous dissatisfaction with the inequities and abuses of corporate capitalism. The slogan "We are the 99%!" has resonated with many people. What is your view of the potential strength of this type of mass protest and its possibility to effect social change?

Noam Chomsky: The Occupy Movement already has had a number of significant successes. One of them, as you say, is to kind of change the national discourse. These concerns and fears and so on were, of course, prevalent for a long time for perfectly objective reasons, having to do with changes in the socio-economic system in the last 30 or 40 years. But they weren't crystallized very clearly until the Occupy Movement put them forward. And now they are kind of common coin. So the 99 percent and 1 percent, the radical inequality, the farcical character of purchased elections, the corporate shenanigans that led to the current crisis and have been crushing people for a long time, the overseas wars, and so on. That's one major contribution.

The other one is not discussed so much, but I think it's pretty important. This is an extremely atomized society. People are alone. It's a very business-run society. The very explicit goal of the business world is to create a social order in which the basic social unit is you and your television set, in which you're watching ads and going out to purchase commodities. There are tremendous efforts made, that have been going on for a century and a half, to try to induce this kind of consciousness and social order.

In fact if you go back say 150 years, in the early days of the Industrial Revolution, right here in Massachusetts, where it started, there was a very lively press at the time, probably the period of the greatest free press in the United States. All kinds of press—ethnic, labor, etc. And the labor press, which was extremely interesting, lively and participatory, had a great many harsh criticisms of the industrial system that was being imposed and to which people were being driven. One of the core criticisms was what 150 years ago they called the "New Spirit of the Age": "Gain wealth, forgetting all but self," which they considered savage and inhuman and was being driven into their heads. Well, 150 years later they are still trying to drive into people's heads, "Gain wealth, forgetting all but self." Now it's considered kind of an ideal, but it's also intolerable to human beings.

One effect of the Occupy Movement has been simply to spontaneously create small social systems of solidarity, mutual support, cooperation, cooperative kitchens, libraries, health services, general assemblies in which people actually interact and so on. That's something that is very much missing in this society. When we talk about potential, part of the potential would be to first of all maintain those bonds and associations after the tactic has outlived its usefulness. And tactics do outlive their usefulness. After that happens, if what has been learned and internalized can be sustained and extended, that would be very important in itself.

The other dimension is how much can you engage the rest of the so-called 99 percent in these activities, concerns, interactions and so on? That's the next big step that has to be taken.

Dada Maheshvarananda: Many in the Occupy movement have realized that political democracy is controlled by big money. Few, however, have expressed that economic democracy is essential for a truly democratic society. The Progressive Utilization Theory or Prout advocates economic democracy to empower people and communities through cooperative management of most enterprises. Economic democracy requires that the minimum requirements of life must be guaranteed to everyone, and decision-making be decentralized so people have the right to choose how their local economies are run. It is the responsibility of all levels of government to promote policies that achieve full employment. Do you think that economic democracy and local economies could move us forward?

Noam Chomsky: First of all, this is the traditional stand of the Left. So if you go back again 150 years to the same newspapers I was mentioning, one of their demands was that those who work in the mills should own them, and of course manage them. That was the slogan of the Knights of Labor, the huge labor organization that developed in the nineteenth century. European socialism was mostly coming from several branches, but the more Left branches if you like, were essentially the same–committed to workers' councils, community organization, guild socialism in England was the same. This is the traditional thrust of the socialist movement. It is not understood here, because, as I said, this is a very business-run society. You're not allowed to know any of these things. So socialism is some kind of bad word.

Well, that is what happens in a highly controlled society, a highly indoctrinated society. But these are very familiar goals. In fact, you can even go to the leading social philosopher in the United States, who everyone recognizes as John Dewey, who just took this for granted. As he put it, unless every institution in society–industry, farming, communication, media, all of them–unless they are under popular democratic control, with wide participation by the workforce and the community, he said politics will just be the shadow cast over society by big business. That's the alternative.

You can't have meaningful political democracy without functioning economic democracy. I think this is, at some level, understood by working people. It has to be brought to awareness and consciousness, but it's just below the surface.

In fact, things are happening. Some of the most interesting are [the Evergreen] cooperatives in Ohio in the Cleveland area. There are dozens, maybe hundreds of, not huge, but significant enterprises that are worker-owned and less frequently worker-managed. The biggest worker-owned conglomerate is Mondragón in the Basque Country [Spain]. That's worker-owned but not worker-managed industries, banks, schools, communities, a very broad configuration. [See reply from Mondragón Cooperatives.²] And there are various other elements of it here and there. A couple of quite good books have just come out about it, one by Gar Alperovitz, *America Beyond Capitalism*, which is about the worker-owned enterprises that are sprouting around the country. This could go much beyond.

So, for example, a couple years ago, the government effectively nationalized the auto industry. It came pretty close to that. There were a couple choices. One choice, which is the choice that is reflexive in a business-run system, is to reconstitute it, hand it back to the original owners or to people very much like them, and let them pursue very much the course they pursued before. That's one possibility; that was of course the choice undertaken without discussion.

But there was another choice. And if there had been a live, functioning Occupy Movement at the time, it could have put that other choice onto the national agenda. It would have to have been much larger and more organized than it is now. It's been only a few months after all. The other choice was to hand the auto industry over to the workers in the community, and have them own and manage and run it. Have it directed to things that the country needs.

There are, after all, things that we very badly need as a society. One of the most obvious is high speed rail. The United States is off the international spectrum in this respect. It's kind of a scandal. It's economically harmful, socially harmful, humanly harmful, ecologically harmful, and everything that you can think of. It's just ridiculous. And the skilled workforce in what is called the "rust belt" could easily be reconfigured to do that. People like Seymour Melman have been arguing for that for years. It might take some kind of federal aid, but nothing like what was poured into the banks.

To make this even more ironic, at the very time that Obama was reconstituting the auto industry and handing it back to the normal ownership, he was also sending his transportation secretary to Spain to get contracts for high speed rail from the Spanish, who are way more advanced than we are, or the French or the Germans. And here you have this industrial system sitting there, workers wanting to work, communities wanting to have their own lively work-based communities, and the country needing things badly. But they can't be put together.

And we have to go somewhere else, like to Spain to get them to help us out. I mean, that's an incredible condemnation of the semi-functioning system. And that's the kind of thing that an Occupy Movement, when it moves beyond this particular tactic, should be addressing.

Things like that are happening all over the country. There was one right here about two years ago. A small but sophisticated manufacturing enterprise that was pretty successful in one of the Boston suburbs was producing specialized equipment for aircraft, and the multinational that owned it wanted to shut it down. Maybe it wasn't making enough profit for them. The union, UE [United Electrical, Radio and Machine Workers of America], a pretty progressive union, and the workforce offered to buy it and run it themselves with community support. Well, the company wouldn't agree. I suspect they lost money on it. I suspect it was just for class reasons. The idea of worker-owned, worker-managed successful enterprise is not appealing. Whatever the reasons, they closed it down, so now that town doesn't have the industry on which it is partly based. Again, with a live, progressive activist movement that reaches out to many parts of the community, that could have been salvaged. And there are things like that all over.

So yes, it is the right thing to do. It is deeply ingrained in the American tradition, and it's been suppressed by the nature of a highly class-conscious business class which is always, without stop, fighting a bitter class war. They know exactly what they're doing; it is very coordinated and controlled. It's true everywhere, but especially so in the United States. It is usual in this respect; we see many consequences of it.

Dada Maheshvarananda: Let's go on about the one percent. Because the physical resources of the planet are limited, the hoarding wealth or using it for speculation rather than productive investment reduces the opportunities of other people and causes poverty. A fundamental principle of Prout is to limit the accumulation of wealth and create a maximum salary that is tied to the minimum wage, just as all the salaries in all the forms of government of the United States have pay scales that do not exceed ten times between the starting salary and what the highest pay scale is for a president or general or judge. What is your opinion about limiting the accumulation of wealth?

Noam Chomsky: First of all, there are much more far-reaching goals than that. Another traditional ideal of the Left movements has been "from each according to his ability, to each according to his need." And actually that's a pretty popular idea. In 1976, on the 200th anniversary of the Declaration of Independence, there were polls taken, asking people, giving them lists of statements, and they were supposed to judge which ones do you think are in the Constitution? Well, nobody knows what's in the Constitution, so the question they were answering is which ones are obvious truths, so they must be in the Constitution. This one got a considerable majority.

A lot of it has to do with the financialization of the economy. This is a new phenomenon. Of course there's always been finance, financial crashes and so on, but there was a big change in the 1970s. The New Deal had instituted an array of regulations, among which were regulations which essentially determined that banks were banks, that is they were to do what a bank is supposed to do in a state capitalist economy. You can argue that's the wrong kind of economy. I would, for example, and I suppose you would. But in that kind of economy, banks have a function. They're supposed to take unused capital–somebody's bank account–and transmit it to some kind of productive action, like starting a business, or buying a house, or whatever it may be. And they more or less did that. There were no crashes in the 1950s or 60s, the biggest growth period in American history. It was also a period of, by our current standards, very high taxation of the wealthy. Very fast growth, egalitarian growth, no crashes.

That changed in the 70s and accelerated under Reagan with a freeing up of constraints on capital. The currencies that had been more or less regulated, were freed. The other constraints on capital were dropped. So you had a huge explosion of speculative capital that overwhelmed capital markets. By 2007, right before the latest crash, and the next one will come later, financial institutions were at 40 percent of corporate profits. And they weren't helping the economy.

In fact, maybe one of the most respected financial correspondents in the English-speaking world is Martin Wolf of the *Financial Times*. He simply describes these institutions as like larvae that attach to a host and eat it away from the inside. The host that he's talking about is the market system, which of course he approves of, and he says they're just eating it away from the inside, and he cites figures showing how harmful they are. But they do accumulate a lot of capital for a very few hands. That's one of the reasons that led to the pretty sharp concentration of income.

The one percent image is a little misleading because it's really one tenth of one percent where you find the enormous concentration of wealth. You go down below in the one percent and the wealth is not by spectacular standards. So concentrated wealth is in a tiny percentage of society, substantially hedge fund managers, CEOs of multinational corporations. And that translates itself, almost reflexively, into political power.

You also had at the same time, in parallel, the sharp rise in spending for elections. So of course by now it's just totally out of sight, it's right on the front pages. But by the early 80s, it was substantially increasing. That compels the parties to dig into corporate pockets. The media say "unions and corporations," but it's essentially corporations, because that's where the money is. And increasingly financial corporations; they increasingly buy the elections.

They also buy Congress in many ways. For example, I suppose the United States is the only parliamentary system where–and very recently, incidentally–before, a position of influence in Congress, a chair of a committee, used to accrue to seniority and service in some fashion. Now you just have to pay the party. Then you can qualify for the chair. So that drives the rest into the same pockets.

The Republicans stopped pretending to be a political party back 20 years ago. Now they are just totally enthralled with the one-tenth of one percent. One of the reasons why the Republican debates are just a total farce is that in order to mobilize voters, they can't come to voters with their actual policies; nobody would vote for them. So they have to appeal to pretty unpleasant tendencies in the population that have always been there, but are now mobilized, and you get the picture. The world can't believe what they're seeing. But it's a natural result of the fact that the party actually abandoned any pretenses of being a parliamentary party in the normal sense and is just driven into the service of the one fraction of one percent.

The Democrats aren't that far behind. The Democrats are what used to be called moderate Republicans, but they've all been kicked out of the party. In fact, someone like Eisenhower looks like a radical Leftist within the current spectrum, Nixon pretty much on the Left. Even Reagan would be more or less on the Left. Those are changes that have taken place since the 70s and 80s.

Another aspect of this was deregulation which of course led, predictably, to repeated crashes since the Reagan years. And another element was the change in rules of corporate governance. So, for example, by now, in fact for the last 30 years, a CEO can effectively choose the board that grants him salary and stock options. Well, you can predict what's going to happen from that. So now if you compare, say, the United States and Europe, pretty similar societies, the ratio of pay to top management as compared to workers is far higher here than in comparable societies, and not because they are more talented, as maybe David Brooks [of *The New York Times*] will tell you, or because they perform any services–in fact they probably harmed the economy–but just because if you tell people, well, you can pick your own salary. So, yes, that's a big problem. If the United States were to, say, just return to what it was, nothing very utopian, or to be like other industrial societies, it's really not a very good model, certainly not utopian, then this vast chasm between the top remuneration and the workforce would sharply shrink.

But my feeling is that's nowhere near enough. We ought to have as an ideal at least the traditional Left ideal. There's kind of a conception of work that underlies this. There are different conceptions of what work is. This comes right out of the debates during the Enlightenment. One conception is that work is something that you have to be driven to do. You wouldn't do it unless you were forced by starvation. It's something you hate but you have to do because you can't live otherwise. That's basically the capitalist conception of work.

There's another conception that says that work is an ideal of life. Free, creative work under your own control is exactly what any human being would choose if they could. There are places where that ideal is practiced. Like if you walk down the halls here at M.I.T., you'll find people working maybe 80 hours a week. They could make a lot more money in the stock market. But they're doing it because they love it. You have things you like to do. I know carpenters that are the same way. In their spare time, they go out in the shed and make interesting things, that's what they like to do. That's a different conception of work.

Now if under the second conception, basically the Enlightenment conception, there's no reason why pay should relate to the amount of work you do. It has nothing to do with it; you do the work even if you're not being paid. If the work is under your own control, under your own choice, I mean. A kind of graphic Enlightenment image of this by one of the founders of classical liberalism, Wilhelm von Humboldt, was that if an artisan produces a beautiful object on command, we admire what he did but we despise what he is, namely a tool in the hands of others. On the other hand, if he creates it under his own will and choice, out of his own concerns and interests, we admire what he did and who he is.

Actually, Adam Smith said pretty similar things. These are traditional, conservative ideas, if the word conservative has any meaning. But the capitalist conception is quite different: you work only under a lash. Therefore those who allegedly work harder–actually they don't–they should get the multimillion-dollar stock options. These are extremely different conceptions, and they lead to all sorts of different ideas of how a society ought to be organized.

Dada Maheshvarananda: You have written, Noam, "Slavery, the oppression of women and working people, and other severe violations of human rights have been able to endure in part because, in various ways, the values of the oppressors have been internalized by the victims. That is why consciousness raising is often the first step in liberation." What do you think are the most important ways to raise consciousness to free us from the values of the oppressors that are stuck inside us?

Noam Chomsky: I should say, again, I don't take any credit for that view. It's a very old one. David Hume, for example, another one of the founders of classical liberalism and a great philosopher, wrote on the foundations of government. He said the first principle of government that strikes him as he looks at history, he was also an historian, is that he is struck by the easiness with which the governed accept the rule of the governors. He says this is paradoxical, because power is in the hands of the governed; power is not in the hands of the rulers. So how is this miracle maintained? He says it's by control of opinion. If the governors can control opinion and attitude, can impose what later was called false consciousness, as you were describing, then they can rule. But if you can break that, then they're gone; they can't stand up against the governed.

So how do you break it? Well, all the ways we know. Take slavery. I mean, there was never a peaceful period of slavery; there were always slave revolts. The slave families found their own ways of constructing islands of freedom within the sadistic society they were part of. Occasionally these led to actual major revolts which were violently crushed. Finally it led, after far too long of course, to abolitionism and formal elimination of slavery. Though we should note, formal. Because in fact in many ways, it still remains. The Civil War technically, with the Constitutional amendments did in fact end slavery, but it was reconstituted about ten years later by the criminalization of black life, in a

North-South Compact. We're going through something like that now; look at the incarceration rate.

Take women's rights. That of course also goes far back. But it didn't really become a substantial movement until the 1970s. There were germs of it in the 60s activism, but the way it began was small consciousness raising groups. Groups of women talking to each other and trying to break through the general assumption that this is the way it has to be. There are no choices; women are supposed to be property. In fact, if you look at American law, women remained essentially property until well into the 1970s. I mean there was no guaranteed legal right for women to serve on juries until about 1975 with a Supreme Court judgment. It developed mostly among women. There was a big crisis inside the activist movement in the sixties, incidentally, when young men who were doing courageous things, like resistance [to military service], had to somehow face the fact that they, too, were oppressors. It was difficult; it led to suicide in some cases. It's a hard thing to deal with. But slowly it spread through much of the society, and now a lot of it is just taken for granted. Not everywhere, not to [presidential candidate] Rick Santorum, but quite broadly. And that's the way things change, with workers' rights and everything else. It's no magic. We know how to do it; it's just a matter of doing it.

Dada Maheshvarananda: I live in Venezuela. Do you have any message for the people of Latin America and the Caribbean who are trying to free themselves from domination by the United States?

Noam Chomsky: What's happened in the last decade south of the border is pretty spectacular. I mean it's of real historic importance. Think over history, for 500 years, Latin America was overwhelmingly dominated internationally by imperial powers, in more recent times by the United States. Internally there's a reflection of that. The typical Latin American society had a small, super wealthy elite, a "one percent" if you like, mostly Europeanized, often white. They concentrated the wealth of the society in the midst of tremendous misery and oppression in pretty rich societies, societies that should be quite wealthy. The ruling elites were Western-oriented. Their capital flowed to the West; they didn't invest at home. They imported luxury goods; their children went to colleges in Europe and the United States; they had second homes on the Riviera, that kind of thing. Basically a European and United States, a Western implant inside their own societies, ruling it very brutally. The countries were separated from one another; they scarcely even had roads connecting each other. They were just oriented to the West and the U.S.

Well, that's changed in the last ten years. This half a millennium pattern is changing, radically. The countries are beginning to integrate, a prerequisite for independence. They're beginning to face some of their internal problems, which are very severe, doing it in different ways in different countries, but it's happening throughout the continent.

The indigenous movements, which are the most repressed part of the population, those who survived, have gained considerable organization, and even power in Bolivia. They run the government. In Ecuador, they are a strong part of the system and the socio-political order. They have conflicts with the government, but are fighting for their own interest.

All of these changes are very important; in fact they may save the planet. Around the world, whether it's Australia or Latin America or anywhere else, the indigenous movements are in the forefront of trying to do something to save the planet and the human species from self-destruction. In Bolivia and Ecuador, the two countries with the strongest indigenous movements, there's now legislation. In Ecuador, I think it's in the Constitution, what is called the "rights of Nature." These are traditional parts of indigenous culture that were totally marginalized by industrialization. And unless that consciousness spreads, we're all doomed. So both for themselves and for the world, some very striking things have happened.

The United States used to take Latin America completely for granted. It was called "our little region over here," our "backyard." It was taken for granted that unless we can control Latin America, we can't control the rest of the world. That was stated repeatedly. Well, the U.S. has lost it, not all of it, but in South America, for example, there isn't a single U.S. military base left, which is a pretty significant fact.

Now the U.S. isn't giving up. The training of Latin American officers has increased. They're being trained to combat what's called "radical populism," which means troublesome priests who organize peasants, human rights activists and so on, and you know how that works in Latin America.

The most interesting case right now is Colombia. That was the last holdout for the United States in South America. The U.S. did, through Presidents Bush and Obama, try to get access to seven military bases in Colombia, and there was a lot of furor about that on the continent, a lot of protest. Well the Colombian Constitutional Court blocked it. But the U.S. is still constructing the bases, so they are evidently hoping they can, somehow, overrule the rulings of the court and get through. There's a significant confrontation going on in Colombia about the legacy of the U.S. domination, which was pretty monstrous.

Central America and the Caribbean are much weaker societies–small, weak, separated. There it's easier, though not totally easy anymore, to control them. So the coup in Honduras, which the United States backed–they claimed not to back it, but they effectively ended up backing it. I'm pretty sure it's related to the fact that Honduras is one of the countries where there are major U.S. military bases, the Palmerola Air Base for one; that was the main base for supporting the contras, for example. There are a number of U.S. bases spread all through that region and the Caribbean islands, but it's not the direction things are going.

One significant move, at least symbolically, was the formation last summer and the first meeting in Caracas of CELAC [Community of Latin American and Caribbean States], an organization which includes every country of the Western hemisphere except for the United States and Canada. That, at least symbolically, is very significant. If it becomes a functioning organization, its intention, I presume, is to replace the OAS, the Organization of American States, which is U.S. dominated. It includes Cuba and excludes the United States and Canada.

All of these things are in the same direction. They're a move towards dismantling the system of external control and internal domination. Both are proceeding in parallel. They are both very significant.

Dada Maheshvarananda: Thank you very much.

Afterword

The Possibility of Creating Another World is in our Hands

by Frei Betto

Frei Betto is one of the major voices for social justice in Latin America. A Dominican friar from Brazil, he was a political prisoner for four years during the military dictatorship in that country, and has lived as an activist with the poorest of the poor. He is the author of more than 50 books, including Fidel and Religion: Castro Talks on Revolution and Religion with Frei Betto *[Simon and Schuster, 1987] which sold more than two million copies worldwide.*

The model of the Progressive Utilization Theory (Prout) presented here in a crystalline way by Dada Maheshvarananda along with other complementary texts, joins many proposals and alternatives to help humanity overcome neoliberal capitalism. The current process of globalization is, in fact, a criminal process of global colonization. It is enough to say that today two-thirds of humanity (about four billion people) live below the poverty line.

The book's core idea, as described in Prout's Five Fundamental Principles as well as in the idea of the "collective body," coincides with the same rules that, for millennia, have been governing the life of monasteries in all religious traditions. Every true monastery is a model community in the original sense of the word: each is given according to his or her need, and each is asked to contribute according to his or her capacity. Everyone in the community enjoys the same rights and opportunities, as well.

I believe that the language of the future will be that of a holistic spirituality, a political spirituality that does not separate the body from the spirit. To experience this, meditation is fundamental. It is a source of life, of revitalization. When I meditate in silence, I feel myself vulnerable to and sensitive to the will of God. Every day I meditate, in the morning and the evening, from forty minutes to one hour. I feel it is little, because when I was in prison I did up to four hours of meditation a day.

It does not matter what we call the paradigm of the future society as long as it allows what is contained in the Christian tradition: God is Father of all and we are all companions. Etymologically, "companions" means "those who distribute or share bread." The theme of the World Social Forum, "Another world is possible", refers to our shared dream for a new world that could be described as post-capitalist, global, Neohumanist, etc. What must be emphasized is that humanity will only have a future if we share the goods of the Earth and the fruits of human work.

The constitutional proposals of Prout contain the ethical summary of everything that humanity needs to accomplish this program of universal fraternity, founded in the sharing of the resources of the planet and the wealth of countries. And the great importance of Prout is that its vision of a new world is not just concerned with political, social and economic relationships, but also with education, gender relationships and spirituality.

Let us now take up the content of this work with daring and faith. Because the future, the matter of our dreams, will only become reality if today, in the present, we plant its seeds.

Appendix A

Discussion Questions

This book can be used for a Study/Action Circle. Before each meeting the group may read one chapter. It would be best if a different participant prepared a short presentation at the start of each meeting about some of the main ideas in the chapter. The group could then discuss some of the following questions. There is no need to discuss them all – different people will find some questions more interesting than others.

There are no right or wrong answers here. The questions prompt participants to think about the ideas in the chapter, and so each reply will be, by definition, their honest opinion. A good idea is to go around the group, allowing each person a chance to answer, and starting with a different person each time. Explain that anyone can choose to pass if they want more time to think, and also can give their opinion at the end if they think of something later.

Chapter 1: The Failure of Global Capitalism and Economic Depressions

1. Do you believe that rich countries became rich because they were smarter and worked harder? Why or why not?
2. Do you believe that rich people became rich because they were smarter and worked harder? Why or why not?
3. What in your opinion is the biggest problem with global capitalism?
4. In what way is your country affected by global capitalism?
5. Do you think that the government of your country supports global capitalism? If so, how?

6. In what ways have multinational corporations caused harm to the economy, human health or the environment in your country?

7. There's a joke: "How many neoliberal economists does it take to change a lightbulb? The answer is none, because Adam Smith's 'invisible hand' of the free market will do it!" In your opinion, how effective and how "free" are free markets?

8. Governments have used tax-payer money to bail out the biggest financial institutions when they were threatened with bankruptcy. Do you think they should? If so, what conditions should be imposed on the banks?

9. Do you know anyone who is unemployed? What effect does it have on their life?

10. Do you know of a community that has experienced or is experiencing a recession? What are the effects on the community?

11. Do you think there is a chance that your national economy could enter a significant recession or depression? Why or why not?

12. If your economy took a significant downturn and you lost your job, what would you do and what advice would you give to others in the same situation?

Chapter 2: A New Social Paradigm Based on Spiritual Values

1. Does your government have a strong ecological and spiritual perspective? What are some things that might be different if it did?

2. "The land does not belong to me; I belong to the land." What is your opinion of this idea compared with legal property rights?

3. "Spirituality is the intrinsic human capacity for self-transcendence, in which the self is embedded in something greater than the self, including the sacred, and which motivates the search for connectedness, meaning, purpose, and contribution." Do you agree with this? Have you ever experienced this?

4. "There is in the living being a thirst for limitlessness." Do you agree with this? Have you ever experienced it?

5. Do you agree that Planet Earth and her wealth of resources are the common inheritance of all living beings? Why or why not?

6. Does materialism bother you? Why or why not?
7. Have you ever experienced dogma, geo-sentiment or socio-sentiment? Describe the situation.
8. Have you ever felt a personal sense of loss about the disappearance of a natural area, animals or plants? If so, describe what happened and how you felt.
9. Have you ever practiced meditation? What was your experience?

Chapter 3: The Right to Live!

1. Can you imagine a world in which no one worried about getting enough money to buy food, clothes, housing, education and medical care for his or her family? What do you think it would it be like?
2. Do you know anyone who receives welfare payments from the government? What has their experience been like?
3. "Pharmaceuticals are the third most profitable industry in the United States." What is your opinion about this fact?
4. Have you or anyone you know been treated by alternative forms of medical treatment, such as homeopathy, naturopathy, herbal medicine, acupuncture or yoga treatments? What was their experience?
5. What is your opinion about Marxism?
6. All government employees have pay scales. The U.S. federal government pays the president 10 times more than a starting worker, while Norway pays 5.3 times more. Do you think it is reasonable to ask the same from private business?
7. "Healthy individuals contribute to a healthy society, and a healthy society fosters the development of healthy individuals." Do you agree with this statement, and that individual interests and collective interests do not have to be in conflict?
8. Mark Friedman lists eight factors that motivate people to work productively: individual ability, personality, the demands of the organization, education, experience, work environment, service culture, and income. What factors motivate you to work hard?

Chapter 4: Economic Democracy

1. Economic democracy stands for the empowerment of people to make economic decisions that directly shape their lives and communities through locally-owned, small-scale private enterprises, worker-owned cooperatives, and publicly-managed utilities. Do you think this is important?
2. A Prout slogan says, "Globalize humanity, localize the economy." What are the benefits of a local economy over a global one?
3. "It is a basic right of workers to own and manage their enterprises, making the economic decisions which directly affect their lives." Do you agree with this? Why or why not?
4. Do outsiders control the economy in your community? If so, to what extent? How many of the popular stores, restaurants, banks and entertainment centers are locally owned or part of a national or international chain? How much of the food is locally grown? How many clothes, bicycles, cars, and other goods the people buy are locally manufactured?
5. Are there many small businesses in your community? How are they doing?
6. Are there cooperatives in your community? How are they doing?
7. Are there public utilities in your community? How are they doing?
8. How is housing in your community? Are home prices low or high? Are apartment rents affordable or expensive?
9. Have you ever experienced barter trade or a form of local currency (such as frequent flier miles)? If so, what was your experience?
10. Some common tax systems are: personal income, corporate income, sales or VAT tax, import tariffs, resource, wealth and inheritance, land, and special-purpose taxes. Some are fair, some are efficient and some are simple. Which do you think are better and why?

Chapter 5: Cooperatives for a Better World

1. In your opinion, is human nature fundamentally competitive or cooperative? Why?

2. Why do you think people don't cooperate more often?
3. Did your school teach you how to cooperate well?
4. Does the mass media encourage cooperation?
5. "Cooperatives are the businesses of the future." Do you agree with this? Why or why not?
6. Have you ever visited a cooperative? What impressed you most?
7. What factors do you think are most important for a cooperative to be successful? Why?
8. If there was a credit union where you could keep your money instead of a commercial bank, would you use it?
9. Do you think your community would benefit if it had more cooperatives? Why or why not?

Chapter 6: An Agrarian Revolution and Environmental Protection

1. What are the biggest problems farmers in your country are facing?
2. How much of the food that you eat is grown locally, and how much is imported from far away?
3. Do you think an agrarian revolution is necessary? Why or why not?
4. Have you ever visited a cooperative farm or a Community Supported Agriculture farm?
5. "Since 1950, the number of farm animals on the planet has risen 500 percent; now they outnumber humans by three to one, consume half the world's grain, and cause more global warming than all cars and other transportation put together." What is your opinion about this?
6. Have you ever eaten food that you planted yourself? How did it make you feel?
7. What percentage of your country's population works in agriculture, industry, and services? What would be the effect if your economy became more balanced?
8. What do you think could be done to save the rainforests of our planet?
9. Have you ever used a medicinal plant? What was your experience?

Chapter 7: A New Perspective on Class, Class Struggle and Revolution

1. Do you personally know people who tend to represent shudras? What are they like?
2. Do you personally know people who tend to represent ksatriyas? What are they like?
3. Do you personally know people who tend to represent vipras? What are they like?
4. Do you personally know people who tend to represent vaeshyas? What are they like?
5. Which of the four classes do you think you represent, and why?
6. In the history of your country, which classes dominated society at what times?
7. Have you ever experienced a time of great social change? If so, what was it like?
8. According to the theory of the Social Cycle, which class is dominating your society now, and what would it take to move it forward?
9. What is your opinion about the condition of women in your country in the past and today?
10. Have you ever experienced sexism directly or indirectly? Describe your experience?
11. What, in your opinion, would be the most positive change for women in your society today?

Chapter 8: Spiritual Revolutionaries

1. Do you think that anyone could become an ideal leader, a sadvipra? Why or why not?
2. Which qualities of the four classes (laborer, warrior, intellectual and entrepreneur) have you developed in your life? What would it take to develop the others?
3. "One's universal outlook is a way to judge whether a person is a sadvipra." Is your outlook completely universal, or do you harbor negative feelings about any group of people?
4. "True leaders empower others to be great. They sincerely listen to the opinions of others, and they encourage and praise the accomplishments of others." Do you?

5. Do you have shadows, inner enemies and bondages: complexes, weaknesses and fears? Are you examining and confronting them?

6. "What we despise in others – the qualities that we hate – are actually within us." What qualities do you hate in other people? Are those qualities also within you?

7. Have you ever felt the "bystander effect", the trap that discourages you from acting?

8. Have you ever been in a situation where you were called on to perform a heroic deed? If so, what happened?

9. Have you ever met someone who was "emotionally intelligent": sensitive, aware and always able to make others feel better?

10. Have you ever met someone you consider to be a true hero? What were they like?

11. Have you ever met a bad leader, who was arrogant? What were they like?

12. What do you need to work on to become a sadvipra, a spiritual revolutionary?

Chapter 9: A New Concept of Ethics and Justice

1. What are some of the moral dilemmas that your country faces today?

2. What are some of the moral dilemmas that you and your friends face today?

3. The American Psychiatric Association concluded that the most common factor among habitual offenders was the tendency to lie. Do you know anyone with this tendency?

4. "Most moral values have reflected the interests of the rich and powerful." Do you agree with this statement? Give an example to support your view.

5. There is a cynical saying, "Every man has his price," which means that a person who is able to resist a small temptation of money might give in if the amount is big enough. Have you ever seen an example of this?

6. Do you feel the 10 universal ethical principles of Yama and Niyama could be a relevant guide to your actions today? Why or why not?

7. Have you ever met someone who claimed to be moral, but was not? How did their actions differ from their words?

8. Have you ever seen a government leader who claimed to be moral, but was not? How did their actions differ from their words?

9. "Accumulating as much money as you can is immoral." Do you agree? Why or why not?

10. "Pornography pollutes the mind." Do you agree? Why or why not?

11. Restorative justice organizes a meeting between the offender and the victim, along with family members, friends and co-workers of both. Have you ever been a victim of crime? If so, would you want to meet the offender in such a meeting?

12. Have you ever been to jail, or do you know anyone who has? If so, what was their experience?

13. "Since 1971, the United States has spent more than $1 trillion on its 'War on Drugs,' and yet drugs are cheaper, purer and more available today than ever." What is your opinion about illegal drugs?

Chapter 10: "Our Culture is Our Strength!"

1. What was your experience in school? Was it mostly positive or negative? How could it have been better?

2. In your opinion, is there a lack of social and economic awareness among the people of your country? If so, why?

3. Are fear and inferiority complexes imposed on people in your country? If so, how?

4. Have you ever experienced racism directly or indirectly? Describe your experience?

5. Have you ever experienced exploitation directly or indirectly? Describe your experience?

6. Are lotteries legal in your country? Should they be? Why or why not?

7. In the past, imperialists used superior weapons to invade and conquer other lands, then they told the defeated people, "Your culture is primitive, your religion is defective, your language is unsophisticated" in order to break people's will to resist. In your opinion, were they successful?

8. Pseudo-culture means that which is fake, imposed, which has a debilitating effect psychologically and spiritually and which lowers the will of people to resist. Can you give examples of pseudo-culture in your society? How can we evaluate what is true culture and what is fake?

9. Do advertisements in your country make young people want to be someone else? Explain.

10. How many popular songs encourage people to rise up and make a revolution? What percentage of pop stars serve as role models in this regard? Why don't more do this?

11. What percentage of popular TV shows encourage people to rise up and make a revolution? Why don't more do this?

12. How many languages do you speak? Do you feel it would be useful to learn another? Why?

13. "Our culture is our strength!" Do you agree with this? Why or why not?

Chapter 11: Prout's Governance

1. What is your opinion about a council of wise elders leading society?

2. "Power tends to corrupt, and absolute power corrupts absolutely." What is your opinion of this statement?

3. Do corporations influence the government of your country through legal or illegal financial contributions?

4. In your opinion, are most political leaders in your country controlled by big money? Explain.

5. Does an examination for voters, like a driver's license examination, make sense to you? Why or why not?

6. Do you think the constitution should give individuals the right to sue the government to force it to provide access to the minimum necessities? Why or why not?

7. Do you think we need a World Constitution with a Universal Bill of Rights? Why or why not?

8. Do you think a world government would be beneficial? Do you think it would be possible to achieve it in next 10 or 20 years?

9. What do you think about sadvipra governance, the "rule of the wise"?

Chapter 12: A Call to Action: Strategies to Implement Prout

1. British Prime Minister Margaret Thatcher said, "There is no alternative," and the mass media reinforces this idea that capitalism is the only good system and it will go on forever. How do you think we could change this collective consciousness?
2. How do you think you could convey Prout ideas to students, professors, writers and intellectuals?
3. How could you use the Internet and social media to spread Prout's message?
4. How could you organize Prout training for activists in your community?
5. "All Proutists should carry out social service, and in this way connect with the common people, experiencing their hardships firsthand." Do you agree? If so, how would you start?
6. Have you ever been a part of a mass movement? If so, what happened?
7. Do you agree that a revolutionary change in society requires young people, who have the vigor and resilience to implement the vision of a new society? If so, how do you think we could attract them?
8. "The forces opposed to revolution possess immense military power. In spite of this, the revolutionaries will achieve victory... because moral and spiritual power is infinitely stronger than physical force." Do you agree? Why or why not?
9. "Nonviolent direct action (civil disobedience) is a revolutionary tactic that creates pressure on the powers that be." Do you agree? Why or why not?
10. "Most NGOs and social movements are focused on a single issue to achieve clear, immediate goals. The Prout movement differs in that it is comprehensive, working for a total transformation of society." What do you think of this?
11. In your opinion, when will hunger, poverty and war end?
12. Can you change the world?

Appendix B

Designing Prout Study/Action Circles

Since Prout began, study circles and training courses have been essential in the effort to develop new Proutists. However, Prout is a vast theory: Sarkar published 1,500 pages of thought on it, and other Proutists are continually adding new ideas and practical examples. Conveying all this information may at times become boring and disappointing unless the theory can be demonstrated to practically solve real problems.

An exciting course first needs a catchy title: "The National Reality and Tools to Change the World." Replace the word "National" with the name of your country. Each module could begin with a short discussion about a current social problem, such as poverty, unemployment, hunger, crime, pollution, corruption, racism and sexism. Most of these problems exist in some form in every country of the world. Present the scope and cause of that problem in your country, and briefly analyze the government responses to it.

Next, present ideas about how Prout principles could be systematically applied nationwide to alleviate the problem. To change the world, we also have to change ourselves. We have to be the change we want to see, "to walk our talk". So each module should also present the importance of Prout lifestyle changes as part of the solution.

To engage participants, we need to ask them to express their opinions through appropriate discussion questions. People remember more when they are physically active, and they become more invested when they are bonding with other people. Cooperative games, group dynamics and artistic expressions should be used to involve participants. Teams of participants can create slogans, projects, activities and campaigns for their community.

The goal should be nothing less than to create a course in which all participants are so inspired that they become actively engaged in their community and so enthusiastic that they bring their friends and family to the next course. To do this, participants need to talk, connect, laugh and create.

Below is a list of 14 possible modules for a course, each with one or more social problems and the relevant Prout solutions. Feel free to combine, rearrange or add other problems.

Social Problems	Prout Solutions
Poverty	Minimum necessities of life
Unemployment	Cooperatives
Crime, violence, police corruption	Ethics, anti-corruption campaigns, drug reforms
Inflation, exploitation, gap between rich and poor	Three-tier economy, tax policies, ceiling on wealth
Hunger, water crisis, dependence on food imports and global markets	Food sovereignty, co-ops
Rural poverty, urban migration	Block-level planning, agricultural revolution, agro- and agrico-industries
Media lies: advertising, consumerism, beauty myth, inferiority complex	Cooperative ownership of media, strengthening traditional cultures and identity
Racism, sexism, broken families	Neohumanism
Problems with schools and universities	Neohumanist education, cooperative games
Inefficient and corrupt leaders	Ideal leadership (Sadvipras)
Emotional depression, bad health, stress	Holistic health, spiritual perspective, meditation
Selfishness, greed, materialism	Biopsychology of cooperation
Pollution, global warming	Five Fundamental Principles, alternative energy, maximum utilization and rational distribution

| Inequality and injustice of global capitalism | Balanced economy, economic diversity |

To get people warmed up and excited, start each session with a 10-minute discussion about the problem. The facilitator should say:

"Welcome. We'd like to begin this session with a 10-minute discussion about how this global problem affects you personally, if at all. Please limit your contribution to one minute at the most, and please do not speak a second time until everyone has spoken, though you have the right to 'pass' if you don't wish to speak. Remember, the purpose is to express how this global problem affects you personally."

The facilitator should focus on watching the time and gently asking people to finish when they reach the one-minute limit. Invite each person to say something.

After 10 minutes, gently close the discussion and start your short presentation about the scope and cause of that problem in your country. Begin with a dramatic "eye-opener." Put numbers in context. Show before and after photos. If possible, show a short documentary clip about the problem. Show the inevitable result if present trends continue. Briefly analyze the government responses and show how other countries are solving the problem.

Gathering this information will be a challenge. Invite different participants in the first course to research the topic that is most interesting to them and design that presentation. Asking the right questions for each module is very important; it's much easier to ask experts for the right data [see Appendix C for a list of some relevant questions]. Invite a professor, expert or the representative of a concerned organization to a special dinner to explain the topic and answer questions about it. Take field trips to relevant sites; for example, to the local garbage dump, to a successful cooperative and to a failed one.

Ask the participants how they would share their ideas with other people. Who do they think most needs to hear this information and how do they think that that person could best comprehend it? We learn at a different level when we have to teach the information to someone else.

Challenge participants to develop a campaign in their community to solve the problem. Create street theater to raise consciousness about the issue. Design posters for the public that highlight the problem and Prout's solutions; these can be displayed at progressive conferences, universities, lectures and other social and educational events. Create banners and signs that can be carried in marches. Learn or compose your own revolutionary, protest and Prout songs.

At the start of the course as well as at other times practice interpersonal, cooperative and team-building exercises to build closeness among group members. Use different media that animate the senses. Serve delicious snacks or a meal. It's also important to celebrate the group's successes with participants.

Some tools to change the world:

- Activist media
- Consciousness-raising
- Movement building
- Marches
- Slogans
- Public speaking
- Community murals
- Street theater
- Theater of the Oppressed
- Building strong organizations
- Organizing community meetings to hear about the community's problems and to prioritize them
- Storytelling
- Listening to the life stories of people in the community
- Petition campaign
- Recruitment
- Working with coalitions
- Organizing young people
- Civil disobedience
- Organizing a concert of revolutionary music
- Organizing a contest of revolutionary art

Appendix C

Economic and Social Questions About Your Area

"Know the area," said P.R. Sarkar. If you understand which are the right questions to ask, you are close to finding the answers. Below is a list of questions for a Prout Study/Action Circle and to kickstart a block level plan. Sources you can consult to find the answers include government statistics, non-governmental organizations, the United Nations and the CIA World Factbook. Check if the data is contested, and whether independent sources support the government statistics. Invite a professor, expert or the representative of a concerned organization to a special dinner to explain the topic and answer questions about it.

Agriculture

How much arable land is there, and what proportion is cultivated?
What fraction of total land is arable?
What proportion of cultivated land is irrigated?
What are the main agricultural products?
Which agricultural products are exported?
How much food is consumed?
What percentage is produced locally? What percentage is produced nationally? What percentage is imported?
1. Cereals and grains (rice, corn, sorghum, barley, wheat, etc.)?
2. Beans (black, pinto, kidney, garbanzo, lentils, etc.)?
3. Milk: fresh, powdered?
4. Produce: vegetables, fruits?
What natural resources exist? How much of each one?
Which raw materials, if any, are exported, and what percentage of each?

Water

Percentage of people with access to potable water in their homes?
Percentage of people with sanitation systems in their homes?

Manufacturing and trade

Which goods are manufactured, and how much of each?
How much is produced for domestic consumption, and how much is exported?
At what level is electricity production and consumption? Is any imported or exported?
At what level is the petroleum production and consumption? Is any imported or exported?
At what level is natural gas production and consumption? Is any imported or exported?
What are the major imports?
What are the major exports?
What is the balance of trade?
Which countries are the major import partners?
Which countries are the major export partners?

Banks

What percentage of banks are cooperatively-owned?
What percentage of banks are national and privately-owned?
What percentage of banks are internationally owned?
What percentage of banks are government owned?
Are banking laws strict or is banking largely unregulated?
Are existing regulations properly enforced?
Do laws allow banks to operate in other markets, such as insurance?
What are the capital reserve requirements? Are these enforced?
Are there large investment banks and are there meaningful regulations to limit high-risk behaviors?
What are the total capital reserves and interest rates for each bank?
What is the demographic breakdown of loans and repayment?
What is the demographic breakdown of bank locations?
What is the commercial bank prime lending rate?

Cooperatives

What is the total number of cooperatives in the country? In each state? In each sector?

What proportion of businesses are organized as cooperatives in each sector?

How many people are members of cooperatives? What percentage of the population?

Over time, is this percentage increasing or decreasing?

Are the laws relating to cooperatives favorable?

Do cooperatives receive tax breaks or other support from the government?

Are there national associations of cooperatives?

Economy

What percentage of the labor force is in agriculture, industry and services?

What types of taxes are collected at the national level, state level and local level?

At each level is the tax system effectively progressive, regressive or flat?

What are the annual tax revenues and expenditures?

What proportion of government expenditure at each level goes for: education, health care, military, police, fire, sanitation, infrastructure, social safety net, agricultural programs, etc.?

What is the budget surplus or deficit as a percentage of the GDP?

Is the surplus or deficit changing quickly or is it relatively stable?

What is the total public debt?

What is the total external debt?

What percentage of any debt is public debt?

What percentage of any debt is external debt?

Combining all taxes at all levels, what percentage of the GDP is collected as tax revenue?

How much foreign exchange and gold reserves are held?

Gap Between the Rich and the Poor

What percentage of wealth is held by the top 20%?

What percentage of wealth is held by the top 10%?
What percentage of wealth is held by the top 1%?
What percentage of wealth is held by the top 0.1%?
What percentage of wealth is held by the bottom 50%?
What percentage of wealth is held by the bottom 20%?
What percentage of income is earned annually by the top 20%?
What percentage of income is earned annually by the 10%?
What percentage of income is earned annually by the top 1%?
What percentage of income is earned annually by the top 0.1%?
What percentage of income is earned annually by the bottom 50%?
What percentage of income is earned annually by the bottom 20%?
How have these distributions been changing over the last 10 years? The last 5 years?
Which is more unevenly distributed, income or wealth?

Poverty

What is the current poverty level as defined by the government?
How many people are under this poverty level? What percentage of the population is this?
How many people are under the absolute poverty level as defined by the U. N.: US$1.25 a day?
How is the poverty rate changing over time?
What is the level of rural poverty? What is the level of urban poverty?
Are some demographic groups experiencing more poverty than others?

Unemployment

What is the official unemployment level as defined by the government?
How many people are unemployed?
What is the real unemployment level?
Are some demographic groups experiencing more unemployment than others?
What percentage of the workforce is underemployed?

What is the minimum wage?
How much is a living wage that is enough to buy the minimum necessities?
Are real wages changing? If so, how?

Crime and Corruption

What are the total figures for violent crimes?
How are these numbers changing over time?
What are the reported rates of domestic violence and rapes?
What are the estimated rates of domestic violence and rapes?
How many corruption cases are filed; how many are pursued and what percentage are convicted?
How many involve police officers, government officials and business owners?
What is the perceived level of corruption?
What is the total prison population? Is the population growing over time?
How many violent incidents occur in prisons?
What proportion of people in prison are people of color?
Are people of color more likely to receive harsher sentences for the same crime?

Media and Advertising

How many TV stations exist? How many are government, private, pro-government, opposition, cooperative, public? How many broadcast over the airwaves and how many over cable?
How many radio stations are there, and what are their affiliations?
What are the 10 largest magazines and newspapers according to circulation? When was each formed?
How concentrated is media ownership? Are TV, radio and print media owned by the same company?
What is the "beauty myth" and how does it affect this culture?
What is the total amount spent on advertising?
How is that divided among TV, radio, print ads, billboard signs and others?
How is that divided among sectors, such as alcohol, fast foods, cigarettes, soda and cars?

How much money is spent on political advertising?
In what ways do advertisers exert editorial pressure?
In what ways does the government exert editorial pressure?
Does the government have direct censorship authority?

Urban Migration

What is the rural population?
What is the urban population?
How have these percentages changed over time?
What are the principal reasons for these migration patterns?

Land Ownership

Who owns most of the land? How concentrated is the ownership?
How much land does the government own, and how is it used?
Is mining, grazing or timber harvesting allowed on government land?
Can foreigners own land?
How is land taxed? Urban? Rural? How is it calculated and what are the rates?
Have there been occupations of rural lands? If so, how many?
Do the media call these "invasions" or "occupations"?
Is there land reform? If so, how many hectares have been redistributed by the government? How many more hectares are being considered for redistribution? Has the government taken land and not redistributed it?

Racism

What are the demographics of the major ethnic groups in the population?
What are the population and languages of the indigenous people?
What proportion of businesses is run by people of color?
What proportion of university professors are people of color?
What proportion of elected officials at each level are people of color?
Do people of color receive equal pay compared to others with equal qualifications?

What are the demographics of all the models and actors in two hours of prime time TV ads?
What are the demographics of all the models in the ads in a popular magazine?

Sexism

What proportion of businesses is run by women?
What proportion of university professors are women?
What proportion of elected officials at each level are women?
How many shelters are there for victims of domestic abuse?
Are there telephone hotlines for victims of domestic abuse, either government or private?
Do women receive equal pay compared to men with the same qualifications?
What is the divorce rate?
How long does the average marriage last?
How many single mothers are there? Single fathers?
Are women and children more likely to live in poverty?
Are unemployment rates higher or lower for women? (If they are higher, consider why this still might be evidence of sexism.)

Education

What percentage of the GDP is spent on education?
What is the expenditure per student?
What is the average teacher/student ratio at different grade levels?
How do teacher salaries compare with other professionals with similar qualifications?
How many students are enrolled in universities?
What percentage of eligible students attend university?
What percentage of students complete high school?
What is the cost of an education in a public university and a private university?
What is the total number of teachers?
What is the total number of schools?
How many schools are public and how many are private?

What are the UN statistics for the number of children not in school and their ages?
What is the literacy rate?

Mental Health

What are the suicide rates for males and females?
What are the facilities for mental health treatment?
What is the number of admissions?
What is the estimated population and proportion of mental health patients?
What are the import totals and consumption estimates of anti-depressant medicines?
What are the drug abuse estimates?
What are the alcohol abuse estimates?

Health

What are the leading causes of death?
What are the major infectious diseases?
What is the infant mortality rate?
What is the population growth rate?
How many people are malnourished? What percentage of the population?
What percentage of children is malnourished?
What percentage of expectant mothers receives prenatal care?
What is the diabetes rate?
What is the average life expectancy?
How many doctors are there per 1,000 people?

Pollution

What are air pollution levels? What are the carbon dioxide levels? What are the main causes of air and water pollution?
What is the estimate of kilometers per capita driven?
Are auto emissions inspections required?
Is carpooling encouraged? (HVO lanes)
Are bicycle lanes available and well maintained?
What public transportation options are available?

What is the trash production per capita?
How much recycling is done by government and by non-governmental organizations?

Global Warming

Which have been the hottest years on record in your country?
Are rainfall and snowfall patterns changing? If so, how?
Are natural storms increasing in number or intensity?
If sea levels rise one meter, how would that change the map of your country? By four meters? How many people live in those low-lying coastal areas? (see http://flood.firetree.net/)

Appendix D

Solutions to Block-Level Planning Exercise in Chapter 6

With 75 percent of the population depending on agriculture, the main focus of planning efforts should be to restore prama (dynamic balance) in the agricultural sphere. As no more people could conceivably be absorbed into agriculture, the development of an industrial base is also essential to create jobs and increase the purchasing capacity of Keyyan's citizens. Areas to concentrate our planning effort:

Agriculture
Industry
Finance
Energy
Transportation
Housing
Education

Agriculture

Though Keyyan is producing a surplus, it still imports food, mostly luxury items like coffee, imported canned goods and other processed foods. Food is both the biggest export as well as the biggest import. The high level of malnutrition is due to inadequate purchasing capacity rather than any lack of food. Though food is available, many people cannot afford to buy it.

The fact that 72% of arable land is under cultivation suggests that there is some possibility to expand the area of agricultural land. However, Keyyan already produces enough food – the problem is that the production methods give farmers a very poor return for their labor. Therefore, this is where we should focus our efforts.

The cost of production is so high that only a marginal profit of $1,667 per annum is left for a two-and-a-half hectare farm. This figure, though, is still too high, because the cost of the labor of the farmer and the family members is not included. If each person was given the minimum wage, we would find that the farmers actually lose money in the venture. We must conclude that most of the farms are uneconomical at present.

So what could we do to increase efficiency?

One way is to organize the farmers in cooperatives. This requires grass-roots organizing that takes time. However, even with the introduction of cooperatives, it is clear that agriculture has to be made more efficient. This means that fewer people will work the land, and the displaced people will need alternative employment. We cannot increase the purchasing capacity of a few by depriving the many of their only source of income.

Then how to increase the purchasing capacity of the farmers? There are a few possibilities.

1. Increase the yield of the land: This was done in the past with the Green Revolution. However, the living standards of the farmers actually declined, since the cost of inputs went up many-fold. It also caused a dependence on outside factors. Previously farmers had been fairly independent, but now the farmers and the country as a whole are heavily dependent on imported fertilizers, pesticides, and genetically modified seeds.

    Perhaps with the help of appropriate, indigenous technology a little improvement in rice yields could be achieved, but it is doubtful this would be significant within the foreseeable future.

2. Reduce the costs of production: As Sarkar recommends, uneconomic land holdings should be consolidated into cooperatives. This takes time to achieve. Subsistence farmers cannot afford to take risks, so they will be suspicious of any innovation that might upset the delicate balance between survival and disaster. On the other hand, if they can see with their own eyes tangible proof that consolidating their land holdings would improve their earnings, they will be convinced. If we can establish successful model cooperatives, people will copy them.

3. Diversify production: This is quite practical. Study is needed to determine what other crops and plants could be grown

profitably. As the block is self-sufficient in staple foods, the excess capacity could be used to grow crops that might be economically profitable even on areas that are too small for growing rice.

Consult successful farmers, rural development NGOs and agricultural colleges to find out which crops would do well in Keyyan. Then test these in a small research plot that farmers can see and imitate. Coconut and palm oil plantations have been successful in other parts of the country. Intensive vegetable gardening can also be done in very small areas that would help reduce malnutrition.

4. Irrigation: Yields can be increased and more crops can be harvested each year through irrigation. In Keyyan, rainfall is adequate, so it is possible to collect run-offs through encatchment ponds that are practical and sustainable. Study carefully the cost of building small check dams on the rivers and their impact on production. Again, start with one or two projects, and when successful, they can be implemented elsewhere.

5. Increasing fish populations: Artificial reefs can be created with used tires. School and media campaigns can solicit the public to bring tires, and the fishermen themselves can be convinced to contribute a half-day of their labor to collectively build the new reefs.

Industry

To solve the problems of unemployment and low purchasing capacity, an industrial base has to be developed. As agriculture becomes more efficient, displaced people will need new jobs. So the reform of agriculture must go hand-in-hand with the development of local industry.

The first focus should be on agro- and agrico-industries that will benefit the farmers. Products made out of rice, such as beaten rice, puffed rice, rice noodles, etc. could be produced, increasing the value of the rice that is harvested. Rice straw can also be used for many applications, including the production of paper. Rice husk can be used in the cement industry.

There is even more economic potential in coconuts and palmnuts, which are both oil seeds; from the oil a number of products can be produced, including soap. A soap factory could therefore be established to supply the local area. Coconut fibers can also be used in making rope, mats, brushes, and many other commodities. By introducing these cash crops and utilizing the products in agro-industries, the productivity of the area can be increased, employment created and the purchasing capacity of the people enhanced. Detailed feasibility studies would have to be done. Keyyan has the raw materials and the labor, but we need to calculate whether the production would be economical, and whether there are markets for the products.

Likewise, the potential of the limestone deposits for cement manufacturing should be carefully studied. Due to the cost of cement and cement blocks, which have to be imported from afar, people usually make temporary buildings from straw, mud and bamboo that last only a few years. With the local production of cement, more permanent structures could be encouraged. Cement could also be exported to neighboring areas which have no limestone.

Cooking oil, rope, soap, cement and other important products are all imported, even though the potential to produce them from local raw materials exists. The principle of matching supply with demand clearly requires us to rectify this imbalance. The principle of maximum utilization of land also suggests that some of these coconut and palm oil plantations could be grown on land that is not presently cultivated.

Detailed studies have to be made as to the cost of the raw materials, machinery, labor and other factors to see if there is a reasonable margin for profit. Labor-intensive technology is often more appropriate in a poor rural community than capital-intensive technology, even if on paper it looks more profitable, because imported machinery might cause long delays while waiting for spare parts and expatriate repair technicians. Furthermore, Prout's goal is to maximize consumption, not profit. With a greater number of workers who are part-owners of the cooperative, the wages paid are profit-sharing, and the money is plowed back to the local people to increase their purchasing capacity. This in turn will make them buy more goods locally, and stimulate the entire local economy.

Finance

In the capitalist economy of Inflatonia, the possibilities of raising credit and funds for development projects are limited. In Keyyan, farmers and rural cottage entrepreneurs are at the mercy of local money lenders, who charge ten percent per month interest.

Therefore, starting cooperative credit unions should be the first step towards solving the problem of credit for farms and small-scale cottage industries. Credit unions will favor cooperatives, thus giving another incentive for farmers to work together. However, credit unions will be unable to finance a major project like the cement factory. Still, if the credit union and the municipal government together approved it, a major bank loan could possibly be negotiated if it was sponsored by an NGO.

Energy

Be sure to consider the energy requirements of the different projects. Study both alternative and traditional energy sources.

Housing, Transportation and Education

In the same way that we treated agriculture and industry, make step -by-step plans for housing, transportation, education, etc. Look at the problems, consider the options, and draw up practical plans. Use Prout's five fundamental principles to direct your planning efforts. Consider the demand and supply of all commodities, and make sure land is properly utilized. For every economic venture, consider the cost of production, and strive for maximum productivity. As an overall goal, try to introduce reforms that will progressively increase people's purchasing capacity, and ensure that the collective needs of the community are being met.

Formulating the plan

With these ideas, you will then have to make detailed planning. This planning involves visiting each village and discussing with the people to assess their problems and potential, to determine which cottage industries could succeed, where roads are needed, and where model projects should be started. All of these assessments must be done in cooperation with the local people.

One of the initial goals is to set up successful models to demonstrate that something works before people will follow it. Master Units and community service projects can play a key role in gaining credibility among the local communities.

Of course if Keyyan was part of a country following Prout policies, its growth towards economic self-sufficiency would be much faster. Credit would be freed up for local projects, and no drainage of wealth would be allowed. Raw materials would no longer be sold to multinationals, and local industries, such as our budding cement and soap industries, would receive economic protection.

Final note

This exercise intentionally chose a block that is impoverished and limited in its potential. The challenge is to do this for an area in the real world to increase the purchasing capacity and quality of life of the people who live there. The planning and the implementation of Prout is still relatively new; we hope you will share your experiences as you put it into practice. Good luck in your planning efforts!

Adapted from *An Introduction to Block-Level Planning* by Caetanya, Prout Research Institute, 1992, 60 pages. Available for free download from www.priven.org Resources.

Appendix E

Prout Slogans

Brief, electrifying slogans, about 5-12 words each, can inspire people and awaken their curiosity about Prout. Choose your favorites, combine them, create your own. Put on banners, signs and T-shirts, with small letters at the bottom: "The Progressive Utilization Theory (Prout)" and the local web page.

A new vision for all living beings.
Basic necessities for all.
Be a flame in the darkness.
Be a revolutionary guided by great feelings of love. - Che
"Be the change you want to see in the world." - Gandhi
Birds need two wings to fly–society needs women's equal and full participation.
Capitalism: Good for the rich, disastrous for the poor.
Capitalist exploitation is killing human beings and the planet.
Capitalist greed is a mental disease–try Prout.
Capitalist greed is destroying our planet!
Co-ops are self-help, not charity.
Co-ops create jobs: 100+ million, more than corporations.
Co-ops empower people to decide their own future.
Co-ops with "coordinated cooperation" is the system of the future.
Cooperative enterprises build a better world.
Cooperatives are enterprises with a soul.
Cooperatives are the businesses of the future.
Corporate stores give your money to rich investors–buy local!
Cultural freedom, economic freedom, spiritual freedom!

Each person here = thousands suffering from global capitalism.
Economic democracy through cooperatives, regional self-sufficiency.
Economic democracy, not political hegemony.
Economic democracy: Cooperatives of the people, by the people and for the people!
Economic democracy: Economic empowerment of people and communities.
Economic democracy: Economy of the people, by the people and for the people!
Economic liberation for all.
Economics from the heart.
Education and jobs will free all women from economic dependence.
End economic exploitation.
End hunger–there's enough food on earth, but not enough will.
Ending repressive regimes starts at home.
Exploitation no more!
Fight for justice, meditate for inner peace.
For an exploitation-free society.
For personal and planetary transformation.
For the good of all beings.
Globalize humanity – localize the economy.
Globalize solidarity.
Grow your local economy.
Human beings of the world–unite!
Human society is one and indivisible.
Humanity is one and indivisible.
It is action that makes a person great.
Meaningful jobs with "living wages" is our right.
Money is a human invention, we CAN change the rules.
Neohumanism: Love for humanity and all living beings.
One billion people aren't wrong: Co-ops work!
One people, one planet, one future.
Our culture is our strength!
Planet Earth has enough for everyone if we share.
Prout, Prout–the only way out!
Prout: Alternative to "global colonialism"!
Rampant materialism is costing us the earth.

Rational distribution of wealth, basic necessities for all.
Real education is that which leads to liberation.
Real solutions for a better world.
Real wealth comes from within.
Reclaim the economy for the community.
Revolution = total transformation.
Save an endangered species: Humans!
Self-reliance, cooperatives and spirituality.
Set maximum wages for the welfare of all.
Share the wealth through local, cooperative-based economies.
Sharing the wealth of our planet.
Support credit unions, not big banks.
The force that guides the stars guides you, too.
There is enough for everyone's needs, not for everyone's greed!
"There's no chance for the welfare of the world unless the condition of women improves." - P.R. Sarkar
Think globally, act locally.
Together we can build a better world.
Transform yourself and transform society.
Transform yourself and transform the world.
Uniting communities for local self-reliance.
Unity in diversity!
We are all connected.
We are all together in this world.
We are one universal family.
We belong to the universe–discover divinity within you.
We have a dream–food for all, jobs for all!
We need a cap on wealth.
Where every life matters.
Working together for a new world.

Notes

Foreword by Marcos Arruda

1   For more information about Solidarity Socioeconomy, see http://www.fbes.org.br. There you will find documents that analyze and describe the innovative practices and proposals related to different fields of the socioeconomy in the context of the present globalization. See also the booklets in the series "Planting Socioeconomy", PACS, Rua Evaristo da Veiga, 47, sala 702, 20031-040 Rio de Janeiro, Brazil, tel/fax (55) 21 2210 2124, adm@pacs.org.br.

2   By compassion I mean, feel with the Other, suffer with the Other, dream with the Other.

3   "In my opinion, the essence of Marx's work is fighting for higher human values. In my books *Humanizar o Infra-Humano: Homo Evolutivo, Práxis e Economia Solidária* and *Tornar Real o Possível: Economia Solidária, Desenvolvimento e o Futuro do Trabalho*, both published by Editora Vozes, I compare the thoughts of four important authors: Sri Aurobindo, Karl Marx, Teilhard de Chardin, and Humberto Maturana of Chile. All of them converge in promoting superior human values, such as growing cooperation, communication, solidarity and love, as the driving force that carries our evolution forward."

Introduction

1   *After Capitalism: Prout's Vision for a New World* (Copenhagen: Proutist Universal, 2003) has been translated into Portuguese, Spanish, German, Italian, Finnish, Polish, Hungarian, Korean and Japanese.

2   My email is maheshvarananda@prout.org.ve

3   While 1921 was listed as the year Sarkar was born in my previous book, the research done by Devashish in his book *Anandamurti: The*

Jamalpur Years (San Germán, Puerto Rico: InnerWorld Publications, 2010) leaves little room for doubt that it was actually 1922.

1. The Failure of Global Capitalism and Economic Depressions

1   P.R. Sarkar, *Problems of the Day* (Calcutta: Ananda Marga Publications, 1968) p. 2.

2   3.14 billion people live on less than $2.50 a day (at 2005 Purchasing Power Parity). *World Bank Development Indicators*, 2008.

3   Howard Zinn, *A People's History of the United States: 1492-Present* (New York: HarperCollins, revised and updated edition, 1995).

4   Walter Prescott Webb, "The Frontier and the 400-Year Boom" in *The Turner Thesis* (Lexington: Heath, 1949) p. 138.

5   For an excellent account of this exploitation, see Eduardo Galeano, *The Open Veins of Latin America: Five Centuries of the Pillage of a Continent* (New York: Monthly Review Press, 1998, 25th anniversary edition).

6   Elikia M'bokolo, "The Impact of the Slave Trade on Africa" in *Le Monde diplomatique*, April 2, 1998. http://mondediplo.com/1998/04/02africa and Eric Williams, *Capitalism and Slavery* (Chapel Hill, NC: The University of North Carolina Press, 1994).

7   Charles Bettelheim, *India Independent* (New York: Monthly Review Press, 1968) p. 47.

8   Walden Bello gives a comprehensive analysis of this agreement in *Capitalism, Nature, Socialism*, March 2000, Vol. 11, Issue 1, p. 3.

9   Tim Weiner, "How the CIA Took Aim at Allende," *The New York Times*, Sep. 12, 1998.

10   Anup Shah, "Structural Adjustment—a Major Cause of Poverty", *Global Issues*, November 28, 2010. http://www.globalissues.org/article/3/structural-adjustment-a-major-cause-of-poverty.

11   Noam Chomsky in *Keeping the Rabble in Line: Interviews with David Barsamian* (Common Courage Press, 2002).

12   2012 Walmart Annual Report, p. 19 http://walmartstores.com/AboutUs/297.aspx

13   http://www.forbes.com/billionaires/

14   "Marketers' Digital Spending to Overtake Print for First Time Ever, According to Outsell, Inc.", March 8, 2010 http://www.outsellinc.com/press/press_releases/ad_study_2010.

15   Humphrey McQueen in *The Essence of Capitalism: How we can learn everything about modern companies and the way the global economy is run by international corporations from the biggest soft drinks maker in the world* (London: Profile Books Ltd., 2001).
16   Rob Mackrill, "Global Mergers and Acquisitions Up to 77% this Year", *The Daily Reckoning*, 24 May, 2007.
17   Richard Thomas DeLamarter, *Big Blue: IBM's Use and Abuse of Power* (London: Pan, 1988) p. 24.
18   Conference papers from "Globalization or Localization: Reclaiming the Economy for the Community" (Nelson, New Zealand: Proutist Universal, 2001).
19   Ibid.
20   *Washington Post*, Dec. 7, 1997.
21   Mark Trumbull, "Lehman Bros. used accounting trick amid financial crisis – and earlier", *The Christian Science Monitor*, March 12, 2010.
22   "CSI: credit crunch". *The Economist*. 2007-10-18. http://www.economist.com/specialreports/displaystory.cfm?story_id=9972489
23   "The End of the Affair". *The Economist*. 2008-10-30. http://www.economist.com/world/unitedstates/displaystory.cfm?story_id=12637090
24   "Warning signs of a bad home loan (Page 2 of 2)". 2008. http://www.bankrate.com/brm/news/mortgages/20040615a2.asp
25   "Senator Dodd: Create, Sustain, Preserve, and Protect the American Dream of Home Ownership". DODD. 2007-02-07.
26   RealityTrac, "Foreclosure Rate Lookup Chart" http://www.realtytrac.com/foreclosure/foreclosure-rates.html
27   Senator Bernie Sanders, "Fed Lifts Veil of Secrecy", December 1, 2010, http://sanders.senate.gov/newsroom/news/?id=02b6e63c-8e86-4a82-8340-7f83c7d329af
28   "Failed Bank List". Federal Deposit Insurance Corporation. United States Government. Archived from the original on 2010-10-17. http://www.webcitation.org/5mrFV7b3r
29   Jeff Green, "Most U.S. Factory Jobs Lost in Slump May Stay Empty in Recovery", *Bloomberg Businessweek*, April 28, 2010.
30   Emily Brandon, "Retirement Accounts Have Now Lost $3.4 Trillion", *U.S. News & World Report: Money*, March 13, 2009 http://money.usnews.com/money/blogs/planning-to-retire/2009/03/13/retirement-accounts-have-now-lost-34-trillion
31   U.S. Department of Labor, Bureau of Labor Statistics http://www.bls.gov/opub/ted_20101207.htm

32   V. Dion Haynes, "U.S. unemployment rate for blacks projected to hit 25-year high", *Washington Post*, Jan. 15, 2010.

33   "Pine Ridge CDP, South Dakota - DP-3. Profile of Selected Economic Characteristics: 2000" U.S. Census Bureau.

34   Jaroslav Vanek, *New Renaissance*, Vol. 5, No. 1.

35   P.R. Sarkar, *Proutist Economics* (Calcutta: Ananda Marga Publications, 1992), pp. 89-90.

36   Scott DeCarlo, "Big Paychecks", *Forbes*, May 3, 2007.

37   Scott DeCarlo, "Special Report: CEO Compensation", *Forbes*, April 28, 2010.

38   AFL-CIO analysis of 292 companies in the S&P 500 Index. CEO pay data provided by salary.com.

39   "World's Richest People", *Forbes*, 2010 list.

40   ECLAC, "Poverty Among the Rural Population in the Region Increases Their Vulnerability to Climate Change", 10 November 2010.

41   "Measuring poverty", Wikipedia http://en.wikipedia.org/wiki/Measuring_poverty

42   Richard Wilkinson and Kate Pickett, *The Spirit Level: Why More Equal Societies Almost Always Do Better* (London: Allen Lane, 2009).

43   Gusmorino, Paul A., III. "Main Causes of the Great Depression." Gusmorino World (May 13, 1996). http://www.gusmorino.com/pag3/greatdepression/index.html.

44   April 2010 report, Bank for International Settlements

45   IMF World Economic Outlook, April 2009 http://www.imf.org/external/pubs/ft/weo/2009/01/index.htm

46   "OTC derivatives market activity in the second half of 2009", Bank for International Settlements, 11 May 2010 http://www.bis.org/press/p100511.htm

47   Gretchen Morgenson, "Given a Shovel, Americans Dig Deeper Into Debt", *The New York Times*, July 20, 2008.

48   The U.S. Federal Reserve "Monthly G.19 Consumer Credit Report", May 7 2012 and U.S. Census Bureau "State & County Quick Facts", Jan 17, 2012.

49   Consumer Credit Counselling Service, press release 21 Jul 2010 http://www.cccs.co.uk/Portals/0/Documents/media/pressreleases/Human-impact-of-debt-survey-press-release.pdf

50   Morgenson, op cit.

51   Administrative Office of the U.S. Courts, "Statistical Tables for the Federal Judiciary", 2010.

52   http://www.federalbudget.com and Congressional Budget Office, "Budget and Economic Outlook: An Update", Aug. 24, 2011.
53   This includes Current Military ($965 billion) and Past Military ($484 billion), which includes veterans' benefits plus 80 percent of the interest on the debt. War Resisters League http://www.warresisters.org/piechart.htm
54   U.S. Census Bureau, Foreign Trade Statistics, Annual 2011 Trade Highlights http://www.census.gov/foreign-trade/statistics/highlights/annual.html
55   U.S. Environmental Protection Agency, Toxics Release Inventory, http://www.epa.gov/tri/
56   The data was collected in 2008 by the U.S. Carbon Dioxide Information Analysis Center (CDIAC) for the United Nations.
57   "Estimated deaths & DALYs attributable to selected environmental risk factors, by WHO Member State, 2002". http://www.who.int/entity/quantifying_ehimpacts/countryprofilesebd.xls.
58   "US oil spill: 'Bad management' led to BP disaster", BBC, January 6 2011.
59   BP Statistical Review of World Energy 2010.
60   IEA World Energy Outlook 2010
61   Jaromir Benes, Marcelle Chauvet, Ondra Kamenik, Michael Kumhof, Douglas Laxton, Susanna Mursula and Jack Selody. *The Future of Oil: Geology versus Technology. IMF Working Paper WP/12/109* (New York: International Monetary Fund, 2012).
62   http://www.starvation.net/

2. A New Paradigm Based on Spiritual Values

1   P.R. Sarkar, "Práńa Dharma", *Prout in a Nutshell Part 6* (Calcutta, Ananda Marga Publications, 1987).
2   A few economists have incorporated spiritual values in their work, including Monsignor John Ryan, author of *A Living Wage, Its Ethical and Economic Aspects* (New York: Macmillan, 1906), E.F. Schumacher, author of *The Age of Plenty, a Christian View* (Edinburgh: The Saint Andrew Press, 1974), Herman Daly, author with J.B. Cobb Jr. of *For the Common Good* (Boston, MA: Beacon Press, 1989) and Charles Eisenstein, author of *Sacred Economics: Money, Gift and Society in the Age of Transition* (Berkeley, CA: Evolver Editions, 2011).

3   John Neihardt, *Black Elk Speaks* (New York: William Morrow & Company, 1932).

4   Eddie "Kookaburra" Kneebone (1951-2009), recipient of the Pax Christi International 2001 Peace Award, quoted in Stan Stevens, *Conservation Through Cultural Survival: Indigenous Peoples and Protected Areas* (Washington, DC: Island Press, 1997), p. 157.

5   Quoted in Rod Giblett, *Living with the Earth: Mastery to Mutuality* (Cambridge, MA: Salt Publishing, 2004), p. 218.

6   George Adams, "Traditional Wisdom Of the Yoruba - African Spirituality", Sep. 20 2010   http://elevatedentity.posterous.com/okun-o-baba-olourun-in-guyana

7   Roar Bjonnes, "Economics as if All Living Beings Mattered" in *UNESCO Encyclopedia of Life Support Systems, Globalization and World Systems*, (Oxford, 2002).

8   Alan Watts, *The Book: On the Taboo Against Knowing Who You Are* (New York: Vintage, 1966).

9   See Fritjof Capra, *The Tao of Physics: An Exploration of the Parallels Between Modern Physics and Eastern Mysticism* (Boulder, CO: Shambhala Publications, 1975) and *Uncommon Wisdom: Conversations with Remarkable People* (New York: Simon and Schuster, 1988), p. 43.

10   P.L. Benson, E.C. Roehlkepartain and S.P. Rude, "Spiritual development in childhood and adolescence: Toward a field of inquiry." *Applied Developmental Science* 7(3) 2003: pp. 205–213.

11   For the convergence of fundamental mystical beliefs amongst the great religions, see Aldous Huxley's excellent work, *The Perennial Philosophy* (New York: Harper & Row, 1945) and Swami Abhayananda, *History of Mysticism: The Unchanging Testament* (London: Watkins Publishing, 2002).

12   P.R. Sarkar, *Problems of the Day* (Calcutta: Ananda Marga Publications, 1987).

13   Peter Meyer, "Land Rush: A Survey of America's Land – Who Owns It, Who Controls It, How Much is Left", *Harpers Magazine*, Jan. 1979.

14   Kevin Cahill, *Who Owns Britain?* (London: Canongate, 2000).

15   P.R. Sarkar, "Agrarian Revolution" in *Proutist Economics* (Calcutta: Ananda Marga Publications, 1992), p. 117.

16   P.R. Sarkar, *Thoughts of P.R. Sarkar* (Calcutta: Ananda Marga Publications, 1981) p. 91.

17   For damning condemnation of the UN from the inside, see Graham Hancock, *Lords of Poverty: The Power, Prestige, and Corruption of the International Aid Business* (New York: Atlantic Monthly Press, 1992).
18   Abraham Maslow, *Eupsychian Management: A Journal* (Homewood, IL: Richard D. Irwin Inc., 1965).
19   Carl Sandburg, "Timesweep", in *Honey and Salt* (Boston: Houghton Mifflin Harcourt, 1967).
20   Paul Hawken, Amory Lovins and L. Hunter Lovins, *Natural Capitalism: Creating the Next Industrial Revolution* (Snowmass, CO: Rocky Mountain Institute, 1999).
21   Thomas Fuller, "League Tables and Update", in his blog Does Human Knowledge Double Every 5 Years?, May 26, 2007. http://newsfan.typepad.co.uk/does_human_knowledge_doub/increase_in_publications/
22   According to the International Union for Conservation of Nature (IUCN). See "Extinction crisis shows urgent need for action to protect biodiversity," UNEP, 3 November 2009.
23   Stephen Leahy, "Runaway Global Economy Decimating Nature", *International Press Service*, Oct 28, 2010.
24   The full text and list of distinguished signatories is available at http://www.commondreams.org/headlines01/1207-01.htm
25   P.R. Sarkar, "Pramá" in *Proutist Economics* (Calcutta: Ananda Marga Publications, 1992) p. 54.
26   "Morbidity and Mortality Weekly Report", U.S. Department of Health and Human Services, Centers for Disease Control and Prevention, June 4, 2010 / Vol. 59 / No. SS-5.
27   U.S. Department of Justice FBI statistics, http://www2.fbi.gov/ucr/cius2009/data/table_32.html.
28   Grossman, P., Niemann, L., Schmidt, S., and Walach, H. "Mindfulness-based stress reduction and health benefits: A meta-analysis", *Journal of Psychosomatic Research* 57:35–43, 2004.
29   McCracken, L., Gauntlett-Gilbert, J., and Vowles K.E. "The role of mindfulness in a contextual cognitive-behavioral analysis of chronic pain-related suffering and disability", *Pain* 131.1:63-69, 2007.
30   Hofmann, S.G., Sawyer, A.T., Witt. A.A., Oh, D. "The effect of mindfulness-based therapy on anxiety and depression: A meta-analytic review" *Journal of Consulting Clinical Psychology* 78:169-83, 2010.
31   Steven M. Melemis, *Make Room for Happiness: 12 Ways to Improve Your Life by Letting Go of Tension. Better Health, Self-Esteem and Relationships* (Toronto, ON: Modern Therapies, 2008).

32 Williams, J.M.G., Duggan, D.S., Crane, C., and Fennell, M.J.V. "Mindfulness-Based cognitive therapy for prevention of recurrence of suicidal behavior", *Journal of Clinical Psychology* 62:201-210, 2006.

33 Roger Walsh, "Asian Psychotherapies", in R. J. Corsini and D. Wedding (eds.), *Current Psychotherapies* (5th ed., Itasca, IL: F. E. Peacock, 1995).

34 Tierney, John, "When the Mind Wanders, Happiness Also Strays", *The New York Times*, November 15, 2010.

35 Reprinted and translated with permission from "Preface by Leonardo Boff" in the Portuguese edition of *Proutist Economics* by P.R. Sarkar (São Paulo: Ananda Marga Publications, 1996).

3. The Right to Live!

1 P.R. Sarkar, "Social Values and Human Cardinal Principles", *Prout in a Nutshell Part 7* (Calcutta: Ananda Marga Publications, 1987).

2 P.R. Sarkar, "The Principles of Prout", *Proutist Economics* (Calcutta: Ananda Marga Publications, 1992), p. 4.

3 From a letter to the author.

4 National Law Center on Homelessness and Poverty, "Homelessness in the United States and the Human Right To Housing" January 14, 2004. www.nlchp.org/content/pubs/HomelessnessintheUSandRightstoHousing.pdf

5 During some part of the year 2010, 60.5 million Americans (19.8 percent) were without health insurance. Robin A. Cohen and Michael E. Martinez, "Health Insurance Coverage: Early Release of Estimates From the National Health Interview Survey, January–March 2011" Division of Health Interview Statistics, National Center for Health Statistics. http://www.cdc.gov/nchs/data/nhis/earlyrelease/insur201109.pdf

6 "Supplemental Nutrition Assistance Program (SNAP): We put healthy food on the table for more than 46 million people each month." United States Department of Agriculture Food and Nutrition Service. http://www.fns.usda.gov/snap/

7 World Health Organization, "Removing Obstacles to Healthy Development", 1999.

8 "Global HIV and AIDS estimates, 2009 and 2010" http://www.avert.org/worldstats.htm

9 Ibid.

10   "Fortune 500 Top industries: Most profitable", CNNMoney.com, May 4, 2009 http://money.cnn.com/magazines/fortune/fortune500/2009/performers/industries/profits/

11   Larry Elliott, "Evil Triumphs in a Sick Society", *The Guardian*, Feb. 12, 2001.

12   "Worldwide HIV & AIDS Statistics", op cit.

13   "Brazil's success in AIDS fight depends on cheap drugs", Agence France-Presse, July 30, 2008.

14   Ibid.

15   Stephanie Nebehay, "Major push could end malaria deaths by 2015 - WHO", Reuters Africa, 14 Dec 2010 http://www.fightingmalaria.org/news.aspx?id=1551

16   David Leonhardt, "Why Doctors So Often Get It Wrong", *The New York Times*, February 22, 2006.

17   Linda T. Kohn, Janet M. Corrigan, and Molla S. Donaldson, editors, *To Err Is Human: Building a Safer Health System* (Washington, D.C.: National Academies Press, 2000).

18   David Leonhardt, op cit.

19   World Health Organization, "10 Facts on Patient Safety" http://www.who.int/features/factfiles/patient_safety/en/index.html

20   P.R. Sarkar, "Various Occupations", *Human Society Part 1* (Calcutta: Ananda Marga Publications, 1959).

21   Devashish, *Anandamurti: The Jamalpur Years* (San Germán, Puerto Rico: InnerWorld Publications, 2010), p. 295.

22   Karl Marx, *Capital Volume 1*, Chapter 1, Section 4, "The Fetishism of the Commodity and its Secret."

23   Sarkar, *Proutist Economics*, p. 4.

24   F. Burlatsky, "Concrete Analysis is a Major Requirement of Leninism", *The Current Digest of the Post-Soviet Press*, No. 30, Vol. 15, August 21, 1963, pp. 7-8.

25   P.R. Sarkar, "Dialectical Materialism and Democracy," *Prout in a Nutshell Part 6* (Calcutta: Ananda Marga Publications).

26   Yanqi Tong, "Mass alienation under state socialism and after", *Communist and Post-Communist Studies*, Volume 28, Issue 2, June 1995, pp. 215-237.

27   Jeffrey Goldberg, "Fidel: 'Cuban Model Doesn't Even Work For Us Anymore'", *The Atlantic*, September 8 2010.

28   Benjamin A. Valentino, "Communist Mass Killings: The Soviet Union, China, and Cambodia" in *Final solutions: mass killing and genocide*

in the twentieth century (Cornell, NY: Cornell University Press, 2005), pp. 91–151.

29   Amnesty International Report 2007. "Countdown to Olympics Fails to Stop Killing in China", American Chronicle, August 12, 2007.

30   P.R. Sarkar, "Nuclear Revolution", *Prout in a Nutshell Part 21* (Calcutta: Ananda Marga Publications).

31   Sarkar, *Proutist Economics*, p. 5.

32   Ibid, p. 58.

33   Ibid, pp. 6-11. Sarkar used slightly different wording for these five fundamental principles at different times, and there is a slight difference between the simple translation of the Sanskrit word Sarkar used and the English term he approved. For example, the mental potential of humans is "metaphysical," and the subtle potential of the universe is "supra-mundane."

34   John Kenneth Galbraith, *Economics and the Public Purpose* (New York: The New American Library, 1973).

35   P.R. Sarkar, *Problems of the Day* (Calcutta: Ananda Marga Publications) Section 27.

36   R. Buckminster Fuller and Anwar S. Dil, *Humans in Universe* (New York: Mouton, 1983) p. 212.

37   Frances Moore Lappé, Joseph Collins and Peter Rosset, with Luis Esparza, *World Hunger: 12 Myths* (New York: Grove/Atlantic and Food First Books, 2nd Edition, 1998).

38   This proposal was first made by Mariah Branch and Dada Maheshvarananda in their article, "The Progressive Utilization Theory (Prout): Alternative Economic and Spiritual Model for the Welfare of All" in *WorkingUSA: The Journal of Labor and Society*, 1089-7011, Volume 13, March 2010, pp. 31–40.

39   Abraham Maslow, *Eupsychian Management: A Journal* (Homewood, IL: Richard D. Irwin, 1965).

40   Ibid.

41   Friedman, Mark, "Living Wage and Optimal Inequality in a Sarkarian Framework", *Review of Social Economy*, Vol. LXVI, No. 1, March 2008, pp. 93-111. A free earlier version of his article is available at: http://priven.org/publications/

42   NFL Player Salaries http://www.buzzle.com/articles/nfl-player-salaries.html

43   Associated Press, "MLB's average salary eclipses $3M", December 13, 2010, http://sports.espn.go.com/mlb/news/story?id=5915468

44   U.S. Library of Congress, "The Business of Soccer", Business & Economics Research Advisor, Issue 3/4, Summer 2005.

45   Ravi Batra, *Progressive Utilization Theory: Prout – An Economic Solution to Poverty in the Third World* (Manila: Ananda Marga Publications, 1989) pp. 58-60.

46   Friedman, op cit.

47   http://www.bevegelsen.no

48   Ibid.

49   Michael Albert, *Parecon: Life After Capitalism* (New York: Verso Books, 2003).

50   Ibid.

51   For more information on Abha Light Foundation, see http://www.abhalight.org.

4. Economic Democracy

1   P.R. Sarkar, "Economic Democracy", *Proutist Economics* (Calcutta: Ananda Marga Publications, 1992), p.236.

2   Conversation with the author, February 21, 2012, Chapter 13.

3   Richard D Wolff, "Economic Democracy, Not Austerity or Keynesian 'Growth,'" Truthout, 10 May 2012. http://truth-out.org/news/item/9026-austerity-vs-keynesian-growth-vs-economic-democracy#.T6xssyufckJ. email

4   P.R. Sarkar, *Problems of the Day* (Calcutta: Ananda Marga Publications, 1968), Chapter 11.

5   Muhammad Yunus with Alan Jolis, *Banker to the Poor: Micro-lending and the Battle Against World Poverty* (New York: Public Affairs, 1999) and http://www.grameen-info.org/

6   Sarkar, *Problems of the Day*, Chapter 11.

7   For a much more detailed explanation of the three-tiered approach, see Michael Towsey, "The Three-Tier Enterprise System" in *Understanding Prout: Essays on Sustainability and Transformation, Volume 1* (Maleny, Australia: Proutist Universal, 2010).

8   "Minimum Wage History", Oregon State University, Nov. 9, 2011, based on Consumer Price Index, US Department of Labor. http://oregonstate.edu/instruct/anth484/minwage.html

9   Sylvia Nasar, "Economist Wins Nobel Prize for Work on Famines and Poverty", *The New York Times*, Oct. 15, 1998.

10   P.R. Sarkar, *Human Society Part 1* (Anandanagar, India: Ananda Marga Publications, 1962, 1998 revised translation), p. 91.

11   P.R. Sarkar, *Liberation of Intellect: Neohumanism* (Calcutta: Ananda Marga Publications, 1982), pp. 39-42.

12   Higgins, Andrew. "Twilight Economy: Lacking Money to Pay, Russian Firms Survive on Deft Barter System." *Wall Street Journal*, 27 August 1998.

13   Mariana Colacellia and David J.H. Blackburn, "Secondary currency: An empirical analysis." *Journal of Monetary Economics*, Volume 56, Issue 3, April 2009, Pages 295-308.

14   The International Reciprocal Trade Association, http://www.irta.com/

15   Raymund Flandez, "Barter Fits the Bill for Strapped Firms", *The Wall Street Journal*, February 18 2009.

16   Mel Hurtig, *The Vanishing Country* (Toronto: McClelland & Steward Ltd., 2002).

17   Robert E. Scott, "The High Price of Free Trade," Economic Policy Institute, 17 Nov. 2003. http://www.epi.org/publications/entry/briefingpapers_bp147/

18   Hazel Henderson, "Sovereign Governments v. Lords of Finance," Inter Press Service, May 2010.

19   Margrit Kennedy, *Interest and Inflation Free Money: Creating an Exchange Medium that Works for Everybody and Protects the Earth* (E. Lansing, MI: Seva International, 1995).

20   "Local Currency", Wikipedia. http://en.wikipedia.org/wiki/Local_currency

21   This section is based on Michael Towsey's essay, "Tax in a Proutist Economy, Version 2.1", Prout Institute of Australia, 24 June 2005, 39 pp.

22   United for a Fair Economy, "End the Bush Tax Cuts for the Wealthy", http://www.faireconomy.org/bushtaxcuts

23   Cato Handbook for Congress: Policy Recommendations for the 108th Congress, 2003.

24   P.R. Sarkar, "Some Specialties of Prout's Economic System," *Proutist Economics* (Calcutta: Ananda Marga Publications, 1992), p. 20.

25   P.R. Sarkar, *Discourses On Prout*. p. 15.

26   Kevin Cahill, *Who Owns Britain?* (London: Canongate, 2002).

27   P.R. Sarkar, "Developmental Planning", *Proutist Economics*.

28   UN Habitat II Action Agenda (Section B.55) http://ww2.unhabitat.org/declarations/ch-4b-3.htm

29   Hartzok, Alanna, "Pennsylvania's Success with Local Property Tax Reform: The Split Rate Tax". http://www.earthrights.net/docs/success.html#2

30   Flomenhoft, Gary, "A Green Tax Shift for Vermont", Vermont Green Tax and Common Assets Project, MPA/CDAE and Gund Institute, University of Vermont, December 2009.

31   http://www.earthrights.net.

32   "In PROUT production is for consumption – our industrial system will be based on consumption. Profit will be minimized so capitalists will not get the scope to exploit the workers.", P.R. Sarkar, "Questions and Answers on Economics – Section C", Proutist Economics.

33   Profit maximization means setting marginal revenue equal to marginal cost. Marginal cost is the cost of producing one more unit of output, marginal revenue is the added revenue from selling one more unit (assuming all units sell at the same price). Average cost is just total cost divided by output. At the output level where marginal revenue equals marginal cost price is greater than marginal cost. This means that the cost of producing more output is less than the value consumers place on added output. This difference is deadweight loss or waste that Prout seeks to eliminate (see the footnote below).

34   Deadweight loss is a measure of economic waste. It generally arises when the benefit and cost of producing one more unit of a good differ. See any microeconomics textbook, such as Thomas Nechyba, Microeconomics: An Intuitive Approach (Boston: South-Western College Publishing, 2010) for more on deadweight loss, profit, taxation etc.

5. Cooperatives for a Better World

1   P.R. Sarkar, Proutist Economics (Calcutta: Ananda Marga Publications, 1992) p. 130.

2   For an deeper analysis of the following debate, see Ronald Logan's "Cooperative Economics: In Russia", opening address at the Symposium on the Humanistic Aspects of Regional Development, held in September 1993 in Birobidzhan, Russia. http://www.proutinstitute.org/pdfs/Why_Russia_Should_Develop_Cooperative-Economics.pdf

3   Thomas Henry Huxley, "The Struggle for Existence in Human Society", Huxley's Collected Essays Volume IX. 1888. http://alepho.clarku.edu/huxley/CE9/Str.html

4   Robert Augros and George Stanciu, *The New Biology: Discovering the Wisdom of Nature* (Boulder, CO: Shambhala, 1987).

5   Quoted in Logan, op cit.

6   Gilbert Gottlieb, *Individual Development and Evolution: The Genesis of Novel Behavior* (Hove, East Sussex, UK: Psychology Press, 2001).

7   Khaled Diab, "Survival of the Nicest", *The Guardian*, 11 March 2009. http://www.guardian.co.uk/commentisfree/2009/mar/10/evolution-genetics

8   Giacomo Rizzolatti and Laila Craighero, "The mirror-neuron system". *Annual Review of Neuroscience 27*: (2004) pp. 169–192. http://www.annualreviews.org/doi/abs/10.1146%2Fannurev.neuro.27.070203.144230

9   Zak, Paul, R. Kurzban and W. Matzner. "The Neurobiology of Trust". *Annals of the New York Academy of Sciences*, 1032: pp 224-227, 2004. See also http://abc.net.au/catalyst/stories/s1481749.htm.

10   Alfie Kohn. *No Contest: The Case Against Competition* (Boston: Houghton Mifflin, 1992), quoted in *Noetic Sciences Review*, Spring 1990.

11   Elinor Ostrom. Nobel Prize Lecture: "Beyond Markets and States: Polycentric Governance of Complex Economic Systems" http://nobelprize.org/nobel_prizes/economics/laureates/2009/ostrom-lecture.html

12   For a deeper, excellent analysis of this topic, see Michael Towsey, "The Biopsychology of Cooperation" in *Understanding Prout: Essays on Sustainability and Transformation, Volume 1* (Maleny, Australia: Proutist Universal, 2010).

13   International Cooperative Alliance homepage, http://www.coop.org/ica.org. This is an excellent cooperatives resource.

14   http://www.ica.coop/ica/index.html.

15   National Cooperative Business Association homepage, http://www.ncba.org. Another excellent cooperatives resource.

16   http://www.amul.com

17   Williams, Richard C. "The Cooperative Movement in India", *The Cooperative Movement: Globalization from Below* (Burlington, VT: Ashgate, 2007), pp. 95-112.

18   Ibid.

19   Ibid.

20   World Council of Credit Unions, Statistical Data: United States Credit Union Statistics, 1939-2002. http://www.woccu.org

21   Williams, Richard C. "History and Theory of the Cooperative Movement", *The Cooperative Movement: Globalization from Below*, pp. 9-35.

22   Williams, Richard C. "Cooperatives in Latin America", *The Cooperative Movement: Globalization from Below*, pp. 125-138.

23   *Mondragon Corporation 2009 Annual Report* http://www.mcc.es/ENG/Economic-Data/Yearly-Report.aspx

24   This and following information is from a class by Mikel Lezamiz, Director of Cooperative Dissemination, Lanki Institute of Cooperative Studies, Mondragón, Spain, for the author on January 3, 2007.

25   *2009 Annual Report*, op. cit.

26   Class by Mikel Lezamiz. See also his careful reply to Noam Chomsky about cooperative management in note 2 of Chapter 13.

27   José Albarrán, "La Experiencia Cooperativa de Mondragón Desde la Visión de Prout". http://prout.org.ve/publications/

28   Personal correspondence by Mikel Lezamiz, Director of Cooperative Dissemination, Lanki Institute of Cooperative Studies, Mondragón, Spain, dated January 3, 2007.

29   Sarkar, op cit, p. 128.

30   A. Perkins, "On the transition from state planning to a cooperative system of production in the former Soviet Union". Unpublished paper.

31   *2009 Annual Report*, op. cit.

32   *National Credit Union Administration 2010 Annual Report.*

33   Marie Trigona, "Factory in the Hands of Workers", Znet, August 14, 2009. http://www.zcommunications.org/factory-in-the-hands-of-workers-by-marie-trigona. See the inspiring documentary "The Take" by Naomi Klein and Avi Lewis at http://thetake.org/.

34   John Restakis, *Humanizing the Economy* (Gabriola Island, BC: New Society Publishers, 2010).

35   "Fábricas recuperadas y también legales", Pagina 12, June 2, 2011.

36   According to Sistema de Informações em Economia Solidária, as reported in Thais Linhares Juvenal, "Empresas Recuperadas por Trabalhadores em Regime de Autogestão: Reflexões à Luz do Caso Brasileiro", *Revista Do BNDES*, Rio De Janeiro, V. 13, N. 26, P. 115-138, DeC. 2006.

37   http://evergreencooperatives.com/

38   The complete article and database are available at: http://priven.org/publications/

39   See Jake Karlyle, "Maleny Cooperatives". *New Renaissance*, Volume 12, No 2 (Winter, 2003-4) and the excellent documentary by Alister Multimedia, "Creating Prosperous Communities: Small-Scale

Cooperative Enterprises in Maleny" http://alistermultimedia.nhlf.org/
creating-prosperous-communities/
40   http://www.malenycu.com.au
41   http://www.maplestreetco-op.com
42   http://www.lets.org.au/qlets.html
43   http://www.amriverschool.org.
44   Carla Farreira, "A cooperative where there are no positions, only
tasks to be done: Cecosesola, Venezuela". http://priven.org/262/
45   Dario Azzellini, "Venezuela's Solidarity Economy: Collective
Ownership, Expropriation and Workers Self-Management." *WorkingUSA:
The Journal of Labor and Society*. Volume 12, Issue 2, June 2009, pp.
171-191.

6. An Agrarian Revolution and Environmental Protection

1   P.R. Sarkar, "Systems of Production", *Prout in a Nutshell Part 14*
(Calcutta: Ananda Marga Publications, 1988).
2   John Seymour and Herbert Girardet, *Far from Paradise* (London:
BBC, 1986).
3   Justin Murphy, "Salinity - our silent disaster", Australian Broadcasting
Corporation, 1999. http://www.abc.net.au/science/slab/salinity/default.
htm
4   Center for Human Rights and Global Justice. *Every Thirty Minutes:
Farmer suicides, human rights, and the agrarian crises in India* (New
York: NYU School of Law, 2011).
5   According to the Census of Agriculture, the number of U.S. farms
was 6.8 million in 1935; by 2002, about 2.1 million farms remained.
"Structure and Finances of U.S. Farms: 2005 Family Farm Report / EIB-
12", Economic Research Service/United States Department of Agriculture.
6   EU Annual Budget for 2010.
7   U.S. Department of Agriculture Economic Research Service, http://
www.ers.usda.gov/briefing/farmincome/govtpaybyfarmtype.htm
8   http://viacampesina.org/en/
9   David Suzuki, *The Sacred Balance* (Australia: Allen and Unwin, 1997).
10   Jerry Mander and Edward Goldsmith, *The Case Against the Global
Economy–And for a Turn Toward the Local* (San Francisco: Sierra Club
Books, 1996).
11   P.R. Sarkar, *Ideal Farming Part 2* (Calcutta: Ananda Marga
Publications, 1990).

12   Food and Agriculture Organisation of the United Nations, "Livestock's Long Shadow–Environmental Issues and Options", Rome, 2006, and "Counting chickens: Global livestock counts", *The Economist online*, July 27, 2011.

13   Vaclav Smil, *Enriching the Earth: Fritz Haber, Carl Bosch and the Transformation of World Food Production* (Cambridge, MA: The MIT Press, 2004).

14   Natural Resources Defence Council, "Facts about pollution from Livestock Farms", 2005. http://www.nrdc.org/water/pollution/ffarms.asp

15   Instituto Brasileiro de Geografia e Estatística. http://www.ibge.gov.br/home/

16   P.R. Sarkar, *Proutist Economics* (Calcutta: Ananda Marga Publications, 1992), p. 36.

17   These benefits were adapted from Acarya Krsnasevananda, "Prout's Concept of Balanced Economy: A Solution for Japan's Economic Crisis", *Journal of Future Studies*, Taipei, Vol. 5, No. 2, November 2000, pp. 129-144.

18   P.R. Sarkar, "Master Units", *Prout in a Nutshell Volume 4 Part 19* [a compilation].

19   Ibid.

20   Daniel Imhoff, "Community Supported Agriculture", in Mander, op cit.

21   USDA data, from a report to the Illinois General Assembly by The Illinois Local and Organic Food and Farm Task Force, March 2009.

22   "Current Unemployment Rates for States and Historical Highs/Lows", Local Area Unemployment Statistics Information and Analysis, U.S. Bureau of Labor Statistics, April 16, 2010.

23   http://foodfarmsjobs.org/

24   Personal correspondance with the author.

25   "Amazon Rainforest, Amazon Plants, Amazon River Animals". World Wide Fund for Nature. http://www.worldwildlife.org/wildplaces/amazon/index.cfm

26   "Amazon River and Flooded Forests". World Wide Fund for Nature. http://www.nationalgeographic.com/wildworld/profiles/g200/g147.html

27   Greenpeace, "Slaughtering the Amazon", 2009.

28   "Killer Inhabitants of the Rainforests" http://trendsupdates.com/killer-inhabitants-of-the-rainforests/

29   Personal correspondance with forestry engineer Edemilson Santos: Email edemilson_santos@yahoo.com.br.

30   Ibid.
31   Ibid.
32   See Norman Lewis, *The Missionaries: God Against the Indians* (New York: Viking Penguin, 1990).
33   http://www.amazonteam.org
34   Mark J. Plotkin, *Tales of a Shaman's Apprentice: An Ethnobotanist Searches for New Medicines in the Amazon Rain Forest* (New York: Viking Penguin, 1993) pp. 285-290.
35   Prof. Ângelo Tiago de Miranda, "Urbanização do Brasil: Conseqüências e características das cidades", Instituto Brasileiro de Geografia e Estatística (IBGE). http://educacao.uol.com.br/geografia/ult1701u57.jhtm
36   http://www.gnhusa.org http://www.felicidadeinternabruta.org.br
37   Future Vision Ecological Park, Porangaba (SP), Tel. (15) 3257-1540, 3257-1520, 3257-1243, Email: mail: visaofuturo@visaofuturo.org.br, http://www.visaofuturo.org.br

7. A New Perspective on Class, Class Struggle and Revolution

1   P.R. Sarkar, "Ananda Marga: A Revolution", *A Few Problems Solved Part 7* (Calcutta: Ananda Marga Publications, 1987).
2   P.R. Sarkar, *Human Society Part 2* (Anandanagar, India: Ananda Marga Publications, 1967).
3   P.R. Sarkar, *Prout in a Nutshell Part 18* (Calcutta: Ananda Marga Publications, 1980).
4   Frei Betto, *Valores de uma Prática Militante* (São Paulo: Consulta Popular, 2000) p. 40.
5   http://www.forbes.com/billionaires/
6   Szu-chien Hsu, "The Economy of the People's Republic of China: The Socialist Syndicate", 2007. http://priven.org/publications/
7   Jones, Bart. *¡Hugo! The Hugo Chávez Story from Mud Hut to Perpetual Revolution* (Hanover, NH: Steerforth Press, 2007) p. 160.
8   A group of 62 retired generals ran full-page advertisements in newspapers attacking the government and supporting the coup leaders. Ibid, p. 163.
9   Dec. 6, 1998: presidential election; April 25, 1999: referendum for a constitutional assembly; July 25, 1999: constitutional assembly members; Dec. 15, 1999: referendum on the new constitution; July 30, 2000:

all elected officials; Dec. 3, 2000: local representatives; Aug. 15, 2004: presidential recall referendum; Oct. 31, 2004: mayors and governors; July 17, 2005: city councils; Dec. 4, 2005: national assembly; Dec. 3, 2006: presidential election; Dec. 2, 2007: constitutional reform referendum (lost by 1 percent); Nov. 23, 2008: regional elections; Feb. 15, 2009: constitutional amendment on term limits; Sept. 26, 2010: national assembly; Oct. 7, 2012: presidential election; Dec. 16, 2012: governors. Thanks to Gregory Wilpert for this list.

10   "Occupy protests around the world: full list visualised", *The Guardian* Data Blog, http://www.guardian.co.uk/news/datablog/2011/oct/17/occupy-protests-world-list-map?newsfeed=true

11   Peter Hayward and Joseph Voros, "The Sarkar Game: Creating the experience of social change" http://www.priven.org/publications/

12   Ibid.

13   P.R. Sarkar, "Matriarchy in the Ksattriya Age", *The Awakening of Women* (Calcutta: Ananda Marga Publications, 1995), p. 3-4.

14   P.R. Sarkar, "The Development of Goddess Worship", *The Awakening of Women*, p. 183. See also PBS documentary, "Joseph Campbell and the Power of Myth with Bill Moyers", 1988.

15   Merlin Stone, *When God was a Woman* (New York: Barnes and Noble, 1976).

16   Brian Levack, in his book *The Witch Hunt in Early Modern Europe* (Harlow, UK: Longman, 2006) showed that the number of known European witch trials which are known for certain to have ended in executions is about 12,000. Multiplying this by the average rate of conviction and execution, he arrived at a figure of around 60,000 deaths.

17   See the excellent work by Diane E. Levin and Jean Kilbourne, *So Sexy So Soon: The New Sexualized Childhood and What Parents Can Do to Protect Their Kids.* (New York: Ballantine Books, 2009).

18   Evelyn Reed, *Woman's Evolution from Matriarchal Clan to Patriarchal Family* (New York: Pathfinder Press, 1975).

19   For gender bias in United States schools, see David Sadker and Karen Zittleman, *Still Failing at Fairness: How Gender Bias Cheats Girls and Boys in School and What We Can Do About It* (New York: Scribner, 2009) and American Association of University Women, "How Schools Shortchange Girls", AAUW Foundation and Wellesley College Center for Research on Women, 1992.

20   Lyn Mikel Brown and Carol Gilligan, *Meeting at the Crossroads: Women's Psychology and Girls' Development* (Cambridge, MA: Harvard

University Press, 1992) and Deborah A. Cihonski, "Finding my voice: Adolescent girls' experiences with speaking up and how recounting these experiences impacts future expression". Theses and Dissertations Paper 2827. 2005. http://scholarcommons.usf.edu/etd/2827

21   Ginette Castro, *American Feminism: A Contemporary History* (New York: NYU Press, 1990).

22   See Robert Bly, *Iron John: A Book About Men* (Boston: Addison-Wesley, 1990).

23   The United Nations Secretary-General's Campaign UNITE to End Violence against Women, "Violence Against Women: The Situation". 2009. http://www.un.org/en/women/endviolence/pdf/factsheets/unite_the_situation.pdf

24   Anti-Slavery International, Annual Review 2005, London.

25   Sylvia Nasar, "Economist Wins Nobel Prize for Work on Famines and Poverty", *The New York Times*, Oct. 15, 1998.

26   Oxfam, Education, and the Beyond Access project http://www.oxfam.org.uk/

27   Chen, M., Vanek, J., Lund, F., & Heintz, J. (2005). "Progress of the world's women 2005: Women, work and poverty." United Nations Development Fund for Women. http://www.unifem.org/attachments/products/PoWW2005_eng.pdf.

28   Sierminska, Eva, Frick, Joachim R. and Grabka, Markus M. "Examining the Gender Wealth Gap in Germany". Institute for the Study of Labor (IZA), 2008. http://ideas.repec.org/p/iza/izadps/dp3573.html

29   The Insight Center for Community Economic Development. Lifting as We Climb: Women of Color, Wealth, and America's Future. Spring 2010. http://www.insightcced.org/uploads/CRWG/LiftingAsWeClimb-WomenWealth-Report-InsightCenter-Spring2010.pdf

30   Much help in this section came from Didi Ananda Rucira's excellent compilation of P.R. Sarkar's writings on women, *The Awakening of Women*.

31   P.R. Sarkar, *The Thoughts of P.R. Sarkar* (Calcutta: Ananda Marga Publications, 1981).

32   P.R. Sarkar, *The Awakening of Women*, p. 113.

33   Published in Sohail Inayatullah and Jennifer Fitzgerald, *Transcending Boundaries: Prabhat Ranjan Sarkar's Theories of Individual and Social Transformation*, (Maleny, Australia: Gurukula Press, 1999), p. 39. See http://www.ravibatra.com.

34   *P.R. Sarkar, Human Society Part 2* (Anandanagar, India: Ananda
Marga Publications, 1963, 1998 revised translation), p. 123.
35   This text is from Dr. Johan Galtung's speech at the University of
California in Los Angeles on October 19, 1996. For more on him and
his work, see http://www.transcend.org

8. Spiritual Revolutionaries

1   P.R. Sarkar, "Nuclear Revolution", 1969, *Prout in a Nutshell Volume
4 Part 21* [a compilation].
2   Ibid.
3   P.R. Sarkar, "The Future of Civilization," *Prout in a Nutshell Volume
2 Part 6* [a compilation].
4   Quoted in "Empowered by the Sacred" by Louise Danielle Palmer
in *Spirituality & Health*, Sept/Oct. 2006, p. 46.
5   P.R. Sarkar, "Dialectical Materialism and Democracy," *Prout in a
Nutshell Volume 2 Part 6* [a compilation].
6   Daniel Goleman, Richard E. Boyatzis and Annie McKee, *Primal
Leadership: Realizing the Power of Emotional Intelligence* (Cambridge,
MA: Harvard Business School, 2002).
7   P.R. Sarkar, "Paincadasha Shiila (The Fifteen Rules of Behaviour)",
Ananda Marga Caryacarya Part 2.
8   Stanley Milgram, "Behavioral Study of Obedience", *Journal of
Abnormal and Social Psychology*, 67 (4), 1963: pp. 371–8.
9   Haney, C., Banks, W. C., and Zimbardo, P. G. "Interpersonal dynamics in a simulated prison." *International Journal of Criminology and
Penology*, 1, (1973) pp. 69–97.
10   Zeno Franco and Philip Zimbardo, "The Banality of Heroism".
Greater Good, Fall/Winter 2006-2007, pp. 30-35.
11   Goleman, op.cit.
12   Amanda Sinclair, *Leadership for the Disillusioned: Moving Beyond
Myths and Heroes to Leading That Liberates* (Crows Nest, NSW, Australia:
Allen & Unwin, 2008).
13   David B. King and Teresa L. DeCicco, "A Viable Model and Self-
Report Measure of Spiritual Intelligence," *The International Journal of
Transpersonal Studies*, Volume 28, (2009) pp. 68-85.
14   P.R. Sarkar, *Human Society Part 2* (Anandanagar, India: Ananda
Marga Publications, 1963, 1998 - revised translation), p. 133.

9. A New Concept of Ethics and Justice

1   P.R. Sarkar, "Remain United with the Supreme Benevolence", *Ananda Vacanamrtam Part 4* (Calcutta: Ananda Marga Publications, 1978).

2   Cited in Eduardo Galeano, *Upside Down: A Primer for the Looking-Glass World* (Montevideo: Picador, 2001).

3   Statistical Abstracts of the United States, 1957-1997.

4   U.S. Department of Justice, Federal Bureau of Investigation, "Crime in the United States, 2009", Sept. 2010.

5   Lt. Col. Dave Grossman, "Teaching Kids To Kill", *Phi Kappa Phi National Forum*, Fall 2000.

6   S.L.A. Marshall, *Men Against Fire: The Problem of Battle Command* (Gloucester, MA: Peter Smith, 1978). Later analysis of Marshall's methodology found many defects; however his conclusions were supported by research into the killing ratios of other wars.

7   Lt. Col. Dave Grossman, "Hope on the Battlefield", *Greater Good: The Science of a Meaningful Life*, Summer 2007.

8   Brandon S. Centerwall, "Television and Violence: The Scale of the Problem and Where to Go from Here", *Journal of the American Medical Association*, Vol. 267, No. 22, June 1992.

9   Ibid.

10   "Joint Statement on the Impact of Entertainment Violence on Children: Congressional Public Health Summit", July 26, 2000.

11   P.R. Sarkar, "Introduction", *A Guide to Human Conduct* (Calcutta: Ananda Marga Publications, 1977).

12   P.R. Sarkar, "Social Defects in Gandhism", *Prout in a Nutshell Part 21* (Calcutta: Ananda Marga Publications, 1992). For a most interesting comparison, see Sohail Inayatullah's "interview" with the two beyond the bondages of time and space, "Gandhi and Sarkar: On Nonviolence, Rural Economy and the Indian Independence Movement," *Global Times*, No. 3, May/Jun., 1998, http://www.proutglobe.org/2012/02/gandhi-and-sarkar-the-interview/.

13   E.F. Schumacher, *Small is Beautiful* (London: Abacus, 1973) p. 23.

14   "USA is the country with the largest per capita footprint in the world -- a footprint of 9.57 hectares. If everyone on the planet was to live like an average American, we would need 5 planets." from "Much Ado About Nothing", October 11, 2006. See also John L Seitz, *Global Issues: An Introduction* (Hoboken, NJ: Wiley-Blackwell, 2001) and Frances Harris, *Global Environmental Issues* (Hoboken, NJ: Wiley, 2004).

15   Quoted in Bo Lozoff, *Deep and Simple* (Durham, NC: Human Kindness Foundation, 1999) p. 65.

16   Sohail Inayatullah and Jennifer Fitzgerald, *Transcending Boundaries: Prabhat Ranjan Sarkar's Theories of Individual and Social Transformation* (Maleny, Australia: Gurukula Press, 1999).

17   U.S. Department of Justice Statistics, 2011, http://bjs.ojp.usdoj.gov/content/pub/press/p10cpus10pr.cfm.

18   According to the Justice Policy Institute, in 2000 there were 791,600 black men in prison and 603,032 enrolled in college. Reported in "Prison Population Exceeds Two Million", Information Please Database, 2007, Pearson Education, Inc. http://www.infoplease.com/ipa/A0881455.html

19   P.R. Sarkar, "Mass Murder", *Prout in a Nutshell Part 15* (Calcutta: Ananda Marga Publications).

20   P.R. Sarkar, "Justice", *Human Society Part 1* (Calcutta: Ananda Marga Publications, 1959, revised edition 1998).

21   James M. Henslin, *Social Problems: A Down-to-Earth Approach* (Boston: Allyn & Bacon, 2007).

22   The Criminal Sanctions Agency of Finland, "The released from prison in Finland 1993-2001 and the re-entered" http://www.rikosse-uraamus.fi/25234.htm

23   Senator Paul Simon and Dave Kopel, "Restore Flexibility to U.S. Sentences", *National Law Journal*, Dec. 16, 1996, p. A15.

24   Lawrence W Sherman and Heather Strang, et al, "Restorative Justice: The Evidence", The Smith Institute, 2007. http://www.sas.upenn.edu/jerrylee/RJ_full_report.pdf and http://www.murdoch.edu.au/elaw/issues/v9n1/haslip91.html

25   Lozoff, "A Nation Behind Bars", *Peace and Social Justice*, Mar. 1998.

26   P.R. Sarkar, "The Neohumanism of Sadvipras", *Neohumanism in a Nutshell Part 1* (Calcutta: Ananda Marga Publications).

27   Sarkar, "Justice", op cit.

28   Nelson Mandela, *Long Walk to Freedom* (New York: Little Brown & Co., 1995).

29   Sarkar, "Justice", op cit.

30   Sarkar, "Justice", op cit.

31   Human Kindness Foundation, P.O. Box 61619, Durham, NC 27715, http://www.humankindness.org

32   Prison Phoenix Trust, http://www.theppt.org.uk

33   Pashupati Steven Landau, MD, and Jagat Bandhu John Gross, "Low Reincarceration Rate Associated with Ananda Marga Yoga and

Meditation", *International Journal of Yoga Therapy*, No. 18 (2008), pp. 43-48. http://prisonyoga.com/downloads/ReincarcerationStudyIJYT.pdf

34   Translated from the Portuguese, "Monk Teaches Yoga to Prisoners in Minas Gerais", *Jornal do Brasil*, Feb. 28, 2000.

35   Translated from the Portuguese, letter to the author.

36   Larry Cohen and Susan Swift, "A Public Health Approach to the Violence Epidemic in the United States", *Environment and Urbanization*, Vol. 5, No. 2, 1993.

37   BBC, "Alcohol 'more harmful than heroin' says Prof David Nutt", Nov. 1 2010. http://www.bbc.co.uk/news/uk-11660210

38   Democracy Now, "'The House I Live In': New Documentary Exposes Economic, Moral Failure of U.S. War on Drugs", Jan. 31, 2012, http://www.democracynow.org/2012/1/31/the_house_i_live_in_new

39   "Budgetary Implications of Marijuana Prohibition in the United States" http://www.prohibitioncosts.org/endorsers.html

10. "Our Culture is Our Strength!"

1   P.R. Sarkar, "Developmental Planning", *Proutist Economics* (Calcutta: Ananda Marga Publications, 1992) p. 198.

2   Dada Maheshvarananda, "Conversation with Paulo Freire, Educator of the Oppressed", in Sohail Inayatullah, et al, eds. *Neohumanist Educational Futures: Liberating the Pedagogical Intellect* (Taipei: Tamkang University, 2006).

3   Acarya Prasiidananda Avt., *How to Introduce the Ideas of Ananda Marga and Prout to the Public* (Manila: Ananda Marga Publications, 1989).

4   Davide Dukcevich, "The Richest of the Rich", *Forbes*, Dec. 12, 2001.

5   Maheshvarananda, op cit.

6   P.R. Sarkar, *Human Society Part 1* (Calcutta: Ananda Marga Publications, 1959 - 1998 revised edition) pp. 12-13.

7   Maheshvarananda, op cit.

8   Dada Maheshvarananda, "Cooperative Games that Teach Solidarity", *New Renaissance*, Vol. 11, No. 3, Autumn 2002, pp. 15-17, http://www.ru.org/maheshvarananda-113.htm.

9   http://www.amurt.org.br.

10   See http://www.gurukul.edu and http://www.nhe.gurukul.edu

11   http://www.wlrp.org

12   Acarya Tadbhavananda Avt., *Samaj: A New Dimension in Politics* (Delhi: Proutist Universal, 1987).
13   http://news.angkasama.info/.
14   http://www.sfmt.org/index.php
15   "The Nobel Prize in Literature 1997". Nobelprize.org. 3 Jun 2012 http://www.nobelprize.org/nobel_prizes/literature/laureates/1997/
16   http://www.commediaschool.com
17   See photos of the Nordic Buffoons at http://www.belef.org/01/galerija/11vece.html and http://www.belef.org/01/prog/012.html. Contact info@commediaschool.com.
18   Letter to the author.
19   Linda Tuhiwai Smith, *Decolonizing Methodologies: Research and Indigenous Peoples* (London: Zed Books, 1999).
20   Quino-Solis, et al., *From a Game of Cards to the Development of Regional Cooperatives*, 2004, pp. 85-86.
21   Ibid.
22   Ibid.

11. Empowering Communities: Prout's Political System

1   P.R. Sarkar, *Problems of the Day* (Calcutta: Ananda Marga Publications, 1968) Chapter 32.
2   This section is partly based on an essay in development, "An Introduction to Sadvipra Governance" by Michael Towsey and Jake Karlyle, not yet published.
3   Qian Sima and trans. Burton Watson, *Records of the Grand Historian: Han Dynasty* (Research Center for Translation, The Chinese University of Hong Kong and Columbia University Press, 1993).
4   Letter to Bishop Mandell Creighton, April 5, 1887 published in *Historical Essays and Studies*, edited by J. N. Figgis and R. V. Laurence (London: Macmillan, 1907).
5   Thomas Hobbes, *Leviathan: With Selected Variants from the Latin Edition of 1668* (Hackett Classics, Edwin Curley, editor).
6   "The US presidential form of government is a better form of government, but there is a shortcoming in the US constitution and that is that individual rights are given maximum scope: this leads to an unrestrained capitalist order... Too much individual freedom should be curtailed in an ideal form of government. Prout will introduce social controls so that collective interests will be supreme. In the US constitution purchasing

power is not guaranteed to the people. The best form of government is the presidential form where the president is elected directly by the electorate and there is less individual liberty." P.R. Sarkar, "Requirements of an Ideal Constitution", *Prout in a Nutshell Volume 3 Part 12.*

7   The Center for Responsive Politics (2010). Election Stats. http://www.opensecrets.org/bigpicture/elec_stats.php?cycle=2010.

8   "Money Meant Victory for Many" by Jonathan D. Salant, Associated Press, Nov. 8, 2000.

9   P:R. Sarkar, "Talks on Prout", *Prout in a Nutshell Volume 3 Part 15,* "Political Parties" section.

10   Cardinal human values, as explained in Chapter 9, are the virtues of honesty, courage, mercy, humility, self-restraint and compassion. According to these cardinal values, the strong should protect the weak, selfishness is unethical, and it is important to try to avoid harming others. This important proposal gives balance to the other rights, guaranteeing that no other right conflicts with the general welfare of humanity.

11   Agrico-industries refers to "pre-harvest" industries that produce what farmers require, such as tools, implements, seeds and fertilizers. Agro-industries are "post-harvest," processing raw agricultural products into flour, oil, textiles, paper, etc.

12   For an excellent comprehensive and comparative analysis of Prout's concept of world government, see Craig Runde, "Beyond Nationalism: Sarkar's Vision of World Government" in *Transcending Boundaries: Prabhat Ranjan Sarkar's Theories of Individual and Social Transformation* (Maleny, Australia: Gurukula Press, 1999) p. 39.

13   Michael Towsey and Jake Karlyle, op cit.

14   P.R. Sarkar, "Dialectical Materialism and Democracy", *Prout in a Nutshell Volume 2 Part 6.*

15   The first part of this essay was excerpted from Sohail Inayatullah, "Conclusion: The Lamp that Illuminates Countless Other Lamps", which appeared in his book, *Situating Sarkar: Tantra, Macrohistory and Alternative Futures* (Maleny, Australia: Gurukula Press, 1999). See http://www.metafuture.org

16   Charles Paprocki, "On Proutist Methodology", unpublished paper.

17   Thomas Khun, *The Structure of Scientific Revolutions* (Chicago: University of Chicago Press, 1962).

18   Richard Slaughter, *Futures Tools and Techniques* (Victoria, Australia: Futures Studies Center, 1987).

19　For more on the methodological framework in this paper, see Sohail Inayatullah, *Questioning the future: Tools and methods for organizational and societal transformation* (Tamsui, Taiwan: Tamkang University, 2007). For information on other books by Inayatullah, see http://www. metafuture.org.

20　For example, see Graeme Taylor, *Evolution's Edge* (Bagriola Island, Canada: New Society Publishers, 2008), Bill Halal, *Technology's Promise* (New York: Palgrave Macmillan, 2008), Sohail Inayatullah, "Positive trends amidst the doom and gloom" May 15, 2009, http://www.metafuture.org

21　See the works of Joseph Campbell at the Joseph Campbell Foundation. http://www.jcf.org/new/index.php?categoryid=31.

12. A Call to Action: Strategies to Implement Prout

1　P.R. Sarkar, "Ananda Vanii", 1975.

2　Personal story told by Dada Abhayananda

3　http://www.forumsocialmundial.org.br/

4　http://shop.anandamarga.org/books/sarkar/eledit70.htm

5　"Beyond Seattle" Teach-in, Washington DC, Apr. 14, 2000.

6　http://www.proutglobe.org/2012/04/persecution -of-proutists-pricks-kolkatas-conscience/

7　http://priven.org/global-conference-2011/

8　http://www.r-evolucionar.eu

9　http://www.economicdemocracyconference.org

10　http://www.irprout.it, http://www.prout.it

11　http://www.prout.org.ar

12　http://www.proutugal.org

13　http://prout-de.net/

14　P.R. Sarkar, "The Role of Youth: Talks on Education – Excerpt G," *Prout in a Nutshell Volume 4 Part 18* [a compilation]

15　Contact Pradeep Sharma at sewa.service@gmail.com

16　Contact Kanhu Behura at kanhu.behura@gmail.com

17　Contact at jivandev@gmail.com. His blog is http://www.hualien-permaculture.blogspot.com.au/

18　http://www.proutjournal.com

19　"Repertorio Forense: Publicación diaria de doctrina, legislación, jurisprudencia, bibliografia, información judicial", Vol. XXXIX, No. 14.541-2, Caracas, 28 Feb. 2007, pp. 2-4.

20   http://priven.org/about/about-the-institute/
21   "Barlovento co-op survey" http://www.priven.org/publications/
22   http://www.youtube.com/watch?v=bgL4WMlzuGU
23   http://priven.org/global-conference-2011/
24   http://www.centromadre.org
25   http://www.proutinstitute.org
26   I personally believe that this small booklet, in the guise of a children's story, is one of the clearest blueprints Sarkar gave as to how a Proutist revolution can develop from the grassroots and achieve victory. I recommend it to everyone. P.R. Sarkar, *The Golden Lotus of the Blue Sea* (Calcutta: Ananda Marga Publications).
27   Peace sign: http://www.flickr.com/photos/aaronfreimark/378454005/sizes/l/in/photostream/
28   Capture the Flag: http://www.youtube.com/watch?v=3UZLgPD_cjk
29   Pillow fight: http://www.youtube.com/watch?v=dmdcjj49hZQ
30   Water fight: http://www.youtube.com/watch?v=foJ6h5iq1lc
31   Mp3 Flashmob: http://www.youtube.com/watch?v=Eq7LiZmpKT8
32   Music video: http://www.youtube.com/watch?v=GSP81Che1Xo
33   Protest rally: http://www.youtube.com/watch?v=ucF7IoASP8g
34   4K!: http://www.negyedikkoztarsasag.hu
35   Interview in *Caros Amigos*, Issue 39, Jun. 2000.
36   P.R. Sarkar, "Nuclear Revolution", *Prout in a Nutshell Part 21* (Calcutta: Ananda Marga Publications).
37   P.R. Sarkar, *Problems of the Day* (Calcutta: Ananda Marga Publications, 1968), Chapter 2.
38   P.R. Sarkar, "Move with Ever-Accelerating Speed", *Prout in a Nutshell Part 17*, (Calcutta: Ananda Marga Publications).
39   Victor Hugo, *Histoire d'un Crime* (The History of a Crime) [written 1852, published 1877], Conclusion, ch. X. Trans. T.H. Joyce and Arthur Locker.
40   "Women's Voices: Quotations by Women" – Margaret Mead, http://womenshistory.about.com/cs/quotes/a/qu_margaretmead.htm
41   P.R. Sarkar, *Ananda Vacanamrtam Part 31* (Calcutta, Ananda Marga Publications), pp. 43-45.

13. A Conversation with Noam Chomsky

1   The Occupy Wall Street film team: Abe Heisler, Mike McSweeney, Katie Davison and Ras Arthemio Selassie, with logistical assistance by

Amal Jacobson and Nir Kronenberg. See the interview: http://studiooc-
cupy.org/#!/media/wewwbk
2   Mikel Lezamiz, Director of Cooperative Dissemination of Otalora,
Mondragon Cooperative Corporation, wrote to the author in reply,
"Practically 100 percent of senior managers in Mondragon cooperatives are co-op members, not outside, salaried, non-member staff. A
very substantial portion have degrees in management or engineering
from Mondragon University and most of the rest from another one of
the Basque universities. Almost all senior managers are developed and
mentored over many years inside the cooperative group; very, very few
are hired from outside at a senior level. We should also take issue with
the claim that the Mondragon co-operatives are not worker-managed.
Note first that governance in the cooperatives is democratic, based on
the principle of one member, one vote. There is a full separation of
governance staff from management staff and the latter are fully accountable to the former. Day-to-day operational decision making is different.
There most certainly is a division of labor, as we think is inevitable in any
viable business organization of more than a handful of people, and the
level of shop floor or office floor autonomy and involvement certainly
varies from co-op to co-op (and over time), but worker participation
in decision making at various levels is widespread in Mondragon and
a continuing priority, both from philosophical and business perspectives. Building and sustaining high levels of participation in complex
organizations competing in intensely competitive international markets
is a challenge for many reasons, and our experience is far from perfect,
but it is a challenge we fully embrace."

Bibliography

Abhayananda, Swami. *History of Mysticism: The Unchanging Testament.* London: Watkins Publishing, 2002.

Albert, Michael. *Parecon: Life After Capitalism.* New York: Verso Books, 2003.

Alinsky, Saul. *Rules for Radicals.* New York: Vintage Books, 1989.

Alperovitz, Gar. *America Beyond Capitalism.* Hoboken, NJ: John Wiley and Sons, 2004.

Augros, Robert and George Stanciu. *The New Biology: Discovering the Wisdom of Nature.* Boulder, CO: Shambhala, 1987.

Aung San Suu Kyi. *The Voice of Hope: Conversations with Alan Clements.* New York: Seven Stories Press, 1996

Batra, Ravi. *Progressive Utilization Theory: Prout: An Economic Solution to Poverty in the Third World.* Manila: Ananda Marga Publications, 1989.

Benjamin, César e Tânia Bacelar de Araújo. *Brasil: Reinventar o Futuro.* Sindicato dos Engenheiros no Rio de Janeiro, 1995.

Bettelheim, Charles. *India Independent.* New York: Monthly Review Press, 1968.

Bhaskarananda, Acarya Avadhuta. *Social Dynamics and Social Movements: Shrii P. R. Sarkar's Vision for Society.* Anandanagar, India: Psychospiritual Research Foundation, 2001.

Bjonnes, Ramesh. *Sacred Body, Sacred Spirit: A Personal Guide to the Wisdom of Yoga and Tantra.* San Germán, Puerto Rico: InnerWorld Publications, 2012.

Bjonnes, Roar. *Principles for a Balanced Economy: An Introduction to the Progressive Utilization Theory.* Copenhagen, Denmark: Prout Research Institute, 2012.

Bly, Robert. *Iron John: A Book About Men.* Boston: Addison-Wesley, 1990.

Bobo, Kimberley et al. *Organizing for Social Change: Midwest Academy Manual for Activists.* Cabin John, MD: Seven Locks Press, 2001

Boggs, Grace Lee. *The Next American Revolution: Sustainable Activism for the Twenty-First Century*. Berkeley, CA: University of California Press, 2011.

Brown, Ellen. *Web of Debt: The Shocking Truth About Our Money System — The Sleight of Hand That Has Trapped Us in Debt and How We Can Break Free*. Baton Rouge, LA: Third Millennium Press, 2007.

Brown, Lyn Mikel, and Carol Gilligan. *Meeting at the Crossroads: Women's Psychology and Girls' Development*. Cambridge, MA: Harvard University Press, 1992.

Caetanya. *An Introduction to Block Level Planning: A Manual for PRI Staff*. New Delhi: Prout Research Institute, 1992. www.proutworld.org/ideology/ecdem/BLP.pdf

Cahill, Kevin. *Who Owns Britain?* London: Canongate, 2002.

— *Who Owns the World: The Surprising Truth About Every Piece of Land on the Planet*. New York: Grand Central Publishing, 2010.

Camacho, Carlos José Molina and Alberto García Müller. *Cooperativas: Principios, Valores, Organización, Manejo*. Caracas: Panapo, 2006.

Capra, Fritjof. *The Tao of Physics: An Exploration of the Parallels Between Modern Physics and Eastern Mysticism*. Boulder, CO: Shambhala Publications, 1975.

— *Uncommon Wisdom: Conversations with Remarkable People*. New Yo: Simon and Schuster, 1988.

Cavanaugh, John and Jerry Mander, eds. *Alternatives to Economic Globalization: A Better World is Possible*. San Francisco: Berrett-Koehler Publishers, Inc., 2004.

Center for Human Rights and Global Justice. *Every Thirty Minutes: Farmer suicides, human rights, and the agrarian crises in India*. New York: NYU School of Law, 2011.

Chomsky, Noam. *Keeping the Rabble in Line: Interviews with David Barsamian*. Monroe, ME: Common Courage Press, 2002.

— *Occupy (Occupied Media Pamphlet Series)*. New York: Zuccotti Park Press, 2012.

— with David Barsamian. *Secrets, Lies and Democracy*. Tucson: Odonian Press, 1994.

Consedine, Jim, and Helen Bowen. *Restorative Justice: Contemporary Themes and Practice*. New Zealand: Ploughshares Publications, 1999.

— *Restorative Justice: Healing the Effects of Crime*. New Zealand: Ploughshares Publications, 1999.

Danaher, Kevin, Shannon Biggs and Jason Mark. *Building the Green Economy: Success Stories from the Grassroots*. Sausalito, CA: Polipoint Press, 2007

Devashish. *Anandamurti: The Jamalpur Years*. San Germán: InnerWorld Publications, 2010.

Dyer, Bruce, ed. *Conference papers from Globalization or Localisation: Reclaiming the Economy for the Community*. Nelson, New Zealand: Proutist Universal, 2001.

Eisenstein, Charles. *Sacred Economics: Money, Gift and Society in the Age of Transition*. Berkeley, CA: Evolver Editions, 2011.

Fuller, R. Buckminster and Anwar S. Dil. *Humans in Universe*. New York: Mouton, 1983.

Gaffney, Mason and Fred Harrison. *The Corruption of Economics*. London: Shepheard-Walwyn, 1994.

Galbraith, John Kenneth. *Economics and the Public Purpose*. New York: The New American Library, 1973.

Galeano, Eduardo. *The Open Veins of Latin America: Five Centuries of the Pillage of a Continent*. New York: Monthly Review Press, 1998 (25th anniversary edition).

— *Upside Down: A Primer for the Looking-Glass World*. Montevideo: Picador, 2001.

George, Henry. *Progress and Poverty: An Inquiry Into the Cause of Industrial Depressions, and of Increase of Want with Increase of Wealth, the Remedy*. Garden City, NY: Doubleday, 1912.

Ghista, Dhanjoo and Michael Towsey. *Self-Reliant Regional Proutistic Development*. Delhi: Prout Research Institute, 1991.

Giecek, Tamara Sober. *Teaching Economics as if People Mattered: A High School Curriculum Guide to the New Economy*. Boston: United for a Fair Economy, 2000.

Goleman, Daniel, Richard E. Boyatzis and Annie McKee. *Primal Leadership: Realizing the Power of Emotional Intelligence*. Cambridge, MA: Harvard Business School, 2002.

Greider, William. *One World, Ready or Not: The Manic Logic of Global Capitalism*. New York: Simon & Schuster, 1997.

Grossman, Lt. Col. Dave. *On Killing: The Psychological Cost of Learning to Kill in War and Society*. New York: Back Bay Books, 1996.

Hahnel, Robin. Panic Rules! Cambridge, MA: South End Press, 1999.

Hancock, Graham. *Lords of Poverty: The Power, Prestige and Corruption of the International Aid Business*. New York: Atlantic Monthly Press, 1992.

Hartzok, Alanna. *The Earth Belongs to Everyone: Articles and Essays by Alanna Hartzok*. Radford, VA: The Institute for Economic Democracy Press and Earth Rights Institute, 2008.

Hawken, Paul. *Blessed Unrest: How the Largest Social Movement in History is Restoring Grace, Justice and Beauty to the World*. New York: Penguin Books, 2007.

Henderson, Hazel. *Ethical Markets: Growing the Green Economy*. White River Jct., VT: Chelsea Green Publishing, 2006.

Hopkins, Rob. *The Transition Handbook: From oil dependency to local resilience*. White River Junction, VT: Chelsea Green Publishing, 2008.

Huxley, Aldous. *The Perennial Philosophy*. New York: Harper & Row, 1945.

Inayatullah, Sohail. *Situating Sarkar: Tantra, Macrohistory and Alternative Futures*. Maleny, Australia: Gurukula Press, 1999.

— *Understanding Sarkar: The Indian Episteme Macrohistory and Transformative Knowledge*. Leiden, the Netherlands: Brill, 2002.

— and Jennifer Fitzgerald, eds. *Transcending Boundaries: Prabhat Ranjan Sarkar's Theories of Individual and Social Transformation*. Maleny, Australia: Gurukula Press, 1999.

— Marcus Bussey and Ivana Milojevic, eds. *Neohumanist Educational Futures: Liberating the Pedagogical Intellect*. Taipei: Tamkang University, 2006.

Jitendrananda, Dada and Paul Wildman. *Here, Together, Now – A Neo-Humanist Guidebook for Human Development*. Auckland, New Zealand: Prosperity Press, 2002.

Jones, Bart. *¡Hugo! The Hugo Chávez Story from Mud Hut to Perpetual Revolution*. Hanover, NH: Steerforth Press, 2007.

Jyotirupananda, Dada. *Meditation: Searching for the Real You*. Washington: O Books, 2009.

Karlyle, Jake and Michael Towsey, eds. *Essays on Sustainability and Transformation: Understanding Prout, Volume 1*. Maleny, Australia: Proutist Universal, 2010.

Katsiaficas, Georgy. *The Subversion of Politics: European Autonomous Social Movements and the Decolonization of Everyday Life*. Oakland, CA: AK Press, 2006.

Kennedy, Margrit. *Interest and Inflation Free Money: Creating an Exchange Medium that Works for Everybody and Protects the Earth*. E. Lansing, MI: Seva International, 1995.

Kohn, Alfie. *No Contest: The Case Against Competition*. 2nd, Revised edition, Boston: Houghton Mifflin, 1992.

Korten, David C. *The Post-Corporate World: Life After Capitalism.* San Francisco: Berrett-Koehler Publishers, 1999.

Krtashivananda, Acarya. *Prout Manifesto.* Copenhagen: Proutist Universal, 1988.

— *Prout: Humanistic Socialism and Economic Democracy.* Copenhagen: Prout Research Institute, 2011.

Lappé, Frances Moore, Joseph Collins and Peter Rosset, with Luis Esparza. *World Hunger: 12 Myths.* New York: Grove/Atlantic and Food First Books, 2nd Edition, 1998.

Levin, Diane E. and Jean Kilbourne. *So Sexy So Soon: The New Sexualized Childhood and What Parents Can Do to Protect Their Kids.* New York: Ballantine Books, 2009.

Lewis, Norman. *The Missionaries: God Against the Indians.* New York: Viking Penguin, 1990.

Lichauco, Alejandro. *Nationalist Economics: History, Theory and Practice.* Manila: SPES Institute, 1988.

Loewen, James W. *Lies My Teacher Told Me: Everything Your American History Textbook Got Wrong.* New York: The New Press, 1995.

Lozoff, Bo. *Deep and Simple: A Spiritual Path for Modern Times.* Durham, NC: Human Kindness Foundation, 1999.

Magnuson, Joel. *Mindful Economics: How the U.S. Economy Works, Why it Matters, and How it Could Be Different.* New York: Seven Stories Press, 2008.

Maheshvarananda, Dada. *After Capitalism: Prout's Vision for a New World.* Copenhagen: Proutist Universal, 2003.

Mandela, Nelson. *Long Walk to Freedom.* New York: Little Brown & Co., 1995.

Mander, Jerry and Edward Goldsmith, eds. *The Case Against the Global Economy: and for a Turn Toward the Local.* San Francisco: Sierra Club Books, 1996.

Maslow, Abraham. *Eupsychian Management: A Journal.* Homewood, IL: Richard D. Irwin, 1965.

McKibben, Bill. *Deep Economy: The Wealth of Communities and the Durable Future.* New York: Henry Holt & Company, 2007.

McQueen, Humphrey. *The Essence of Capitalism: How we can learn everything about modern companies and the way the global economy is run by international corporations from the biggest soft drinks maker in the world.* London: Profile Books Ltd., 2001.

Melman, Seymour. *After Capitalism: From managerialism to workplace democracy.* New York: Alfred A. Knopf, 2001.

Neihardt, J. *Black Elk Speaks.* New York: William Morrow & Company. 1932.

Nichols, John. *Uprising: How Wisconsin Renewed the Politics of Protest, from Madison to Wall Street.* New York: Nation Books, 2012.

Ormaechea, Jose Maria. *The Mondragon Cooperative Experience.* Mondragón, Spain: Mondragon Corporacion Cooperativa, 1993.

Plotkin, Mark J. *Tales of a Shaman's Apprentice: An Ethnobotanist Searches for New Medicines in the Amazon Rain Forest.* New York: Viking Penguin, 1993.

Prasiidananda, Acarya. *How to Introduce the Ideas of Ananda Marga and Prout to the Public.* Manila: Ananda Marga Publications, 1989.

— *Neo-Humanist Ecology.* Manila: Ananda Marga Publications, 1990.

Proceedings of the Proutist Universal Global Convention, 20-27 July 2009, Ananda Gaorii, Denmark. Copenhagen, Denmark: Proutist Universal, 2010.

Prout Research Institute. *Togo: A Proutist approach for solving the problems of lowered living standards, unemployment and rural poverty.* Togo: Prout Research Institute, 1991.

Proutist Writers' Group of New York Sector. *A Comprehensive Guide to the Study of Prout.* Second Edition. Washington: Proutist Universal, 1999.

Restakis, John. *Humanizing the Economy.* Gabriola Island, BC: New Society Publishers, 2010.

Runde, Craig E. and Tim A. Flanagan. *Becoming a Conflict Competent Leader: How Your Organization Can Manage Conflict Effectively.* Sausalito, CA: John Wiley & Sons, Inc., 2007.

Rynn, Jon. *Manufacturing Green Prosperity: The Power to Rebuild the American Middle Class.* Santa Barbara, CA: Praeger, 2010.

Sadat, Anwar. *In Search of Identity: An Autobiography.* New York: Harper Collins, 1987.

Sarkar, Prabhat Ranjan. *The Awakening of Women.* Calcutta: Ananda Marga Publications, 1995.

— *Human Society Part Two.* Anandanagar, India, Ananda Marga Publications, 1963, 1998 (revised translation).

—*The Liberation of Intellect: Neo-Humanism.* Calcutta: Ananda Marga Publications, 1982.

— *Ideal Farming: Part 2.* Calcutta: Ananda Marga Publications, 1990.

— *Proutist Economics*. Calcutta: Ananda Marga Publications, 1992.

Sharp, Gene. *The Politics of Nonviolent Action, Vol. 2: The Methods of Nonviolent Action*. Boston: Porter Sargent Publishers, 1973.

Schumacher, E.F. *Small is Beautiful: Economics as if People Mattered*. London: Abacus, 1973.

Schweickart, David. *After Capitalism (New Critical Theory)*. Lanham, MD: Rowman & Littlefield Publishers, 2011.

Sen, Amartya. *Poverty and Famine*. Oxford: Oxford University Press, 1981.

Seymour, John and Herbert Girardet. *Far from Paradise*. London: BBC, 1986.

Shafarman, Steven. *We the People: Healing Our Democracy and Saving Our World*. California: Gain Publications, 2001.

Shambhushivananda, Dr. *PROUT: Neo-humanistic Economics*. Mainz, Germany: Dharma Verlag, 1989.

Shostak, Arthur B. ed. *Viable Utopian Ideas: Shaping a Better World*. New York: Armonk, 2003.

Smith, Linda Tuhiwai. *Decolonizing Methodologies: Research and Indigenous Peoples*. London: Zed Books, 1999.

Stiglitz, Joseph E. *Making Globalization Work*. New York: W. W. Norton, 2006.

Survival International. *Disinherited: Indians in Brazil*. London: Survival International, 2000.

Suzuki, David. *The Sacred Balance*, Australia: Allen and Unwin, 1997.

Tadbhavananda, Acarya. *Samaj: A New Dimension in Politics*. Delhi: Proutist Universal, 1987.

Teasdale, Wayne. *A Monk in the World: Cultivating a Spiritual Life*. Novato, CA: New World Library, 2002.

Weatherford, Jack. *Indian Givers: How the Indians of the Americas Transformed the World*. New York: Fawcett Books, 1988.

Wilkinson, Richard and Kate Pickett. *The Spirit Level: Why More Equal Societies Almost Always Do Better*. London: Allen Lane, 2009.

Williams, Richard C. *The Cooperative Movement: Globalization from Below*. Burlington, VT: Ashgate, 2007.

Yunus, Muhammad with Alan Jolis. *Banker to the Poor: Micro-lending and the Battle Against World Poverty*. New York: Public Affairs, 1999.

Zinn, Howard. *A People's History of the United States: 1492-Present, Revised and Updated Edition*. New York: HarperCollins, 1995.

Index

Guinea Bissau 4
Gulf of Mexico 28, 125
Gulf Stream Current 28
Gurukula Network 224–223
Gusmão, Xanana 184
Haiti 275
Halliburton 28
Hartzok, Alanna 98–99
Harvey, Andrew 183
Hass, Liila 231–232
Havel, Vaclav 184
Hawaiian language 225
Hawken, Paul 43
Hayward, Peter 166–170
health care 15, 26, 30, 44, 54, 55, 58,
67, 76, 77, 78, 85, 87, 93, 97, 148,
147, 148, 173, 174, 195, 196, 233,
244, 254, 255, 90
HealthGrades 58
Hebrew 225
Henderson, Hazel 93
herbal medicine 58, 77
hierarchy of human needs 42
Hispaniola 12
HIV/AIDS. See AIDS
Hobbes, Thomas 240
Hollywood entertainment 103, 201,
221
homeopathy 58, 76, 77
Honduras 105, 291
Hopis 46
Hsu, Szu-chien 164
Hugo, Víctor 279
humanism 41
Human Kindness Foundation 214
Humboldt, Wilhelm von 287
Hume, David 288
Hungary 200, 271–273
hunger 29, 162, 258, 277, 278
Huxley, Thomas Henry 102
IBM 18
Iceland 21
illiteracy 15

immigrants 89
imperialism 41, 220
imprisonment 8, 25, 60, 61, 209, 214
Inayatullah, Sohail 250–256
India 7, 9, 13, 16, 39, 56, 57, 61, 98,
99, 105, 106, 126, 134, 137, 153,
157, 173, 176, 177, 200, 205, 209,
218, 222, 224, 225, 226, 227, 243,
244, 261, 262, 264, 90
indigenous cultures 146–147, 157,
239, 290
Indignados Movement 6, 166
Indonesia 222, 225, 275
Industrial Revolution 13, 281
infectious diseases 29, 49, 55
inflation 15, 34, 83, 87, 91, 94, 150
Inquisition 171, 208
inspiration 188–190
Institute for Cultural Action 4
Institute of Medicine 58
International Cooperative Alliance
(ICA) 105
international dumping 126
International Energy Agency 29
internationalism 42
International Monetary Fund (IMF)
15, 16, 26, 29, 72, 84, 92, 126, 149,
150, 275, 276
Interpol 199
Iran 165
Iraq 124, 165, 186, 226
Ireland 21, 214, 226
Italy 13, 21, 104, 105, 107, 263
Japan 13, 105, 135, 138, 200
Jordan 165
Judeo-Christian values 199, 240
Kenya 75, 75–78, 76, 77
Keynesian economists 73, 80
Khmer Rouge 60, 66
King, Martin Luther 184
Kneebone, Eddie "Kookaburra" 36
Knights of Labor 282
knowledge 44

patriarchal societies 170–173
Paula, Carlos Roberto de 215
peak oil 28, 29
people power 162, 275–276
Pérez, Carlos Andrés 165
permaculture 129, 265, 268
Peru 61, 143
petroleum 15, 27, 28, 29, 72, 84, 267
pharmaceutical corporations 19,
  55–57, 77, 146
Philippines 61, 221, 222, 227, 275
Pickett, Kate 24
Pine Ridge Indian Reservation 22
Pinoche, Augusto 14
Pino, Darlin 262
Pioneer Hi-Bred Corporation 126
Plotkin, Mark J. 146
Poland 94
political parties 243
pornography 46, 155, 172, 198, 228,
  270
Portugal 6, 14, 21, 157, 215, 262,
  263
poverty 11, 24, 30, 36, 54, 55, 77, 80,
  83, 98, 121, 128, 133, 150, 158, 172,
  199, 202, 212, 219, 245, 258, 277,
  278, 284, 90
pramá (dynamic balance) 44–48,
  51–52
Prayer of Saint Francis 208
predatory pricing 17
Premier League 71
prisons 211–215, 216
profit maximization 100–101
progress 3, 42–44
property rights 35, 36, 39, 128
Prout: A Journal of Proutistic Views
  and Neohumanistic Analysis 266
Prout College 260
Prout Community Settlement Co-op
  120
Prout Institute (Eugene, Oregon,
  USA) 268–269

Prout movement 7, 250–255,
  250–256, 252, 257, 278
Prout (Progressive Utilization
  Theory); amenities 52, 72, 80, 91;
  as "progressive socialism" 60; balanced economy of 134–136; comparison with participatory economics (parecon) 73–75; comparison
  with welfare economics 89–101;
  concept of ownership of 39; constitutional proposals of 244–246;
  decentralized economy of 88–89;
  democratic reform proposals 241,
  241–244; economic democracy,
  requirements of 80–81; education 222–223; ethics of 201–210;
  Five Fundamental Principles of
  62–67; Fundamental Principles to
  evaluate policies 67; governance
  of 239–249; ideal farming of 131;
  in comparison with Marxism and
  communism 58–61, 176; justice
  system of 211–215; language policy
  of 224, 224–225; Master Units of
  136–137; maximum utilization of
  63–65; minimum requirements of
  life 80; monetary system of 93;
  on classes 152–179; on trade 92;
  philosophical base of 36, 36–39; rational distribution of 64; revolution
  159–162; revolutionaries 180–192;
  Small-scale private enterprises
  82–83; socio-economic regions of
  88, 88–89; taxation of 94–98, 100;
  three-tier economy of 81–84; world
  government proposal 246–247
Prout Research Institute of Venezuela 109, 116, 121, 263, 267, 266–268,
  267–268, 268, 271
Prout Research Institutes 265–268
pseudo-culture 220–222
psychic exploitation 218–219
purchasing capacity 22, 55, 80, 85,

CPSIA information can be obtained at www.ICGtesting.com
Printed in the USA
BVOW07s2002051113

335539BV00001B/52/P